VOLUME TWO

Direct
Psychotherapy

28 AMERICAN ORIGINALS

VOLUME TWO

Direct
Psychotherapy

28 AMERICAN ORIGINALS

Edited by
Ratibor-Ray M. Jurjevich

University of Miami Press
Coral Gables, Florida

Designed by Mary Lipson and Anne Hertz

Manufactured in the United States of America

We acknowledge permission to reprint copyright material for the following
chapters in these volumes. Chapter 20, "Reality Therapy," condensed and
modified from *Reality Therapy* by William Glasser, M.D. Copyright © 1965 by
William Glasser, M.D. Reprinted by permission of Harper & Row, Publishers,
Inc. Chapter 26, "Synanon," reprinted with permission of The Macmillan
Company from *The Tunnel Back: Synanon* by Lewis Yablonsky. Copyright ©
by Lewis Yablonsky, 1965. Chapter 28, "Recovery, Incorporated: Mental Health
Through Will Training," reprinted with permission of The Christopher Publishing
House from *Mental Health Through Will Training* by Abraham A. Low. Copy-
right © 1960.

Contents

VOLUME ONE

Foreword by Hans J. Eysenck   *ix*
Acknowledgments   *xiii*
Introduction   *1*

Part One. Physiological and Behavior Therapy Approaches   33

1   Assertion-Structured Therapy: A Behavioral Position   *35*
E. LAKIN PHILLIPS

2   Verbal Behavior Therapy   *67*
H. A. STORROW

3   Implosive Therapy   *83*
THOMAS G. STAMPFL AND DONALD J. LEVIS

4   Conditioned Reflex Therapy   *106*
ANDREW SALTER AND RATIBOR-RAY M. JURJEVICH

5   Therapy #52—The Truth (Operant Group Psychotherapy)   *129*
WILLARD A. MAINORD

6   Attitude Therapy: A Behavior Therapy Approach   *165*
EARL S. TAULBEE AND JAMES C. FOLSOM

7   Group Behavior Therapy with Offenders   *190*
FREDERICK C. THORNE

8   Therapy for Scrupulosity   *221*
V. M. O'FLAHERTY, S.J.

9   A Physiologic Therapy for the "Neuroses"   *244*
GERHARD B. HAUGEN

Part Two. Cognitive Restructuring Methods   255

10   Assumption-Centered Psychotherapy   *257*
CAMILLA M. ANDERSON

11   Rational-Emotive Therapy   *295*
ALBERT ELLIS

12   Confrontation Problem-Solving Therapy   *328*
     HARRY H. GARNER

13   Transactional Analysis   *370*
     ERIC BERNE, CLAUDE M. STEINER, AND JOHN M. DUSAY

14   Fixed Role Therapy   *394*
     GEORGE A. KELLY

15   An Introduction to Gestalt Therapy   *423*
     JAMES S. SIMKIN

16   Some Powerful Tools and Techniques for Positive Psychotherapy   *433*
     ERNEST M. LIGON

17   The Illumination Method: A Specialized Type of Psychotherapy   *464*
     JOHN A. BLAKE

18   Problem-Centered Guidance   *485*
     HENRY WEITZ

VOLUME TWO

Part Three. Emphasis on Personal Integrity   *513*

19   Integrity Groups Today   *515*
     O. HOBART MOWRER

20   Reality Therapy   *562*
     WILLIAM GLASSER

21   A Program of Recovery for the Alcoholic   *611*
     ARTHUR H. CAIN

Part Four. Religion in Psychotherapy   *637*

22   Christian Psychotherapy   *641*
     DONALD F. TWEEDIE, JR.

23   Behavioral Pastoral Counseling   *678*
     JOHN M. VAYHINGER

24   Essential Therapies and Catholic Practice   *696*
     VINCENT V. HERR, S.J.

25   Spiritual Therapy with "Alcoholics"   *717*
     GEORGE W. BURROUGHS

Part Five. "Lay" and Self-Therapy 745

26 Synanon 747
    LEWIS YABLONSKY

27 Alcoholics Anonymous 795
    LESTER R. BELLWOOD

28 Recovery Incorporated: Mental Health Through Will Training 818
    ABRAHAM A. LOW

    Conclusion: An Eclectic Evaluation of Psychotherapeutic
       Methods 847
    FREDERICK C. THORNE

    Name Index 885
    Subject Index 891

Part Three

EMPHASES ON
PERSONAL INTEGRITY

Even in antiquity a good life and a strong conscience were associated with inner health and strength, and an immoral life was considered to lead to personality deterioration. Only in the last two hundred years has moral integrity been regarded as separable from the integrity of mental life. However, the last decade or two has brought a reversal in the morally uncommitted attitude of many mental health professionals. Today one hears less about the "overstrict superego" and the need to "relax" it, except in strictly Freudian circles, which still display a practical difficulty in distinguishing between the irrational, neurotic aspects of the superego, which needs to be relaxed, and the rational, socially meaningful superego function, which needs to be strengthened in both the patient and the therapist.

Mowrer (4) has performed a great service in this field by showing various facets of the alienation of morally immature individuals from the core of their personality and from a meaningful existence. The selections from *Morality and Mental Health* indicate that the morally unintegrated therapists produce, or at least leave untouched, similar moral immaturities in their patients.

Indeed, all three therapists represented in this section have attacked the alleged moral neutrality of the psychoanalyst and the counselor as one of the fictions of the Freudian and nondirective therapy. All three therapists possess a working knowledge of "psychodynamic" views and precepts, and all three have found them ineffective as therapy and futile as theory and a view of life. In his three useless psychoanalyses, Mowrer (3) discovered that the nondescript Freudian morality could push the patient further toward moral irresponsibility and thus aggravate his mental troubles. The turning point in Mowrer's own search for emotional stability came when he abandoned psychoanalytic misconceptions and began guiding himself by the demands of his conscience. Integrity therapy encourages the "patient" to examine his moral failures and inconsistencies as the source of his instability, depression, and conflicts within himself and with others.

Early in his residency training, Glasser (1) found that "psychodynamic" techniques produced quite undynamic therapeutic effects. He discovered that he achieved much more wholesome results when he first established a responsible relationship with his patient (involvement) and then insisted that the patient abide by his avowed moral values as a way of healing his life as well as his mind. Glasser sees the danger of encouraging the patient's resistance to psychological improvement by allowing him to dwell on the ways others had hurt or misdirected him; rather, Glasser insists that the patient concentrate on what he can do to assume more responsible attitudes and behavior.

Cain (2) chose to work with entrenched character disorders and alcoholics, people with whom psychoanalytically oriented therapists or psychoanalysts would prefer not to deal since these therapists and analysts are aware of the ineffectiveness of their skills in rebuilding such disordered lives. Instead of endless analyzing of "early traumas," a process that tends to bog down the patients in their pathology, Cain demanded intellectual and moral effort from his patients and friends. Instead of pushing them further toward the existential impotence of a hedonistic, self-centered attitude, Cain demanded they abandon their "sissified," morally relativistic culture and assume a traditionally manly, responsible, and energetic role in life.

REFERENCES

1. Glasser, W. *Reality therapy: a new approach to psychiatry.* New York: Harper and Row, 1965.
2. King, A. *Seven sinners.* New York: Harcourt, Brace and World, 1961.
3. Mowrer, O. H. *Abnormal reactions or actions? An autobiographical answer.* Dubuque, Iowa: Brown, 1966.
4. Mowrer, O. H. (Ed.) *Morality and mental health.* Chicago: Rand McNally, 1967.

Chapter 19

Integrity Groups Today

O. HOBART MOWRER

O. Hobart Mowrer: b. 1907, Unionville, Missouri.
A.B., in psychology, University of Missouri, 1929. Ph.D., in psychology, Johns Hopkins University, 1932.
Research Professor of Psychology, University of Illinois, 1948–date. Assistant and Associate Professor of Education, Harvard University, 1940–1943, 1945–1948. Research Assistant, Institute of Human Relations, Yale University, 1936–1940. Fellowships, National Research Council and Sterling, 1932–1936.
President: American Psychological Association, 1955–1956; American Psychological Foundation, 1955–1956; Division of Clinical Psychology and Division of Personality and Social Psychology, APA, 1952–1953.
Books: *The New Group Therapy* (1964). *The Crisis in Psychiatry and Religion* (1961). *Learning Theory and the Symbolic Processes* (1960). *Learning Theory and Behavior* (1960). *Learning Theory and Personality Dynamics* (1950). (Editor) *Morality and Mental Health* (1966); *Psychotherapy—Theory and Research* (1953).
Articles: Nearly 200 articles on psychotherapy, psychopathology, learning theory, language, and other subjects. New evidence concerning the nature of psychopathology. In J. Feldman (Ed.), *Studies in psychotherapy and behavior change*, 1968, 111–193. Loss and recovery of community—a guide to the theory and practice of integrity therapy. In G. M. Gazda (Ed.), *Innovations to group psychotherapy*, 1968, pp. 130–189. Psychoneurotic defenses (including deception) as punishment-avoidance strategies. In B. C. Campbell and R. M. Church (Eds.), *Punishment and aversive behavior*, 1969. New York: Appleton-Century-Crofts, 1969. Conflict, contract, conscience, and confession. *Transactions* (Department of Psychiatry, Marquette School of Medicine), 1969, **1**, 7–19. The behavioral vs. disease model of psychopathology—Do we need new patterns of training and treatment? (Mimeographed, to be published). The problem of good and evil empirically considered, with reference to personal and social adjustment. (Mimeographed, to be published.)

Originally, my plan for this paper was to make a sort of survey of many types of group therapy, including residential or "live-in" programs, and empirically derive the behavior modification or learning

515

principles which are in visible and manifest operation in Integrity Therapy. But the magnitude of this task soon struck me as somewhat overwhelming; and, what was in some ways even more determinative, I found that this was not what I actually wanted to do. I found that what more actively appealed to me was the prospect of singling out the particular form of group therapy and the type of therapeutic community that I know best and scrutinizing and analyzing them in relation to the psychology of teaching and learning.[1] The type of group therapy to which I refer is what is known as Integrity Therapy—or, as some of us prefer to say, simply Integrity Groups; and the type of therapeutic community I have in mind is exemplified by Synanon Foundation, which originated at Santa Monica, California, and Daytop Village, Inc., with headquarters in New York City.

COMMON DENOMINATORS IN INTEGRITY GROUPS AND THE SYNANON–DAYTOP COMMUNITIES AND SOME PRELIMINARY DEFINITIONS AND DISCLAIMERS

It so happens that Integrity Groups and the residential programs just mentioned accept and make extensive use of three cardinal concepts or principles: In Integrity Groups the terms we most commonly use in this connection are: honesty, responsibility, and emotional involvement. These terms are sometimes also used at Synanon and Daytop; but more often honesty is referred to as "saying where you're at" or "telling it like it is," responsibility is referred to as "doing your thing" or "tending to business," and emotional involvement is called "having heart" or "caring." When I once addressed a group of Daytop residents, I was gently chided for "not having enough little words." Many of the drug addicts, of which the Daytop and Synanon communities are largely composed, come, as they say, "from off the streets" (with a minimum of formal education), and they speak a kind of Basic English, with a relatively limited vocabulary composed mainly of "little words"; but they manage, as is also possible in Basic English, to put a few of these "little words" together in such a way as to get something that is just as good as—and often much more graphic and colorful than—the more formal, polysyllabic terms that we academic and professional people are likely to use.

---

[1] Under the title of "Group Therapy and Therapeutic Communities Examined in the Light of Behavior Modification Principles," this paper was originally presented as the opening address at the First Southern California Conference on Behavior Modification, Los Angeles, California, October 9, 1969. Also to appear in a forthcoming issue of *The Counseling Psychologist.*

So, as I have indicated, what I propose to do in this paper is to take the concepts of honesty, responsibility, and involvement and examine them in relation to the basic tenets and principles of Behavior Modification or what might equivalently be termed Psychosocial Functionalism. I have several reasons for wishing to do this, among them the following. One of the commonest and most exasperating criticisms which has been made of our approach in Integrity Groups is that this approach is "moralistic" and thus, in the minds of some persons, to be peremptorily discredited and dismissed. "Moralistic" is a pejorative term and, in this context, is clearly intended to be; so I have no hesitation in dismissing it and substituting the term moral. Our approach is indeed a moral one, or at least tries to be, and we make no apology for this. Morality we believe, despite all that psychoanalysts and others have said against it and the current vogue of "situation ethics," is psychologically, sociologically, and humanly essential, and anyone who seriously denigrates it is inadequately informed regarding the social sciences and basic human nature (69, 70). Here I shall not attempt to delineate or further defend this position, except to say that we find that the Contract Psychology of Pratt and Tooley provides an excellent scientific underpinning and rationale for our position regarding morality or ethics, and I would refer interested persons to their various writings (e.g., 83, 84, 85; see also 71 and 94).

Also, our approach has been termed "highly religious" and dismissed, out-of-hand, by many individuals who have broken with conventional churches and creeds and who hold a naturalistic, humanistic world view. Because the Old Testament says, "Thou shalt not bear false witness," and the New Testament says, "Seek ye the truth, and the truth shall make you free," the fact that we too stress honesty is interpreted by some to mean that we do so "on authority," because the Bible "says so." The Judeo-Christian ethic likewise stresses responsibility as well as "loving your neighbor" and "bearing one another's burdens." So, on the face of it, we are suspect of a sort of Trojan Horse strategy, of trying to smuggle conservative Biblical teachings into academic and professional circles (63, 64).

Perhaps we have a surprise for our critics on this score. Integrity Groups as well as Synanon–Daytop are totally nontheistic; there are no prayers of the usual kind, no formal worship, no appeal to deity. Yet we are religious—seriously, enthusiastically, and determinedly religious. "But how can that be?" our critics will ask. "Doesn't being religious mean believing in God?" This is a common and, I think, really quite unfortunate misconception. Religion, in terms of its derivation from Latin sources, simply means re-connection. And in Integrity Groups and at Daytop and Synanon, that is our main business: helping lonely, frightened, alienated persons to be converted (turned-with), to "join-up," "plug-in," become socially integrated, reconciled, reconnected, fully and truly. Thus religion in its literal sense—and that is the sense in which we use it—has no necessary relationship at all with theology, which means "the discussion of God." We have no interest in the latter, although one often hears people, both in Integrity Groups and in the cognate therapeutic communities, attest that in groups they have come closer to having an experience of the holy, the numinous, the godly than they have ever had in conventional churches. Individual members may have any private theistic belief they wish, and they may and often do belong to and are active in the church of their choice; but these considerations do not enter, implicitly or explicitly, into either our theory or our practices (65, 66).

So, for these and other reasons, I welcome the occasion to try to describe and analyze what occurs in Integrity Groups and in the two special therapeutic communities alluded to in terms of learning theory or Behavior Modification, i.e., to operationalize their programs and, hopefully, lay the ghost, once and for all, of the imputation that we are either "moralistic" or "theistic." In passing, I should perhaps say that although there is a large miscellaneous literature on Synanon and Daytop [including a book by Casriel (18) and one by Endore (33)], I shall take Lewis Yablonsky's 1965 book, *The Tunnel Back: Synanon,* as the point of reference for the statements I make about these communities, and I suggest that this be the document consulted by persons who have had no direct contact with either of these organizations and who are not well versed in the miscellaneous writings about Synanon. Yablonsky (see Vol. Two, p. 747) spent three years as a nonaddict member of Synanon, married a Synanon girl, and was for a number of years a member of the Synanon Board of Directors. These considerations, plus his formal training in sociology and in psychodrama under Moreno, qualify him uniquely, I feel, to speak with authority concerning Synanon; and I have personally confirmed many of his observations and inferences during several rather extended stays in the Daytop "family" (I am presently on the Daytop Board of Governors) and one visit of a few days at the Synanon house in San Francisco and an evening at the Santa Monica house.

There is now a sizeable and growing literature on Integrity Groups which I have recently compiled and published (71), but probably the best integrated, synoptic description is to be found in Drakeford's *In-*

tegrity Therapy (24), published in 1967 (see also 25). I have been personally associated with this type of group therapy since its inception more than 20 years ago and have read as well as contributed to the pertinent literature.

OUR APPROACH VIEWED IN A BROAD AND REALISTIC CONTEXT WITH SPECIAL REFERENCE TO THE SOCIAL AND HISTORICAL SIGNIFICANCE OF THE SMALL-GROUP MOVEMENT

Despite the many virtues of conventional forms of behavior therapy, one criticism, I believe, can legitimately be leveled against this approach: it is often parochial, dogmatic, and doctrinaire. Both the virtues and the narrowness of behavior therapy are vividly portrayed in a new textbook entitled *A Psychological Approach to Abnormal Behavior,* by Leonard Ullmann and Leonard Krasner (104). The book as a whole witnesses eloquently to the virtues, power, and many applications of behavior therapy; but, it so happens that the narrow, parochial nature of the approach comes out in the first two sentences of the prologue. Here the authors say: "The central idea of this book is that the behaviors traditionally called abnormal are no different, either quantitatively or qualitatively, in their development and maintenance from other learning behavior. This book will trace the conceptual, research, and therapeutic implications of not labeling any behavior *ipso facto* as abnormal or as an indication of 'mental illness' " (104, p. 1).

If this position were advanced as an hypothesis to be tested and extended as far as empirical evidence warrants, there could be no objection to it; but, when it is put forward as a more or less firmly established and all-inclusive truth which is to be relentlessly propagated, I, for one, take exception to it—a stance in which I suspect I am joined by many others. More than a hint of the evangelical fervor of behavior therapists is supplied by the name of the professional organization that represents their special interests. This organization is called "The Association for the Advancement of Behavior Therapy." Now the word "advancement" can be interpreted as implying improvement; and, to that there can surely be no objection. But the term also carries the implication of promulgation; and, if it be objected that this meaning is not intended, I would point out that at a recent meeting of the Board of Directors of this organization the proposal was seriously put forward (but fortunately voted down) that the Association set up a special committee on publicity and public relations.

Having voiced these criticisms, I wish to say that I am myself a member of the Association for the Advancement of Behavior Therapy, am presently on its Board of Directors, am an editorial consultant for two of its journals, and am, in still other ways, identified with the Association's assumptions and aims. But I do enter a disclaimer when either individual members or the association as a whole overreaches what seem to me to be the legitimate boundaries of this discipline. In a paper entitled "The Behavioral vs. Disease Model of Psychopathology: Do We Need New Patterns of Training and Treatment?" (73) which I presented at the 1969 annual meeting of the Association, I set forth what appears to me and many others as very substantial evidence of genetic factors in the etiology of schizophrenia and cyclothymia; and such evidence is more concordant with the so-called disease model than with the behavioral or learning model. In preparing the paper, I also reviewed a considerable literature on recent researches on psychopharmacology and am persuaded that biochemical factors (be they constitutionally or environmentally induced) often enter into the etiological picture. There is likewise abundant evidence to show that certain ecological or epidemiological variables contribute significantly to psychopathology: e.g., it is well established that psychopathology is positively correlated with population density (a finding which, incidentally, has striking parallels throughout the animal kingdom, as indicated, for example, by the common phenomenon of "territoriality").

I am sure that many behavior therapists are well aware of all these considerations and at least tacitly accept the eclecticism they suggest; but, both by implication and explication, other practitioners and theorists in this field actively deny the relevance of genetics, biochemistry, and ecology and would make their art and science the alpha and omega, not only of psychotherapy, but of all remedial measures in this field. In the paper just cited, I present a diagram that seems to me to put the behavioral approach in an appropriately comprehensive context while at the same time giving it a suitably modest position with respect to the field as a whole. This diagram is shown in Figure 1. Behavior therapy manifestly belongs in Quadrant IV, as do all other forms of psychotherapy, individual and group, however similar to or different from behavior therapy. In other words, if this general scheme is valid, reeducation, retraining, teaching is only one of four possible and potentially profitable approaches to the field of psychopathology, and behavior therapy, in the restricted sense of that term, is only one of many other reeducative and change-producing measures.

In Quadrant IV we also put the theory and procedures of Integrity

	PHYSICAL FACTORS	PSYCHOLOGICAL FACTORS
Populations	Genetics (Eugenics) I	Ecology (Social Planning) III
Individuals	Biochemistry (Medication) II	Bad Choices & Habits (Re-Education) IV

Figure 1. Schematic representation of the four "areas" which contribute to psychological disorders (with relevant corrective measures shown in parentheses).

Groups and of the Synanon and Daytop communities, with their common emphasis on honesty, responsibility, and emotional involvement with other people. As I have already indicated, Integrity Groups and the related residential communities differ virtually not at all with respect to these three major principles or precepts. Their major difference, on quite another level, is that the Daytop–Synanon communities are for persons who would probably not come into or stay in Integrity Groups (or, for that matter, in a residential community without compulsion of some sort) and who need more intensive and continuous help than Integrity Groups can provide. And two other secondary differences are worth noting. Whereas, in Integrity Groups, we now have no objection to individuals being on properly monitored medication, Synanon and Daytop tend to be extremely strict on this score, because of the addictive tendencies of their members. We are now also probably taking genetic influences more seriously than Synanon and Daytop have, to date, done. But there is certainly an actively shared interest on the part of both the residential communities and Integrity Groups, which extends up into Quadrant III, the one having to do with ecology, environment, and social organization. It will take a moment to explain what I mean.

In his presidential address to the American Psychiatric Association in 1958, Dr. Harry Solomon said: "Large mental hospitals are antiquated, outmoded, and rapidly becoming obsolete. . . . I do not see how any reasonably objective view of our mental hospitals today can fail to conclude that they are bankrupt beyond remedy. I believe therefore that [they] should be liquidated as rapidly as can be done in an orderly and progressive fashion" (98, p. 7).

And in a book published in 1963 entitled *Moral Treatment in American Psychiatry,* J. S. Bockoven (16) gave further substance to Solomon's strictures by showing that as the state mental hospital system developed during the latter part of the 19th century and the first half of this century the recovery and discharge rates progressively declined and the problem of chronicity became increasingly serious. (Today, traditional custodial hospitals are often referred to opprobriously as "human warehouses.")

At last it has become clear that to take a person whose social integration is already tenuous in his home community and "put him away" in a prisonlike environment where his identity and sense of self-worth are still further impaired is only to make bad matters worse; some alternative arrangement must be found. Since the Solomon and Bockoven blasts, "hospitalization" has no longer been very energetically defended as the optimal way of handling most persons with so-called psychiatric disorders. But what is to be the alternative? The advent of the psychotropic drugs has been of some assistance but has also created certain new hazards (73); these drugs are obviously not the total answer. As a result of the efforts to find an alternative, over the course of the last decade or so the terms Community Psychiatry, Social Psychiatry, and Community Mental Health have all come into common usage; but no one has seemed to be very clear about their meaning, except that the operations they presumably denote are in some way to provide the sought-for alternative to incarceration in (commitment to) a so-called mental hospital. George Albee, in one of the many papers he has written on this subject, has testily summed up the situation regarding the Community Mental Health movement by likening it to the side show of a circus which displays a new sign and a new name but which, upon entering, one discovers contains "the same old performers going through the same old routines" (1, p. 498).

I understand that at the 1969 meeting of the American Psychological Association in Washington, D. C., Division 27, for Community Psychology, spent a good deal of time on this issue. Unfortunately, I was not able to attend any of these sessions; but, I would independently suggest that the expression Community Psychiatry or Community Psychology is used today with at least five distinct but not necessarily unrelated meanings:

1. The expression Community Psychiatry (Psychology) is sometimes used to indicate that emotionally disturbed persons should some-

how be gotten out of existing mental hospitals and back into their home communities and that these communities ought to be responsible for them, instead of big, impersonal, state-operated institutions.

2. Sometimes this expression is used in such a way as to imply that society at large (which is composed of innumerable local communities) ought to "be changed" so as not to be so pathogenic. This is the domain of social action, social planning, ecological improvement.

3. Sometimes the term seems to suggest any means whereby the mental health of a community can be improved, by medication, mental hygiene programs in schools (see next section), or any other device.

4. Community Psychiatry or Psychology can also be used to denote the psychology and sociology of special therapeutic communities, such as Daytop and Synanon, but it can also include such related endeavors as those about which Maxwell Jones (48) and many others (see, for example, 34) have written.

5. And finally, Community Psychiatry or Psychology can be used to refer to the phenomenon of personal alienation or loss of community and procedures for effecting social reintegration.

Alienation has been called the basic psychiatric problem of our time [Anant (3), Elliot and Scott (31), Heath (44), Nettler (79), and Sager (91)], and both Integrity Groups and Synanon and Daytop are centrally concerned with this matter. For these two related approaches there is an especially important connection between Quadrant IV and Quadrant III. And I personally believe that in combination these two approaches offer great promise of implementing community mental health, in several of the senses identified in the preceding list.

MEANING OF THE SMALL-GROUP MOVEMENT IN RELATION TO COMMUNITY MENTAL HEALTH AND BEHAVIOR MODIFICATION

How are we to understand the remarkable development, in recent years, of the so-called "small-group movement"—or what is sometimes referred to simply as "grouping"? I believe it arises from the fact that the great traditional primary social institutions of home, church, school, and community (neighborhood) are today in varying states of transition and disintegration and that laymen and professionals alike, feeling the need for greater human intimacy, identity, and support, have begun, in a variety of contexts, to come together in special or "artificial" groups to satisfy otherwise unmet emotional and interpersonal needs.

The resulting groups may be a temporary phenomenon that will disappear as the more conventional primary institutions readjust to changing times and develop a new stability. Or, as I am more inclined to suspect, it may be that the many new small groups now in existence are here to stay, a permanent product of our largely urbanized and highly mobile society, or, if you will, a new type of primary group (see also 37 and 108).

I have recently been surprised and delighted to discover the extent to which guidance and counseling in secondary schools and colleges are shifting from the one-to-one type of situation associated with classical client-centered therapy to what is today being called group counseling, and to find that many graduate schools of education are offering excellent programs of training for leadership in this area and that quite sophisticated textbooks are appearing, such as those of Mahler (60) and Ohlsen (80). The benefits of this line of endeavor can already be seen as twofold:

1. Group counseling in schools is providing young people with learning experiences and skills which help them function more satisfyingly in school, in their own families, and in other social groups.

2. If special small groups are indeed here to stay, the schools thus provide our citizens, at an early age, with understanding of and experience in such groups which may stand them in good stead in later life.

In the final analysis, the objective of group counseling or group therapy, in whatever setting, is to effect behavior change. So the question that therefore arises is this: Is behavior change more quickly and expeditiously brought about by means of what may be called the "classical" techniques of behavior therapy or through properly guided experiences in groups, be they recurrent or continuous (residential)? I would readily concede that the classical behavior therapy methods, involving work with single individuals, are uniquely indicated for certain types of problems; but I would also hold—and in this I think a good many behavior therapists would in turn agree—that the group setting offers a range and intensity of motivation and reinforcement rarely if ever achieved in the one-to-one relationship characteristic of behavior therapy (cf. 7, 15)—and, we may add, classical Freudian psychoanalysis—as commonly taught and practiced. For a combination of classical behavior-therapy methods and group procedures, see the work that Wesley Becker et al. (9, 10) and William Glasser (39) are currently conducting in the public schools and the work that Sidney Bijou and associates (12) are doing with classes of "exceptional" children.[2]

But, to return to the original question of the relative effectiveness of individual behavior-modification procedures as compared with group methods, it is my feeling that, in the long run, group methods are likely to prove more powerful and generally more influential. "Hard" data are not yet available in this score (cf. however, 73), and one must suspend final judgment. Also, I should admit to what I fear are rather obvious biases in this connection. I like being in groups and find the group process endlessly interesting and personally salutory. By contrast, I would find a learning-therapy procedure, such as "systematic desensitization," very tedious (107). And in the event one practiced the particular type of desensitization that Thomas Stampfl (99, and here, chap. 3) calls Implosive Therapy, it would be much too strenuous for my taste. I once witnessed Stampfl conduct an Implosive Therapy session, and at the end of 50 minutes he was drenched with perspiration and looked exhausted. I have long had certain reservations about the whole matter of fee therapy, but I had no doubt in this situation that the laborer had, at least in terms of exertion, been worthy of his hire. Group therapy calls for skill, perception, wisdom, and courage, and is sometimes stressful; but it can also bring joy, delight, humor, and fellowship of a kind that, for many people, can be found in no other way.

Another consideration which favors group therapy is that, if it is properly structured and conducted, the participating members are not merely "treated," they are also trained. While an individual is becoming comfortable as a result of his ongoing experience in a good group, he is simultaneously acquiring skills that he or she can then employ with others. There is a widespread assumption that personality disorders cannot be remedied without the intervention of one or another type of paid professional; but there never seems to be enough of these to meet the needs of those who can pay, and that leaves hardly anyone at all to help those who cannot. This is the crux of the so-called mental-health manpower shortage, which promises to become more rather than less acute in the years ahead. With this problem groups that produce what have been termed "indigenous workers" are of special relevance and value. [For at least an oblique approach to this problem see Ells-

---

2 See also a film made by Arnold Lazarus (56) entitled "Broad-Spectrum Behavior Therapy." In his introductory comments Lazarus says: "In addition to involving the usual range of behavioral techniques, broad-spectrum behavior [group] therapy teaches *a way of life* to include empathy, self-disclosure, and authenticity" (italics added).

worth (32). For a somewhat more direct discussion, see Reissman (87) and Mowrer (75).] When the professionals failed to deal effectively with alcoholism, alcoholics themselves banded together in such a manner as to become uniquely helpful, through Alcoholics Anonymous (A.A.), to one another. And the victims of drug addiction, who had also been pronounced "hopeless" by the professional healers, have created Synanon and Daytop Village, whose concepts and methods of producing personal change have in some measure already permeated our entire culture and even had considerable impact upon some professionals.[3] Integrity Groups have considerable affinity with this tradition; and, as has been indicated earlier, their members believe that they are not merely being helped and helping others, but that they, along with many related organizations and movements, are developing a new, basic social institution—the group—which provides not only "cure" but is also, and perhaps more importantly, a continuously redemptive way of life.

Many young people who are "looking for a profession" are "put-off" by the concept of the indigenous worker and of self-help and mutual-help movements. They are looking for a way to "make a living"; and, if A.A.'s slogan is correct, that "you can't keep it unless you *give* it away," this concept is manifestly not the young professional's dish. In Integrity Groups (I. G.), it is our hope and confident expectation that the labors of I. G. members as such will continue, in most instances, on an avocational rather than vocational basis. But there is also a place, we feel, for the professional in our line of endeavor. In groups, the professional has the same status as anyone else; and, his skills and dedication may actually be less than those of many lay members. But the professional who is persuaded of the validity of I. G. principles can be of enormous help in other capacities, in writing about or teaching these principles, in publicly supporting and encouraging the I. G. approach to "problems of living," and in this way perhaps making a highly significant contribution to the advancement of community mental health through groups that help lost, confused, alienated persons again, or perhaps for the first time, find community (cf. 74).

---

[3] On the evening of Oct. 12, 1969, I visited the "Mother House" of Synanon in Santa Monica, California, with a psychiatrist friend and his wife and was told—and later, upon attending the Sunday evening Orientation Lecture, personally observed—that "squares" (nonaddicts) were applying at the rate of 150 a week for admission to Synanon-led therapy groups ("Synanon Games"). The psychologist friend who invited us to visit Synanon with him is a full-fledged nonaddict member.

BASIC PRESUPPOSITIONS AND PRECEPTS IN INTEGRITY GROUPS AND RELATED PROGRAMS

Earlier in this paper we have posited, at least as a working hypothesis, that there are four major types of influence or "factors" which may predispose a person to mental health or mental illness (maladjustment): (I) genetic, (II) biochemical, (III) ecological, and (IV) educational or "decisional." Most clinical psychologists and educational counselors, although they may recognize the importance of factors I and II, do not ordinarily have any special competence in these two areas; and, if they feel that Factors I and II are important in a particular situation, they will "make a referral" to (or at least seek the professional cooperation of) a geneticist, physician, or psychiatrist. With respect to ecological (environmental) influences, psychologists and counselors may be more interested and effective. But their main area of concern and endeavor is Quadrant IV, in Figure 1, which is labeled "Bad choices and habits." This label is as general and neutral a phrase as I could think of for the "content" of this quadrant; and it goes without saying that under this rubric, specific assumptions as to what is wrong with a given individual who "comes for help" may vary enormously. For example, classical Freudian analysts posit unrealistic fears or fixations that they attempt to "work through in the transference," really a form of extinction; and a very similar assumption is commonly made in classical (Wolpean) behavior therapy, namely, that the individual is again victim of unrealistic fears (commonly referred to as phobias) and that these can best be eliminated by means of "reciprocal inhibition" (counterconditioning) or "systematic desensitization" (a form of extinction).

By contrast, in Integrity Groups the "diagnostic" presuppositions are usually very different. We do not categorically deny the presence and possible influence of unrealistic fears (which have failed, rather inexplicably, to extinguish spontaneously). But our major and overriding supposition is that the suffering individual (to the extent that his difficulties do not involve Quadrants I, II, and III) is uncomfortable ("neurotic") because he has been behaving dishonestly, irresponsibly, and without proper emotional involvement with and concern for other persons. And our "treatment" or, better said, "teaching" objectives are to help the person in question become more honest, responsible, and involved. Our goals are thus typically positive rather than extinctive, substractive, negative—unless one wishes to invert terms and say that we try to help the individual get rid of his dishonesty, irresponsibility, and uninvolvement. Also, we recognize that behavior therapy may take more than one form and that instead of counterconditioning or extinction, positive operant conditioning or behavior shaping (instrumental learning) may be fostered. However, we doubt that our particular objectives are very often the ones that behavior therapists pursue in this connection (see, for example, the case history which constitutes the next to the last section of this paper), although we would be pleased to discover that we are mistaken in this surmise.

Now in order to simplify and facilitate discussion from this point on, I am going to limit the discussion specifically to Integrity Groups, but with the understanding that much of what will be said applies, at least in principle, to the programs found in such residential communities as Synanon and Daytop and in a number of group-therapy situations that have other names but are operationally very similar. I do not wish to identify the originators and practitioners of any types of group therapy with Integrity Groups which do not wish such an affiliation, but it is objectively true that as early as 1962, Willard A. Mainord published a paper on group therapy in which he stressed precisely the same three cardinal principles: honesty, responsibility, and involvement.[4] In his book, *The Transparent Self,* Sidney Jourard (49) has emphasized honesty and involvement; in *Reality Therapy: A New Approach to Psychiatry* (38, see also next chapter), William Glasser puts heavy emphasis upon honesty and responsibility; in 1966, Henri F. Ellenberger (30) published a paper entitled "The Pathogenic Secret and Its Therapeutics"; and in 1964 and 1967, Kazimierz Dabrowski (22, 23) published books which stress the concept of "positive disintegrating" and have much in common with the other works just cited, as does Merle Ohlsen's book *Group Counseling* (80). As already pointed out, Lewis Yablonsky's 1965 book, *The Tunnel Back: Synanon,* shows repeatedly how these three variables are stressed in Synanon; and miscellaneous writings too numerous to mention (see 95, 19, 101; see also 20, 51, 55, 92, 96) indicate (as I myself can attest) that much the same situation holds in Daytop Village.

Thus, it will be clear that in talking in a specific and delimited way about Integrity Groups we are, by implication at least, covering a wide spectrum of experience in clinical psychology and psychiatry, and self-directed therapeutic enterprises (see 5, 45, and 81). At the same time, we recognize that there are other group-therapy operations that involve very different premises and procedures; and, if any of the authors or

---

4 See his paper here, Volume One, p. 129.

organizations specifically cited wish to disavow the communalities suggested, they are certainly free to do so.

PRINCIPLES AND PROCEDURES OF INTEGRITY GROUPS: THE INTAKE INTERVIEW

The most economical way of getting into the material to be covered in this and the following sections will, I think, be to start with a description of what is involved when a person applies for membership in an Integrity Group. As a result of personal conversation, a telephone call, or a letter, an individual (on the basis of often quite varied sources of information and motivations) indicates that he has decided he would like to be considered for membership in one of our groups. This message is conveyed to the total I. G. community at its next regularly scheduled general meeting (composed of several "groups"); there is brief discussion of the information available concerning this person; and if there are no glaring counterindications, the chairman of the meeting will call for someone to volunteer to chair an ad hoc Intake Committee for the applicant, and then three other members volunteer or are appointed, so that the Committee consists of four persons, usually two men and two women. A convenient time for the Intake Session is decided upon, then and there; and the prospect is immediately contacted by phone and the proposed time confirmed or rescheduled. Ordinarily, the Intake is held within the next few days at the home of one of the Committee members, so that, if the meeting proceeds satisfactorily, the new person can start attending regular group meetings the following week.

These Intake meetings are very unlike a social case-work intake interview. There is no note taking, and no specific effort is made to obtain a personal "anamnesis" or "family history" for subsequent "diagnostic" or "disposition" purposes. Our procedure is much more like the procedure followed in intakes at Synanon or Daytop. "Therapy," in the sense of attempting to help the new person to change, starts at once; the initial effort is usually in the direction of trying to get him or her to "level" with the Committee, "come clean," "get honest." Different I. G. members have different styles of chairing Intakes, and they may also vary what they do from time to time. For example, a chairman may begin by asking the prospect to describe the nature of the problems or suffering that motivated him to ask for help. In which event, members of the Committee may respond to the newcomer's story by saying, "I can identify with what you are saying," and then speak of mistakes that they have made and the difficulties they have encountered. Or the chairman may start out by himself "modeling," i.e., telling his own story, other Committee members may follow this lead, and eventually the prospect will be asked to tell the group something about himself (see 6, 15, 57, 66, 68 for further discussion of modeling). In any case, the sharing which thus occurs (and would be most unusual in a professional setting) commonly has the effect of releasing, relieving, encouraging, and reassuring the prospect. This sharing puts him at ease and indicates to him that he is with people who have first-hand knowledge of the types of problems which are burdening him. That is to say they are not asking him to do anything they are not able and willing to do themselves, and he starts identifying with them.

But eventually a point is likely to be reached where one or more of the members of the Committee feel that the prospect is being evasive, inconsistent, or defensive in certain areas; and he or she may be specifically, and very directly, "challenged" on this score. If the prospect divulges the material he has been hiding, i.e., "comes clean," the "heat" subsides, and approval and admiration will be generously expressed. And if the prospect seems to feel deeply about his disclosures—fearful, sad, or perhaps deeply relieved—the group may encourage "reaching out." That is, the candidate is asked if he feels especially warmly toward one or more members of the Committee and would like to go to them, say how he feels about them, and embrace them. Or a member of the group who has been particularly moved by the "work" the new person has done may get up, go over to him or her, and say "I think you're great!" or "I'm beginning to like you very much!" and embrace the person. There may be a good deal of confrontation and encountering in an Intake, but there is also always a lot of support, if and when it is indicated. This is, of course, just another way of saying that candidates are actively pressed toward truth-telling; and, when they cooperate, they are powerfully reinforced and rewarded.

If, on the other hand, a person remains supercilious or stubbornly uncooperative during an Intake, if he is intoxicated or medicated beyond a reasonable point, he is likely to be told that the Committee is not satisfied with his performance and is not going to recommend, at least not immediately, his admission to the group; and the process, by which such a decision is reached, goes on right in the presence of the candidate! In other words, he is never asked to "withdraw" while the Committee "deliberates." Rarely, however, is a person categorically rejected. He may be told to make application for another Intake in a stipulated number of months, or sometimes he will be asked to consult a psychiatrist of our choosing, or the Committee may say it is not sure yet what its action ought to be and will schedule another interview within the next few days.

But if the Committee members feel good about an interview and indicate that they wish to recommend the new person for membership, and if the individual himself indicates that he is ready and willing to join and make some "investments" in the group, then the I. G. "contract" is explained, i.e., the few simple ground rules that govern and structure the activities of our group. These are:

1. There is no physical violence or threat of physical violence. Violation of this rule may be just cause for summary expulsion of the offending individual from the group.

2. No one leaves a group session when he is under challenge or "upset." Persons freely come and go for any minor reason, but if a person is having a "run" and becomes "involved" with another individual or the group as a whole, he stays on and sees it through before leaving the room.

3. There is no Red-Crossing or rat-packing. When one individual is under challenge, another person does not go to his aid until the nature of the challenge has been made completely clear and the merits of the case reviewed. Also, if a person is spontaneously expressing emotional or moral pain, he is not to be given spurious assistance, or reassurance. On the other hand, we are very concerned about justice and never want a group to "gang-up" on a member or Intake prospect.

4. There is no restriction as to what language may be used in a group. In fact, persons are sometimes encouraged to use "gut-level" language, both as a means of getting in touch with their own feelings and of communicating their feelings to others. A person does not even have to use language; if he wants to, he can moan, yell, scream, or make any other type of bizarre sound he chooses.

5. There is no "subgrouping," i.e., what is called whispering in grammar schools. If someone has something to say, then it is ordinarily said to the group as a whole. Nor is there to be too much one-on-one-ing outside the group. Both procedures drain off energy and content that need to be channeled into the group process. Extended private conversation between members outside the group is to be reported at the next regular group meeting.

6. All conversation and action that transpire in a group are strictly confidential. Members of a subgroup are free to talk about such material outside group meetings with each other or members of other subgroups, but they are not to say anything about another member to a nonmember. (This goes for nonmember husbands and wives and is one of several reasons why we encouraged both spouses to be in the group if at all possible.) Members are, however, free and even encouraged to "tell their own story" and become more open and honest

with the "significant others" in their lives and thus extend and consolidate the greater personal authenticity they gradually develop in groups.

7. And finally, each newcomer is asked to commit himself to the three principles of honesty, responsibility, and involvement—and to be open to challenge in regard to his nonpractice of any of these. He also commits himself to attend six consecutive weekly meetings of the group (allowing for prior obligations), at the end of which time he may leave if he chooses, without so much as explaining why. If, however, after this probationary period, the person continues to attend meetings, he is automatically considered a regular member, with the privileges of occasional absences, if explained and announced in advance. (A more detailed and complete list of I. G. concepts and practices is given at the end of this paper.)

When our total membership was small, business and policy issues were discussed by the total membership; but now most routine business is taken care of by a Council (consisting of one elected representative from each of the groups comprising the entire I. G. community and two ex-officio members), but the Council is always careful to refer innovations in policy back to the total membership for ratification or rejection. Once a month there is a Saturday evening potluck supper, a purely "social" event, to which friends and relatives may be invited, but there is no "grouping," properly speaking, on these occasions. Or, instead of the potluck supper, there may be a "talk-fest," where matters of general concern are informally discussed. At our regular weekly meetings, there are, I would say, never any visitors.

At the present time, our local I. G. community has more than fifty members, a circumstance which makes it necessary to have six groups (the members of which are shuffled every three or four months). A city in Texas has—typically!—the largest known Integrity Group, consisting of upward of 100 members, with ten or more operating subgroups.

My associates and I have started an academic I. G. seminar which involves a two-hour didactic session each week and a three-hour practicum (actual group experience). In connection with this venture, six groups, which have their own council, are in operation. Students who have previously taken this seminar help "seed" the new practicum groups each semester.

Now a word, perhaps not really necessary at this point, about the advantage of having new persons come into the larger group, or community, or "tribe" by way of an Intake Committee. These advantages, as we see them, are:

1. The special Intake procedure provides newcomers with a long "run," i.e., much more time than they could ordinarily have at a regu-

lar group meeting. Instead of having a turn of a few minutes or half an hour, the prospect can be the center of attention and concern for two or three hours, or even longer if necessary.

2. Having been through Intake, a new person comes into the group with considerable knowledge as to how the group operates and some actual, though preliminary, group experience. (A few pamphlets and booklets are used to provide supplementary information, especially "theory.")

3. When the individual appears in the larger group, he sees some familiar and friendly faces. This makes him more secure, and often he shows real pleasure at this reunion.

4. The operation of Intake Committees spreads responsibility and experience on the part of group members. Usually an Intake Committee will consist of two experienced and two less-experienced members. In fact, a person may be put on an Intake Committee after having "grouped" only a few weeks. In short, it is good "training." (A considerably modified type of Intake is used in the seminar groups discussed in the preceding paragraph.)

At this point, two objections are likely to arise. The first of these may take the form of a question: Why all these rules, all this "structure"? The answer is: We are just plain "square" and take democratically derived group rules and mutually accepted contracts very seriously. We accept the basic tenets of Pratt and Tooley's "Contract Psychology" and believe that contracts—and the more explicit they are, the better—are absolutely essential for the orderly and satisfactory functioning and survival of any human group or association. However, I shall not attempt to elaborate this thinking here but instead refer interested persons to the several pertinent references cited near the beginning of this paper.

"But why," someone else will ask, "all this fuss about honesty? Isn't it because the group really thinks dishonesty is 'bad' in the medieval sense of 'sinful,' and may even take a perverse pleasure in hearing other people 'dump their garbage'?" We take the position that we do because we believe that honesty is indeed the best policy, i.e., that it is humanly and socially functional and that dishonesty is, in the long run, very nonfunctional and destructive. Naturalistic and empirical evidence for this position can be spelled out at considerable length—a task which I am now undertaking in a paper in preparation (74) as a commentary on Ellenberger's (30) previously cited article, "The Pathogenic Secret and Its Therapeutics," so I will not repeat the same considerations here. Often, however, applicants ask: "But isn't it enough if you're honest with yourself?" We do not really understand how a person can be honest with himself and a liar with others; but rather than chop logic on this point, we say, in return: "Perhaps so, but how has that practice been working out for you? Remember where you are and think carefully about why you are probably here."

Willard Mainord says that his approach to group work has sometimes been called "brutality therapy," and Integrity Therapy has been dubbed, by one especially clever fellow, "Nudity Therapy." And both approaches have, on occasion, been equated to "brain-washing." In response to the latter charge, I can do no better than repeat a story that Yablonsky tells in his book on Synanon. One day Charles Dederich, founder and then also director of Synanon, was challenged on the grounds that the Synanon program was nothing more than Chinese torture and "brainwashing" in disguise. Good-naturedly, Dederich replied: "Yes, that's right! We do engage in a good deal of 'brainwashing.' Most of the people who come in here have very dirty brains, and we try to clean them up a bit!"

Some people who are in emotional difficulties have sick brains, and every ounce of relief and restoration they can get in the form of medication is a blessed balm to all concerned (73). But the people who come to see us and are really "our kind of folks" usually just have dirty brains, or dirty as well as sick brains, fouled up by what members of Alcoholics Anonymous call "stinkin' thinkin'"; and we make no apology to anyone as to the specificity and effectiveness of our program and approach for such persons.

PRINCIPLES AND PROCEDURES: REGULAR GROUPS, WITH SPECIAL REFERENCE TO RESPONSIBILITY

In this and the following section (which will deal with our third principle, emotional involvement), I shall have to be highly synoptic. One could not only write a book about what goes on in our regular Integrity Group meetings and those of related groups; it would, as a matter of fact, take a book-length document to report and explain what goes on in a single session. (I should say that our Thursday night sessions officially run from 7:30 to 11:00 P.M., at which point a bell is rung and anyone may legitimately leave, but groups often continue on for another hour or more). In this paper only a few pages are available, and my first response to this dilemma is to recommend, for those who want a reasonably fine-grained picture of our type of group process, a book already repeatedly mentioned: Yablonsky's *The Tunnel Back: Synanon*. There are other books and any number of related articles, some of which I have mentioned; but, in my judgment, the Yablonsky book, for reasons already given, is the most graphic, conceptually astute, and generally valuable. Here even the tie-up with the psychology of learning is implied or made quite explicit in any number of passages (pp. 88, 110–111, 162–163, 164, 169, 177, 188, 189, 190, 217–218, 262, 274, 278, 368, 388), including one in which Charles Dederich is quoted as saying that he felt, at least in the early years of Synanon, that his main function was essentially that of a teacher (cf. 15). Now he is largely preoccupied with administrative and related matters.

In this section I am not even going to describe the format of the meetings of our Thursday evening Urbana group except to say that we assemble (promptly) at the appointed time, such general business as is absolutely essential is transacted, and the groups go into their assigned meeting rooms. There someone volunteers or is asked to serve as chairman; and then there is usually a quick "go round," during which each member quickly reports how things have gone for him recently, how well he has kept previously made "commitments," and whether he wants "time." This procedure lets the chairman determine who is under pressure and gives him a basis for deciding how he will sequence various people's "runs." Then the chairman will say something like this: "All right! Tom, maybe we'd better start with you." And the group is under way, bound only by the constraints and restraints already mentioned, but with broad latitude within this general structure.

In connection with the discussion of the Intake Interview in the preceding section, I have spoken, at least sketchily, about our first basic principle: honesty. This is the point most heavily stressed. In coming into his particular group, the new member is encouraged, both by admonition and by the example of others, to extend his honesty, both in breadth and in depth. When this extension occurs, a person, regardless of how much approval he gets for being honest, almost always finds himself uncomfortable and motivated to do something about his situation as he now reexamines it as shared knowledge instead of a carefully hidden secret that he could privately deal with in ways (rationalization, self-deceit, etc.) which he finds the group will now not permit.

Sometimes a person will find himself sufficiently uncomfortable after having had just the Intake Interview that between then and the first regular meeting he attends, he will already have started being responsible and making amends (see the brief case history reported later in this paper). If after a few sessions in the larger group, an individual does not move spontaneously toward action, someone is likely to say to him, perhaps a little roughly: "All right now! You've dumped your garbage. What are you going to do about it? How are you going to clean it up?" The group will often press for a formal commitment, with stipulated sanctions if it is not kept. (We have a Commitment Book in which an individual himself records his commitments, or at least the more important ones, so that there is no later ambiguity or dispute as to the precise nature of the agreement he has made.) Contemporary psychoanalysis has put great stress upon the importance of "ego strength," but it has never been very successful in developing methods of increasing this psychic force or will power. It is quite remarkable how one's ego strength increases, after a significant confession and a relevant commitment, at the prospect of facing a group the following week without having followed through as agreed.

In some would-be therapeutic and redemptive approaches, confession is followed by acceptance, reassurance, forgiveness, absolution, with little or no emphasis upon restitutive action. But we do not regard "cheap grace" (to borrow Bonhoeffer's apt phrase) as either good therapy or good religion and have always insisted that, in the long run, the hard way is really the easiest and best. The guilt and embarrassment released by personal confession of major magnitude is never, we believe, fully allayed without appropriate restitution; and so central has this conviction been in our work that at one time we seriously considered calling our approach Action Therapy, and one of our slogans was "Act right, feel right." Weinberg (106) published a book entitled *The Action Approach: How Your Personality Developed and How You Can Change It*. The following passage from the book's dust jacket shows the remarkable parallelism between his thinking and our own:

> The Action Approach is a way of meeting life—of seeing the power in your action. It explains how personality originates and what can be done to change it. Dr. Weinberg tells about the feelings, attitudes, and beliefs that stem directly from present behavior, and shows how the seemingly small choices a person makes today determine the way he's going to feel about himself and the world tomorrow.
>
> Recognizing that men cannot easily control the emotions that produce neurotic behavior patterns, the author shows readers how they *can* alter their actions, and in so doing, can eventually modify the feelings themselves. This profound insight into the way people's feelings are dependent on their actions is the basis of Dr. Weinberg's immensely successful, practical, and speedy method of psychotherapy—a therapy that usually does not require professional help. (See also references 29 and 85.)

Faced by the reality of having been both a cheat and a liar, and motivated to do something to relieve the resulting discomfort, one can do many self-defeating and destructive things: one can leave the group, physically or psychologically; become defensive or hostile; play sick; get drunk; etc. The useful and constructive response is, of course, to "get responsible." But what, more precisely, does this mean?

For a moment let us drop back to the dynamics of lying. With considerable regularity we find that lying occurs because (a) it enables the liar to get something positive which he does not deserve or (b) it enables him to avoid something negative which he does deserve. Both situations involve a form of cheating. "Being responsible" in the first instance calls for restitution (which literally means putting something back where it belongs, replacing it), and in the second instance, it involves being willing to accept the negative consequences, of whatever nature, that the lying has averted. In the Recovery Program of Alcoholics Anonymous, step 4 says: "Made a searching and fearless moral inventory of ourselves." And step 5 says: "Admitted to God, to ourselves, and to another human being the exact nature of our wrongs." These are the confessional or honesty steps. And steps 8 and 9 read: "Made a list of all persons we had harmed, and became willing to make amends to them all; made direct amends to such people whenever possible, except when to do so would injure them or others." These are the responsibility steps.

Circumstances obviously alter cases and no two situations are ever exactly alike, but the over-all picture is clear: When a person has cheated and then lied to hide the cheating, confession must be followed by restitution and amendment of life. This step is the first aspect of responsibility which we would emphasize.

This type of responsibility grows out of confessions that are made concerning mistaken past actions. Confession of another sort is also highly desirable: i.e., "confession" of intentions, plans, contemplated future actions. If one is responsible in a second sense of the term, he engages in confession of this sort—which is commonly called seeking counsel. This is a good way to avoid both errors of judgment or simple ignorance and the folly of yielding to temptations, which often cease to be very interesting when they are openly acknowledged. Persons in high office, whose decisions have far-reaching political or business repercussions, always, if they are wise, have and heed their cabinets, boards, and consultants. We hold that a private individual, no matter how humble his station in life, can also profit by following the same practice. And Integrity Groups will serve this function for anyone who desires it and is willing to make the investments required for entry into such a group. Such an individual, after he has listened to the feedback of his group, is in no way obliged to take the implied or stipulated advice.

If he does take such advice, he does so on his own initiative and cannot hold the group accountable if the advice proves ill-founded; but such a person will be censured if he makes unilateral (undisclosed and undiscussed) decisions and gets into trouble and then comes asking the group to help him.

There is another even more rudimentary meaning of the term responsibility, and that is simply keeping one's word, doing what one says he will, or if for any reason that proves impossible or highly undesirable, going back to the other party or parties to the agreement and renegotiating the contract. We expect members of Integrity Groups to be men (and women) of their word. This not only helps consolidate a person's integrity and good feelings about himself; it also improves his integration, his social, interpersonal integration, acceptance, and trust. Another term for this type of responsibility is dependability.

The fourth and, for our purposes, final meaning of responsibility is more subtle but not less important. Its inverse is the kind of irresponsibility that involves alibying, excusing oneself, "cleaning it up," "copping out," saying "Yes, I did it, but. . . ." As an almost certain corollary, there is the tendency to blame others. In Integrity Groups, one of the first types of assault made on this form of irresponsibility is to insist that "You really can't do much about changing other persons, but you can change yourself or at least open yourself up to the possibility of change. Others are not your primary responsibility, but you are. So start 'acting like a man' and accept the consequences of your own indolence, folly, perversity. Ask no quarter, and you soon won't need any."

In trying to get people to give up this kind of infantilism and invalidism, it is also often pointed out to them that a mature person is not just a reactor—he is also an actor, with initiative, choice, volition (67). But we must, of course, concede that freedom and responsibility at this level of analysis are relative, not absolute. If one happens to be in the wrong place at the right time and gets struck by lightning, his only "choice" is to die. Lesser forces impinge upon us all from the sources represented in Quadrants I, II, and III of Figure 1. But the individual himself is also one of the variables in the total equation that determines behavioral outcome. It is disastrous to let a person play the game of pretending that he has no control over or accountability for his own conduct and destiny. If this supposition were generally accepted, there would be no justification for holding anyone responsible for anything, no basis for either reward or punishment; and the whole educational and socialization enterprise would, on principle, have to be abandoned.

Some persons are of such low intelligence, so badly brain-damaged, or so debilitated by certain forms of "mental illness" that the prospect of education or significant change may be practically nil. It is ridiculous, however, for the average person to "bag-up" in the theory of total determinism and thus defend himself against benign social pressures which, if accepted, would help him "straighten up and fly right." In Integrity Groups, until it is proven otherwise, the assumption is that even though a given individual in the beginning may truly not be able to control himself in certain areas, he can acquire this control if he will trust the group and let it teach him some of the facts (and feelings) of life which, up to this point, he has successfully prevented himself from learning (cf. 6, 40, 71, 90, 105).

I would be the last to hold that the foregoing in any sense disposes of the problem of freedom vs. determinism in the ultimate, philosophical sense of the term (cf. 62, 64; the Contract Psychology of Pratt and Tooley is again relevant here); but the position outlined in the foregoing paragraphs proves remarkably workable in our groups and in everyday life as well.

Perhaps the essence of our position in this connection is best captured by the statement: "You alone can do it, but you can't do it alone!" By this we mean that a person is not likely to change without the concern and help of others but that others are unable to bring about such change unless the person who is the object of their efforts is willing and eager to be changed. In secular terms this change involves (a) anguish on the part of the individual himself and (b) the development of trust in some community or group. Christian writers often deal with this problem under the rubrics of "hardness of heart" (pride) and "surrender" (conversion). A Hindu aphorism puts it this way: "The breeze of God's redeeming grace blows continuously through the Universe, but some sailors are too lazy to hoist sail and be moved by this force." Our assumption, along with that of George Herbert Mead, Harry Stack Sullivan, and others is that human personality is primarily a social phenomenon and that without adequate social interaction a kind of moral entropy (secrecy, isolation, withdrawal) sets in and this process of decay can be reversed and converted into growth only by membership in and openness to the values and ethos of some human community, often called a reference group. Integrity Groups are willing and eager to "adopt" individuals who, for whatever reason, have lost or never found a natural reference group and who need an artificial, but nonetheless meaningful and vital, one. In this way the erstwhile lost and anomic individual finds a new personal identity through a new social identification.

INTEGRITY GROUPS: THE PRINCIPLE AND PROBLEMS
OF EMOTIONAL INVOLVEMENT

Until a few years ago, those of us who were identified with Integrity Groups understood the significance of honesty and responsibility very much as sketched in the two preceding sections of this paper, but we were not much interested in and paid relatively little attention to involvement, in the emotional and interpersonal sense. The significance of emotions and feelings had, we felt, been very much overstressed both by Freudian psychoanalysts and by the proponents of Carl Rogers' client-centered form of counseling. We felt that exclusive preoccupation with the purely affective side of human experience provides, at best, a very partial and imperfect approach to the problem of personality transformation, and we would still, I think, maintain much the same position. But we now feel that our own approach was, at that earlier stage, almost as one-sided and unbalanced as the approaches that concentrated so heavily upon emotions and feelings. Recently we have learned a good deal in this area both from Synanon and Daytop, from the groups that operate in New York City under the direction of Dr. Daniel Casriel, and from places like—but as remote from one another as—the National Training Laboratory at Bethel, Maine, and the Esalen Institute, Big Sur, California.

The situation was, in a sense, brought to a head by the following incident. Some three or four years ago a bright woman graduate student came into my office one day and said she had been reading William Glasser's book, *Reality Therapy,* that she had already read Sidney Jourard's *The Transparent Self,* and that she also knew something about Integrity Therapy. She then went on to observe that between these three approaches there was an emphasis on all three basic principles—honesty, responsibility, and involvement—but that no one of the three approaches she had designated stressed more than two of the three principles. Glasser, she noted, had written at length about responsibility and involvement but had little to say about honesty. Jourard, she said, like Glasser, also stressed involvement, but talked about honesty (openness, transparency) rather than responsibility. And in Integrity Therapy, she reminded me, we were preoccupied with responsibility and honesty, to the virtual exclusion of involvement. To have a "stool" that was stable and could support a heavy burden, we need to use all three of these principles as "legs." The young woman's logic immediately struck me as impeccable; I then recalled that in his 1962 paper Willard Mainord had reported that he was already using all three of these principles in setting up the "contracts" that he established with all persons who entered into his type of therapeutic groups (cf. 28). Since that conversation with the graduate student, we have been making a self-conscious attempt to learn as much as we can from others about, and by our own experimentation in, the area of involvement. What we can now say about this matter is still tentative, but we believe we have identified and incorporated into our group work some of the major parameters of the involvement phenomenon.

Over the years we had often observed, quite independently, that when a person is painfully authenticating himself, simply in respect to his past behavior and misbehavior, he often becomes quite emotional, sometimes weeps, and that this emotion causes the other members of the group to feel closer to him. In other words, mere behavioral honesty can have the capacity to release feelings and cause interpersonal involvement. Recently we have realized a second form of honesty and dishonesty quite distinct from the first. A person may give a highly detailed and accurate account of his overt activities during the course of a given day but not say a word about the emotional interplay that accompanied these activities. From various other groups we have learned that it is often extremely useful to ask a person to say how he has felt or feels now about incidents, other persons, or himself, instead of just stating objective facts. In the beginning when a person is pressed for this kind of material, he may resist and evade by lapsing into intellectual rather than affective language. But when a group finally succeeds in getting the person to verbalize his real feelings, fully and in nonsanitized terms, i.e., be emotionally honest, there is often a flood of feeling, some of it perhaps quite new to the person himself. This, in other words, is a second way in which a person may "get in touch with his feelings" and establish more meaningful interaction with others.[5]

Then we had also noticed that affect was often aroused in members after they had already leveled with the group and were now being pressed to take action, in the form of restitution or apology; and this affect was especially striking when the person was being importuned to extend his newfound openness to significant others in his life. Also, if and when such actions were in fact carried out, further feelings, often

---

[5] When a person confesses or is challenged in regard to an objectionable and self-defeating bit of behavior, he is often asked to give the "gut-level" term that best characterizes him with respect to such a situation. Recently in a group, when a woman characterized her own action as "hypocritical and phoney," the effect was, I am sure, much greater than if these terms had merely been hurled at her by someone else, as epithets.

in the nature of first fear and then relief, were reported. Recently we have also become interested in certain special "exercises" that can be used in groups, often to excellent effect, with persons who are emotionally blocked—and, likely as not, also behaviorally resistant. Sometimes very striking results can be obtained by simply asking a person to move around the circle formed by the group and stop in front of each person in turn, call him or her by name, and say something that the group has reason to believe is emotionally charged for him. This exercise may take the form of admitting to inordinate pride, ambition, vengefulness, or brutal domination of others; or the person may be encouraged to say, "I am in pain and need help!" or "I am very lonely and frightened and need your love." Such statements very commonly release weeping and bring much relief; and sometimes anger can be tapped by encouraging the person to yell, "I'm angry!" or "I'm angry at you," over and over again at the top of his voice. Although the latter type of exercise, in the beginning, may seem silly to the person who is asked to carry it out, very commonly the yelling releases first the emotion of anger itself and then relief and weeping. Innumerable other exercises have been tried as means of getting at feelings; but, beyond those mentioned, we are not yet persuaded of the particular effectiveness of any of them. I am certainly in favor of continued experimentation along these lines, in our groups and elsewhere, and am sure that all possibilities in this area have not yet by any means been fully explored and exploited.

I think that most of us who are working in Integrity Groups would agree that, of the various approaches to emotional release and "loosening-up" which we have discussed, the practice of "reaching out" is the most powerful and effective. We treasure this privilege very highly and take every precaution to see that it is not misused or spoiled. It does not take place in private, unless immediately reported to the group, and although there is no formal rule on this score, there is strong sentiment against lip kissing. These physical contacts are intended primarily for use in and before a group, with all the restraints and safeguards this use implies. They have something of the quality of rituals, which are not to be practiced privately or perversely but are nevertheless appropriate and powerful given the proper circumstances (cf. the practice in certain early Christian congregations of the ritual of the "holy kiss").

After some measure of experience in reaching out, one makes an interesting discovery. In our culture, physical contact is commonly freighted with sexual overtones and intimations. In the practice of what I have alluded to as "ritualistic" embracing, one discovers that a type of love (of a very deep and dynamic kind) can be facilitated in this way which is sharply differentiated from specifically sexual feelings or ideas. In other words, we have found that human beings can learn to feel very warmly toward each other without becoming sexually aroused or involved; and this emotional warmth powerfully promotes a sense of acceptance, support, and belongingness in the group.

Similarly, we have learned—again something which seems not to be generally realized—that one can, and should, make a distinction between anger and aggression. We have already indicated that our I. G. ground rules involve a strong taboo on aggression, or even threats thereof; but, at the same time we have said, somewhat paradoxically it may seem, that we often encourage persons to get in touch with and verbalize their anger. The paradox, if any, is resolved by taking the position that an individual, no matter what the circumstances, has a right to experience anger and to talk about it; and that if he has anger and cannot experience it, it may very well "come out sideways" (be disguised) or converted into psychosomatic symptoms, such as headache, fatigue, indigestion, etc. Thus, it is important to know when one is angry and to be able to experience the emotion directly, not in some muted, circuitous form. This is not, however, to say that one should act out his anger, i.e., convert it into physical attack. Verbal aggression is admissible and is often all that is necessary to discover that behind the person's anger there is fear, not infrequently connected with deep caring for the other person and a belief that the relationship has been or is about to be ruptured. So the emotion of anger and aggressive actions are sharply separated, just as love and personal closeness are not expected to go over into sexually directed behavior. (Unattached members of our group are completely free to date outside the group if they simply inform the group of these developments, but any "hanky-panky" between married persons or a married person and a single person is contrary to our ethics and conception of integrity unless there is openness and mutual agreement on the part of all concerned.)

Although we still have much to learn in this whole area of feeling and mutual caring, our explorations of it have already paid handsome dividends, and we intend to continue to investigate and experiment, prudently we hope, along these lines.[6]

---

[6] For a series of articles with such titles as "The Taboo against Touching" and "The Uses of Intimacy" see the Fall 1969 issue of *Psychotherapy: Theory, Research and Practice;* see also Azorin (4) and the many studies by Professor Harry F. Harlow of the University of Wisconsin on the importance of infant–mother contact in the normal psychological development in monkeys.

SOME FINAL REFLECTIONS

At an earlier point in this paper we conjectured that the small-group movement has come into existence and is today growing so rapidly because the traditional primary groups or institutions of home, church, school, and community are undergoing changes which, as yet, we do not know whether to interpret as regenerative or degenerative. In any case, small, artificial, "intentional" groups have come into existence under a wide variety of circumstances to fill the void thus created in the lives of many persons, not only in this country, but also abroad (see 2, 26, 52, 88, and 89).

In light of these considerations it is instructive to look, somewhat more closely, at Integrity Groups and similar social aggregates to see what is going on therein. There is, it seems, something of all four of the traditional primary social groups in such organizations. One sees (1) something like a family but yet different, more like a tribe—as Dederich had the insight to realize with respect to Synanon (108). These groups are also (2) somewhat like churches yet significantly different—intensely religious in the literal sense of the term but, on the whole, not theistic. These groups (3) function as schools—certainly a lot of learning goes on, but the content is largely about how to "get along with people," not that of ordinary "school subjects." And (4) these groups have a strong sense of community, fellowship, and neighborliness (cf. 76, 77). How different, incidentally, the relationship between the members of such groups and the "social distance" that classical Freudian analysts thought they had to maintain between themselves and their patients!

In likening our Groups to a school, I am reminded of a recurrent dream I had between the ages of perhaps 35 and 50. I would, it seemed, be in a classroom, always the *first* grade; and, although a full-grown man and so dressed, I would be sitting in one of the little seat and desk arrangements, along with a regular class of six-year-olds. In the dream I was always very perplexed as to just what I was doing there, and I was embarrassed and wanted to get out of the situation, and then I would usually wake up. Could this dream have been premonitory of the fact that, although I had already attained the highest possible academic degree, I still needed to "go back to school" in certain areas of my life? (One is reminded of the New Testament injunction that adults cannot change, learn, be saved, "enter the Kingdom of Heaven lest ye become as a little child." We often describe our groups as offering inadequate, wayward adults a second chance at socialization, if they will let down their defenses and become open, i.e., childlike.) In any case, Integrity Groups have afforded me that chance, and I am deeply grateful for it. But our groups are not like a school in another, especially important way: eventually, if one does not drop out, one graduates from a school. We do not think in these terms as far as Integrity Groups are concerned. As already indicated, participation in such groups does not have a definite terminus, nor are the groups a form of "treatment" that one hopes will soon be completed. They are instead a way of life designed to help anyone meet what Sullivan has aptly called the "problems of living," and in this respect they are more like a church, where one may be "confirmed" but from where one never "graduates."

In this paper I have not been able to say as much as I would like about the more conventional forms of behavior modification and the ways in which they are related to or perhaps differ from Integrity Groups and similar operations.[7] This is in part because I have not yet managed to cover a segment of the Behavior Modification literature which is specifically concerned with the creation and operation of groups, more or less explicitly on the basis of learning and conditioning principles (17, 27, 35, 41, 42, 43, 48, 59, 82, 93, 100, 103). For this inadequacy I can only apologize and hope to rectify it in the future. But to one book I must, in closing, call attention in a not entirely favorable way. I am referring to Donald J. Levis' volume, *Learning Approaches to Therapeutic Behavior Change* (58). I quote from the publisher's advance announcement of the book:

> The term "behavior therapy" is applied to many techniques and strategies (some theoretically based, some not) unified by a common goal: the application of learning principles to the treatment of psychopathology. The learning approach is *the only major new therapy in clinical psychology,* a field dominated for the last sixty years by Freudian and neo-Freudian therapy. . . .
> Professor Levis provides an introduction into the history, principles, and theory underlying this new field, *raising the question as to whether behavior therapy is the "fourth therapeutic revolution"* (first

---

[7] A lay member in one of our groups, upon hearing the term "Behavior Modification" as currently used in academic circles, exclaimed: "But I thought that was what we were doing—modifying behavior—our own and others!" Manifest behavior change is indeed the common goal in both instances. In ways which have not been fully analyzed, there are, however, both similarities and differences in the specific objectives sought and in the procedures used to reach them. This area is challenging and potentially very fruitful for further inquiry. As far as Integrity Groups are concerned, despite a good deal of "face validity," we would like to have much more "hard data" concerning their effectiveness than are presently available. There are, unfortunately, some rather formidable, but hopefully not insurmountable, obstacles (see 74).

Pinel, second Freud, third, Community Mental Health). (Aldine Fore-
cast, Fall–Winter, 1969–1970, p. 18. Italics added).

The assumption that behavior therapy is the Fourth Psychiatric (or
Therapeutic) Revolution [a manner of speaking introduced by Zilboorg
(110) in referring to what he termed the First and Second Psychiatric
Revolutions], has already superseded and supplanted the Community
Mental Health movement (the Third Psychiatric Revolution) is, at the
very least, premature; and there is perhaps even justification for calling
it arrogant. I do not wish to become involved in invidious comparisons;
but I do not believe the author of *Learning Approaches to Therapeutic
Behavior Change* has any real conception of the ubiquity and vigor of
the small-group movement, which is certainly a facet, perhaps the most
important one to date, of the Community Mental Health movement, in
the sense of mental health through a return to (or, perhaps for the first
time, the discovery of) community; and I see behavior modification as
both implementing and, in certain important respects, supplementing
this movement but not supplanting it. I, therefore, deplore Professor
Levis' implication of incompatibility and mutual exclusiveness. I do not
believe his view of our present situation is really congruent with existing
realities; and, if taken seriously, it can, I feel, be very misleading and
abort the friendly and constructive interaction between behavior therapy and the small-groups movement which I envision and which I hope
this paper, in at least some small measure, will help to bring about.

A BRIEF I. G. CASE HISTORY

Recently a professional colleague and friend mentioned to me informally one evening when he and his wife happened to be in our home
that he had been seeing a woman with depressive tendencies for some
months, felt he was not getting anywhere with her, and said he would
like to refer her to our Thursday evening groups. My wife and I agreed
that we would be glad to take the matter up at the meeting the following Thursday evening and would ask that an ad hoc Intake Interview
Committee be set up for Mrs. Ames (as we shall call her). We suggested
to the psychologist making the referral that he get in touch with Mrs.
Ames, tell her that he had made the referral, and give her the name
and telephone number of the chairman of the Intake Committee, which
we would provide shortly after the Thursday evening meeting. If Mrs.
Ames felt she would like to have a preliminary conference with three

or four of our members about the possibility of attending our regular meetings, she should then call the Intake Chairman and work out a mutually agreeable time for the interview.

I was not on the Intake Committee, but Mrs. Ames—let us now call her Madeline—after she had gone through the Intake and had made a commitment to attend six regular meetings on an exploratory or trial basis, was assigned to the subgroup of which I was then a member. (I might say that our entire I. G. community then comprised about 25 persons, and each Thursday evening, after a brief general session, we broke up into three subgroups, which have a revolving chairmanship and which are reconstituted every four months.) When we were in our subgroup and Madeline's turn came to speak, she said that in the Intake one of the first questions she was asked was whether she was hiding anything from her husband. In response to this question (which she later said neither of her two former therapists had ever asked her), Madeline had said No! But this answer, she said, was a lie; she had, in fact, had an extended affair with and then been "chucked" by another young man just before she started dating her present husband, Richard. Richard, who had had a strict religious upbringing, had often talked during their courtship of how important it was that both bride and groom come to the altar without prior sexual experience. They, themselves, nevertheless had a premarital affair, which was the first for Richard; Madeline did not admit to any prior experience in this area.

In her first regular group meeting, Madeline said that in the Intake situation someone had presently asked her: "What do you regard as the worst thing you have ever done in your life?" She said her mind immediately went back to the situation just described. She admitted she had lied to the previous question and then told a straight story. But she insisted that she did not want her husband to have an Intake Interview or come into the Group.

However, between the Intake on Sunday and the following Thursday evening meeting, Madeline went through a process which not infrequently occurs. She had found some relief in "coming-clean" with the Intake Committee; and she was thrown into a dilemma as to how she should present herself the following Thursday night when assigned to her subgroup, which would consist of seven or eight persons including one or two members of her Intake Committee. She did not want to resort to lying again, and she felt she could not come in and tell the truth about herself without having first done something to improve the situation. So she took her courage in her hands and gave her husband a full and honest account of her premarital history, including the fact that she had married Richard somewhat on the rebound and as a means, so to say, of making an "honest woman of herself." At times she was not sure whether she really loved him or would have married him had it not been for these circumstances; she certainly had not been truly married to him, in the sense of being fully open and honest with him, "of one flesh and one spirit." (Officially they had been married 13 years.)

When Madeline reported this sequence of events at her first Thursday evening meeting, she did it in a very straightforward and nondefensive way that made her subgroup respond very warmly to her. She said that she felt much relieved—and showed it. At this point she was asked if she felt particularly warmly toward any member of her group and would like to "reach out" and ask for their love (these terms were explained to her). She declined on the grounds that she had grown up in a very undemonstrative family and that she "just couldn't do this." We explained that this procedure of "asking for love" often helped emotionally constricted persons get in touch with their feelings—very commonly they wept and experienced a great sense of relief and well being—but we did not press her to go through with the procedure. However, it was apparent that she had found her interaction with the group very rewarding, as evidenced by the fact that before the evening was over she had said she would like her husband to have an Intake Interview and then join her group. (When both husband and wife become I. G. members, they have the option, at least in the beginning, of being either in the same or different groups. Madeline wanted Richard to be in her group.)

To recapitulate, Madeline in the Intake had become honest; between the Intake and her first regular group meeting, she acted responsibly by extending her honesty to her husband; and when she came to the group and reported these developments, the group felt very empathic and involved with her and gave her a lot of support and approval for what she had done and offered a physical expression of their love for her, which she was not yet able to accept. But she did reveal increased trust in and affection for the group as indicated by her expressed desire to have her husband go through Intake and join this group as soon as possible. She wanted him to be in the same subgroup that she was in.

That night an ad hoc Intake Committee was set up for Richard, who had from the outset indicated his willingness to come into the group. The following Thursday night he joined our group, which included one of the persons who had been on his Intake Committee. He had apparently not had a very good Intake, in that he was somewhat supercilious and would preemptorily dismiss suggestions or ideas put forward by the members of the Committee. Nevertheless, he told the group that Madeline had been "a different woman" since she had made her confession to him, that he was more in love with her than ever before, and wished to join the group and would work hard in it.

During the preliminary "go-round" which we usually have at the beginning of each subgroup session, Madeline said she had been feeling good but that Richard was upset and that the two of them ought to have some time later to discuss their situation. After the "go-round," the Chairman gave Richard the first opportunity to talk. What came out was this. When Madeline had made her confession to him, he reciprocated by telling her of his having once gone to a prostitute, several years ago, when their marriage was, as he put it, "at its lowest ebb." This exchange, this mutual confession between Madeline and Richard had apparently had a wonderfully releasing effect on both of them, and they had arranged to leave their two children at home for a weekend and go for a sort of second honeymoon. Richard was nevertheless mysteriously upset afterward and went back to see the psychologist who had originally referred Madeline and had spent most of the hour with him weeping uncontrollably, something that Richard said he had been brought up to believe a man did not do and which was very much out of character for him. Madeline was perplexed by this behavior and showed just a trace of doubt as to whether she should, despite its manifest advantages, have leveled with her husband.

As the work of the group proceeded, this picture became somewhat clarified. Richard was something of a self-righteous prig. Before he married Madeline, two of his old buddies came to him and told him about her affair with the other man. He pretended he did not believe them and apparently there were some brief fisticuffs over the incident. He said he really did not believe this story about Madeline and had "pushed the whole thing" out of his mind. She had initiated the self-revealing talk with him after her Intake by saying: "There is something I want to tell you." He had said, "Yes, I know what it is." She said, "Then you say what it is." And he replied, "No, it will be better if you tell it."

Thus, all along Richard had "had something" on his wife and was in a sense silently "blackmailing" her with it—or at least using it to rationalize some of his own less-than-perfect behavior, including the incident with the prostitute. But Madeline had had the character to be severely uncomfortable about the incompleteness and dishonesty in her relationship with Richard; and when, in the context of our Integrity Groups, she had a chance to really clear the whole thing up, she threw Richard badly off balance, and he was beginning to look at himself as the "heel" he really was, rather than secretly capitalizing upon his wife's moral inadequacies. This seemed to put the proper words on Richard's feelings, and he saw the picture "like it was."

But then events took an unexpected turn. At this point someone went back to the episode of Richard's admitting his encounter with the prostitute and asked him what Madeline had said when he made this disclosure. He said that Madeline had said, "I couldn't care less!" This response was obviously very ungracious on her part and had evidently hurt Richard far more than he had been willing to admit. It took only a little further discussion of this situation for Madeline to see she had been hard-hearted and in the wrong in this situation and to ask Richard to forgive her for her poor conduct on this score. Richard and Madeline were soon in each other's arms and seemed genuinely reconciled.

What then came out was that, over the years, Madeline had become pretty domineering in the relationship and often "wore the pants." It also emerged that Richard, although an intelligent and competent man, was excessively dependent upon her, often calling her at work as many as two or three times a day and trying to arrange to have lunch with her almost every day, at times when it would have been more convenient for Madeline to eat with the other girls with whom she worked.

We were now moving down into the area of specific behaviors and laying the groundwork for some commitments to specific behavior changes. When asked how often she would like her husband to call her at work, Madeline said once a day, and she added, "And as far as the luncheons with Richard are concerned, I'd like him just to lay off and let me tell him when I'd like to meet him for lunch." Richard accepted these stipulations by his wife as reasonable and wrote them into our Commitment Book.

Then Madeline was asked if she felt she was "missing the boat" in any way, and she said she was sure she was not giving enough attention, time, and love to her two children; she committed herself to spending a minimum of five minutes (and as much more time as possible) each day in the company of her two girls, just "relating" to them.

At this point the question of the preceding week was repeated to Madeline: "Is there anyone in the group toward whom you feel especially warmly and would have the courage to ask for their love." This time, she looked at one of the older women, got up and walked over to her and stood in front of her and said: "Molly, will you love me?" This woman rose and took the younger woman in her arms and held her closely for a brief time. When Madeline returned to her seat, tears were rolling down her cheeks, and she was encouraged to "let go" and weep freely if she wanted to but she stifled any further emotion. However, she had gone further than she had been able to the preceding week. At this point, it was suggested that she and her husband again embrace each other. After that, Richard said he too felt very warmly toward Molly and "reached out" to her.

Both Madeline and Richard then took an active part in the discussion of the problems which other persons presented, and when the meeting ended, both of them were radiant and obviously "high." But just before the end of the meeting, it came out that Madeline had been feeling so much better the past week that she had gone off of the medication she had been taking (Elavil and some tranquilizer) without conferring with the family physician who had prescribed it upon the recommendation of the psychologist with whom Madeline and, intermittently, Richard had been working. We asked Madeline to repeat the name of our groups, *Integrity* Groups, and asked if she thought she had acted with integrity in this matter. She then agreed to go back on the medication and seek to have it terminated or reduced by orderly renegotiation with the psychologist and the physician.

The story of the Ames family is, of course, not at an end, and they will continue to have work to do in the group as long as they are members, which can be for the rest of their lives as far as we are concerned. But they will quickly become "strength" in the group, start serving on Intake Committees, chairing occasional Thursday evening meetings, and moving into increasingly responsible roles in the total structure of the local I. G. community and the movement.

Again let me point out that the kind of "psychosurgery" which occurs in our groups often starts with the disclosure of festering secrets, and this process is often facilitated in the Intake by the chairman "modeling" first and then asking the other members of the committee to briefly disclose themselves in some depth. Soon after the new member moves into his or her subgroup, the guilt thus revealed points to the need for specific behavior changes, and here is where the matter of contract, commitments, and responsibility come in. Then as the members of the group offer their love and support—or express their concern in the form of anger and disgust—the process of involvement begins and grows.

The Sunday following their third Thursday night meeting, Richard and Madeline were at the potluck meal which the group has together once a month, and both of them were in obviously good spirits and said things had been going well.

One year later: Richard and Madeline are still faithful and hard-working I. G. members; Madeline's depression has largely cleared up, and Richard has become a "better husband" in a variety of ways. Now their motivation, in addition to continuing to "work on themselves," is to use their newfound skills to help others.

BASIC PRINCIPLES, GROUND RULES, AND GUIDELINES FOR INTEGRITY GROUPS

Originally known as Integrity Therapy, Integrity Groups or the I. G. Process, along with a growing number of related movements and organizations, is concerned, not directly or primarily with changing others (the professional model—"psychotherapy," Behavior Modification, etc.), but with self-change. However, in changing oneself in desirable ways, one almost invariably begins to evoke more positive behavior from others and one also learns how to help others achieve self-change. Sometimes referred to as a self-help approach, this is more accurately characterized as a mutual-help process, or the peer-group model. Unlike "therapy" and formal education which are normally time-limited, Integrity Groups become for many a distinctive subculture and way of life.[8]

Integrity Groups are based upon three cardinal principles: honesty, responsibility, and involvement (sharing one another's pain and joy). Members commit themselves to these three principles as a condition of their entrance into and continued participation in Integrity Groups. Members are always subject to challenge for possible deviation from or violation of these principles. These principles, their rationale and implementation, are discussed in detail in this paper. They are also stressed orally in I. G. "Intakes."

Ground Rules

1. An I. G. member may be summarily expelled for physical violence (directed at another person or persons or at material objects) or threat thereof.
2. If a person arbitrarily "walks out" during a "run" (i.e., while he is trying to work through a problem or feeling and is in active

---

[8] "To make a better world, make yourself a better individual." Berkeley, California, street poster.

interchange with the group), he has automatically and permanently resigned from the group.

3. During a group session, a member is free to use any language he wishes or to make wordless noises (such as yelling, groaning, crying, etc.).

4. If a person is, for any reason, unable to attend a meeting of his group, he is to notify some other member, who will in turn inform the group as a whole of the anticipated absence and the reasons for it.

5. If a person, without having called in, arrives more than a few minutes late for a group meeting, he is, at an appropriate point, subject to challenge: i.e., a "pull-up" and a request for an explanation of his lateness.

6. During a meeting, there is no subgrouping, i.e., everyone listens to and participates in what is going on in the group as a whole.

7. Members of a group are permitted, indeed encouraged, to associate on a friendly basis outside of meetings and, if need be, to talk about matters pertaining to themselves or other members of the group. However, such conversations are to be reported at the next group meeting.

8. Members are encouraged to increase their sphere of openness concerning their lives with relatives or other significant persons outside the group; but they are, under no circumstances, to tell another member's story. This is regarded as a breach of confidence and, if repeated, may be cause for expulsion of the offender.

9. Integrity Group meetings nominally last for three hours but often run somewhat longer. A member is, however, free to leave at the end of the stipulated three-hour period.

10. If he decides to do so, a member may unceremoniously quit a group, i.e., "split." But the more fitting procedure is to discuss his contemplated action with his group; and if, after having done this, he is still so disposed, he should submit a letter of resignation or request a leave of absence of stipulated duration. (Normal university rules apply if a group meets in an academic context.)

11. If a group is not able to meet the needs of its members in the regularly scheduled meeting each week, one or more extra, "extended-time" meetings may be called.

12. If an individual feels he is not making satisfactory progress or a crisis arises, he may request a Special, i.e., an extra meeting,

primarily for himself to which the members of his regular group are automatically invited plus "extra strength" from other groups. A Special without a minimum of eight persons is not recommended.

13. The chairmanship of meetings rotates weekly, usually on an alphabetical basis. A chairman may start a meeting in any of several ways: he may "go 'round" and ask each member in turn to tell the group "where he is" and whether he wants time to talk at the meeting; he may follow a less structured procedure and merely say, "Who is hurting and wants to start?" or "Who has a feeling [or problem]?" Flexibility and inventiveness are encouraged on the part of chairmen.

14. If one person has a grievance against a person in another group and if he cannot settle it by talking directly to the other person (or feels that it is unwise to "one-on-one" in the situation), he should first run this problem in his own group and then, if his group concurs, go to the other person's group and ask for the privilege of challenging that person when it will be convenient with the group for him to do so.

15. When two or more groups are operating together as part of a larger I. G. community, experience has shown that it makes for more rapid progress if group membership is reassigned or shuffled every few months. Groups may also accept new persons into membership in keeping with their particular provisions for doing so.

16. At the end of a group session it is highly desirable to have feedback. This involves "going 'round" and each person giving his over-all reactions to the session, commenting positively or negatively on his own and other persons' behavior, or saying anything else on his mind. This procedure helps prevent members from leaving a meeting with unresolved tension and ensures that all pertinent reactions will impinge upon the group and facilitate its development.

Suggestions and Guidelines

1. Don't interrupt! Show the other person the courtesy of listening to him. He will certainly feel better if you hear him out instead of interrupting him. (Besides, it may give you time to think of a better answer.)

2. Don't blame! You rarely change other people by complaining about them. But if you change, so also will their reaction to

you. (This does not mean, of course, that you cannot, under proper circumstances, challenge the behavior of other persons.)

3. Don't "act-off" negative emotions (e.g., resentment, jealousy, depression, etc.). It's important to get in touch with your feelings and talk about them instead of repressing or suppressing them. However, it is one thing to tell another person that you are angry at him and quite another to "run an indictment" on him (i.e., try to damage or destroy him verbally).

4. Don't "one-on-one"! If you are up-tight or baffled about something, (i.e., need help), by all means telephone or talk individually with one or more members of your group (and later report this in your group). But don't argue or fight verbally. This nearly always makes bad matters worse—unless you have learned certain "rules" in the group. One major reason for marital failure is husband and wife "one-on-oneing" each other and not having, or denying they need, a group.

5. Don't "Yes . . . but!" If you are trying to effect a reconciliation with (get rid of resentments toward) someone, the first question to ask is: "What contribution did I make to this situation?" When you have seen your error, "cop to it." But you will lose the whole game if you say: "Yes, I did thus and so, but. . . ." and then proceed to justify, alibi, disavow your accountability, your responsibility. Instead, simply say, "I did it. I goofed. I'm sorry, wish to make amends, and will not do it again. Period."

6. Don't "talk back." At Daytop Village and in Integrity Groups, the correct response to a "pull-up" (being caught and corrected when you are off base) is "Thank you!" You will never start an argument or fight with this response. If, upon reflection, you think the pull-up was unwarranted, run it in group with the other person.

7. Don't mind-read or expect others to read yours! Let the other person state his own position and take the responsibility for having done so, as you yourself are expected to do. Don't try to second guess him (especially as a means of justifying what you want to believe and do).

8. Don't fudge! If you have an agreement with another person, keep it or else renegotiate the agreement (before rather than after you violate it).

9. Don't double talk! This often passes as clever or witty but can wound. Have the courage to talk straight rather than ambigu-

ously. Sometimes people "come out sideways" without knowing what they are really doing. They need help.

10. Don't tit-for-tat! When another person challenges you on some aspect of your behavior, it is far better to accept the challenge (if valid) and mend your ways than to try to nullify the challenge by reminding the other person of some of his shortcomings.

Rarely have we seen a husband and wife (or other closely associated persons) "in trouble" who are not violating all, or at least most, of these ten simple maxims.

REFERENCES

1. Albee, G. No magic here: a review. *Contemp. Psychol.*, 1965, **10**, 497–498.
2. Allport, G. W. Autobiography. In E. G. Boring & G. Lindzey (Eds.), *A history of psychology in autobiography.* New York: Appleton-Century-Crofts, 1967.
3. Anant, S. S. The need to belong. *Canadian Ment. Health*, 1966, **14**, 21–27.
4. Azorin, W. A. *Superficial living, or the fear of deep feelings.* New York: Auxiliary Council to the Association for the Advancement of Psychoanalysis, 1957.
5. Bach, G. R. The marathon group: intensive practice of intimate interaction. *The Dis-Coverer*, 1967, **4**, 1–6.
6. Bandura, A. Behavior modification through modeling procedures. In L. Krasner & L. P. Ullmann (Eds.), *Research in behavior modification.* New York: Holt, Rinehart, & Winston, 1965.
7. Bandura, A. Modeling approaches to the modification of phobic disorders. In R. Ported, (Ed.), *The role of learning in psychotherapy.* London: J. & A. Churchill, Ltd., 1968.
8. Bandura, A. Vicarious and self-reinforcement processes. In R. Glaser (Ed.), *The nature of reinforcement.* Columbus: Merrill, 1971.
9. Becker, W. C., Madsen, C. H., Jr., Arnold, C. R., & Thomas, D. R. The contingent use of teacher attention and praise in reducing classroom behavior problems. *J. Spec. Ed.*, 1967, **1**, 287–307.
10. Becker, W. C., Madsen, C. H., & Thomas, D. R. Rules, praise, and ignoring: Elements of elementary classroom control. *J. Appl. Behav. Anal.*, 1968, **1**, 139–150.
11. Bernstein, S., Wacks, J., & Christ, J. Effects of group psychotherapy on the psychotherapist. *Amer. J. Psychother.*, 1969, **23**, 271–282.
12. Bijou, S. Implications of behavioral science for counseling and guidance. In J. D. Krumboltz, (Ed.), *Revolution in counseling.* Boston: Houghton-Mifflin, 1966.
13. Bijou, S. W. Reinforcement history and socialization. Paper presented at symposium on "Social Behavior: Early Experience and the Process of Socialization," Miami University, Oxford, Ohio, November, 1968.

14. Bijou, S. W. What psychology has to offer education—now. *J. Appl. Behav. Anal.,* 1969.
15. Bixenstine, V. E. Community House and its groups: a new approach to community mental health. Mimeographed. Department of Psychology, Kent State University, Kent, Ohio, 1970.
16. Bockoven, J. S. *Moral treatment in American psychiatry.* New York: Springer, 1963.
17. Bronfenbrenner, U. Soviet methods of character education: some implications for research. *Amer. Psychol.,* 1962, **17**, 550–564.
18. Casriel, D. *So fair a house: the story of Synanon.* Englewood Cliffs, N. J.: Prentice-Hall, 1963.
19. Casriel, D. H., & Deitch, D. New success in cure of narcotics addicts. *The physician's panorama,* October 1966.
20. Collier, P. The house of Synanon. *Ramparts,* 1967, **6**, 47–54.
21. Coons, W. H. & Peacock, E. P. Interpersonal interaction and personality change in group psychotherapy. Mimeographed. Whitby Psychiatric Hospital, no date available.
22. Dabrowski, K. *Positive disintegration.* Boston: Little, Brown & Co., 1964.
23. Dabrowski, K. *Personality-shaping through positive disintegration.* Boston: Little, Brown & Co., 1967.
24. Drakeford, J. W. *Integrity therapy—a Christian evaluation of a new approach to mental health.* Nashville: Broadman Press, 1967.
25. Drakeford, J. W. *Farewell to the lonely crowd.* Waco, Texas: Word Books, 1969.
26. Dreikurs, R. Early experiments in social psychiatry. *Intern. J. Soc. Psychiat.,* 1961, **7**, 141–145.
27. Dunphy, D. C. Planned environments for learning in the social sciences: two innovative courses at Harvard. *Amer. Sociol.,* Nov. 1967, 202–296.
28. Egan, G. *Encounter: group processes for interpersonal growth.* Belmont, Calif.: Wadsworth Publishing Co., 1970.
29. Eitsen, L. Confrontation action psychotherapy with religious-moral values. *J. Pastoral Care,* 1969, **23**, 26–35.
30. Ellenberger, H. F. The pathogenic secret and its therapeutics. *His. Behav. Sci.,* 1966, **2**, 29–42.
31. Elliot, O., & Scott, J. P. The development of emotional distress to separation, in puppies. *J. Genet. Psychol.,* 1961, **99**, 3–22.
32. Ellsworth, R. B. *Nonprofessionals in psychiatric rehabilitation.* New York: Appleton-Century-Crofts, 1968.
33. Endore, G. *Synanon.* Garden City, N. Y.: Doubleday, 1968.
34. Fairweather, G. W., Sanders, D. H., Cressler, D. H., & Maynard, H. *Community life for the mentally ill: an alternative to institutional care.* Chicago: Aldine Publishing Co., 1969.
35. Frank, J. D. The influencing process in psychotherapy (a tape). New York: McGraw-Hill, 1969 catalogue, p. 35.
36. Franks, C. M., Susskind, D. J., & Franks, V. Behavior modification and the school psychologist. In *Professional school psychology.* Vol. 3. New York: Grune & Stratton, 1969.

37. Gendlin, E. T. Psychotherapy and community psychology. *Psychother.: Theory, Res. Prac.,* 1968, **5,** 67–72.
38. Glasser, W. *Reality therapy: a new approach to psychiatry.* New York: Harper & Row, 1965.
39. Glasser, W. *Schools without failure.* New York: Harper & Row, 1969.
40. Goldiamond, I. Stuttering and fluency as manipulatable operant response classes. In L. Krasner & L. P. Ullmann (Eds.), *Research in behavior modification.* New York: Holt, Rinehart, and Winston, 1965.
41. Goldstein, A. P. Psychotherapy research by extrapolation from social psychology. In I. W. Sarason (Ed.), *Contemporary research in personality.* Princeton, N. J.: D. Van Nostrand, 1969.
42. Goldstein, A. P., Heller, K., & Sechrest, L. B. *Psychotherapy and the psychology of behavior change.* New York: John Wiley & Sons, 1966.
43. Hastorf, A. H. The "reinforcement" of individual actions in a group situation. In L. Krasner & L. P. Ullmann (Eds.), *Research in behavior modification.* New York: Holt, Rinehart and Winston, 1965.
44. Heath, D. H. Youth alienation. *Academy [of Religion and Health] Reporter,* 1969, **14,** 3–4.
45. Hurvitz, N. Peer self-help groups and their implications for psychotherapy. *Psychother.: Theory, Res. Prac.,* 1970, **7,** 41–49.
46. Jakobovits, L. A. *Effects of repeated stimulation on cognitive aspects of behavior: some experiments on the phenomenon of semantic satiation.* Doctoral dissertation, McGill University, 1962.
47. Jakobovits, L. A. Utilization of semantic satiation in stuttering: a theoretical analysis. *J. Speech & Hearing Disorders,* 1966, **31,** 105–114.
48. Jones, M. *The therapeutic community: a new treatment method in psychiatry.* New York: Basic Books, 1953.
49. Jourard, S. *The transparent self.* Princeton, N. J.: D. Van Nostrand, Company, 1964.
50. Kanfor, F. H. The use of self-regulation in behavior therapy. Paper presented at the First Annual Southern California Conference on Behavior Modification, Los Angeles, Calif., Oct. 10–12, 1969.
51. Kerr, W. They grow their own play. *New York Times,* June 2, 1968, Section 2, pp. 1, 3.
52. Knobloch, F. On the theory of a therapeutic community for neurotics. *Intern. J. Group Therapy,* 1960, **10,** 419–429.
53. Knobloch, F. The system of group-centered psychotherapy for neurotics in Czechoslovakia. *Amer. J. Psychiat.,* 1968a, **124,** 1227–1231.
54. Knobloch, F. Toward a conceptual framework of a group-centered psychotherapy. In B. F. Reiss (Ed.), *New direction in mental health.* New York: Grune & Stratton, 1968b.
55. Langguth, J. California's gift to psychotherapy. *Harper's,* June 1967, **234,** 52–56. (reprint)
56. Lazarus, A. A. Broad-spectrum behavior therapy in a group (30-min. film). Audio-visual Service, Pennsylvania State University, University Park, Penn., 1969.

57. Lederer, W. Dragons, delinquents, and destiny. *Psychol. Issues,* 1964, **4,** 1–83.
58. Levis D. J. *Learning approaches to therapeutic behavior change.* Chicago: Aldine Publishing Co., 1970.
59. Liebson, I. Conversion reaction: a learning theory approach. *Behav. Res. Ther.,* 1969, **7,** 217–218.
60. Mahler, C. A. *Group counseling in the schools.* Boston: Houghton-Mifflin, 1969.
61. Mainord, W. A. A therapy. *Res. Bull. Ment. Hlth.,* Research Institute, Fort Stilacoom, Washington, 1962, **5,** 85–92.
62. Mowrer, O. H. Freedom and responsibility: a psychological analysis. *J. Legal Educ.,* 1953, **6,** 60–78.
63. Mowrer, O. H. *The crisis in psychiatry and religion.* Princeton, N. J.: D. Van Nostrand, 1961(a).
64. Mowrer, O. H. The rediscovery of responsibility. *The Atlantic Monthly—a special supplement on psychiatry in American life,* July, 1961(b), pp. 88–91.
65. Mowrer, O. H. *The new group therapy.* Princeton, N. J.: D. Van Nostrand, 1964(a).
66. Mowrer, O. H. Freudianism, behaviour therapy and "self-disclosure." *Behav. Res. Ther.,* 1964, **1,** 321–337. (b)
67. Mowrer, O. H. Abnormal reactions or actions? (an autobiographical answer). In *Introduction to general psychology (a self-selection textbook).* Dubuque, Iowa: Brown Publishing Co., 1966. (a)
68. Mowrer, O. H. The behavior therapies, with special reference to modeling and imitation. *Amer. J. Psychother.,* 1966, **20,** 439–461. (b)
69. Mowrer, O. H. Christianity and psychoanalysis: is a new synthesis needed? In J. C. Feaver & W. Horose (Eds.), *Religion in philosophical and cultural perspective.* Princeton, N. J.: D. Van Nostrand, 1967. (a)
70. Mowrer, O. H. (Ed.) *Morality and mental health.* Chicago: Rand McNally, 1967.(a)
71. Mowrer, O. H. Conflict, contract, conscience, and confession. *Transactions.* Milwaukee: Marquette School of Medicine, Department of Psychiatry, 1969.(a)
72. Mowrer, O. H. Psychoneurotic defenses (including deception) as punishment-avoidance strategies. In B. A. Campbell & R. M. Church (Eds.), *Punishment and aversive behavior,* New York: Appleton-Century-Crofts, 1969.(b)
73. Mowrer, O. H. The behavioral vs. disease model of psychotherapy. *Proceedings of the Third Annual Meeting of the Association for the Advancement of Behavior Therapy.* New York: Academic Press, 1970. (a)
74. Mowrer, O. H. Belated "clinical" recognition of the pathogenic secret. In A. Mahrer & L. Pearson (Eds.), *Creative developments in psychotherapy,* Vol. 2, 1970.(b) Also available in a longer mimeographed version.
75. Mowrer, O. H. Peer groups and medication—the best "therapy" for

professionals and laymen alike (Mimeographed.) Department of Psychology, University of Illinois, 1970.(c)

76. Mowrer, O. H. Group counseling in the elementary school: a specialized service *to* students or a new "subject" and learning experience *for* them? In M. M. Ohlsen (Ed.), *Group counseling in the elementary schools.* New York: Holt, Rinehart & Winston, 1971.(a)

77. Mowrer, O. H. Peer groups and medication, the best "therapy" for professionals and laymen alike. *Psychother.: Theory, Res. Prac.*, 1971, **8** (1), 44–54 (b).

78. Murray, E. J., & Jacobson, L. I. The nature of learning in traditional and behavioral psychotherapy. In A. E. Bergin & S. L. Garfield (Eds.), *Handbook of psychotherapy and behavior change.* New York: Wiley, 1969.

79. Nettler, G. A measure of alienation. *Am. Soc. Rev.*, 1957, **22**, 670–677.

80. Ohlsen, M. M. *Group counseling.* New York: Holt, Rinehart and Winston, 1969.

81. Parlour, R. R. *Responsibility therapy: some ways to mental, spiritual and social health.* Mimeographed. Claremont, Calif.: Parlour Medical Group, 1968.

82. Paul, G. L., & Shannon, D. T. Treatment of anxiety through systematic desensitization in therapy groups. *J. Abnorm. Psychol.*, 1966, **71**, 124–135.

83. Pratt, S., & Tooley, J. Contract psychology and the actualization transactional field. *Internat. J. Soc. Psychiat.*, 1964, Congress Issue, 51-69.

84. Pratt, S., & Tooley, J. Human actualization teams: the perspective of contract psychology. *Amer. J. Orthopsychiat.*, 1966, **36**, 881–895.

85. Pratt, S., & Tooley, J. Action psychology. *J. Psychol. Studies,* 1967, **15**, 137–231.

86. Pratt, S., & Tooley, J. Toward a metataxonomy of human systems actualization: The perspective of contract psychology. Mimeographed Jacksonville (Illinois) State Hospital, 1968. To be published, in abridged form, in *New approaches to psychodiagnostic systems,* (A. H. Mahrer, Ed.) Chicago: Aldine Press, 1968.

87. Reissman, F. *Up from poverty; new career ladders for nonprofessionals.* New York: Harper & Row, 1968.

88. Rogers, C. R. Autobiography. In E. G. Boring & G. Lindzey (Ed.) *A history of psychology in autobiography.* New York: Appleton-Century-Crofts, 1967. (a)

89. Rogers, C. R. The process of the basic encounter group. In J. F. T. Bugenthal (Ed.), *Challenges of humanistic psychology.* New York: McGraw-Hill, 1967. (b)

90. Rogers, C. R., & Skinner, B. F. Some issues concerning the control of human behavior: a symposium. *Pastoral Psychol.*, 1962, **13**, 12–40.

91. Sager, C. J. Alienation can be said to epitomize our times. *Roche Report,* 1968, **5**, 1, 2–11.

92. Samuels, G. Where junkies learn to hang tough. New York Times Co., May 1965. (Reprint)

93. Saslow, G. A case history of attempted behavior manipulation in a

psychiatric ward. In L. Krasner & L. P. Ullmann (Eds.), *Research in behavior modification*. New York: Holt, Rinehart and Winston, 1965.

94. Shapiro, S. B. Some aspects of a theory of interpersonal contracts. *Psychol. Reports,* 1968, **22,** 171–183.
95. Shelly, J. A., & Bassin, A. Daytop Lodge–a new treatment approach for drug addicts. *Corrective Psychiat.,* 1965, **11,** 186–195.
96. Shubin, S. Therapeutic "village." *SK&F Psychiatric Reporter,* March–April, 1967. (reprint)
97. Skinner, B. F. Freedom and the control of men. *Amer. Scholar,* 1955–56, **25,** 47–65.
98. Solomon, H. C. The American Psychiatric Association in relation to American psychiatry. *Amer. J. Psychiat.,* 1958, **115,** 1–9.
99. Stampfl, T. G., & Levis, D. J. Essentials of implosive therapy: a learning-theory-based psychodynamic behavioral therapy. *J. Abnorm. Psychol.,* 1967, **72,** 496–503.
100. Stevenson, I. Processes of "spontaneous" recovery from psychoneuroses. *Amer. J. Psychiat.,* 1961, **117,** 1057–1064.
101. Sugarman, B. Daytop Village: a case study of moral education in a self-help community of former drug addicts. (Mimeographed.) Oxford University, 1969.
102. Thomas, D. R., Becker, W. C., & Armstrong, M. Production and elimination of disruptive classroom behavior by systematically varying teachers behavior. *J. Appl. Behav. Anal.,* 1968, **1,** 35–45.
103. Ullmann, L. P., & Krasner, L. Introduction. *Case studies in behavior modification*. New York: Holt, Rinehart and Winston, 1965. Pp. 1–64.
104. Ullmann, L. P., & Krasner, L. *A psychological approach to abnormal behavior*. Englewood Cliffs, N. J.: Prentice-Hall, 1969.
105. Walters, R. H., & Parks, R. D. Direct and vicarious punishment as antecedents of self-control. Paper presented at the Annual Meeting of the American Psychological Association, Chicago, 1965.
106. Weinberg, G. *The action approach: how your personality developed and how you can change it*. New York: World Publishing Co., 1969.
107. Wolpe, J. The systematic desensitization treatment of neuroses. *J. Nerv. Ment. Dis.,* 1961, **132,** 189–203.
108. Yablonsky, L. *The tunnel back: Synanon*. New York: Macmillan, 1965.
109. Zeitlyn, B. B. The therapeutic community—fact or fantasy. *Intern. J. Psychiat.,* 1969, **7,** 195–212.
110. Zilboorg, G. *A history of medical psychology*. New York: W. W. Norton, 1941.

Chapter 20

Reality Therapy

WILLIAM GLASSER

William Glasser: b. 1925, Cleveland, Ohio.
M.D., Western Reserve Medical School, 1953. Residence in Psychiatry,
Veterans Administration and University of California hospitals,
1954–1957.
Private practice in psychiatry, 1957–date. Consulting Psychiatrist, Ventura
School for Girls, 1956–1967. Consultant, Public Schools of Los Angeles,
Palo Alto, and Watts, California, 1967–date. President and Founder,
Institute for Reality Therapy, and its Division of Educator Training
Center, both in Los Angeles, California.
Books: *Schools Without Failure* (1969). *Large Group Counseling: A Manual
of Procedure and Practice* (1966). *Reality Therapy* (1965). *Mental
Health or Mental Illness* (1961).

Toward the end of my psychiatric training I found myself in the uncomfortable position of doubting much that I had been taught. My
teachers implied that there was a great deal more to be learned in
the field, but only a very few questioned the basic tenets of conventional psychiatry. One of these few was my last teacher, Dr. G. L.
Harrington. When I hesitatingly expressed my own concern, he reached
across the desk, shook my hand, and said "Join the club." For the
past eight years as I progressed from student to colleague he has continued to work with me to develop the concepts of Reality Therapy.[1]

Reality Therapy is an effective psychiatric treatment different from
that generally accepted today. Based on psychiatric theory, which also
differs greatly from conventional or traditional psychiatry, it is applicable to all people with psychiatric problems.

Difficult as the principles of Reality Therapy may be to apply in
practice, now at least I know fairly well what they are. This has not
always been the case. Dissatisfied with traditional therapy as early as

---

[1] The text consists almost exclusively of selections from Dr. William Glasser's
Reality Therapy: A new approach to psychiatry. New York: Harper & Row,
1965. Published with permission of the publishers and the author, and with
modifications to conform to the style adopted for this book.

my last year of training, I was groping for a better way to treat people than what was being taught. It was during this period that a small, unhappy boy was assigned to me for treatment. It was to be many years before I was able to understand why this boy changed so drastically, but if there was a time when Reality Therapy began for me, it was with Aaron.

Aaron was the highly intelligent eleven-year-old son of an unemotional, overly intellectual, divorced woman who worked as a mathematician at one of the Los Angeles missile and space laboratories and a father who lived in another part of the country and had no contact with him. Aaron was often left home in the care of a neighbor while his mother went away on weekends with her boyfriend. At the time I saw him he had been seen by two other therapists over the previous two years, both third-year residents in a psychiatric training facility. He was assigned to me for treatment when I was also a third-year resident; he was my first child outpatient. The other therapists had treated him conventionally with play therapy. Most of their time was spent interpreting the meaning of his play to him. For example, if he struck a female doll repeatedly, the therapist would ask him if he would like to hit his mother and hoped Aaron would confirm the truth of his guess. Having also been trained in traditional psychiatry, I attempted at first to follow in the footsteps of the previous therapists. When Aaron confirmed his anger and hostility against his mother, I wondered, as they must have, why this insight did not help him. He wanted to learn better ways to act, but until then all of us had avoided teaching him what he needed to know.

One way to describe Aaron and his behavior is to say that although he was pleasant in appearance he was the most obnoxious child I had ever met. I dreaded Monday and Thursday mornings because those days started with Aaron. He evidently had been treated very permissively by his previous therapists who, besides interpreting his behavior to him, accepted everything he did. And what he did was horrible. He ran pell-mell from game to game and toy to toy, never letting me help him to enjoy what he was doing. He seemed to be almost desperately avoiding my offer to play as if my joining in the play might deprive him in some way of some of his pleasures. He acted aggressively in a completely haphazard, unpredictable way, crying for my attention but turning nasty and withdrawing when I gave him some warmth. He discussed his mother in a highly critical way, making her into an ogre of psychiatric rejection. His angry comments paraphrased the words of the previous therapists, especially in his use of adjectives like hostile and rejecting as he described his mother. Criticizing the previous therapists at the clinic in their treatment of him as well as the clinic toys, playrooms, and lack of entertaining facilities, he also rattled on about all the destructive things he did and was planning to do at home.

He blamed his failure to be happy on his mother, her boyfriend, his missing father, or his previous therapists. His school did not escape his critical wrath: it was very bad, his teachers did not understand him, and the other kids picked on him. As time went on, however, he blamed more and more of his predicament upon me. He was preoccupied with his mother's current boyfriend, who had been the subject of voluminous psychiatric interpretations in the past. He had learned to blame many of his problems on the boyfriend, always ending on the martyred note that this man took his mother away from him. A reading of the record showed that his repetitious complaint was almost verbatim from what previous therapists had told him.

Regardless of how he behaved, no one had ever attempted to put a value judgment on his behavior, no one had ever told him he was doing wrong. Everything he did was accepted as something to be explained or, in psychiatric terms, "interpreted" ad nauseam.

Because no one had attempted to set limits for him either in his home or in treatment, he was erratic and unhappy. His behavior was a desperate attempt to force someone to direct his behavior and discipline him so that he might behave better and achieve something worthwhile. All he felt was that no one really cared; he was involved with no one, and lacking the necessary involvement, he acted almost totally on impulse.

In his attempt to get someone to set some limits, he tried everything, producing grossly inconsistent behavior. Vocally and physically aggressive at times, he might with equal suddenness become withdrawn and almost detached from reality. He would start a game, then destroy it if he suffered even one minor setback. He walked away from our outdoor play and then would come back to beg me for candy. He would run away, hide, and try to make me look for him all over the clinic. Continually begging for ice cream or for money, he became detached when he was refused. He made it a point never to talk about anything meaningful, that is, what he was doing and feeling. If it came up naturally in conversation, he would stop suddenly and run, scream, or begin to talk gibberish. Several times during each session he would tell me that his mother did not like him and that her dislike caused his troubles. It was some time before I began to realize that he was well aware of his behavior, even to the extent that in his own erratic, impulsive way he devised new tests for my patience. He actually planned some of his misconduct, which must have been exhausting and difficult for him to keep up as long as he did.

His mother was an impersonal, detached individual who raised Aaron as an object rather than as a person. Instead of reacting to his behavior and setting some limits, she discussed it with him objectively. Essentially a cold woman, she did contribute to his frustration, but if our hope was for her to change, Aaron had little chance. Basically Aaron felt worthless and unloved. From material in the record it was apparent that the school had given up trying to reach this intelligent boy and was just trying to live with him. He made fair grades in subject matter, but he was a disrupting influence in the classroom and in all his social contacts. The other children in school and around his neighborhood shunned him like the plague, precipitating further anger and obnoxious behavior, which in turn caused them to shun him even more. At home or in school he interrupted their play, destroyed their creative attempts, and broke into their recitations in class with snide remarks.

Although Aaron was desperate for some change, I was advised by my supervisor to continue to work with him in play therapy and to interpret his "anal retention and oral aggression." A firm believer in psychoanalytic theory, my supervisor was convinced that the child needed to know "why." Once his behavior was interpreted to him in terms of the transference—that he was reacting to the therapist as a good father and also as a bad abandoning father—he should be able to change. My supervisor also thought that many of Aaron's problems could be solved if his mother, through weekly conferences with a social worker, could gain insight into her role in his difficulties and improve her treatment of him; two years of traditional social work conferences, however, had produced only more intellectualizing from her. My supervisor failed to recognize the desperate, present situation in which Aaron was doing his best to change.

Although it was to be many years before Reality Therapy became definite in my mind as a method of treatment, it was with Aaron that I first discovered the dramatic force of confronting a child with present reality. This confrontation, fortunately made after we had gained some involvement, solidified our relationship into a deeper therapeutic involvement that produced great changes in Aaron.

I realized dimly that in following the principles of orthodox therapy I was contributing to Aaron's present desperation rather than relieving it, and I made up my mind to change my approach. Against all my training and reading, and without telling anyone what I planned to do, I began a kind of Reality Therapy. The explaining was over. From now on, we were going to emphasize reality and present behavior.

When Aaron arrived the following morning, I took him into my office, nudging him gently past the playroom when he tried to stop there as usual. Telling him to sit down and listen, I explained that I was not interested in anything he had to say, only that he listen to me this morning. He whined and tried to get away, but I held him and faced him toward me. I told him to shut up and for once in his life to listen to what someone had to say. I informed him that the play was over, that we would sit and talk in an adult fashion, or if we walked we would walk as adults. I explained clearly that I would not tolerate any running away or even any impolite behavior while we were walking. He would have to be courteous and try to converse with me when I talked to him. He was to tell me everything he did, and I would help him decide whether it was right or wrong.

When he immediately attempted to leave, I forcibly restrained him. When he tried to hit me, I told him I would hit him back! After two years without restraint, he was probably shocked by the suddenness of this approach into going along with me. After some brief initial testing, he did not resist much, probably because he had been anxious for so long to be treated in this realistic way. Also, apparently sensing my own desperation, he was afraid that if he pushed me too far I would leave, and he needed me very much.

I wanted to know what he did in school and at home and what he could do that was better. When I told him frankly that he was the most miserable and obnoxious child I had ever met, he was greatly surprised. He had thought all therapists must automatically love their patients. I informed him that if he stayed in therapy he was going to have to change because neither I nor anyone else could possibly care for him the way he was now.

What happened next was most dramatic. First of all, he became likeable, talking to me courteously. He seemed to enjoy being with me, and surprisingly, I began to look forward to seeing him. Even though we were now becoming involved, he complained to his mother about my tactics. He knew that she would be upset, and he wanted to find out if she could make me change my new approach to him. If his mother had been able to change me then, it would have proved that I did not really care, and our involvement would have been broken. She sought me out as he knew she would and asked me what I had in mind. When I told her that I was definitely going to continue with my new method, she threatened to take my "unpsychiatric behavior" to my child psychiatry supervisor. I bluffed her by telling her to do so. Had she told him, I would have been in trouble, but the bluff worked. Aaron did not complain further, and she never took any action against me. I discussed other cases with my supervisor, mentioning Aaron only to say he was doing much better.

Rapidly Aaron and I grew more involved. Criticizing him for all his old weaknesses but praising him when he did well, I stood in his path whenever he tried to revert to his old ways.

In about six weeks he changed remarkably. I heard from his school that his work had suddenly risen to straight A and that his behavior had also become excellent. The teachers could not understand what had happened. I told them to be firm with him, treat him as kindly as they could, and not to make any comments about his changed performance. At home his mother noticed the changes that began to occur there also and, while she liked his new behavior, she was uncomfortable because he was "so different." Having always seen him as some kind of a miserable little boy creature, she found it difficult to relate to him as a responsible boy because of her poor attitude toward men in general.

Her attitude did not seem to bother Aaron at all. He was only slightly involved with his mother, and he was now getting satisfaction from his relationships with other people. He rather enjoyed his mother's discomfort and her inability to understand what had happened to him. I told her very little other than to treat him as an adult and to expect good behavior. After a while she began to get used to her different son, and eventually their relationship became a little better. Theirs will never be a warm, good, mother–son relationship, but it became far better than it had been in the past. As he began to play constructively with other children, for the first time in his life playmates began to seek him out.

About three months later he was discharged from therapy. He had developed a good relationship with his mother's boyfriend, and it was their new relationship that was going to make marriage between his mother and this man possible. Aaron would benefit because he certainly needed a father. After the marriage had been decided on, I thought it was a good time for him to quit therapy. School was almost over, Aaron had made some friends, and he needed me much less. I was able to follow the case for six months, and he continued to do well. Not only had Aaron benefited greatly from the therapy, but I had learned the valuable lesson that breaking with teaching and tradition as I had done could be beneficial.

THE BASIC CONCEPTS OF REALITY THERAPY

What is Wrong with Those Who Need Psychiatric Treatment?

What is it that psychiatrists attempt to treat? What is wrong with the man in a mental hospital who claims he is Jesus, with the boy in and out of reform schools who has stolen thirty-eight cars, with the woman who has continual crippling migraine headaches, with the child who refuses to learn in school and disrupts the class with temper outbursts, with the man who must lose a promotion because he is afraid to fly, and with the bus driver who suddenly goes berserk and drives his busload of people fifty miles from its destination in a careening, danger-filled ride?

Do these widely different behaviors indicate different psychiatric problems requiring a variety of explanations, or are they manifestations of one underlying difficulty? We believe regardless of how he expresses his problem anyone who needs psychiatric treatment suffers from one basic inadequacy: he is unable to fulfill his essential needs. The severity of the symptom reflects the degree to which the individual is unable to fulfill his needs. No one can explain exactly why one person expresses his problem with a stomach ulcer while another fears to enter an elevator; but whatever the symptom, it disappears when the person's needs are successfully fulfilled.

In their unsuccessful effort to fulfill their needs, no matter what behavior they choose, all patients have a common characteristic: they all deny the reality of the world around them. Some break the law, denying the rules of society; some claim their neighbors are plotting against them, denying the improbability of such behavior. Some are afraid of crowded places, close quarters, airplanes, or elevators, yet they freely admit the irrationality of their fears. Millions drink to blot out the inadequacy they feel, but that feeling need not exist if they could learn to be different; and, far too many people choose suicide rather than face the reality that they could solve their problems by more responsible behavior. Whether it is a partial denial or the total blotting out of all reality of the chronic backward patient in the state hospital, the denial of some or all of reality is common to all patients. Therapy will be successful when these patients are able to give up denying the world and to recognize that reality not only exists but that they must fulfill their needs within its framework.

A therapy that leads all patients toward reality, toward grappling successfully with the tangible and intangible aspects of the real world, might accurately be called a therapy toward reality, or simply *Reality Therapy*.

As previously mentioned, helping a patient face reality is not enough; he must also learn to fulfill his needs. Previously when he attempted to fulfill his needs in the real world, he was unsuccessful. He began to deny the real world and to try to fulfill his needs as if some aspects of the world did not exist or in defiance of their existence. A psychotic patient who lives in a world of his own and a delinquent boy who repeatedly breaks the law are common examples of these two conditions. Even a man with a stomach ulcer who seems to be facing reality in every way upon investigation is often found to be attempting more than he can cope with, and his ulcer is his body's reaction to the excess stress. Therefore, to do Reality Therapy, the therapist must not only be able to help the patient accept the real world, but he must then farther help the patient fulfill his needs in the real world so that he will have no inclination in the future to deny its existence.

How Do We Fulfill Needs?

Before discussing the basic needs themselves, we must clarify the process through which they are fulfilled. Briefly, we must be involved with other people, one at the very minimum, but hopefully many more than one. At all times in our lives we must have at least one person who cares about us and whom we care for ourselves. If we do not have this essential person, we will not be able to fulfill our basic needs. Although the person usually is in some direct relationship with us, as a mother is to a child or a teacher is to a pupil, he need not be that close as long as we have a strong feeling of his existence and he, no matter how distant, has an equally strong feeling of our existence. One characteristic is essential in the other person: he must be in touch with reality himself and able to fulfill his own needs within the world. A man marooned on a desert isle or confined in a solitary cell may be able to fulfill his needs enough to survive if he knows that someone he cares for cares about him and his condition. If the prisoner or castaway loses the conviction that this essential human cares about what is happening to him, he will begin to lose touch with reality, his needs will be more and more unfulfilled, and he may die or become insane.

Without the key person through whom we gain the strength and encouragement to cope with reality, we try desperately in many unrealistic ways to fulfill our needs. In doing so our efforts range throughout the whole gamut of psychiatric problems from mild anxiety to complete denial of reality. Therefore, essential to fulfillment of our needs is a person, preferably a group of people, with whom we are emotionally involved from the time we are born to the time we die. Much of what we call senility or senile psychosis is nothing more than the reaction of aged people to isolation. They may be physically near many people, but no one is any longer involved with them. A beautifully written example is the play *The Silver Whistle* in which a young ne'er-do-well disguises himself as an old man in order to get into what he thinks is the warmth and comfort of an old folks' home. Here he finds the occupants unnecessarily decrepit and senile. By helping them to become involved with each other, he restores them to functioning much better than they had dreamed possible. Having had a similar experience working with a ninety-five-year-old patient, I can testify to the almost miraculous effect of getting a very old man involved in life again after he had thought it impossible. From a weak, bedridden, senile man he became a vigorous, self-sufficient, active member of the sanitarium patient group, all in a period of a little over three months.

The Basic Needs

It is generally accepted that all humans have the same physiological and psychological needs. Competent people may describe or label these needs differently, but no one seriously disputes that in all cultures and in all degrees of civilization men have the same essential needs. It is also generally accepted that needs do not vary with age, sex, or race. A Chinese infant girl has the same needs as a Swedish king. The fulfillment of the physiological needs for food, warmth, and rest are rarely the concern of psychiatry. Psychiatry must be concerned with two basic psychological needs: the need to love and be loved and the need to feel that we are worthwhile to ourselves and to others. Helping patients fulfill these two needs is the basis of Reality Therapy.

Although men of all societies, classes, colors, creeds, and intellectual capacity have the same needs, they vary remarkably in
their ability to fulfill them. In every area of the world, including the
most economically and culturally advanced, there are many people
whose psychological needs are not satisfied, who are unable to give
and receive love, and who have no feeling of worth either to themselves or to others. These people are the concern of psychiatry, either
because they directly present themselves for help or because their
behavior leads their family or the community to compel them to
seek outpatient help or be placed in a psychiatric or correctional institution.

First is the need to love and be loved. In all its forms, ranging
from friendship through mother love, family love, and conjugal love,
this need drives us to continuous activity in search of satisfaction.
From birth to old age we need to love and be loved. Throughout
our lives, our health and our happiness will depend upon our ability
to do so. To either love or to allow ourselves to be loved is not
enough; we must do both. When we cannot satisfy our total need
for love, we will without fail suffer and react with many familiar
psychological symptoms, from mild discomfort through anxiety and
depression to complete withdrawal from the world around us.

Equal in importance to the need for love is the need to feel that
we are worthwhile both to ourselves and to others. Although the
two needs are separate, a person who loves and is loved will usually
feel that he is a worthwhile person, and one who is worthwhile is
usually someone who is loved and who can give love in return. Although this is usually the case, it is not always so. For example,
although an overindulged child may receive an abundance of love,
the parents do not make the critical distinction between loving him
and accepting his behavior, good or bad. Certainly the child should
be loved, but love need not mean a blanket approval of everything
he does. The child knows the difference between right and wrong behavior, and he is frustrated because receiving love for behavior that
he knows is wrong does not allow him to feel worthwhile. In this
situation he reacts in all the familiar spoiled-child patterns in an
effort to get his parents to enforce some behavioral limits and some
achievement standards along with their love. When the parents do
so, the child's behavior improves. A beautiful and capable woman
often finds herself in a similarly uncomfortable position when she is
recognized only for her beauty. Therefore, an important part of fulfilling our need to be worthwhile depends upon the ability to see

that being the object of someone's love does not in itself give us worth.

But, whether we are loved or not, to be worthwhile we must maintain a satisfactory standard of behavior. To do so we must learn to correct ourselves when we do wrong and to credit ourselves when we do right. If we do not evaluate our own behavior, or having evaluated it, we do not act to improve our conduct where it is below our standards, we will not fulfill our need to be worthwhile and we will suffer as acutely as when we fail to love or be loved. Morals, standards, values, or right and wrong behavior are all intimately related to the fulfillment of our need for self-worth.

Learning to fulfill our needs must begin early in infancy and continue all our lives. If we fail to learn, we will suffer, and this suffering always drives us to try unrealistic means to fulfill our needs. A person who does not learn as a little child to give and receive love may spend the rest of his life unsuccessfully trying to love. A woman, for example, may become involved in series of unhappy romances in which she uses sex in an unrealistic attempt to gain and give love. Only when she learns that there are better ways to attain love will she give up her unhappy, unsatisfactory behavior. A related example is a happily married woman whose husband dies. If she cannot adjust to her loss realistically and fulfill her need for love, she may follow the course of the woman in the previous example.

We know, that at the time any person comes for psychiatric help he is lacking the most critical factor for fulfilling his needs, a person whom he genuinely cares about and whom he feels genuinely cares about him. Sometimes it is obvious that the patient has no close relationships. Many times, however, especially in patients who are functioning fairly well and come to a psychiatrist in private practice, the lack of involvement is not apparent. Patients may have devoted wives, friends, and family, but they still are unable to fulfill their needs. Despite the presence of people who claim they care, the patient is either not able to accept their love or he does not care for them. What appear to be satisfactory relationships are not satisfactory for him, a condition often graphically illustrated by the case of many suicides. A person who commits suicide may have many people who care about him and he may be successful in his work, yet still leave a note describing the overwhelming loneliness and isolation he feels. Therefore, to obtain help in therapy the patient must gain or regain involvement, first with the therapist and then with others. His problem and the accompanying symptoms will disappear once he is able to become involved and fulfill his needs.

Fulfilling his needs, however, is a part of his present life; it has nothing to do with his past no matter how miserable his previous life has been. It is not only possible, it is desirable to ignore his past and work in the present because, contrary to almost universal belief, nothing which happened in his past, no matter how it may have affected him then or now, will make any difference once he learns to fulfill his needs at the present time.

Having established that we are concerned with involvement and what the patient is doing now in contrast to the usual emphasis on his past life, we must also state that we do not concern ourselves with unconscious mental processes. We do not deny that they exist as demonstrated vividly by our dreams, but they are unnecessary to the essential process of helping a patient fulfill his needs, a process which we have found must be completely conscious to be effective.

RESPONSIBILITY

Responsibility, a concept basic to Reality Therapy, is here defined as the ability to fulfill one's needs, and to do so in a way that does not deprive others of the ability to fulfill their needs. To illustrate, a responsible person can give and receive love. If a girl, for example, falls in love with a responsible man, we would expect him either to return her love or to let her know in a considerate way that he appreciates her affection but that he does not share her feelings. If he takes advantage of her love to gain some material or sexual end, we would not consider him responsible.

A responsible person also does that which gives him a feeling of self-worth and a feeling that he is worthwhile to others. He is motivated to strive and perhaps endure privation to attain self-worth. When a responsible man says that he will perform a job for us, he will try to accomplish what was asked, both for us and so that he may gain a measure of self-worth for himself. An irresponsible person may or may not do what he says depending upon how he feels, the effort he has to make, and what is in it for him. He gains neither our respect nor his own, and in time he will suffer or cause others to suffer.

Acquiring responsibility is a complicated, lifelong problem. Although we are given unchanging needs from birth to death, needs which, if left unsatisfied, cause us or others to suffer, we are not naturally endowed with the ability to fulfill them. If the ability to fulfill our needs were as much a part of man as are the needs themselves, there would be no psychiatric problems. This ability must, however, be learned. We are not directly concerned with those who have learned to lead responsible lives. Our concern is with those who have not learned or who have lost the ability—those who fill our mental hospitals and prisons, our psychiatric clinics and offices.

Throughout the remainder of this paper, these people are described as irresponsible. Their behavior is their effort, inadequate and unrealistic as it may be, to fulfill their needs.

Dispensing with Psychiatric Labels

In consonance with our emphasis on responsibility and irresponsibility, we who practice Reality Therapy advocate dispensing with the common psychiatric labels, such as neurosis and psychosis, which tend to categorize and stereotype people. Limiting our descriptions to the behavior that the patient manifests, we would, for example, describe a man who believes that he is President Johnson as irresponsible, followed by a brief description of his unrealistic behavior and thinking. Calling him psychotic or schizophrenic immediately places him in a mental illness category that separates him from most of us, the label thereby serving to compound his problem. Through our description we can immediately understand that he is unsuccessful in fulfilling his needs. He has given up trying to do so as John Jones and is now trying as President Johnson, a logical delusion for a man who feels isolated and inadequate. The description irresponsible is much more precise, indicating that our job is to help him to become more responsible so that he will be able to satisfy his needs as himself. It is evident, however, that neurotic, psychotic, schizophrenic, and other similar terms are a part of our language, both popular and scientific. Because dispensing with them suddenly would be artificial and misleading to many readers, they are used occasionally in the remainder of this paper. We suggest, however, that these labels be considered only as descriptions of irresponsibility, nothing more. We hope that the reader will try to substitute responsible for mental health and irresponsible for mental illness and its many subcategories. Accepting this change in terminology will in itself help us approach those we treat not as mentally ill but as people who need to become involved with us to fulfill their needs and thereby improve the behavior that brings them to our attention.

The Teaching of Responsibility

As the many instances of abandoned children show, man is not driven by instinct to care for and teach responsibility to his children.

In place of instinct, however, man has developed the intellectual capacity to be able to teach responsibility well. Children ordinarily learn by means of a loving relationship with responsible parents, an involvement which implies parental teaching and parental example. In addition, responsibility is taught by responsible relatives, teachers, ministers, and friends with whom they become involved. The responsible parent creates the necessary involvement with his child and teaches him responsibility through the proper combination of love and discipline. Although the means by which every responsible man was exposed to love and discipline may not be apparent, careful investigation will, we feel, always show that it did occur. People who are not at some time in their lives, preferably early, exposed intimately to others who care enough about them both to love and discipline them will not learn to be responsible. For that failure they suffer all their lives.

The words "preferably early" used in the preceding paragraph are important; they mean that the younger we are exposed to love and discipline the easier and the better we will learn responsibility. That it can be taught only to the young is not true; responsibility can be learned at any age. Nevertheless, it is easier to learn correctly at first than to overcome previous bad learning. Consider the problems in trying to correct a defective golf swing, bad grammar, or poor manners. Learning how to study in college is much harder than learning in primary or even secondary school. Similarly, responsibility should be learned early at home and in school rather than later from a psychiatrist.

Parents, who are willing to suffer the pain of the child's intense anger by firmly holding him to the responsible course are teaching him a lesson that will help him all his life. Parents who do not do so are setting the pattern for future irresponsibility which prevents the child from fulfilling the need to feel worthwhile.

When discipline is reasonable and understandable, and when the parents' own behavior is consistent with their demands on the child, he will love and respect them even though his surface attitude may not always show it. The parents must understand that the child needs responsible parents and that taking the responsible course will never permanently alienate the child.

In essence, we gain self-respect through discipline and closeness to others through love. Discipline must always have within it the element of love. "I care enough about you to force you to act in a better way, in a way you will learn through experience to know, and I already know, is the right way." Similarly, love must always have an element of discipline. "I love you because you are a worthwhile person, because I respect you and feel you respect me as well as yourself."

We learn responsibility through involvements with responsible fellow human beings, preferably loving parents who will love and discipline us properly, who are intelligent enough to allow us freedom to try out our newly acquired responsibility as soon as we show readiness to do so.

Therapy is a special kind of teaching or training which attempts to accomplish in a relatively short, intense period what should have been established during normal growing up.

Easy or difficult as its application may be in any particular case, the specialized learning situation that we call Reality Therapy is made up of three separate but intimately interwoven procedures. First, there is the involvement; the therapist must become so involved with the patient that the patient can begin to face reality and see how his behavior is unrealistic. Second, the therapist must reject the behavior that is unrealistic but still accept the patient and maintain his involvement with him. Last, and necessary in varying degrees depending upon the patient, the therapist must teach the patient better ways to fulfill his needs within the confines of reality.

The Involvement

How does the therapist become involved with a patient so that the patient can begin to fulfill his needs? The therapist has a difficult task, for he must quickly build a firm emotional relationship with a patient who has failed to establish such relationships in the past.

The ability of the therapist to get involved is the major skill of doing Reality Therapy, but it is most difficult to describe.

One way to attempt an understanding of how involvement occurs is to describe the qualities necessary to the therapist.

The therapist must be a very responsible person—tough, interested, human, and sensitive. He must be able to fulfill his own needs and must be willing to discuss some of his own struggles so that the patient can see that acting responsibly is possible though sometimes difficult. Neither aloof, superior, nor sacrosanct, he must never imply that what he does, what he stands for, or what he values is unimportant. He must have the strength to become involved, to have his values tested by the patient, and to withstand intense criticism by the person he is trying to help. Every fault and defect may be picked apart by the patient. Willing to admit that, like the patient, he is far from perfect, the therapist must nevertheless show that a person can act responsibly even if it takes great effort.

The therapist must always be strong, never expedient. He must withstand the patient's requests for sympathy, for an excess of sedatives, for justification of his actions no matter how the patient pleads or threatens. Never condoning an irresponsible action on the patient's part, he must be willing to watch the patient suffer if that helps him toward responsibility. Therefore, to practice Reality Therapy takes strength, not only the strength for the therapist to lead a responsible life himself, but also the added strength both to stand up steadily to patients who wish him to accede to their irresponsibility and to continue to point out reality to them no matter how hard they struggle against it.

Finally, the therapist must be able to become emotionally involved with each patient. To some extent he must be affected by the patient and his problems and even suffer with him. The therapist who can work with seriously irresponsible people and not be affected by their suffering will never become sufficiently involved to do successful therapy.

Developing a therapeutic involvement may take anywhere from one interview to several months, depending upon the skill of the therapist, his control over the patient, and the resistance of the patient. Once the involvement occurs, the therapist begins to insist that the patient face the reality of his behavior. He is no longer allowed to evade recognizing what he is doing or his responsibility for it. When the therapist takes this step—and he should start as soon as involvement begins—the relationship deepens because now someone cares enough about the patient to make him face a truth that he has spent his life trying to avoid: he is responsible for his behavior. Now, continually confronted with reality by the therapist, he is not allowed to excuse or condone any of his behavior. No reason is acceptable to the therapist for any irresponsible behavior. He confronts the patient with his behavior and asks him to decide whether or not he is taking the responsible course. The patient thus finds a man who cares enough about him to reject behavior that will not help him to fulfill his needs.

Concentrating on Realistic Behavior

In Reality Therapy we are much more concerned with behavior than with attitudes. Once we are involved with the patient, we begin to point out to him the unrealistic aspects of his irresponsible behavior. If the patient wishes to argue that his conception of reality is correct, we must be willing to discuss his opinions, but we must not fail to emphasize that our main interest is his behavior rather than his attitude.

Suppose an adolescent girl has continual temper tantrums over her mother's unwillingness to let her date a certain boy. If in therapy we had attained a good involvement with the girl, we would ask her to try just once to discuss the subject with her mother without losing her temper. She may say there is no point in talking to her mother, that even if she holds her temper, her feelings about the situation will be unchanged. On the other hand, she may agree to take our advice, and the whole problem may suddenly disappear, a very common occurrence.

This incident actually happened and not because we made a magic suggestion but because the girl had learned a valuable lesson in need fulfillment. She had become willing to try a new pattern of behavior, regardless of her conviction that it would not work.

The change had a dramatic effect on the girl's mother. She saw her daughter in a different light. The mother grew calmer, and for the first time the question of dating the boy could be discussed on its merits. The conflict between the mother and daughter began to disappear when they could talk to each other reasonably. As they felt more love for each other and more worthwhile themselves, the problem was quickly solved.

This brief example demonstrates how waiting for attitudes to change stalls therapy whereas changing behavior leads quickly to a change in attitude, which in turn can lead to fulfilling needs and further better behavior. The Negro groups fighting for their civil rights use the same argument. If they wait for the attitude of the people of Mississippi to change, they may wait forever.

Along with the emphasis on behavior and as a continuing part of the involvement, the therapist freely gives praise when the patient acts responsibly and shows disapproval when he does not. The patient demands this judgment, which is a natural expression of faith between two people, as a test of the sincerity of the relationship. The patient rather than the therapist must decide whether or not his behavior is irresponsible and whether he should change it. If a boy thinks that he cannot help stealing cars, no therapy is possible. If a man thinks that it is all right to overeat and be fat, no obesity treatment will work. The skill of therapy is to put the responsibility upon the patient and, after involvement is established, to ask him why he remains in therapy if he is not dissatisfied with his behavior. In private practice, where the patient comes voluntarily, the timing of this question is vital. It must not be asked before the involvement is deep enough to force the patient to stop defending his irresponsible actions rather than leave therapy. Even a skillful therapist may lose a patient if he asks this question too soon. Usually a patient who leaves office therapy under these circumstances will return because, of course, nothing will change to make his life better. In treatment the skillful therapist does not make the point blatantly; rather, it is implied during the whole process of therapy.

As therapy proceeds, the therapist must teach the patient that therapy is not primarily directed toward making him happy. Accepting the premise that people can find happiness only for themselves, the therapist must guide the patient toward understanding that no one can make another person happy for long unless this person becomes more responsible. Happiness occurs most often when we are willing to take responsibility for our behavior. Irresponsible people, always seeking to gain happiness without assuming responsibility, find only brief periods of joy but not the deep-seated satisfaction that accompanies responsible behavior. When they have a problem, they may try to ignore it, drown it in alcohol, or rationalize it away—all in an effort to gain brief happiness. When they are finally faced with reality, when they can no longer ignore or rationalize their action, they suffer and run for help. However, the only help that will do any good is that which guides them toward the responsibility they are so steadfastly avoiding.

The therapist who accepts excuses, ignores reality, or allows the patient to blame his present unhappiness on a parent or on an emotional disturbance can usually make his patient feel good temporarily at the price of evading responsibility. He is only giving the patient "psychiatric kicks," which are no different from the brief kicks he may have obtained from alcohol, pills, or sympathetic friends before consulting the psychiatrist. When these kicks fade, as they soon must, the patient with good reason becomes disillusioned with psychiatry.

We must never delude ourselves into wrongly concluding that unhappiness led to the patient's behavior, plausible as it may seem, or that a delinquent child broke the law because he was miserable and therefore our job is to make him happy. He broke the law not because he was angry or bored but because he was irresponsible. The unhappiness is not a cause but a companion to his irresponsible behavior.

The reader may wonder what the conversation between patient and doctor consists of if the latter is not interested in the patient's history, his unconscious mind, or even in making him happy. As part of becoming involved, the therapist must become interested in and discuss all aspects of the patient's present life. Relating discussion to his behavior whenever possible, the patient and the doctor talk about the patient's interests, hopes, fears, opinions, and particularly his values— his own personal ideas of right and wrong. We are interested in him as a person with a wide potential, not just as a patient with problems. In fact, one of the best ways not to become involved is to discuss his problems over and over. Although continually listening to misery is one way of giving the patient sympathy, he soon discovers that with all the talk the therapist can do nothing directly to solve his problems.

We must open up his life, talk about new horizons, expand his range of interests, make him aware of life beyond his difficulties. Anything two people might discuss is grist for therapy: politics, plays, books, movies, sports, hobbies, finances, health, marriage, sex, and religion are all possible topics.

When values, standards, and responsibility are in the background, all discussion is relevant to therapy.

Because the patient must gain responsibility right now, the focus is always on the present. The past has certainly contributed to what he is now, but we cannot change the past, only the present. Recounting his history in the hope that he will learn from his mistakes rarely proves successful and should be avoided. From past mistakes the patient learns only that he knew better at the time yet still did not act on his knowledge. Past errors with friends or family may be interesting to talk about, but discussing them with the therapist is a waste of time. The present, the right now, is the critical task, not the easy job of recounting the patient's historical irresponsibility and looking for excuses. Why become involved with the irresponsible person he was? We want to become involved with the responsible person we know he can be.

In Reality Therapy emotions and happiness are never divorced from behavior. Gaining insight into the unconscious thinking that accompanies aberrant behavior is not an objective; excuses for deviant behavior are not accepted, and one's history is not made more important than one's life. We never blame others for the patient's irresponsibility or censure mother, father, or anyone deeply involved with the patient no matter how irresponsible they are or were. The patient cannot change them; he can only learn better ways to live with them or without them. We never encourage hostility or acting out irresponsible impulses, for that only compounds the problem. We never condemn society. If a Negro, for example, feels limited by the white society, he must still take a responsible course of action. Blind hatred of his oppressors gains nothing for him or anyone else in a similar position.

In Reality Therapy, therefore, we rarely ask why. Our usual question is What? What are you doing—not why are you doing it? Why implies that the reasons for the patient's behavior make a difference in therapy, but they do not. The patient will himself search for reasons; but, until he has become more responsible, he will not be able to act differently, even when he knows why. All the reasons in the world for why he drinks will not lead an alcoholic to stop. Change will occur only when he fulfills his needs more satisfactorily. Then the reasons become unimportant because the need to drink will have disappeared. All aberrant behavior is either an attempt to evade or an inability to take the responsibility of doing right, of fulfilling our basic needs. Alcoholics Anonymous, for example, is successful in many instances because it fulfills the needs of the alcoholic, but first he has to give up all evasions and admit he is an alcoholic. The therapist's job is to point out the reality of what the patient is doing now, not to search with him for the "why" that he will always grasp in an effort not to change. Thus, in our effort toward helping him gain more conscious responsible control over what he does, we adhere closely to the reality of the present.

Learning New Ways

When the patient admits that his behavior is irresponsible, the last phase of therapy—relearning—begins. Actually no definite change in therapy occurs; relearning is merged into the whole treatment. The patient must rely on the therapist's experience to help him learn better ways of behavior. When he can do so, when the young delinquent learns the value of working and experiences the good feelings that accompany responsible action, therapy is approaching an end. It is only a matter of time until the patient, with his newly acquired responsible behavior, begins to fulfill his needs. He finds new relationships, more satisfying involvements, and needs the therapist less. Visits become less frequent as both therapist and patient are aware of the approaching end. Parting is a pleasant time, but it is not necessarily final nor should it be. The stress and strain of living may cause the patient to return, but not for more than brief relearning periods. Once the specific situation is responsibly handled, the patient leaves again.

THE DIFFERENCES BETWEEN REALITY THERAPY AND CONVENTIONAL THERAPY

Having described Reality Therapy in the previous section, I now wish to make clear the major differences, both in theory and practice, between Reality Therapy and what is widely accepted as conventional psychotherapy. Conventional therapy, based either strictly or loosely upon the psychoanalytic beliefs and teachings of Sigmund Freud, is taught in almost every major college and university in the United States and Canada.

CONVENTIONAL PSYCHIATRY

1. Conventional psychiatry believes firmly that mental illness exists, that people who suffer from it can be meaningfully classified, and that attempts should be made to treat them according to the diagnostic classification.

2. Conventional psychiatry holds that an essential part of treatment is probing into the patient's past life, seaching for the psychological roots of his problem because once the patient clearly understands these roots he can use his understanding to change his attitude toward life. From this change in attitude he can then develop more effective patterns of living which will solve his psychological difficulties.

3. Conventional psychiatry maintains that the patient must transfer to the therapist attitudes he held or still holds toward important people in his past life, people around whom his problems started. Using this concept, called transference, the therapist relives with the patient his past difficulties and then explains to him how he is repeating the same inadequate behavior with the therapist. The patient, through the therapist's interpretations of the transference behavior, gains insight into his past. His newly attained insight allows him to give up his old attitudes and to learn to relate to people in a better way, solving his problems.

4. Conventional psychotherapy, even in superficial counseling, em-

REALITY THERAPY

1. Because we do not accept the concept of mental illness, the patient cannot become involved with us as a mentally ill person who has no responsibility for his behavior.

2. Working in the present and toward the future, we do not get involved with the patient's history because we can neither change what happened to him nor accept the fact that he is limited by his past.

3. We relate to patients as ourselves, not as transference figures.

4. We do not look for unconscious conflicts or the reasons for them.

phasizes that if the patient is to change he must gain understanding and insight into his unconscious mind. Unconscious mental conflicts are considered more important than conscious problems; making the patient aware of them through the interpretation of transference, dreams, and free associations, and through educated psychiatric guessing, is necessary if therapy is to succeed.

A patient cannot become involved with us by excusing his behavior on the basis of unconscious motivations.

5. Necessarily accompanying the conviction that mental illness exists, conventional psychiatry scrupulously avoids the problem of morality, that is, whether the patient's behavior is right or wrong. Deviant behavior is considered a product of the mental illness, and the patient should not be held morally responsible because he is considered helpless to do anything about it. Once the illness is cured through the procedures described in Points 2, 3, and 4, the patient will then be able to behave according to the rules of society.

5. We emphasize the morality of behavior. We face the issue of right and wrong, which we believe solidifies the involvement, in contrast to conventional psychiatrists who do not make the distinction between right and wrong, feeling it would be detrimental to attaining the transference relationship they seek.

6. Teaching people to behave better is not considered an important part of therapy in conventional psychiatry, which holds the patients will learn better behavior themselves once they understand both the historical and unconscious sources of problems.

6. We teach patients better ways to fulfill their needs. The proper involvement will not be maintained unless the patient is helped to find more satisfactory patterns of behavior. Conventional therapists do not feel that reaching better behavior is a part of therapy.

In the detailed discussion that follows, it will be clear that each of the six points of difference between Reality Therapy and conventional psychiatry contributes to the difference between the way we as Reality therapists become involved with our patients and how conventional psychiatrists relate to theirs. With the overall difference of involvement in mind, let us examine in detail the six major beliefs of conventional psychiatry and compare them to the theory and practice of Reality Therapy.

First, and very important from a treatment standpoint, both the theory and practice of Reality Therapy are incompatible with the prevalent, widely accepted concept of mental illness. We [the pronouns we and our are used by the author to refer to himself and his colleagues who endorse and practice Reality Therapy] believe that this concept, the belief that people can and do suffer from some specific, diagnosable, treatable mental illness, analogous to a specific, diagnosable, treatable physical illness, is inaccurate and that this inaccuracy is a major roadblock to proper psychiatric treatment. Scientific and lay literature are both filled with the idea that anyone who behaves and thinks in a way unacceptable to the majority of the society is mentally ill or, in popular terms, "sick," a concept as prevalent to our culture as the flatness of the earth was to the Middle Ages.

Those who believe in mental illness assume incorrectly that something definite is wrong with the patient which causes him to be the way he is. Most psychiatrists believe that the patient was all right at one time and then fell victim to a series of unhappy life experiences that now cause his deviant behavior. We believe this concept misleads the doctor, the patient, and those concerned with him into the false belief that the doctor's job is to treat some definite condition, after which the patient will get well. This attitude was graphically illustrated by a patient whom I treated some years ago, an imposing woman who sat down, looked directly at me, and stated in all sincerity, "I'm here, Doctor. Do psychiatry!"

Those who believe in mental illness try to remove some specific internal psychological cause (the often heard "root of the problem") which they believe is responsible for the patient's present deviant behavior. Conventional psychiatry, almost without fail, relates this cause to instances in his previous life when the patient was unable to cope with stress. We believe that there is no noxious psychological causative agent to remove. Our job is to help the patient help himself to fulfill his needs right now.

If there is a medical analogy that applies to psychiatric problems, it is not illness but weakness. Although illness can be cured by removing the causative agent, weakness can be cured only by strengthening the existing body to cope with the stress of the world, large or small as this stress may be.

By dispensing with the idea of mental illness and calling a man irresponsible, and then describing how he is irresponsible, Reality Therapy defines the situation much more precisely. Using the latter description, one sees that the cause of the psychiatric patient's condition is different from that of a patient with a physical illness, who is more truly the victim of forces outside himself. Regardless of past circumstances, the psychiatric patient must develop the strength to take the responsibility to fulfill his needs satisfactorily. Treatment, therefore, is not to give him understanding of past misfortunes that caused his "illness" but to help him to function in a better way right now.

Philosophically, as well as practically, from the patient's standpoint there is a world of difference between being cured of illness and helping oneself. With typhoid fever, one may be as motivated as possible and still die unless some capable physician gives the proper medical treatment. A car-stealing juvenile delinquent, however, treated by a psychiatrist for years on the basis of mental illness, will not change as long as he is allowed to play the misunderstood or mistreated child who does not understand all that has happened to him. He and all other irresponsible people now wrongly labeled "mentally ill" must clearly understand that they must help themselves regardless of what has happened to them in the past (and we should be the last to deny that they have suffered). As long as the mental illness concept prevails and patients continue to see themselves as the recipients of help, we will make little progress in psychiatry. With the hazy conception that most patients and their families have of mental illness, the responsibility for change lies less with them than with the treating agency, be it doctor, social worker, correctional institution, or hospital.

Psychiatrists discovered long ago that as much as they would like to follow the medical parallel and cure the patient of his brain disease, they were unable to do so because no brain pathology existed. Instead of giving up the illness concept, psychiatrists seized on the discovery of unconscious conflicts as the cause of mental illness. It was the conflicts that caused patients to be the way they are, mentally ill. Patients are led on long, expensive trips back through their childhood, often discovering that mother was the cause of it all. Once the patient is helped to wrest his childhood resentments against mother from his unconscious mind, cure is theoretically in sight.

For example, an obese young woman who has a compulsive overeating problem may find out through psychotherapy that her mother wanted a more beautiful daughter. Because obesity in a young woman is never desirable, she overeats in order to avoid facing the truth that her mother would reject her even if she were slim. She can accept the mother's rejection because she is indeed fat and unattractive, perhaps so much so that her mother and others may have given her sympathy, if not acceptance. In traditional therapy, being accepted as mentally ill and having learned why, the patient will attempt to throw herself upon the therapist. Learning from him that the source of the problem is past and present unresolved conflict with her mother, she continues to eat, her appetite undiminished by this knowledge. This not uncommon situation, where the unchanging fat and miserable patient damns her mother for years in psychotherapy, has discredited psychiatry in the minds of many people. Under these too-familiar circumstances, where the mental illness is accepted and the cause is sought and discovered to be outside herself (in this case her mother's rejection), the patient is relieved of the necessary responsibility for her part in the therapy. The fat girl's only chance of being helped is to learn that she is irresponsible, not that she is mentally ill, and that her unattractiveness is important primarily to her. Her mother is only an excuse for her irresponsibility. To help this girl we must scrupulously avoid giving her excuses for the way she is, rather, we must help her give up excusing her inability to fill her needs and guide her toward the reality that she must fulfill them regardless of her mother.

Also misleading but an important part of the mental illness concept is the use of psychiatric diagnoses to label a wide variety of "mental illnesses." The purpose of diagnosis is to select proper treatment. If we diagnose that a headache is caused by a brain tumor, a logical sequence of treatment is suggested. The treatment, which often includes brain surgery, is far different from the treatment that might be given to a severe headache caused by eyestrain or alcoholic hangover. Where treatment logically and necessarily follows diagnosis, correct diagnosis is vital; in the case of so-called mental illnesses, however, treatment by any one doctor, whether psychoanalyst or Reality therapist, is essentially the same. Psychotherapy lacks the specific and individual treatment that follows the diagnosis of scarlet fever, syphilis, or malaria. Even where there is no specific treatment, as in the common cold, the correct diagnosis hopefully will avoid improper treatment with antibiotics and other detrimental medications.

With Reality Therapy there is no essential difference in the treatment of various psychiatric problems. The treatment of psychotic veterans is almost exactly the same as the treatment of delinquent, adolescent girls. The particular manifestation of irresponsibility (the diagnosis) has little relationship to the treatment. From our standpoint, all that needs to be diagnosed is whether the patient is suffering from irresponsibility, no matter with what behavior he expresses it, or from an organic illness.

Under the heading of "mentally ill" are numerous diagnoses, such as schizophrenic, neurotic, depressed, sociopathic, and psychosomatic, all describing some kind of irresponsible behavior. All these various terms only describe the best the patient has been able to manage in his effort to fulfill his needs. The psychotic patient who believes he is Jesus Christ seems very different from a man with a stomach ulcer, but we should not be fooled by appearances. Like the blind mens' descriptions of the elephant, each variety of irresponsible behavior seems much different from all others. Irresponsibility, however, is as basic to the various kinds of behavior as the elephant is basic to his trunk, tail, or legs, and it is the irresponsibility, the whole elephant, that must be treated.

Unfortunately for taxpayers as well as patients, almost all teaching of psychiatry, psychology, and social work follows traditional thinking that considers the diagnosis of mental illness to be essential to successful treatment. Millions of dollars are spent annually in an attempt to diagnose types of mental illness in the vain hope that the diagnosis will be helpful in treatment. It is pathetically common to hear young psychiatric residents argue whether a certain patient is neurotic because he fears to leave the house or psychotic because he imagines that an unseen enemy will attack him if he steps outside the door. In either case he suffers from the inability to fulfill his needs. Whether he is afraid of reality (conventionally described as neurotic) or denies reality (psychotic) makes little difference in his life and no difference in treatment. The argument over labels helps no one. Conventional psychiatry wastes too much time arguing over how many diagnoses can dance at the end of a case history, time better spent treating the ever-present problem of irresponsibility.

Necessarily closely related to eliminating the concept of mental illness is the somewhat more radical idea of dispensing with any major inquiry into the patient's past history, ordinarily considered as essential to psychiatry as the scalpel is to the surgeon. Both professional and lay people often ask us, "How can there be any therapy if the therapist does not probe deeply into the patient's past life and uncover each twist and turn?" Light must be cast on each dark corner in the patient's previous life or you cannot help him. The most frustrated critics ask what the patient and the psychiatrist talk about if case history is eliminated from the discussion. Although what has happened to a person may be important as information contributing to developing psychological generalizations (such as perhaps finding out that boys who have poor relationships with their fathers are more apt to become homosexual), this information has little to do with therapy. Studies of how to raise children to be more responsible are valuable, but finding out how poorly a patient was raised will never change his upbringing. The most complete history possible, perhaps a sound motion picture of the patient's whole life plus a tape recording of every unconscious thought, would be no more helpful in treating a patient than a short description of his present problem. The history merely details ad infinitum the patient's unsuccessful attempts to fulfill his needs.

Without denying that the patient had an unsatisfactory past, we find that to look for what went wrong does not help him. What good comes from discovering that you are afraid to assert yourself because you had a domineering father? Both patient and therapist can be aware of this historical occurrence, they can discuss it in all of its ramifications for years, but the knowledge will not help the patient assert himself now. In fact, in our experience the more he knows why he cannot assert himself, the less inclined he will be to do so because he now understands that self-assertion is psychologically painful. Most patients will then lean on the psychiatrist, saying, "Now that I know why I can't assert myself, what will make me lose the fear?" The psychiatrist's reply is necessarily weak, "You don't have to be afraid because your father is no longer in the picture." It would be wonderful if therapy were that simple, that knowing the root of the fear would allow the patient to become unafraid.

For Reality Therapy it makes little difference what relationship the patient had with his father. We want to know what is going on now in all aspects of the patient's life. When the patient tells all the details of his past to the therapist, he overemphasizes his inadequacy to the point where it is difficult for him to believe that the therapist can really accept him. Attaining involvement is hampered because involvement can start only on the solid ground of your being able to accept him as he is right now. As therapists, however, we do find it helpful to find out how long his current problem has been going on, not for historical information, but to help us gauge whether he will need brief or more extended therapy.

The conventional psychiatrist depends far too much on the ability of the patient to change his attitude and ultimately his behavior through gaining insight into his unconscious conflicts and inadequacies. In Reality Therapy we emphasize behavior; we do not depend upon insight to change attitudes because in many cases it never will. Once we become involved with a patient and teach him new ways of behavior his attitude will change regardless of whether or not he understands his old ways, and then his new attitude will help promote further behavioral change. What starts the process, however, is an initial change in behavior, and it is toward this event that the therapist must work.

Conventional psychiatrists, led by Freud, have also learned that insight derived from the past is not by itself an effective instrument for change. They have, therefore, developed another concept through which they implement the insight gained through a study of the past. This concept, called transference, is an attempt to tie the insight more closely to the present and hopefully make it more useful to the patient.

Although a conventional psychiatrist tries to stay personally un-involved with the patient during therapy, he certainly does not avoid involvement completely. Instead of a single, intense personal in-volvement of doctor with patient, he attempts to gain a series of involvements, such as mother to patient, father to patient, brother to patient, teacher to patient, and employer to patient. He does so, according to Reality Therapy, in the mistaken belief that the patient must reexperience in therapy his attitudes toward the important peo-ple in his life, past and present. Using transference, the conventional psychiatrist does not tell the patient that he is afraid to assert himself because his father treated him harshly. Instead, he goes halfway to-ward becoming personally involved with the patient by saying. "You are treating me as if I were your father and blaming your failure to assert yourself upon me." Ironically, the patient is indeed blam-ing his failure to assert himself upon the psychiatrist, but not because the psychiatrist is like his father. It is because of the difficulty of be-coming involved with a therapist who, instead of establishing a close personal relationship with the patient in his own capacity, sometimes plays the role of someone else and sometimes acts as himself.

Psychiatric patients are not seeking to repeat unsuccessful involve-ments past or present; they are looking for a satisfying human in-volvement through which they can fulfill their needs now. In con-ventional therapy an involvement that can benefit the patient may occur if therapy lasts long enough because the patient will eventually relate to the psychiatrist as himself no matter how the psychiatrist protests at the time that he is acting as someone else. The psychia-trist must reject the untherapeutic concept of transference and relate to the patient as a new and separate person with whom the patient can become involved, and through the new involvement teach him to fulfill his needs in the real world of the present.

Closely allied to transference is the concept of the unconscious. Conventional psychiatry contends that the unconscious motivation is highly important and that for successful therapy the patient must become aware of previously unconscious reasons for the way he behaves. In the transference relationship the therapist is able to point out behavior and thought processes of which the patient was not aware. Besides the transference, he uses projective tests, free associations, dream analysis, and slips of the tongue. These methods all give the therapist insight into the patient's unconscious mind, but they do not help therapy.

Certainly patients, like everyone else, have reasons of which they may be unaware for behaving the way they do. Talking in one's sleep, slips of the tongue, phobias, and compulsions are examples of behavior obviously based upon unconscious mental processes. But we are doing therapy, not research into the cause of human behavior, and we have found that knowledge of cause has nothing to do with therapy. Patients have been treated with conventional psychiatry until they know the unconscious reason for every move they make, but they still do not change because knowing the reason does not lead to fulfilling needs. It is wishful thinking to believe that a man will give up a phobia once he understands either its origin or the current representation of its origin in the transference relationship. He continues to have the phobia because of some present irresponsible behavior that may or may not be directly related to the origin of the phobia. If we examine his present life in detail, we will find behavior of which he is fully conscious that does not lead to fulfilling his needs. When we help him through Reality Therapy to act in ways that will fulfill his needs, his phobia will disappear. Emphasis upon the unconscious sidetracks the main issue of the patient's irresponsibility and gives him another excuse to avoid facing reality. We cannot emphasize enough that delving into a man's unconscious mind is detrimental to therapy.

An example will help clarify the point that investigating the unconscious is detrimental to therapy. A man who is educated and qualified to practice law fails in his own practice, but does well when he is a subordinate research clerk in a large law firm. Although he says he would like to achieve success, whenever he attempts to strike out on his own he becomes nervous, anxious, and unable to function. Diagnosed as neurotic, he consults a conventional psychiatrist. Eventually he may discover that in his childhood he greatly feared his strong father, a fear accompanied by many fantasies of murdering his father and taking his father's place as the head of the house. These fantasies caused him at that time to fear retaliation, and they still remain in his subconscious mind to produce the conflict between his desire to assert himself and his fear of doing so.

According to traditional theory, this unconscious conflict is the obstacle to his getting ahead, since even now he fears to assert himself as a man. Twenty-five years later, whenever he steps from his subordinate, almost child-like role of law clerk, he is unable to function. He is nervous, upset, and ineffective until he retreats from the danger of his independent position to the safety of his clerk's job. According to accepted psychiatric thinking, his (now unconscious) childhood conflict, never resolved and continuing throughout his life, thwarts his success. Maintaining that resolving the conflict is the crux of therapy, the conventional therapist works in the man's past, delving into his unconscious through dreams and free associations in the hope that once these conflicts are uncovered the patient will be able to move ahead successfully.

We accept the fact that a very small portion of his problem may be based upon his past, but we believe that most of it is due to his inability to face what he is really doing now. Because no one lives a life where his needs are always fulfilled, it is impossible not to find a wealth of buried conflicts which, being similar to present difficulties, seem to explain a person's inability to fulfill his needs now. This kind of unconscious material comes forth readily under the pressures and skills of the conventional psychiatrist. In addition, the patient soon learns that he can gain the psychiatrist's approval by giving him reams of conflict-causing material. Besides psychiatric approval, the patient likes nothing better than to be relieved of the responsibility for his present behavior by his wonderful storehouse of unconscious conflicts derived from his past failures.

Actually, however, what is really below the level of consciousness is what he is doing now. In a sense the patient is aware of his present behavior, but it is only a meager awareness. Incorrectly assuming that the patient is fully conscious of his present behavior, the conventional therapist emphasizes the past; in so doing he misses the extent to which the patient lacks awareness of what he is doing now.

The Reality Therapist insists that the patient face his present behavior. We go over and over what he is doing now to make him understand that his present behavior does not fulfill his needs.

A further important difference between Reality Therapy and conventional psychiatry concerns the place of morality, or to be more specific, the place of right and wrong. Conventional psychiatry does not directly concern itself with the issue of right and wrong. Rather, it contends that once the patient is able to resolve his conflicts and get over his mental illness, he will be able to behave correctly. We have found that this view is unrealistic. All society is based on morality, and if the important people in the patient's life, especially his therapist, do not discuss whether his behavior is right or wrong, reality cannot be brought home to him. It is unrealistic to ask a delinquent girl why she stole a car, why she is pregnant, why she smokes marijuana, hoping that once she discovers the reasons she will be able to resolve her conflicts and change her behavior. We believe that to stop her unsatisfactory behavior she must fulfill her needs, but that to fulfill her needs she must face the real world around her that includes standards of behavior.

Admittedly, the introduction of morality into psychotherapy may draw criticism from many sources. Some people argue that a great strength of conventional psychiatry is that it does not involve itself with this age-old question. It would be easier for us if we could avoid the issue also, but we cannot. People come to therapy suffering because they behave in ways that do not fulfill their needs, and they ask if their behavior is wrong. Our job is to face this question, confront them with their total behavior, and get them to judge the quality of what they are doing. We have found that unless they judge their own behavior, they will not change. We do not claim that we have discovered the key to universal right or that we are experts in ethics. We do believe, however, that to the best of our ability as responsible human beings we must help our patients arrive at some decision concerning the moral quality of their behavior. To do so, we have found that for the purpose of therapy the following definition seems to be extremely useful. (Whether our definition could stand the test of scholarly debate with great moral philosophers of the world is questionable, but at least it has provided us with some framework upon which to focus our therapy discussions.)

We believe that almost all behavior which leads to fulfilling our needs, within the bounds of reality is right, or good, or moral behavior, according to the following definition: When a man acts in such a way that he gives and receives love, and feels worthwhile to himself and others, his behavior is right or moral.

The psychiatrist sees hundreds of patients who have some conflict between their needs and would like to use this conflict as an excuse for irresponsible behavior. For example, a man who is unhappily married gives lip service to continuing the marriage for the sake of his children, but he begins to drink heavily and neglect his work. His income falls off, his family suffers, and his self-respect disappears.

No outsider could solve the problem of such a patient's marriage. He must do that alone. But the psychiatrist who helps him to face the cause of his behavior, curtail his drinking, and resume his adult responsibility toward the support of his family can make a real contribution to this man's development. This is Reality Therapy in action. The patient regains his self-respect and is able to make a decision that is in the best interests of everyone concerned.

A Reality Therapist treating a patient is not afraid to pose the question "Are you doing right or wrong?" or "Are you taking the responsible course?" In psychiatric treatment, strengthening the patient's recognition that his present behavior is wrong or irresponsible is a powerful motivation toward positive change. When we point out what the patient is doing that may be wrong instead of helping him look for excuses, he finds out that therapy is not an intellectual psychiatric game of conflict, conflict, what can be the conflict? He discovers that we really care about him, an essential step toward gaining the involvement necessary for therapy.

Therefore, in order to do therapy successfully, the therapist must acknowledge that standards of behavior exist, standards accepted by both individuals and society as the best means of meeting basic human needs. Patients must be confronted by the disparity between the values they recognize as the acceptable norm and the lives they lead.

For example, many delinquent girls maintain that there is nothing wrong with prostitution. Rather than argue, I ask if they would help their daughters become prostitutes. They always answer no, but in the next breath they protest that prostitution is the only way they can earn a living—it is all they know.

Getting a patient to acknowledge the values he really believes in is part of the art of therapy, but once these values are acknowledged, the major task is to help him live by these standards. Unfortunately, in their effort to avoid the issue of morality, many conventional therapists accept behavior that does not lead to need fulfillment in the mistaken belief that this is the best effort the patient is capable of making.

Where standards and values are not stressed, the most that therapy can accomplish is to help patients become more comfortable in their irresponsibility. Because our effort is always directed toward helping patients fulfill their needs, we insist on their striving to reach the highest possible standards.

We are looking for neither conformity nor mediocrity in the guise of normal behavior. The most responsible men, such as Abraham Lincoln or Albert Schweitzer, are those farthest from the norm. Our job is not to lessen the pain of irresponsible actions but to increase the patient's strength so that he can bear the necessary pain of a full life as well as enjoy the rewards of a deeply responsible existence.

The final major difference between Reality Therapy and conventional therapy is our emphasis upon the therapist's role as a teacher. In conventional therapy, teaching is limited to helping the patient gain insight into the causes of his behavior. From then on it is assumed that he will either learn better ways by himself or from someone else; the therapist's job is limited to making clear the conscious and unconscious determinants of his problems.

In Reality Therapy we do not search for the insights so vital to conventional psychiatry. Instead we take every opportunity to teach patients better ways to fulfill their needs. We spend much time painstakingly examining the patient's daily activity and suggesting better ways for him to behave. We answer the many questions that patients ask and suggest ways to solve problems and approach people. Patients who have not been able to fulfill their needs must learn both how to approach people so that they can become more involved and how to accomplish enough so that they can gain an increased feeling of self-worth.

To summarize, we should say that in the six major areas covered, Reality Therapy differs markedly from conventional therapy. Reality Therapy is not another variety of the same approach but a different way to work with people. The requirements of Reality Therapy—an intense personal involvement, facing reality and rejecting irresponsible behavior, and learning better ways to behave—bear little resemblance to conventional therapy and produce markedly different results [as is shown in the examples given in the book *Reality Therapy*] with delinquent girls, hospitalized psychotics, school children, and in private practice. The application of the method to psychotics is illustrated in the concluding section.

REALITY THERAPY ON A PSYCHOTIC WARD

Building 206, composed of four wards totaling 210 patients, has been in existence for almost twenty years at the Veterans Administration (V.A.) Hospital in West Los Angeles. Until recently, when Dr. G. L. Harrington introduced the concepts of Reality Therapy, it housed the patients who were most chronic, psychotic, and resistive to treatment. It had the traditional mental hospital approach in which the patients were accepted as mentally ill and were given good standard care. Any active treatment, however, was oriented toward helping them maintain themselves at as high a level as possible within the hospital. No dramatic change in their condition was expected, and the average discharge rate was about two patients a year. The patients' problems were categorized into the standard, meaningless, hospital diagnoses: paranoid schizophrenia, catatonic schizophrenia, and the old wastebasket diagnosis of chronic, undifferentiated schizophrenia. Labeled with these antitherapeutic terms, the patients did about what was expected of them. They hallucinated a little, suffered from a few delusions, but mostly they sat around in the relatively plush V.A. mental hospital environment waiting out their lives. Most patients stayed in the ward indefinitely; fifteen years was the average length stay in Building 206.

Here over 210 men lived separated from the world, both through their own choice, and by the traditional mental illness concepts that prevailed there and still prevail in most mental hospitals. Symbiosis had been established. The patients were no longer actively crazy, they needed little care, and the hospital accepted them as mentally ill people who had arrived at their permanent station in life. For all practical purposes, a contract had been signed that both sides were scrupulous in fulfilling.

It was this contract, the concurrence of the staff with the patients' agreement to stay peacefully psychotic, that Dr. Harrington broke when he took over the ward in 1962. Stepping down at his own request from an administrative position, he returned to his more congenial post of ward physician. Completely in charge of Building 206, he introduced a total Reality Therapy program into the lives of the staff and patients with the help of one social worker and one psychologist.

The impact of the new program quickly began to show on the ward. Increasing numbers of patients began to be discharged. A few at first, and then at a steadily ascending rate, the releases climbed from the average of two per year to twenty-five in 1962. In 1963, seventy-five patients were released with only three returning. Over the following years this rate climbed to approximately two hundred a year, which meant a complete turnover of the ward each year.

The spectacular increase in discharge rate has been accomplished with less psychiatric time devoted to the ward than before. Dr. Harrington, replacing a full-time psychiatrist, spends only twenty hours a week at the hospital; the rest of the staff has remained the same. The average patient has spent an increasing number of years in mental hospitals because the emptied beds are continually filled by the almost inexhaustible supply of veterans transferred from state hospitals. A veteran whose disability is not service connected is eligible for V.A. care when there are no veterans with service-connected disabilities requesting admission. The average transferee has been a patient in a state hospital for over fifteen years. Men who have been hospitalized for twenty years are not uncommon as it is now more than thirty years since the draft began in 1940.

As indicated in working with delinquents at the Ventura School for Girls, the first and perhaps most important step in applying Reality Therapy in Building 206 was to convince each staff member that because it is a total program he is just as important to the success of the program as is the ward psychiatrist. Dr. Harrington carefully taught and retaught each staff member to forget the concept of schizophrenia and mental illness and to consider the patients as people who are behaving this way because that is the best they have been able to do up to now. He instructed them, however, not to respond to the abnormal behavior and thinking, but to treat each patient as if he is capable of not being crazy now; in this ward he does not have to be.

Every staff member is taught that, at one time in his life, each long-term patient had been unable to fulfill his needs and was, therefore, unable to function in a responsible manner. Because he could not fulfill his needs in the real world, sometimes suddenly but more often gradually, the patient began to deny the existence of the real world and live in a world of his own, trying thereby to fulfill his needs. Perhaps it was a completely crazy world full of hallucinations and delusions; perhaps it was just a numb denial of reality and a withdrawal into a world of nothingness, a vegetative existence in which the patient goes through only the bare motions of life. No matter what his behavior, it was his way of trying to fulfill his needs or denying that he had needs to fulfill. Sooner or later someone began to notice that he was acting peculiarly. If he was grossly disturbed, he was immediately hospitalized, but often he gradually drifted into a world of his own and on into the hospital.

Once hospitalized, however, no matter how the patient behaved he was accepted as mentally ill, according to the usual teachings of modern psychiatry. He was considered to be suffering from a psychotic reaction for which he needed help.

Now, however, the staff has been trained to understand that there is a better world for the patients than the world of the mental hospital. They have been thoroughly instructed that they must never accept the situation as hopeless, that each patient can be taught better ways to act, and that there is some place for him in the world. The staff of Building 206 no longer believe that mental illness exists; the patients can, therefore, do better if they can be helped to help themselves slowly but surely to act more responsibly. Toward this end, Dr. Harrington set up a specific program, one that is remarkably similar in principle to the program at Ventura School (as described more fully in my book *Reality Therapy*).

Prior to 1962, Building 206 was known as the chronic or "crock" ward. All patients had received therapy of various kinds without success and had been sent to Building 206 for custodial care. The building was an open ward with off-building privileges but few off-building responsibilities. Because it was so easy to live in the hospital, there was little incentive to change. Tender, loving care was the order of the day. Off-building privileges, passes into town, passes home for weekends, Thanksgiving, Christmas, and the Fourth of July were considered to be every patient's dream. All patients' requests and demands were fulfilled whenever possible, a marked difference from any world they would have to live in if they left.

Group therapies were organized around the principle of making conscious the unconscious in the traditional sense. The great insight into their "illness" that many patients obtained did not increase their responsibility; when they understood why they were mentally ill, it made even more sense to them to stay as they were.

Dr. Harrington instituted the Reality Therapy program when he took over Building 206. Rather than concentrating on making the patient happy, the program stressed carefully graded increments of responsibility so that the patient could slowly work his way back to reality. The building was divided into a fifty-man closed ward, a fifty-man semiopen ward, and a one-hundred-man open ward. All personnel, including the clerk-typist, clothing-room clerk, aides, nurses, social worker, and psychologist, were given responsibilities of reporting behavior concerning the patients' readiness for movement either in the direction of greater or lesser responsibility. During a regular building meeting attended by both staff and patients, patient problems were discussed, ward assignments were made (usually along the progression from closed to semiopen to open-ward status), and individual patient programs were established. The results of all meetings were typed and placed on the patients' bulletin boards.

On the day the program was put into force, Dr. Harrington had had a forty-five-second meeting with the least responsible and most crazy patients, who had been selected for the closed ward. The patients were told simply that in the doctor's judgment they needed a rest on the closed ward as they were not yet ready for the open ward. At the conclusion of the meeting, one patient raised his hand and asked the doctor if he could have a pass into town. When the request was denied, he said "Thank you, Doctor."

As Dr. Harrington left the ward, a patient who was evidently disturbed because he was left in open status approached him, asking if he could be transferred to Building 205, the maximum security ward. Dr. Harrington asked him if he had not been selected to be placed on the closed ward. The patient said no, as far as he knew he was still on open status, to which Dr. Harrington responded, "You're on closed status now." The patient shook hands and said, "Thank you," and the program was under way. It is Dr. Harrington's contention that patients recognize their need for closed status even more acutely than does the staff, as was demonstrated by his exchange with the last patient.

Critics have argued that the procedures of Reality Therapy would make no sense to the patients after all their years of hospital life. In practice such criticism proved to be invalid, further bolstering our conviction that mental illness does not exist. The patients sensed from the total ward attitude that something new was happening, that someone really cared, and that they were involved in a very different hospital experience than any they had known before. In the locked ward, patients who were violent or destructive were put in a belt and cuffs because crazy behavior is not tolerated. Hyperactive patients were given sedation. The aides and nurses worked toward becoming involved with the patients and then asked them to give up their crazy symptoms.

The involvement now becomes critical. The men selected for the closed ward were those least involved with others and most isolated from reality. Here the aides and nurses engage in a continual therapeutic effort to involve the patient first with them and then with the minimum closed ward program. In a totally accepting protected atmosphere, the ward staff used patience, humor, and persistence to force themselves into the patient's life. Attaining the initial involvement takes anywhere from a few weeks to as long as six months, but sooner or later the effort by the ward staff begins to show. The patient responds either by increasing his symptoms or by decreasing them and thus changing to more reasonable behavior. In either case his response shows that the first part of therapy, the initial involvement, has been accomplished.

Now the attitude can be changed toward continued acceptance of the patient but rejection of the symptoms. For the first time in years the patients genuinely respond to human efforts. Those who show an increase in symptoms are trying to avoid involvement, but this behavior indicates that they are already beginning to be involved. They also may be testing the intent and persistence of the ward staff, for many therapists had tried in the past to get them involved, but these therapists had not devoted enough time or effort, nor had they worked in the proper closed ward atmosphere. Little attention is paid to an increase in symptoms or to withdrawal, and these patients soon change their response and begin to give up their symptoms.

The final step on the closed ward is to help the patients begin to function; that is, to eat, bathe, shave, brush their teeth, change clothes, and take needed medicine. Even in cuffs they are expected to take some responsibility for their personal care, awkward as it might be. Available but not required of patients are television, ward games, and a weekly trip to the canteen accompanied by an aide. When they can perform the minimum functions, the patients no longer need cuffs and sedation. When they are able to act sensibly most of the time, they are ready for step two.

Recommendations for a patient to move to the semiopen ward are made by the staff at the building meeting, although Dr. Harrington makes all the decisions and the patients know this. He becomes a vital part of their world, and it is on his training and judgment that the patients, as well as the staff, learn to depend. They trust him not to move them until they are ready, yet they strive for progress because they can and do understand that the Reality Therapy program is the start of a new life for them. It is the whole ward attitude, where everyone is involved, but where mental illness is not accepted, that brings the understanding home to them.

Between two and six months are usually needed to prepare patients for the semiopen ward where they are told that they must stay in the ward although it is not locked. Here they are expected to attend a group meeting run by aides in which their responsibility within the ward program is discussed. With the addition of at least an hour of ward detail to their closed ward duties, they are slowly but surely given increased responsibility and told that they now have an opportunity to make progress.

By taking steadily increasing responsibility, they begin to gain self-respect and self-worth. Now they are easier for the staff to like, and thus they are more likely to fulfill their need for love. They start to feel better and to look and act like men, not like permanent mental hospital residents. Next they get a ground privilege card which entitles them to go outside but which carries with it the obligation to do an outside work detail. Emphasis continues on constructive, realistic work activity. Patients do not wander the grounds as docile inmates, nor do they engage in play or "therapeutic" make-work aimed at making them happy. The goal is to return them to reality, not to make them well adjusted to hospital life. Soon they are ready to go off grounds with the family, if it is judged to be beneficial. Later in the semiopen ward program, patients may go to off-building activities and have off-ground passes, both accompanied and unaccompanied.

In contrast to therapy on the closed ward, which is essentially continuous, therapy now becomes more structured. An important part of the new program is a daily meeting of a therapy group led by an aide trained in Reality Therapy in which the patients discuss their progress in detail. Here they experience the good feeling that results from expressing themselves in a group. All the problems of taking responsibility are patiently and repeatedly gone over as the initial involvement gained in the closed ward is expanded. Relearning how to live in the world beyond the ward for short periods, the patient is carefully prepared for the measured increase in responsibility of each step. The doctor uses his judgment to regulate the speed of the process.

Because it has been discovered that the patient is usually ready to move downstairs to a completely open ward in about ninety days, this time limit is made a condition of the group on the semiopen ward. Downstairs the patient enters another time-limited group led by either a social worker or a psychologist specially trained in Reality Therapy, who actively prepares groups of patients for the next step, the move out of the hospital. Setting time limits of ninety days motivates the patients to work harder toward the goal of leaving. If they do not succeed in ninety days, they are moved back; but well over 90% do succeed. Dr. Harrington believes that those who succeed should increase to almost 100% as everyone learns more about applying the principles of Reality Therapy.

Patients who cannot manage the rapid movement are moved backward, even to the locked ward. Such regression is neither failure nor admission that the craziness was too well established but rather a sign that the ward doctor had erred in his judgment. The patient in his characteristic way communicates his feelings by acting crazy or irresponsible. But whether or not regression occurs, movement generally continues forward.

Downstairs in the open ward, with many privileges earned by taking responsibility, the patient is deeply involved with the program because he knows that in three months he must leave the hospital. The social worker or psychologist leads the group in learning how to live without the protection of the hospital. Entering a carefully planned outside situation, the patient in many cases returns during the day to work and to receive the support of the hospital program; however, he is primarily dependent upon himself.

When a patient is finally moved out to his family, a foster home, an apartment (or, if he is old and feeble, to the old soldiers' home), he is instructed not to look for work. In the beginning, after ten or twenty years in the hospital, it is enough just to leave. Work comes later. To expect too much too soon from men who have been separated so long from the real world will produce a return of irresponsible behavior. Timing and judgment are critical; but, if the patient is not yet ready, he can retrace as many steps as necessary—just as a girl who cannot succeed on parole returns to the school as a part of a continuing program that in the end will produce permanently increased responsibility.

Building 206 sets a standard for proper treatment of chronic mental patients. Its program takes less money and less time than do traditional methods, but it does demand a high degree of skill and training for the staff. Vital to the program on Building 206 but difficult to describe are the detailed plans and the intricate personal relationships which help each man to move over critical hurdles. The ability of the doctor to make the correct decisions, to time each move properly, is part of the skill of psychiatry learned only through experience.

As long as the traditional mental illness concepts prevail, Building 206 will be the exception. Time devoted to programs other than sensitively retraining patients to be responsible will neither prevent half of all admissions from becoming chronic patients nor bring back to reality those who do become chronic. Millions of dollars will continue to be spent to investigate the causes of a nonexistent disease, mental illness, to find answers already graphically demonstrated in Building 206. The same money spent in other hospitals to set up similar programs would return a much greater dividend. But the mental illness concept is deeply entrenched in mental hospitals, and it will take public pressure to change it. Psychiatry is seemingly too close to the problem to take action itself.

ROY

Roy is an example of a patient who has been in both the old and new programs[2] in Building 206.

By midsummer of 1944, Roy was finished with the war in Europe. He was twenty-four years old with a left leg three-quarters as good as new. He had come through a particular man-made kind of hell with flying colors. The not remarkably proud possessor of the Purple Heart and a personal citation for heroism, he felt that he had done only what the circumstances demanded. Whatever was heroic about it had to do with the time, the place, and the minds of other people. His widowed mother was not surprised at his heroism because, as she put it, "He'd been the man of the house since he was eight years old, when his father died."

He had never been a problem as a child, helping to care for the three younger children. At ten (two years younger than any other paper carrier in the hometown) he had acquired a paper route, and for the next seven years he never failed to get up at 4 A.M., winter or summer, to carry his papers. He turned his weekly $5.00 paycheck over to his mother for the family fund. He made good grades in school. No, his mother was not surprised at his heroism

---

[2] The description of Roy was contributed by Dr. G. L. Harrington.

for she knew that he would always conduct himself properly and do right, no matter what the situation.

Just two days before Roy was to board a ship to return to the States, it happened without warning. He ran amuck. He was captured by guards as he ran through the hospital compound, screaming that the Nazis were pouring in the south gate and crying out orders for hand grenades and bayonets. Some of his bunk mates remembered that he had been pacing around the ward more than usual and that he probably had not slept too well for a few nights, but no one could believe what was happening to this mild-mannered, quiet, considerate member of their group.

In the psychiatric unit Roy was grossly disturbed, requiring heavy sedation. Obviously hallucinating, he heard voices accusing him of being a homosexual; he lashed out at the voices continuously, smashing his head and his hands through walls, doors, and windows. After several days of observation, doctors concluded that the patient was suffering from dementia praecox (paranoid type) acute, manifested by ideas of reference, delusions of persecution, and hallucinations. Shortly thereafter he was started on a course of electric shock treatment. After fifteen treatments he had improved enough to allow the therapy to be stopped. At the end of one month the patient appeared to be in a state of good remission. Unable to remember exactly what had happened, he spoke of it all as a bad dream.

Six weeks after the onset of his acute illness the patient was discharged from the service, going to his mother's home in the Midwest. When he arrived home he had changed. According to his mother, he was not the boy she had known. He had no interest in the house or his younger brother and two sisters. He paced the floor, did not sleep for three nights, and on the fourth day had to be corraled by the local police for smashing furniture and windows. Hospitalized on an acute, intensive treatment service in a local V.A. hospital for the next three months, he received forty electric shock treatments with what were considered to be excellent results. The patient was anxious to leave the hospital to go home to pick up where he had left off before the war. His mother, realizing something was still wrong, nevertheless insisted on taking him home and doing everything she could to help him back to health. He was at home ten days before another psychotic episode occurred. This time taken to another V.A. hospital in the area, his treatment again began on the acute, intensive treatment service. The patient, very disturbed, was kept in seclusion. Before preparations for him to receive insulin coma treatment were finished, his acute episode subsided, and the staff decided to withhold this form of therapy.

Within six weeks Roy appeared to be in a state of fair remission. He was transferred from the acute service to an open convalescent service where he could receive psychotherapy. Two hours after his arrival on the open service he became acutely psychotic, with hallucinations and his old destructive behavior. Returned first to the acute, intensive treatment service, where his symptoms subsided within a week, he was transferred to a closed, chronic service for custodial care.

During the next four years, Roy made only a marginal adjustment to the ward routine. Spending most of his time sitting, looking off into space, he did not communicate or otherwise socialize with other patients. On direct questioning by his ward doctor, he just answered the questions, offering nothing to the conversation. When asked whether he heard voices, he replied that he did; when asked what they told him, he said they called him a queer; when asked where the voices came from, he said he was not sure, but he thought it was some Nazi organization.

In 1950 the patient escaped from the hospital. For the next four years nothing was known of his whereabouts, although later his mother reported that he had visited home briefly in 1952 but again disappeared. Recently, he revealed that he had spent these four years wandering around the country.

In 1954 he was picked up by the Los Angeles police, disheveled, confused, and totally disoriented. When it was discovered that he was a veteran, he was transferred from Los Angeles County Hospital to the local V.A. hospital, where he was placed on the acute, intensive treatment service. His new doctor, a first-year resident, was a warm, kindly, born-to-be-a-doctor young man who read the glassy, distant stare in Roy's eyes as fear. Roy must have sensed his doctor's warmth and interest, for almost immediately he began to follow the doctor's instructions by eating better, keeping cleaner, and improving his appearance. Completely oriented within a month, he had gained ten pounds and was busy making ashtrays for the ward in the occupational therapy shop.

Shortly thereafter, his doctor decided to see Roy in individual psychotherapy. The conduct of the therapy was supervised by an experienced psychoanalyst who was a consultant to the residence training program. The sessions between the resident and his super-

visor dealt with helping the young psychiatrist gain a deeper understanding of the structures of the mind (the superego, the ego, and
the id), the principles of psychosexual development, the relationship
between latent homosexuality and paranoid schizophrenia, and techniques for helping patients solve intrapsychic conflicts by means of
insight into unconscious impulses. Roy's therapy progressed rapidly
and satisfactorily. Deeply interested in what his doctor had to say,
he offered much to the therapy in terms of feelings, thoughts, and
memories from his past life. He spent much time when not in
therapy thinking about his newfound knowledge of the mind, and
once offered a possible fifth proposition to Freud's original four
propositions concerning the mechanism for the development of para-
noia to ward off homosexuality.

Roy's progress in understanding was equally impressive to himself, to his doctor, and to his doctor's supervisor. Finally, after eight
months of intensive work, the doctors agreed that he was no longer
schizophrenic, that he was a sensitive, stable human being ready to
take his place in the world. At his supervisor's suggestion, the resident doctor told the patient of the conclusions and wrote an order
transferring him to an open ward from which he would soon be discharged. Thirty minutes after he arrived on the open ward he was
screaming out loudly against the voices and had to be restrained; he
was placed in seclusion on the closed unit. The resident, a most dis-
traught young man, declared that everything had gone along perfectly until the damn voices came back and spoiled everything, as if
the voices were in truth a visitation from outer space.

Roy's destructive, disturbed behavior could not be controlled on
the acute, intensive treatment service, and he was therefore transferred to a maximum security ward. Although his acute episode subsided the day after his arrival on the maximum security ward, he
communicated with no one and did no more than meet the basic demands of the ward. His former resident doctor visited him once before
moving to another service, but Roy did not recognize him.

By 1957, two years later, Roy was adjusting well to the ward
routine, including participating in the occupational therapy program.
His mother, who had now raised the other children and moved to
California to be near her son, visited regularly on visiting days.
There was little conversation between them, but the meetings appeared to be quietly pleasant. On occasions she would bring a picnic
lunch and they would eat together on the grounds.

During 1958, it was concluded that the patient's psychosis had stabilized at as high a level as he could attain and that he might be able to live in a family care home if it were a well-organized, protective environment. His mother was not happy to have him go to someone else's home, but she agreed to it hoping it would help her son. Roy stayed in the home three days, became tense, and complained that the voices were returning. Although he did not become destructive, he insisted that he had to return to the hospital. Back at the V.A. hospital, he remained in the maximum security building until the fall of 1960 when he was transferred to Building 206 for custodial care.

During the first three months in Building 206, the patient made a satisfactory adjustment to the closed ward. He spoke only when spoken to and did not socialize with other patients, yet he seemed rather complacent and satisfied with his condition. Later, placed on an open ward and given certain hospital privileges, he was assigned to corrective therapy, a program aimed at sponsoring interplay between patients in such team sports as volleyball and basketball. After about a year in the program, the patient had changed little in his ability to mix with people. He did what he was told and no more.

At this time Dr. Harrington took over Building 206 and started Reality Therapy. Roy was presented to the weekly building staff meeting on the insistence of the corrective therapy worker who complained that he was unable to get anywhere with him. Roy behaved as if he were vegetating, and the corrective therapy worker wanted a reevaluation of the patient's status and program. The building psychiatrist was taken aback when Roy walked into the room, well-groomed, composed, dignified, an early middle-aged man. The greeting was cordial, the handshake firm, and the silence that followed was forever until the doctor asked the patient how long he had been on corrective therapy. The response was a quick "Twelve months." Another pause, and the doctor asked how long he had been bored with corrective therapy. With the impassive face of a straight man, the patient responded "Eleven months." The room broke up in laughter matched in warmth only by Roy's restrained smile. He was then told that his activity was going to be changed from corrective therapy to the sidewalk detail, which consisted of digging, placing forms, mixing concrete, and pouring concrete for new sidewalks about the hospital grounds. Believing that Roy was not responsible enough for open status even though he was now tolerating it, Dr. Harrington moved Roy back to semiopen status on the second floor. Asked for his opinion of the changes, Roy said that he thought it was a good idea.

This three-minute interview signaled the breakthrough, small as it was, which started Roy in Reality Therapy. Until then he had been a patient in a hospital that was trying very hard to do something for him. In the past, when Roy seemed better it had meant only that he had accepted what the hospital was doing for him, whether it was shock treatment or psychoanalysis. He was mentally ill, and he was being treated. When he became quiet and apparently rational, his acceptance of the status quo was interpreted wrongly to mean that he was ready to leave the hospital. Each time, however, he was no more ready to fulfill his needs than before, so he behaved irrationally to emphasize how unready he was.

After years of the same reaction to the same program in various guises, he reached the point where he was vegetating in corrective therapy. Still unable to fulfill his needs in corrective therapy, he had now even given up trying to accept what was being done for him. To say that Roy was bored was a masterpiece of understatement, but in doing so Dr. Harrington showed recognition of Roy's predicament and started their involvement. Roy sensed that here was a doctor who knew that there must be a better life for him than the one he was living, and he certainly knew that he had been at a dead end.

The initial involvement would have gone for naught had not Dr. Harrington given him less responsibility by moving him from the open to the semiopen ward. In the past when contact was made Roy had been pushed ahead; now the opposite occurred. Roy could only interpret this change as understanding, caring, and acceptance. Instead of reacting with irrational fear, he was able to get into the new program of Building 206 as an active participant. Recreation was finally over; he accepted the assignment of working as a part of a crew building a concrete sidewalk, and he remained in the ward when he was not working. Except for the work, little was expected of him unless he himself asked for more responsibility. In group therapy led by a 206 aide he was given a chance to talk of what he was doing now, but he was not pushed to do more. If anything he was restrained; any push would have to come from him.

This treatment was new to Roy. When, as soon occurred, he sought out the doctor and asked for more freedom, he was told to wait. "You are not ready," was Dr. Harrington's refrain over and over again for the next two months. Although Roy asked for more freedom, he was really testing whether his new doctor would fail by granting him freedom before he was ready to fulfill his needs, as had happened so many times in the past. On the ward and at work his aides and nurses were friendly and interested in what he was now doing. They gave him praise, but they did not push. On the job, however, he demonstrated his capability and was promoted to foreman of the sidewalk crew. Especially helpful in starting new men on the job, he showed real skill in taking this additional responsibility.

After about three months on the semiopen ward, Roy was very changed. Now it was not only Roy who was pushing Dr. Harrington; he was joined in his efforts by the aides and nurses. Increasingly involved with Roy and impressed by his progress, they began to badger Dr. Harrington to move him to the open ward and into a discharge group. This occurrence, when both staff and patients join together to press for more responsibility, is a critical point on the semiopen ward. When this joint push occurs, it is the time to move the patient. If only the patient or only the staff urge a change, it is too early. Dr. Harrington resisted until the pressure grew intense, and then he told Roy that he was ready to take a Sunday pass to Santa Monica and report the following day to talk over how it went.

On Monday, Roy reported that he had done some window shopping in town. He was amazed at prices. He had eaten lunch on the pier, watched others fish, and had taken a sightseeing ride along the beach in a little bus. He enjoyed the outing and would like to repeat it regularly. The following week he was transferred from the second floor to the open ward on the first floor. Anticipating the outbursts he had had previously when he was put on open status, Dr. Harrington told him that it might be frightening but that he thought he could make it. His program outside the building would remain the same, and the personnel on the first floor knew him well. If the change proved to be too much for him, he would simply return to the second floor. During his first three days on the first floor, Roy seemed a bit preoccupied and a little distant, and he requested to see the doctor about some vague difficulties in swallowing. Without showing apprehension, Dr. Harrington treated him routinely. He was given some aspirin for his throat and reassured that he could make it on the open ward.

During the next two months, the patient's work record on the sidewalk detail continued to improve. He was actively involved in the open ward therapy group, which was directed toward planning to leave the hospital. Encouraged by everyone, he continued to take day passes to Santa Monica each week, accompanying other, more fearful patients on their first outing. Finally, it was decided that Roy should be seen in the staff meeting as a possible candidate for the day hospital program. His mother had been impressed by his progress; nevertheless, she feared the future and worried about his leaving the hospital on unaccompanied day passes. She sought out the building social worker and doctor many times, both of whom attempted to clarify for her the program in Building 206. She did not interfere in his day passes and she continued visiting, but now only one day a week, during visiting hours.

At the interview that decided whether or not Roy would go into the day hospital program, he was first asked what he saw for himself in the future. He declared that when we felt he was ready to leave the hospital he would go and live with his mother. He was told that because of his history and his own experience the staff had a different plan in mind. The day hospital program, in which a patient is placed on trial separation from the hospital, was explained. Finding himself a place to live near the hospital, he would return by day to continue his same hospital program. Again the responsibility was slowly and carefully extended.

Following this explanation, Roy paused and then admitted that he had escaped previously from a hospital and tried to make it on his own, but he had been unable to do so. The difference between that experience and his present program was discussed. In addition, he was told that if he were selected for the day hospital program, he would be placed in a discharge group with the building social worker. Meeting twice a week for three months, the group would discuss the problems of living outside of the hospital. The interview was concluded by Dr. Harrington telling the patient to think about the new program for another week and then to come to the staff meeting for a final decision on whether or not he would enter the program.

During the week the patient explained the whole program to his mother. After discussing it at length with the social worker, she gave her approval. At the staff meeting the following week Roy said that he would like to try the program, and he was assigned to it.

A total of twenty-three patients from Building 206 have been placed in the three-month treatment program for living outside the hospital and working in. The building psychologist has one therapy group and the social worker has two. Both leaders report that they are having a hilarious time. Some patients moan that it cannot be done; others use the newspaper to quote prices on penthouses in Beverly Hills as evidence that a man with a pension cannot afford to live outside the hospital. All are going on passes to look for places to live. Some want to move now and not wait three months. Roy has surveyed the local area with a fine-tooth comb, and he has a file on rental that would be the envy of any local rental office. They have discussed and checked the price of food and compared cooking in with eating out. Roy's group has enrolled en masse in a cooking school program offered by the hospital dietetics department. One group member excused the building doctor's Reality Therapy program on the grounds that the federal government must be going broke. There is no doubt in the minds of the staff of Building 206 that Roy will make this step satisfactorily. There is no doubt in the mind of the building doctor that twenty-three started and twenty-three will make it.

As of April 1964, Roy and twenty-one others in the group had been out of the hospital over six months. The twenty-third member, ready to go with the others but held because of lack of funds, had been out four months. This one group represents a total of over three hundred years of hospitalization.

Chapter 21

A Program of Recovery
for the Alcoholic

ARTHUR H. CAIN

Arthur H. Cain: b. 1913, Atlanta, Georgia.
B.S., 1953, M.A., 1956, and Ph.D., 1960, in psychology, Columbia University,
  Teachers College.
Private counseling practice, 1956–date.
Books: *Young People and Sex* (1967). *King's Rebellion* (1967). *Young
  People and Smoking* (1964). *The Cured Alcoholic* (1964). *Young People
  and Drinking* (1963). *Seven Sinners* (1959). *The Cigarette Habit* (1959).

The vocabulary of alcoholism which has cluttered the pages of our literature and the air waves of both radio and television is one of the greatest reasons for the almost complete confusion surrounding this behavior disorder today. This statement means, of course, that the conceptualization of this problem by persons untrained in psychology and other appropriate disciplines has been inaccurate, helter-skelter, and completely confusing. In other words, the semantic confusion in the field of alcoholism is a direct indication of the intellectual confusion in the minds of alcoholism authorities; this confusion has a snow-balling effect and further compounds the confusion.

I have arbitrarily defined "recovered alcoholic" as being a drinker who had habitually lost control of his drinking; who has stopped drinking completely, but who no longer needs to work at his sobriety in any way. The truly recovered alcoholic does not need to go to Alcoholics Anonymous (A.A.) meetings, to psychotherapists, to pastoral counselors, or do anything else in order to maintain his complete abstinence from alcohol. This is not to say that he may not continue A.A. work or psychotherapy or religious training, but he is no longer dependent upon any of these disciplines to maintain his sobriety.

In my own group of recovered alcoholics, alcohol and alcoholism are simply not problems any more. They seldom if ever talk about alcoholism; rarely do they think of themselves as alcoholics, recovered or

611

otherwise. Their uncontrolled drinking is a phase of their lives which is now over. They are concerned entirely with the present and the future.

And these are "goal-oriented" people. They are not paralyzed by such concepts as "one day at a time" or "easy does it" or any other such restrictive clichés. The very opposite of these withering slogans is the rule with my recovered alcoholics.

I make it a habit of telling my clients at the very beginning of our reeducational, retraining relationship that they must start searching for a goal in life: a goal which will require the optimum effort of the individual, as this is the only conceivable way he can begin living up to his full potential as a man. I do not demand perfection, but I do demand the individual's very best effort. He must go all out in our program or we will not accept him in the group. One of our few maxims is "99% is not enough!"

This conception of educative psychotherapy is a direct result of my conviction that conventional therapy today too often urges the patient to live down to some imaginary norm of society when he should be living up to his own individual potential. I have heard the expression of becoming "adjusted to society" too frequently over the past few years. I have been thoroughly involved with almost every segment of New York City society for the past twenty years and, believe me, if you can bring me a person who regards himself as being well adjusted to this society I will show you a person who is really ill. It is a sick society, and becoming adjusted to it is only going to aggravate the mental, emotional, social, and spiritual illness of the individual.

One of the arguments for this effort on the part of some psychotherapists to achieve a uniform mediocrity in our culture is that some people have delusions of grandeur, are arrogant, have Messianic complexes and so on. These therapists feel that the patient must be brought down to earth; he must learn to accept himself as he is; he must rid himself of guilt feelings and frustrations; he must learn to live with his neurosis much as the A.A. alcoholic must learn to live with his abiding desire to control his intoxication as he once did.

Should this approach to the solution of human problems be permitted to continue there will be no need to worry about automation, Big Brother, or even the atomic bomb. I am sure that these therapists, defeatists all, will have devised a new jargon that will superimpose a new mythology over the patients' neuroses, and we shall have become a nation of zombies.

On the other hand, one hears very little about treating the patient who has habitually sold himself short as a human being. In a society where such words as chivalry, honor, courage, daring, and adventure are almost passé, this is not surprising. But it is truly dreadful, particularly to the younger man, to read the books of Joseph Conrad, for instance, and watch some of the old movies of gallantry and derring-do and then to rise meekly the next morning and tiptoe into a post-Christian matriarchate which is dedicated to permissiveness.

I hope I have made it clear that the complete recovery of my own former alcoholics is not predicated in any way upon acceptance of their society's weaknesses or of their own personal sickness, past or present.

Our basic questions in our *Seven Sinners*[1] therapy are: What is the most you can do with your life? What is the most you can put into life? For that determines what it is you can get out of life.

I should point out here that there is nothing easy, nor is there anything comfortable about the Seven Sinners program. It requires hard work, and lots of it. But this hard work is necessary, and I think that the individual who goes into this program with open eyes knows that it could not possibly be any other way. We are concerned with solving problems, not learning to live with them.

And it is rewarding. There is the same kind of satisfaction that one gets in infantry basic training or boot camp in the Marine Corps or Navy. There is the satisfaction of knowing that one is going all out in a life-or-death struggle, and the program is precisely that. It is the life of the potential man as compared with the lifelessness of the man who is predominantly a child.

This is always the problem, without exception. Within a very few days, particularly if psychodiagnostic tests have been made, I am able to tell my new "colleague" that he is, roughly speaking, about 10% man and 90% baby: the typical product of the matriarchate which went into action full force in 1920. The clinical problem is how to build on the 10% man? And the 10% man is never going to let the 90% baby alone.

This phenomenon is the basic conflict of too many American men today. They have been mentally, emotionally, socially, and spiritually maimed and crippled by their women to the point where they are among the most incredible psychological freaks the world has ever

---

[1] From Arthur King, *Seven Sinners*. New York: Harcourt, Brace and World, 1961. This work, based upon Arthur H. Cain's Ph. D. dissertation at Columbia University, was published under the pseudonym "Arthur King" to preserve the anonymity of the clients described therein.

known: men without manhood; men who are forever boys; boys forever babies.

F. Scott Fitzgerald's prophetic statement (2), which "The Senator"
in *Seven Sinners* found so shattering, comes to mind at once: "the
American Woman, aroused, stood over him; the clean sweeping irrational temper that had broken the moral back of a race and made a
nursery out of a continent, was too much for him . . ."

I can look across my consulting room and very vividly perceive my
40- to 50-year-old colleagues still clad in their babyhood diapers. Most
of their neurotic behavior, including the habitual uncontrolled drinking
we call alcoholism, can be traced to this man/baby conflict. The Bottle,
ironically enough, will resolve the conflict temporarily. It anesthetizes
the baby and it magnifies the fractional man. Later in his alcoholism
the baby asserts himself, and we have the disgusting spectacle of the
biologically adult man struggling helplessly in his crib, crying for his
bottle, spoiling his bed clothes, "mewling and puking in the nurse's
arms"—symbolically if not actually. This, by the way, is the real story
beneath Natalie Anderson Scott's wonderful book, *The Story of Mrs.
Murphy* (4).

This book, along with Henry de Montherlant's *Costals and the Hippogriff* (3) are the only two books that I urge my colleagues not to read
until they and I are absolutely certain they are truly recovered alcoholics. The latter volume is specifically directed toward the problem of
the male–female relationship in Western civilization today.

The shortest period of time required to become a thoroughly recovered alcoholic has been nine months. Other cases required as long
as five years, but I believe that this maximum period can now be reduced to two years even in the most difficult cases, due to the continuing perfecting of techniques, new knowledge of alcoholism and
human behavior in general, and more helpful books directed specifically to the problems with which we are confronted.

The point of recovery is, I think, that point when I as therapist suddenly realize that my colleague knows as much about his specific problems and how to solve them as I do. This is not to say that he has
become a professional psychologist, of course, but that he has had
sufficient training and has gained sufficient knowledge to solve his
problems without further professional help or guidance.

This point of recovery may be attained in some cases without professional help. For the person who is unable for whatever reason to
obtain appropriate professional guidance, books, discussions with other

congenial colleagues (especially if one or more of these individuals is himself a recovered alcoholic), and private application of the Seven Sinners program may enable him to work out his own recovery.

The colleague himself usually reports, in retrospect, that he felt he became completely recovered when he realized that a fairly long period of time, at least a month, say, had elapsed without his having given any thought whatsoever to his own problems of alcoholism.

Many of our recovered alcoholics report that at about this time of their programs they "try on for size" the notion of drinking and if the idea of being able to indulge in "controlled intoxication" does not appeal to them in the least, they become convinced they are truly recovered alcoholics. No longer do they harbor any desires, conscious or unconscious, to become "high"; to achieve that nice warm glow of alcoholic relaxation; or any other of the pleasures they once derived from the consumption of beverage alcohol.

They have learned that reality, with all its ups and downs, is more pleasurable, more exciting, more "high," more warmly relaxing than alcoholic intoxication ever was.

In short, reality has become—for the recovered alcoholic—better than intoxication in any form.

This sentence sums up the recovered alcoholic: He does not wish to drink at all—even normally.

We have already described the basic point of return to normalcy as being the acceptance of a goal-directed life. We must explicate this a bit more clearly before we go on.

It goes without saying that the basic psychological point, the psychodynamics involved, is that the individual has directed his attention outside of himself, which is the direct opposite of the egocentric, self-preoccupied state that is the common denominator of so many neuroses. The recovering alcoholic is set upon a new course of action, one that is primarily concerned with getting the job done—a job in which the man fully believes—rather than the introverted orientation of the neurotic man/baby who is preoccupied with assuaging the needs of the baby in terms of physical, mental, and emotional comfort.

A truly recovered alcoholic is, usually, bored stiff with the subject of alcoholism unless he has become professionally interested in helping other alcoholics become recovered. Usually he is bored stiff, too, with his (former) personality problems or neuroses. He is entirely interested in achieving his goal, whatever it may be.

Perhaps the best general statement concerning the criteria of a suitable goal for any man is expressed in Judeo-Christian scripture, "You shall love the Lord your God with all your heart, with all your strength, and all your soul, and all your mind."

The attention of the special kind of person to whom the Seven Sinners program appeals is invited to the word "mind" in this scripture.

The second part of this great commandment as spoken by Jesus of Nazareth is, of course, an integral part of the Seven Sinners program: "You shall love your neighbor as yourselves."

Which commandment, incidently, points up one of the absolute essentials of any program of recovery whether it be from alcoholism or any other uncontrolled behavior: that the individual cannot achieve recovery entirely on his own. It will be remembered that I stated in a previous paragraph that individuals could work out their recoveries without professional guidance, but I did not say that this could be accomplished in the vacuum of one's individuality. At least two other human beings are necessary to this enterprise; three people comprising a group; and, in my experience, groups of three plus a leader, professional or experienced layman, is the ideal combination.

We have found consistently over the past eighteen years that groups larger than three or four delimit the time allotted to individuals to such an extent that they are unable to satisfactorily ventilate anxieties and confusions and to express their constructive criticisms of the other group members. On the other hand, granting additional time to extra members of such groups makes for too lengthy, too fatiguing group sessions.

None of the foregoing is intended by any means to suggest that this complete recovery from alcoholism or other psychological problems is exclusive with the Seven Sinners program. Many, many alcoholics and many, many other neurotics have achieved this kind of recovery by various means.

There are many fully recovered alcoholics in the fellowship of Alcoholics Anonymous. These are the members who have found over the years that they need no longer work on a day-to-day basis fighting for their sobriety; they may do less and less twelfth step work; they attend fewer and fewer meetings. They have learned that they are no longer dependent on A.A. for dear life as an alcoholic lifesaver.

Other individuals have found their recoveries in psychoanalysis and other techniques of psychotherapy; still more have found the self-understanding and satisfactory worldview they need through counseling in all of the world's great religions.

A few rare and gifted persons have solved their problems and achieved this state of recovery by reading, by discussion, by meditation and—more often than not—by prayer, whether they used this word to describe the phenomenon or not.

The many fine organizations in our society, such as the YMCA, the Salvation Army, Synanon, and Gamanon, are all helpful to many persons in their efforts to find the meaning and purpose in life that is so necessary to their true, complete recovery.

Actually, it seems to be the destiny of the Seven Sinners program to serve as a sort of "psychological court of last appeal" to a relatively small group of men and women dedicated to helping those individuals who have been unable to find sufficient help in any of the preceding movements.

Here are some of the common characteristics of people who have recovered:

1. They are a group of nonjoiners.
2. All are well above average intelligence, meaning at least 110 to 120 I.Q. scores on the WAIS (Wechsler Adult Intelligence Scale) tests.
3. All are well above average in education, although nearly all are unevenly educated in that a great deal of their education has been self-training by reading, attending lectures, and becoming informed about significant issues outside the academic milieu.
4. All are victims, in one way or another, of "Momism": all of them felt that their mothers had influenced their lives adversely. In almost every case of the seventy clients who have become fully recovered in this program, the mother was the dominant parent in the family.
5. All are victims of one of the most epidemic problems of our times: an almost total confusion concerning the opposite sex and the changing status of women in our society.
6. All colleagues come to our group voluntarily.
7. All members, without exception, have stated in retrospect that they feel that, "If this all-out program didn't work, then nothing would." This program was truly a last-ditch stand for every one of our members.

All members were given definite and realistic hope that recovery could be achieved; that it must be achieved; that it would be achieved. They were further convinced that such a road to recovery would be exciting and rewarding, not a matter of drudgery and boredom.

Above all, they were assured, truthfully, that although life had indeed been passing them by, the best years of their lives were still ahead of them. This idea has proved to be true even when the new colleague passed the customary retiring age of 65. It has also been true of colleagues as young as 21.

I should now like to point out in more explicit detail what I mean by an all-out, comprehensive approach to the problems of the colleagues.

As I said in *Seven Sinners,* the heart of the program rests somewhere in those activities we have described as Educative Counseling and Reading.

I use the term "Educative Counseling" for two reasons: (1) I wished to distinguish what we did from formal, orthodox psychotherapy, or consulting or counseling psychology; and (2) the educational part of this activity was most important.

Our method has several aspects, but before I discuss them, I wish to say a word about the fundamental role played by semantics. Semantics, as we use the term, means simply the deliberate systematic re-examination of familiar but difficult words that purport to express concepts basic to human behavior. It is, in short, a discipline and, as an educational device, its value has proved to be incalculable. Without exception, members of the group feel that the habit of scrutinizing their words more carefully—particularly emotional and religious words—has been the single most important lesson they have learned. They feel, furthermore, that the program as a whole, or any other course of therapy, would be unsuccessful without this discipline. Several have attributed their religious conversions to the use of semantics. Without it, they feel, they could not have found their way through the intellectual labyrinths through which certain individuals must necessarily work their way before they can "let in a little faith." We therefore made it a rule that the newcomer begin his program with readings in semantics, usually starting with a book by Stuart Chase or S. I. Hayakawa. The member of the group is also convinced that this discipline has therapeutic value as a purely psychological exercise.

Educative Counseling consists of a weekly two-hour session with the colleague and the therapist. The first hour belongs entirely to the colleague. He may talk about anything he likes. He is also free not to talk—the latter has never happened, though it was frequently threatened. (After a time, I introduced a modification in the second half of the colleague's hour, which I will discuss in a moment.) During the third half hour, the therapist, working from notes, expresses his thoughts about what the colleague has said in the preceding period. He may point out logical or factual errors in the colleague's monologue; he may make specific recommendations for behavior; or he may admit that he sees no immediate solution to a given problem and table it for further consideration. In the fourth half hour the patient and the therapist have a give-and-take discussion.

A word about specific recommendations for behavior: this procedure might not be suitable for many people. It seemed to be necessary for the individuals I was counseling. Any sick, confused person needs and wants to be told what to do during the early days of treatment. I have found time and again that to withhold opinions or insights, particularly on the assumption that they might be injurious to the patient, is self-defeating. Members of my group were instantly aware if I did hold something back, and this awareness had a worse effect than any opinion or insight I could have imparted. Moreover, I have never found that a colleague could not handle my comments, no matter how shattering they might seem to me. Of course, there were outraged denials and colorful recriminations, but no traumatic episodes. And, sooner or later, the colleague would find it possible to consider the opinion or insight rationally and to accept or reject it as the case might be.

In an effort to speed up the therapeutic process I introduced a modification in the second half of the colleague's hour; the modification was also a radical departure from orthodox procedure. It grew out of my conviction that the patient's hour should be more productive. The sick alcoholic cannot wait months and months for analysis to take effect, for when he has a relapse it can mean edema of the brain, psychosis, or death. I felt that the colleague's free talk about himself should have some direction. This sounds like a contradiction in terms, but our old standby, the minute semantic examination, came to the rescue, and we found that actually the colleague's talk could be both free and directed.

Knowing that we had, theoretically, the breadth and depth of human knowledge and experience to cope with, we simply took the logical step of dividing our inquiry into categories as follows:

1. Anthropology, or the colleague's origins and early history
2. Sociology, or the colleague's current relations with society
3. Economics, or the colleague's material status
4. Psychology, or the colleague's emotional responses to all the other categories
5. Philosophy, or the colleague's way of explaining his changing worldview

6. Religion, or the colleague's way of relating himself to whatever he feels is ultimate in his life and in the world
7. Physiology, or how the colleague feels physically

(We put Physiology last because we found that the colleague always felt better physically at the end of the session than he did at the beginning. It was astonishing how many bodily complaints vanished in the course of an hour.)

The colleague talked about whatever he liked for the first half hour. During the second half hour he talked as he liked, first about his childhood, then his relations with other people, then about his economic situation, and so on down the list.

No colleague at any time reported feelings of being coerced. On the contrary, the new procedure made him feel that the half hour had a meaning and purpose it had lacked before. As for myself, I have no doubt whatever that much more "material" came out than in orthodox free association. I also found that in every case the individual became more perceptive of the psychosocial environment in which he was learning to balance himself and more aware of the underlying meaning of his existence.

Once again, the reader must be reminded that the members of the group were special, as far as their drinking problems were concerned, and had tried other techniques unsuccessfully. Nevertheless, I think that this procedure or some variation of it might be useful to many people.

One final comment about Educative Counseling: We all found that great value inhered in the writing each member was required to do, particularly his logging or diary. It seemed to have value simply as a discipline. The mere act of writing everything down, and the self-examination and self-control this entailed, worked wonders. In addition, as an objectifying, externalizing device it gave the patient a new degree of control over the demons—his "latent homosexuality," his alcoholism, his tendency toward anxiety—with which he was beset. For a client to put down on paper and then see the thoughts that have been surging about in his mind for many years seems to have what someone called a "radar effect": the goblins are perceived as goblins and can then be vanquished. We found, too, that such writing was excellent "emergency therapy." When anxiety or depression threatened and the time was inappropriate for personal contacts, the act of "writing it down" proved efficacious in nearly every case.

The mechanics of this writing may be of interest. On one side of a large sheet of paper the client jots down his "stream of consciousness," his thoughts and feelings as they occur. On the reverse side he writes his intellectual appraisal of these thoughts and feelings. These pages are, it goes without saying, invaluable to the therapist as clinical material and research data.

The mere act of concentration upon the written word unquestionably had a salubrious effect on most of the colleagues. When one's thoughts "run wild," as the alcoholic's do during the first days of detoxication, such concentration is almost essential to the maintenance of sanity. Talking is the more common device in this situation, but though reading may not be as cathartic as talking, it definitely helps in getting the client's thoughts back onto something resembling a logical track. "Escape" reading at this time serves a useful purpose too; it seems to hold off the demons until the client is better able to cope with them.

Now we come to the heart of the matter: The effect of reading upon the alcoholic client.

For certain individuals, exemplified by the "seven sinners," I am convinced that the only effective approach to emotional and spiritual difficulties is the intellectual approach. I think it can be shown that intellectual blocks are causative factors in alcoholism and other neuroses and not merely symptoms. It is true, of course, that prolonged abnormal emotionality affects the intellectual process, usually adversely. But this is not the point. What we look for in our minute examination of the client's etiology is (1) the original point of departure from healthy behavior and (2) what it takes to get the patient back on the road to rationality, emotional health, and thinking for himself.

That alcoholism and other disorders have physiological concomitants I should be the last to deny. No one who has watched the withdrawal symptoms of either the alcoholic or the drug addict would say that either affliction is "purely" psychological. No disease—no thing—may be perceived as being "purely" anything. But that physiological pathology occurs in alcoholism and other neuroses, that it may, in turn, prolong, agitate, and even precipitate neurosis, does not affect my conviction that "intellectual pathology" is the prime mover in many cases. Intellectual medicine is required to cure it. Other treatments may supplement the basic medicine; they may even arrest the disease and render it tolerable to the patient. But if he is to cross the bridge into the promised land of total cure, the "total organism," about which so much has been said in the last decade in every field of science, must be considered. For the whole man consists not only of his physical and his emotional life but also of his intellectual life. And we must treat the whole man.

What a man thinks, not just how: this is the problem we must face. In the program we began to face it early for we had no choice. All other avenues of investigation had been explored and found wanting. Fortunately, deliberately, we had adopted an attitude of experimentation: we would make ourselves "receptacles" for all new ideas—good and bad, sensible and nonsensical, rational and irrational, religious and irreligious. Answers began crowding their way through the moment we opened our minds.

Emerson, I believe, said that no matter what great event in history took place it was always, somehow, first a thought in the mind of a man. I would enter a reservation: many things seem to happen as the result of psychosocial and other influences, and then a man perhaps perceives their occurrence, if not their meaning. But we must not throw out the baby with the bath water; some great events (revolutions, discoveries, inventions, even religions) did first take place in the minds of men. Many human destinies are directly traceable to single thoughts of individual human beings.

But ideas are limitless in number. Good books, too, are almost limitless. How to choose the ideas and the books that might help the client?

It seemed hopeless at first, truly like looking for a needle in a haystack. But I had to start somewhere, so I simply began giving the colleagues books that had been assigned to me in reading courses with the late Reverend Otis R. Rice, Bishop James A. Pike, Professors Reinhold Niebuhr, E. La B. Cherbonnier, Goodwin Watson, and others. Some had been important to me, some had not. I presented to the colleagues a list of titles from which to choose. I confess I had a sense of futility about the whole enterprise. What chance was there, really, of a given person stumbling across the word, the shining insight, that would make the difference between night and day in his particular life?

The astonishing thing was that the insights came, and came regularly, almost as if there was some hidden, mysterious system at work in our random choice of books. What this pattern might be we had no idea.

We think now that we have a glimmer of understanding of what was going on. Here was a group of human beings deliberately and desperately searching for just the things that great poets, great novelists, great thinkers, and scientists have always tried urgently to bring to mankind: understanding of and insights into profound truths. What truths? The

truths of Faith and Reason, of Science and Sanity, of Love and Destruction, of Life and Death. In short, the "eternal verities," which, as
we began to perceive, though infinite in depth are finite in number.

In retrospect, we feel that if one were wise enough about the literature of the world one could almost predict when a given person, reading
Plato and Aristotle, Aquinas and Augustine, Dante and Milton, would
strike the spark of inspiration for which his particular need called.

At any rate, it worked out that way for every member of the group.
The Biblical injunction "Seek and ye shall find" is, of course, the perfect parallel. And as the search plumbed the great pool provided by
poets and philosophers, it was as if the ideas contained therein were
rising slowly to the surface, seeking minds in which to perpetuate themselves.

THREE OF THE SEVEN SINNERS

Sol Friedman

Solomon Friedman came to my attention while he was taking part
in group analysis at a clinic at a large New York City hospital.[2] He
had been referred to the clinic as an alcoholic and was being treated
by orthodox Freudian methods. He was not considered to be severely
neurotic, despite the symptoms that had led him to ask for examination at a Veterans Administration hospital. When he came to me, he
told me that he felt that he was making little progress in the group. He
could not afford individual psychoanalysis, he said. Before coming to
the clinic he had tried Alcoholics Anonymous for well over a year without success; he was a Jewish agnostic and refused to consider seeking
guidance from pastoral counselors of any faith. After I told him what
his relationship with me would be, he began work at once on the program.

This man was well muscled, a white American Jew, thirty-five, in
good organic health, and of good appearance. He had attended public
school through the eleventh grade and earned his living in New York
City making prosthetic devices. He was unmarried, had two siblings,
and lived with his parents. Though he continued to participate in all the
other activities of the program, Sol's energies were focused on the reading. Reading is, of course, simply a short cut in any search for truth.
Sol had aired his emotions and found out some things; he had "medi-

---

2 These next three sketches represent extracts about crucial events in the case
studies fully given in Arthur King, *Seven Sinners.*

tated" and discovered others; he had talked with me and with his fellow group members and had learned still more. But by reading books, he could spend ten full hours a week with thinkers, scientists, and poets who, through the centuries, have influenced men's minds, moved their hearts, and altered their behavior. Havelock Ellis, for example, received from reading James Hinton a "religious conversion . . . the intellectual and emotional spheres which had been in constant friction were suddenly united in harmony," and he never had any more moods of religious depression (5, p. 121). Conversions may range from a minor alteration in attitude to a sweeping change in sympathies, knowledge, and behavior (1). They may take a short time or a long time.

Sol's took two years.

The change in Sol's personality did not take two years, of course; that began almost at once. Not long after his new beginning he told me that I was being "too damned Freudian" and that, after all, what we were looking for was truth wherever we found it, not more psychological gimmicks for Sol Friedman's salvation! For Doormat Sol this was a major revolution. He was dead right, too.

But it was about two years before things really happened. One evening at twilight, Sol Friedman and I sat talking about science and religion. This was during the last half-hour of one of our two-hour sessions. Both of us were tired, and the violet, translucent light of New York harbor at dusk had an almost magical effect. Sol was droning along hypnotically, and I was doing my best to maintain the conscious state, when a remark literally leapt into brightness and light. "You know," said Sol, "something Einstein said about the universe being finite first got me to thinking that maybe there was a God after all."

I sat upright and asked him to repeat what he had said. He repeated it.

How long has this been going on, I asked him.

"Well," said Sol, "it was like this." The following transcript, based on notes, is accurate if not verbatim.

> You remember that I started out with H. G. Wells' *Outline of History,* and then I read about anthropology and sociology and economics and science. This was all fine; I needed to know about these things, and reading the books gave me a feeling of confidence that I didn't have before. At least I didn't feel so ignorant. Some of the things I read applied to me too—then and there. For instance, when I got through with the history book I felt like my own problems, and even my own race's problems, were not so bad after all, considering what all humanity had been through.
>
> But I couldn't see how reading all this solved my problems in

any way; it just made them more bearable. We want to solve the problems of the Sol Friedmans of the world, don't we? So that they can go on to bigger and better things, not just endure their lot in life. We Jews have been enduring life for about five thousand years already.

The books on psychology, philosophy, and religion started making more sense to me, but still I couldn't believe in God, and if there wasn't a God how could there be a hereafter? And if there is no hereafter, what's it all about anyhow? It's all very well for people who are gifted and smart. They seem to get enough out of life to make it worthwhile, at least for a while. People like me can't. So why should we behave in certain ways, just because these other people say it's "ethical"? Or "moral"? We've got to behave whatever way we've got to behave to keep the others from beating us out of the little we do have. Ethics is a luxury we can't afford.

And faith. How can I have faith in something which can't be proved? Nobody can ever prove God, can they? I didn't say there wasn't one; I just said I wasn't able to believe there was one.

Then I started reading those books you gave me when we started all over again. *Your God is Too Small, The Great Divorce,* and *Campus Gods on Trial.* Remember? Well, these got me to thinking that what I had been rejecting wasn't God but just my childish ideas of God. The fact that there wasn't any Santa Claus didn't necessarily mean there wasn't a God. I got this kind of thinking from reading Aristotle and then later from Stuart Chase writing about Aristotle. This reminds me, now I've got to do some reading of somebody writing about Stuart Chase.

But still, by this same kind of thinking, I shouldn't jump to the conclusion that there is a God.

So I went on reading, figuring that if I'd gotten that far with just a few books maybe if I kept going I'd get even further. Just like we decided to start building with a little bit of motivation, I decided on my own to start building with a little bit of faith. Like you said, I could at least "try on the idea of God for size."

One thing I'd better tell you first: I went back to the Will Durant book (*The Story of Philosophy*) and started taking sides in the arguments like you said and, for the first time, the philosophies became personal to me. Just reading about them isn't enough. You've got to be Plato and Aristotle and Francis Bacon.

Anyway, I kept on reading, and pretty soon I decided I'd start pretending there was a God. That way if there wasn't one, no harm would have been done, and if there was—well, I wouldn't be pretending any more. I think I got this from reading the Pike and Pittenger book (*The Faith of the Church*) about imitating Christ; I'm not sure. What's more, I didn't keep waiting for a "religious experience" to hit me like I'd always done in the past. I realized by this time that I'd have to go looking for the proof if I was ever going to find it. Nobody was ever going to show me. I'd have to show myself.

Then I got off the track for a while. Reading the book by Bouquet (*Comparative Religion*) got me off the beam. He said that it was no longer a question of whether a man had religion, but rather which of the great religions of man he must choose. This isn't so. I can still reject all of them. And *Intelligible Religion* didn't help any either, not in this way it didn't. It said that a man's religion was whatever he considered holy and all that. Well, I didn't consider anything to be holy. And they said in *The Faith of the Church* that there wasn't any such thing as an atheist. Well, I say that there can be. A man who believes that there is no supernatural god is an atheist, period. And a man who doubts that there is one is an agnostic. I know. I was one or the other for twenty-five years.[3]

But after a while I got to thinking away back to that science book I read (*Science in Our Lives* by Ritchie Calder). I think that was it, or maybe it was something you said, or Stuart Chase. It had to do with what Einstein said about light not just going on indefinitely. It bends, and therefore the universe is not infinite. So maybe some of those philosophers were right; maybe there has to be order in the universe. If so, then maybe it was all planned out by somebody. If so, then that somebody has to be God.

The room was quite dark now, but I could still see Sol Friedman's face as he tilted with the idea of God.

I do not suggest, by any means, that Solomon Friedman had arrived at a mature, permanently sustaining belief in God. Nor would I assert that his new ideas of God were solely the result of his reading. I would definitely say, however, that his reading, for which all other aspects of his research provided a favorable mental and emotional climate, did indeed expedite his arrival at those beliefs. He might have arrived at some conception of God eventually, program or no program, who is to say? He himself states unequivocally, however, that he would never have attained even his tentative belief in God without reading Calder's book on science—which had brought his knowledge of science up to date—in more or less close conjunction with the various semipopular books on religion—which straightened out his semantic confusions concerning the words "God," "hereafter," "faith," "self," and "ethics." For Sol these books formed a necessary bridge of understanding.

Sol's struggle with problems of church and of concepts of worship and, consequently, with the problems of psychological and ethical behavior that partially constitute his "self" was just beginning. But he had

---

[3] He did not notice at the time that he had used the past tense. When told about it later, he was shocked, and insisted that it was a "Freudian slip." I agreed, but pointed out that if this were so he was still arguing against himself.

crossed his Rubicon. He thought that there might be a God. He had hopes that there would be a continuing, identifiable Sol Friedman after death, and his hope was great enough to influence his behavior and demeanor noticeably. He behaved as if a great burden had been removed from his shoulders. He walked straighter and with a lighter tread, and, when he talked, he sounded like a man who was going somewhere. If there was a God, Sol Friedman was no longer alone in the world.

The Senator

"The Senator" was one of the few members of the group I "knew" before the group began. I "met" him while I was still in the Army. My overuse of quotation marks will be excused, I hope, when I explain that the Senator was not really a Senator; the man I knew in the Army was not the same man I knew in the group, and "met" is hardly the word to describe my first encounter with this remarkable individual.

The circumstances of our first meeting, as it turned out, were prophetic.

After V-J Day, I was stationed at a small elite Army post in the East. Here was barracks duty at its best, or worst: strictly spit and polish, close-order drill, formal parades, and "chicken." This is the short form of an Army expression in which the word "chicken" was originally followed by a four-letter word we all knew. It meant overemphasis on the small and the piddling, and this could be overpowering in large quantities. But for that very reason the post was a model military installation, the logical place to serve as official headquarters for visiting V.I.P.s, military and political.

The Senator was one of these V.I.P.s. He had been given the red-carpet treatment, taken on a brisk tour of inspection of the base, and established with pomp and circumstance in a private house on a hill overlooking the parade ground. He was on official business from Washington. Perhaps he was investigating something, but he spent all of his time at the fancy quarters, not snooping around.

One night I received a call from the Catholic chaplain. Would I kindly drop over to the V.I.P.'s residence? Without mentioning it to anyone, of course.

Unaccustomed as I was to being asked so solicitously to do anything by an officer, even a sky pilot, I went over to the guest house on the double without stopping to wonder what was wanted of me. My only real fear was that one of my Catholic men was dying some strange and sudden death and I would be buried in red tape for weeks.

628 ARTHUR H. CAIN

I rapped on the door, opened it, saw no one, took one step forward, and fell over a body just inside the doorway.

Whoever it was—a quick look showed me that it was not one of my men, for which I praised the Lord—was out like a light. An unbelievable reek of alcohol, stale beer, sweat, vomit, urine, and feces engulfed me, and I knew at once what the trouble was and why I had been called. But who was the bum?

I dragged the 200-pound mess into the foyer, kicked it into something resembling a human shape, wiped my hands on my handkerchief (there was not a clean spot on his clothing), and went into the nearest room. It was the living room, and there I saw what is, now, to me, a fairly familiar tableau: troubled priest, baffled physician, and anguished wife.

As a boy the Senator sang in the choir and accepted the values of the Church completely. He loved his parents and kept the Ten Commandments. In due time he graduated from law school. At twenty-six he married an attractive Irish-American girl and settled down to the business of getting ahead. While he was establishing a law practice, he had a position with a business firm. He seemed destined to achieve exactly what his mother and father wanted for him: happiness, respectability, security, sanctity, and salvation.

The atom bomb was dropped on Hiroshima, and the Senator came home. Like others who had distinguished themselves in prolonged tours of combat duty, he found his travel orders cut suddenly. He was flown to San Francisco and sent to a separation center for discharge as a major. He was back in Middletown before his letter from the coast arrived, and he found Moira living secretly in another section of town with another man.

He got very drunk, a feat he had mastered in the Pacific, and soon left for New York City. He heard a year later that Moira was getting a divorce, in spite of the ban on divorce by the Catholic Church. He severed all his connections with Middletown: neither his law practice nor his parents nor Moira nor Sunday-morning Mass existed for him any more.

The Senator settled down to civilian life in Washington. There, by reason of his military experience, his legal training, his brilliant mind, and his driving energy—when he was sober—he soon became one of the most influential men in the District of Columbia.

He married again and was devoted to his new wife, Phoebe. He worked hard. He also drank hard. And he was able to do both—for a time. Then, for awhile he found he could manage somehow by alternating sustained bursts of work, which astonished even elder statesmen in the Capital, with benders that left barkeepers in awe. Finally, of course, the bursts of work became less effective and the benders more violent and frequent.

He was about at the end of the line when I fell over him in the V.I.P. quarters overlooking the parade ground.

It took the Senator a while, of course, to become accustomed to the idea. The rest of us, it turned out, had put into our notebooks a mounting pile of evidence pointing to the Senator's petite, long-suffering, martyred wife as the secondary mover if not the creator of her husband's alcoholism. It was a bitter pill for the Senator to swallow, but the one that made him well once he was able to keep it down.

As always, it seemed abundantly clear in retrospect. The picture of the Senator's wife, once we unraveled it and put it together again, looked something like this:

First stage: Immersed in the life of Middletown, U.S.A., he had accepted the dictates of his parents, his church, and his society without serious question. All three were woven into a comfortable pattern of affection, security, and approval. At twenty-seven, he was still his parents' child and his church's choirboy; Moira was a beautiful amalgamation of Mother, Mary, and Middletown.

Second stage: World War II. The realities of jungle warfare. The resort to alcohol.

Third stage: The shock of finding that his wife was a fallen woman. Family, Jesus, and the Joneses fell with her. They were all suddenly ugly, dishonest, foul.

Fourth stage: The discovery of alcohol as a palliative, hard work as an escape, and Phoebe. Phoebe provided him with a strange mixture of the things he had lost and his ways of forgetting them. She was sweet, gentle, forgiving, virginal, and, above all, not a Catholic. She encouraged his work, and she tolerated his drinking. More than that, she made it easier and easier for him to adopt the role of "ordinary husband," the Elbert Hubbard image of himself that he had been trying to live up to in Middletown fifteen years before. He transferred his always active, always inadequately repressed need for religious devotion to Phoebe. He married her. He worshiped her.

Fifth stage: Alcoholism, somewhat ambiguously referred to by Alcoholics Anonymous and other groups working on the problem as a "progressive disease" (it is the aging process that is progressive), began to catch up with him. His alcoholic episodes became more uncontrolled and more prolonged; inevitably he reached the classic impasse of the alcoholic: he could not endure sobriety, and he could not continue drinking and still live and retain his sanity.

Sixth stage: His attempt to solve the problem. It was in the fifth and sixth stages that Phoebe's actual role in his life began to emerge. Here are some of the notes taken by myself and the colleagues during eight months of the Senator's work with the group; they include some recollections of my earlier acquaintance with him.

"Why does the Senator seem to release his repressed rage against Phoebe during his benders?" (The answer to this one, as noted earlier, seemed to be that he was getting even with Moira.)

"Why, in spite of the fact that he throws her downstairs in drunken fits, does he call for her so pathetically at other times during a binge?" (Remorse? Guilt?)

"Why did Phoebe object so strenuously to her husband's giving the group a try, if she was so anxious for him to cure his alcoholism? Why did she appear to be under more strain than ever during his period of sobriety in Alcoholics Anonymous?"

Recollection: A strange conversation that took place on the screened-in porch of the V.I.P. quarters at the post. The Senator, who had been sober for about a week, remarked, "Thank God, that's over. I feel fine again," or words to that effect. Phoebe replied softly, "Don't even think about it, Dear; it might make the next spell come on even quicker. Let's just forget it ever happened, hear?" she added, with all the forgiveness of an understanding heart in her voice. The Senator flinched almost convulsively. I am sure the thought of another bender had not occurred to him. Now it had been inserted in his mind.

I doubt whether Phoebe knew what she was doing, and the question of moral judgment does not arise. Why she was doing it is a pertinent question. A plausible hypothesis is that she felt uncomfortably inferior to her husband in intellect, achievement, and personal vitality, and consciously or unconsciously encouraged his alcoholism, which reduced him to a blubbering hulk and made him cry out to her in entreaty and reverence.

Still, this is not really the place to analyze Phoebe's motives. Sufficient to say that she abetted the Senator's alcoholism and that she is by no means unique in our society.

The important thing was the Senator's reaction to his sudden discovery that his devotion to Phoebe was a form of idolatry, that he had placed her before God, or ultimate reality, or whatever he chose to call it.

Having discovered that the idol, Phoebe, had been as much a crutch as work and the bottle, he became, for the first time in his life consciously concerned with Ultimate Reality and, for him, the ultimate alternatives: God and life or drink and death.

Seventh stage: This period, at the beginning, was the grimmest of all. The Senator went into a profound depression during which he cared about nothing. He blindly followed instructions of the group; we were all he had left. He seemed without hope, but he had not the strength or the motivation to do away with himself. He showed up at group sessions and private sessions like an automaton. He did his calisthenics, but without enthusiasm; he kept his log, but the entries were sparse and routine; he read steadily, reporting dutifully but dully on whatever book I gave him. He refused to speak with or even write to Phoebe during these weeks. She, in turn, blamed me for "maliciously breaking up her home through a basic hostility toward women."

Finally, after about six weeks, the Senator began to come out of his depression. We could not point to any particular activity or to any spectacular insight derived from his reading or educational sessions that could account for it. But the program was now his whole life, and it is reasonable to suppose that it combined the necessary elements in the right way to start the process of resurgence. This has occurred with a number of the colleagues. It would seem as if, after a certain period of time, "psychic fatigue" sets in: having suffered as long as he is capable of suffering, the patient's depression and anxiety simply give out as a disease runs its course. We kept the patient as warm and as comfortable as we could, so to speak, and when he began to feel better we helped him out of bed.

Eighth stage: One day near the end of his nine-month commitment, the Senator announced that he might as well go the whole hog and look into religious investigation, after all. He had read Richardson's *Christian Apologetics,* then Hansen and Fuller's *The Church of Rome,* and he thought he might like to go a little further. After all, he said, he did not have to assume that the Church rejected him just because he had once thought it was beautiful and loved it for that reason, and then thought it was defiled because of Moira. That fellow Richardson made a lot of sense about Christianity, in general, and those Catholic writers made it sound as if it was still pretty beautiful, "though in a different kind of way. Now is seems beautiful because it's true. Not the other way around."

Paul

Paul, as I shall call him, was born in the deep South of parents who made a religion of social aristocracy, breeding, gentility, and little else. Manners, not morals; graciousness instead of grace.

His mother and father were divorced when he was three. He was the only child. He was the "sissy" of the neighborhood. A childhood portrait shows us a golden-haired boy who looks like a girl.

He became an atheist at the age of eight, when he discovered that Santa Claus was not real. Characteristically, he did not reveal his disillusionment to his mother, thus continuing to reap the worldly benefits of Christmas.

He took his first drink, smoked his first cigarette, and "had his first date," as he euphemistically put it, on his fourteenth birthday.

At fifteen, he had enough money to assure that his mother would be taken care of, having acquired the funds for this "Grand Gesture" (his life was a series of grand gestures) by running corn whiskey from a nearby mountain still to hotels and clubs in the city at a profit of four dollars a gallon. Then he ran away from home.

At twenty-one, Paul was a foreign correspondent for a southern newspaper, making one of those vagabond journeys around the world made popular by Richard Halliburton. He traveled, mostly on foot, in 57 countries in Africa, Europe, the Middle East, and the Orient. This took him two years.

A year after his return he was a vice-president of one of the South's largest newspaper advertising syndicates, a columnist for a daily paper, an associate of a national radio broadcasting system, and a professional gambler.

Now came another of the grand gestures. Paul suddenly chucked it all, spent all his savings on a truly king-sized binge, and left for the Far East—and alcoholism.

As might be expected, he turned first to psychiatry for help. He had faith that he would receive it, too. And he might have, had he been able to go into full-time psychotherapy with a competent therapist when he needed it. Like many other desperate alcoholics, however, he could afford neither the time nor the money for such a lengthy and expensive proposition. He went to a few practitioners, had a few necessarily superficial sessions, and went right on drinking. The futile search for an individual analyst or a clinic added to the frustrations that were steadily shortening the periods between benders.

Finally, after one memorable binge during which he was picked out of the ocean off Coney Island fully clad and singing the "Ode to Joy" in German, he woke up in Knickerbocker Hospital in New York. Alcoholics Anonymous sponsored a ward there.

Paul stayed dry in Alcoholics Anonymous for six months, the longest period of sobriety he had had since that first drink on his fourteenth birthday. He accepted A.A. "to the best of his ability," although he was unable to accept the religious aspect of the program. He practiced A.A. principles in all his affairs and helped a number of sick alcoholics attain sobriety. Then, being one of those alcoholics who were constitutionally unable to abstain from a critical evaluation of the principles that were keeping him sober, he began studying the problem of alcoholism. How could the greatest thinker in the world do otherwise?

"I think I first started analyzing because of a very commonplace remark in A.A. One day someone said, smugly and pontifically, 'There is an aggregate of four hundred years' drinking experience in this meeting room. If we don't understand alcoholism, then nobody does!' Naturally, to an old philosopher-scientist-logician this was a non sequitur of the lowest order. I thought, There's not a man in this room who has the faintest notion of the meaning of alcoholism. They were all staying sober on faith, blind faith. 'Utilize, don't analyze,' said A.A. But this was like waving a red flag at a philosophical bull. Blind faith was to me *ipso facto* objectionable, fundamentally wrong in principle. Sobriety or no sobriety, it was obviously (here we go again!) up to me to dig into the matter and find out what was really going on. Categorical Imperative, you know.

"Within two weeks I was back in the hospital, drunk as an owl." Suitable simile for a potted philosopher.

Like the Senator, Paul tried vainly to return to the A.A. fold. But a few weeks of working hard at A.A., and again he was in a hospital. (Paul and the Senator first met in such a hospital and have been close friends ever since. They had much in common, although Paul's contempt for women was in direct contrast to the Senator's reverence for them.)

It was upon leaving the hospital that Paul had his next revelation, as he might now put it.

"God knows, I'll never forget it. I was only able to stay in the hospital two days, and I was still in the horrors when I left. I was making my way, shaking and retching, along a street which was being reconstructed. It was raining, and the street was full of mud and slush. It was just about dawn.

"Suddenly I heard myself saying, 'No matter if it kills me. No matter what happens to me, I'll find out how to quit drinking, so help me God!' As I said this—and it was as if someone else had put the words in my mouth—I came out from behind the shadows of the buildings, and the lights of the city across the harbor shone brightly in my path. I was able to move forward more quickly, and I picked up a fallen branch to use as a cane. Then the first true light of dawn appeared in the eastern sky, and I went on home. The next day, sick as I still was, I went to a library and got out everything I could find on alcoholism. I outlined a plan for my new project. I went to work on it. Then I met you and the group was started.

"I haven't had a drink since," said Paul. "Not since saying, 'No matter what happens to me,' that is."

But although Paul, like the other "sinners," had indeed achieved sobriety, he kept on with the program. Simple sobriety was not enough, not enough for lasting peace of mind and soul. Sobriety, after all, is but the absence of intoxication, although many members of A.A. and others are prone to speak of it as a thing-in-itself to be loved and cherished. It is, of course, what one does in the absence of intoxication that is meaningful, not sobriety per se. There are many sick, unhappy, neurotic people in the world who have never touched alcohol in their lives, and it is absurd to speak of them as "dry" alcoholics.[4] Sobriety as such can never be a way of life, although it is doubtless an essential condition. A.A. is a wonderful bridge from the jail or hospital to true recovery. But one cannot live on a bridge forever.

For Paul, as for all the others, the group was also a bridge, nothing more. The colleagues crossed over it and never needed a bridge again. They reentered the business of life, the mainstream of life. It is seldom that I hear a colleague speak of his own alcoholism at all. It is no longer a problem, let alone a full-time job. I do not intend here to make an invidious comparison between the Alcoholics Anonymous and the group. I do intend, however, to take advantage of every opportunity to point out that true recovery from alcoholism is possible. Seventy members of the group are living proof of this contention.

Alcoholics Anonymous is not the only bridge to peace and serenity that is mistaken for a permanent way of life. Another is psychotherapy. Indeed, it would seem that at the present stage of development in that embryonic science, mistaking a bridge for a way of life is the rule. I speak now of nonalcoholics as well as alcoholics. Too often a patient says, "Therapy is my religion, my way of life" or "I live my life on Freudian principles," or "I have learned to live with myself as I am." Thus a psychologically frail, unhappy, defensive person is deluded by pseudoscientific word magic into a belief that further progress is not available to him. This is the cult of psychological determinism at its

---

[4] In some "alcoholism circles," including A.A., there is an occasional assertion that so-and-so is a "dry drunk": He is an alcoholic even though he never took a drink in his life. He has the "alcoholic personality." This illustrates the absurdities which have penetrated these semantics.

stultifying worst. Mental and emotional health, like sobriety, is a necessary condition for human growth, not an end in itself. In the same way, the church may be only a bridge—to religion.

My seventy colleagues are also living proof that psychotherapy is a bridge that can be crossed. Wholehearted submission to the fundamentally sound rules of psychotherapy in the early stages of treatment is a good and necessary thing. But the patient must, eventually, come up for air. Psychoanalysis is not a religion; Freud and his followers are neither prophets nor philosophers, scientists nor logicians.

The final rule in therapy should be: "Utilize, then analyze." Analyze the analysis, that is, and move forward.

Which is what Paul did.

He is fond of saying how glad he is that he was not driven to accept any of the higher concepts he now holds by his desperation to stop drinking. He had arrived at them after he had already achieved sobriety and a good measure of success and happiness.

"I just kept on looking for even bigger and better things—because I could," he says. "I found them too."

This is the way he put it.

> As you know, I kept on thinking and I kept on reading long after alcoholism had ceased to be a problem. I was still dedicated, of course, to the pursuit of truth—to me the highest possible good. This was inherent in my program for becoming the greatest thinker in the world. It was with this ideal before me that I turned to religion along with the rest of the group in the effort to find out what we could about human suffering in general so that we might help our particular kinds of alcoholics recover from the illness we had conquered. I personally didn't need religion. [How often we heard that expression in the group!]
>
> But I kept on studying the 'bridge' books: *Christian Apologetics,* the Tillich book, and all the others on the group's list. Then I came up against Kierkegaard's *For Self-Examination.* This one demanded point-blank that I, the reader, examine, not my intellectual concepts, but my own actual position in relation to Angst, and the "fear and trembling and the sickness unto death" and the other phenomena attributed to religious anxiety by the theologians.
>
> I thought, if I'm really going to be thorough in my efforts to become "perfectly wise," I must explore these possibilities just as I let myself be swept into the horrors of alcoholism and narcotics. I must certainly accept the challenge and try on these religious notions for size. It was the only thing I could do if I was really devoted to scientific thoroughness in my investigations and in my training.
>
> This rather casual emendation to my program proved to be my undoing as an atheist. It was just as all the great religions of the world had said. Fundamental religious truths, as well as the religious

experience, are ineffable. That is, no really meaningful description of them is possible until they have been experienced. I arrived at this experience in two stages, and again I'm happy it happened this way. First I unraveled the semantic difficulties that had been blocking my intellectual comprehension of the concept of God; then I went away to the wilderness and tried to experience Him, or It, whichever word you want to use. My point is that I had no reason to suspect that I had sold myself a bill of goods because of any urgent emotional need to believe in a higher power, or in a hereafter, or in any of these ideas. Remember, I was already riding high in those days and didn't need a belief in God. My kind of humanism was good enough for Erich Fromm, and it was good enough for me.

I reached the first stage while I was reading a book called *The Truth of the Gospel*, by a man named Caird. The title nearly scared me off, and I don't remember much about the book, but it made me understand for the first time a phrase that the group used all the time but which had just been an expression with me. This was "Ultimate Reality." Now, for some reason, it rang a bell. Somehow, without emotional fanfare, I realized that I had been trying very hard to comprehend a God that the theologians hadn't been trying to explain at all. God was in truth a simple concept, not the complex one I had denied because it seemed logically impossible. God was the Ultimate Reality—that which was most real, most enduring, most true. God was simply another word to describe what I had always been seeking: the highest truth available to man. Of course, I believed in God. I had always believed in God. What I had so bitterly, and so unnecessarily, fought was a series of childish conceptions of God.

It was that simple. Almost anticlimactic.

All this meant, of course, was that I had an intellectual readiness for God. A necessity but not a sufficiency. I thought I had arrived but I hadn't.

My zeal for scientific truth carried me through—on across the bridge. Ironic? Why? Isn't science one way of seeking the truth? Of course. Just as long as we remember the "one way" part of it. Science isn't a way of life any more than psychotherapy—a scientific enterprise, perhaps; or Alcoholics Anonymous—a religious enterprise, surely. Anyhow, my maxim of trying anything and everything with a "willing suspension of disbelief" led me on to what finally happened.

REFERENCES

1. Diamond, S. A study of the influence of political radicalism on personality development. *Archives of Psychology*, 1936, No. 203.
2. Fitzgerald, F. S. *Tender is the night*. New York: Scribner's, 1933.
3. Montherlant, H. de. *Costals and the hippogriff*. New York: Knopf, 1940.
4. Scott, N. A. *The story of Mrs. Murphy*. New York: Sutton, 1947.
5. Waples, D. *What reading does to people*. Chicago: University of Chicago Press, 1940.

Part Four

RELIGION IN PSYCHOTHERAPY

Some physicians tend to become victims of their self-centeredness and professional parochialism. They ascribe an essential role to their medical activities and blind themselves, at least for a time, to much more potent curative effects contributed by health educators, sanitary technicians, dietetic experts, and the culturally sanctioned rules of healthy living. If by some magic power these self-deluded physicians were able to abolish the socially based health care, they would soon see how little their personal medical skills availed.

Some conceited psychotherapists have developed similar ideas of grandeur quite inappropriate to the levels of reality testing which could be expected from them. These puffed-up psychologists and psychiatrists have lost their sense of proportion; they appreciate only what is being produced in their little corner and lose sight of the accumulated wisdom of centuries and the psychotherapeutic effects that are conserved in religious, mystical, and philosophical traditions. The self-infatuated psychotherapists have deluded themselves and misled others by their exaggerated accent on the merits of their techniques and their equally exaggerated disparagement of other approaches to stabilizing emotionally and characterologically unbalanced individuals. By what might be

637

called a perversion of judgment, some psychotherapists have come to think of the sources of personal stability that can be found in philosophical and ethical systems and in religious practices and precepts as expressions of supposed psychopathology. There is no support in research for such philosophical prejudice. It stems from a naturalistic, positivistic orientation of the previous century.

Psychotherapists who do not have an ideological axe to grind discern readily that psychotherapy is, in ultimate analysis, always carried within a religio-philosophical and social context. It actually obtains its potency from relating the patient to higher values than contained in the medical counseling itself. Jaspers writes:

> We cannot rid ourselves entirely of some basic philosophical viewpoint when formulating our psychotherapeutic goals. This may get obscured or undergo chaotic changes but we cannot develop any psychotherapy that is purely medical, self-contained and appears to be its own justification. . . . Prinzhorn . . . explicitly argues that it is impossible for any psychotherapy to be autonomous from philosophy . . . the therapist can only mediate through his unique personality, through a mental suppleness that lacks objectivity, lacks any sanction for what is done or said; or else because he is a member of some intimate, cultural community, religious, national or party-political; only thus is he able to return firm answers when questions of authority arise.
>
> Therapeutic effort is limited both by the reality of the environment and by the patient being "thus and no other". Because of this, therapy in the end always becomes some kind of philosophical undertaking. Should it choose to illumine rather than obscure, it will have to teach humility and renunciation as well as the need to grasp at positive possibilities. Obviously this is not something that psychology or medicine can accomplish but only the close collaboration of doctor and patient in a mutual philosophic faith. (1, pp. 25, 27)

The earliest psychotherapeutic activity in this country was performed in clinics under the religious auspices of the Emmanuel Movement. This tradition has never died out; it was only overlaid by the dominant psychoanalytic philosophy, which continued in the direction set by Freud's atheism. With the decrease of Freudian influence, religiously oriented psychotherapists have been able to develop techniques more in keeping with the religious concept of man, his nature, and his role in the world.

Tweedie describes a method based largely on evangelical traditions. Herr's approach to therapy is based on classic Christian views of man, partly expressed in the idiom of the existentialist and of Thomist anthropology. Vayhinger develops a method combining broad Christian concepts and some of the learning theory principles. Burroughs de-

scribes a method which grew out of his experiences in reclaiming alcoholics through religious awakening and participation in church practices.

These methods may not boast of sophisticated and complicated
theory. Perhaps their theoretically simplified approach is their strength,
and possibly these methods will be practiced long after other psychotherapeutic theories with all their elaborate, if misleading, speculations
have been forgotten. Their strength lies exactly in what psychologists
and psychiatrists of doctrinaire mentality might consider their weakness: instead of analyzing, they challenge the will and relate the patient to the essential, to the numinous. They avoid the *"egocentric attitude to life"* arising out of analysis and that *"specific brazenness . . .
to display one's psychic entrails"* (1, p. 34). Jaspers comments on the
dangers of an analytic "psychological atmosphere":

> There is a dangerous tendency in psychotherapy to convert the psy-
> chic actuality of an individual into an end in itself. The person who
> turns his psyche into a god because he has lost both world and God
> finds himself standing finally in the void.
>
> He misses the gripping force of things themselves, of objects of
> faith, images and symbols, tasks to perform, of anything absolute
> in the world. Psychological self-reflection can never achieve that which
> only becomes possible through a surrender to being. Here lie the
> radical differences between the purposeful manipulations of psycho-
> therapists directed upon the psyche and the practices of priests, mys-
> tics and philosophers of all times, directed through the ages towards
> God or Being; between confidences, self-revelations given to the doc-
> tor and confession in church. The transcendent reality marks the
> difference. (1, p. 3)

A majority of contemporary psychotherapists, schooled in the learned
naturalistic and rationalistic preconceptions, have a blind spot for the
value of religion in maintaining mental health or establishing the inner
balance and strength. By adopting the current philosophical superstitions against religion, many psychotherapists have cut off themselves and
their patients from the healing resources of religion. They concentrate
on theology as if it were all of religion, and reject it, missing in that
way the wider living effects of religious convictions and practices. They
fail to appreciate the prophetic interpretation of human mental and
social troubles: That humans are sick within their personalities because
they have cut themselves off from the rich resources of God dwelling
in the psyche, in community experiences, and in the universe. The current upheaval of multitudes searching for healthier, nonrationalistic experiences through mind-changing (and mind-twisting) drugs is a reaction
to naturalistic strangulation of religious affects. Most of these persons

appear to be seeking an unknown God, within and without; they cannot yet make the act of faith which would bring them in contact with the known God of religious traditions. They have not reached the mature view of established religious channelization to which Jung witnessed by discharging from therapy patients who had shown genuine religious awakening or dissuading from entering therapy those who were already practicing an active faith. The four therapists of this section demonstrate the potent effects a mature and disciplined religious involvement may have in both the therapist and his "patient."

REFERENCES

1. Jaspers, K. *The nature of psychotherapy.* Chicago: The University of Chicago Press, 1965.

Chapter 22

Christian Psychotherapy

DONALD F. TWEEDIE, JR.

Donald F. Tweedie, Jr.: b. 1926, Salem, Massachusetts.
A.B., in philosophy, Gordon College, 1950. Ph.D., in philosophy and psychology, Boston University, 1954. Clinical Affiliate, Vienna City Polyclinic, Austria, 1959–1960.
Clinical Professor of Psychology, Fuller Seminary Graduate School of Psychology, Pasadena, 1964–date. Professor of Psychology, Gordon College, 1952–1964. Research Specialist, V.A. Hospital, Lexington, Kentucky, 1962–1963.
Fellow, American Scientific Affiliation.
Books: Of Sex and Saints (1965). The Christian and the Couch (1963). Logotherapy and the Christian Faith (1961).
Articles: Psyche's sawdust trail. Contemp. Psychol. (Review of Depth psychology and salvation by W. Daim), 1964, 9. Failure in forgiving: behavior manifestations. Proceedings of the Christian Association for Psychological Studies, 1964. Marriage counseling. Proceedings of the Christian Association for Psychological Studies, 1963. Die Logotherapie und der Christliche Glaube. Zeitschrift für Psychotherapie und Medizinische Psychologie, January, 1961.

Historically, psychotherapy is a direct outgrowth of the two major psychological movements that have characterized American psychology—psychoanalysis and behaviorism.[1] From the beginning psychotherapy has been frustrated by the inadequacy of a procedure that analyzes the historical factors relating to personality disorder but finds no satisfactory means by which to synthesize these factors. This limitation is the problem of psychoanalysis. On the other hand, the contemporary resurgence of behavioristic psychotherapy, with an extremely truncated view of man, is devoid of both the insight of the past and a meaningful value orientation for the future. In spite of the present polemical strivings of these two polar forces, it is obvious that any satisfactory psychotherapeutic system will entail both an understanding of the personal past of

---

[1] This paper is based upon, and adapted from, my book, The Christian and the Couch. Grand Rapids: Baker Books, 1963.

641

the patient and a dynamic hope for his future. At the same time it must be recognized that all psychotherapeutic techniques manipulate behavior in order to alleviate present painful symptoms (18).

A community of opinion is arising with reference to the development of psychotherapy that neither of these two approaches, nor a mutant variation of them, is adequate. This "third force" proposes that, in addition to dynamics and techniques, an adequate psychotherapy must also include a place for responsibility for one's past and an objective value system to sustain healthy personal growth. This seems to call for a moral order not available in either psychoanalysis or behaviorism.

An attempt to resolve this apparent dilemma has renewed an old option. The growing tendency has been to look to religious goals and values for a solution. This trend is noteworthy if for no other reason than that both psychoanalysis and behaviorism, in their initial formulations, were dogmatically irreligious. The trend does not imply that most psychotherapists are becoming religious counselors, but it does indicate that religious experiences are no longer looked upon as necessarily neurotic processes. In fact, religion is increasingly being perceived as resourceful rather than detrimental.

Admittedly, even today a multitude of psychotherapists would consider their therapeutic effort a failure should a patient experience a religious conversion or cling to prior convictions of faith. Nonetheless, the body of literature relating psychology and religion has begun to abound. Study groups and formal organizations, formed to effect a rapprochement, are at every hand. For instance, the Academy of Religion and Mental Health, numbering its members in the thousands, publishes a significant journal and holds periodic enclaves of leaders in the fields of psychology, psychiatry, and religion for the purpose of discovering values for living that will give substance to psychotherapy.

At the same time, there is an increased demand for psychotherapeutic services. The statistical reports and prophecies concerning the incursion of emotional disorders into our society are both fascinating and fearsome. The more ominous indicate that at least a tenth of our populace will spend some time in neuropsychiatric hospitals. In addition, a much greater number will be receiving outpatient professional assistance.

In the light of this burgeoning social need and the *ad hoc* proliferation of the psychotherapeutic profession, what shall be the Christian's involvement? Prompted by his own emotional straits or challenged by the demand to be his brother's keeper, he must have at least a minimal personal investment in the mental health movement.

At this point there should be a clarification as to how the term Christian will be used in this paper. It has a very wide application in our culture and sometimes communicates a rather vague meaning. I use it to refer to those who give allegiance to the Bible as the authoritative Word of God and who have made a personal commitment of trust in the person and work of Jesus Christ. This definition will be too narrow for most and too broad for some, but it has the virtue of being succinct and having a clear historical precedent.

My intention is to investigate the relevance and relationship of psychotherapy to a Biblically oriented faith. I have collated a number of essays and books whose authors appear to reflect such a viewpoint, and I have quoted copiously from them. In addition, I have cited and quoted several authors, such as Frankl and Mowrer, who do not identify their theories as Christian but whose ideas are, in my opinion, significant in their positive bearing upon a Christian critique. Judgment as to whether a literary viewpoint is Christian, in the light of my definition, or whether it entails the conclusions that I have drawn, is my own responsibility. This paper is intended to be provocative rather than definitive; a challenge for research rather than a final answer.

MENTAL ILLNESS

There is a long-standing debate as to whether the causes of mental illness are to be found in physical or psychological components. The non-Freudian European tradition has generally tended to classify neuroses as psychologically based, or psychogenic, and psychoses as physically caused, or physiogenic. Freudian dynamic psychology has tended to psychologize most disorders, whereas behavioristic psychology has inclined toward a physiological basis for all psychopathological problems.

Caution would no doubt dictate some sort of a middle of the road perspective, holding that both physical and nonphysical factors are significant for the functional problems. Orville Walters (52), a Christian psychiatrist, takes this stance: "Both views of schizophrenia (physiogenic-psychogenic) may be correct. Perhaps habitual fear, anger, or other stressful experiences upset an already unstable body chemistry inherited by the schizophrenic, thus bringing on the characteristic disturbance in the thinking. If this is true, the basic defect is a chemical one and the trigger mechanism is psychological stress" (52).

In the psychiatric tradition of Europe, a strong philosophic foundation underlies the diagnosis of neurosis. R. Allers avers, "At the bottom of every neurosis there is a metaphysical problem" (2). Waterink, a conservative Christian psychologist in the Netherlands, believes that "many neuroses are the expression of a more or less unsuccessful attempt at attaining the realization of one's own self, from the perfection of one's own potentialities" (56). Frankl (9, 47), while insisting upon the physical basis for psychotic reactions, convincingly argues for a "noogenic neurosis" which takes root and flourishes in a meaningless life.

Walters (53) names four probable causes for mental illness: organic (due to structural changes in brain cells), metabolic (from a disturbed brain chemistry), psychologic (based on emotional disruptions), and developmental (faulty childhood patterns of behavior persisting into adult life).

Heerema sees the roots of mental illness as an imbalance in developmental years: "The affective roots of most mental illness we have found to be in faulty conditioning in earlier years. The two main factors bearing on the proper actualization of the personality's affective energies are control and expression, or discipline and emotional security, or determination and freedom. These two forces must be in the proper balance in the molding of the young affective life" (11, p. 30).

A conflict theory of mental illness is also held among Christians. Ernest White in *Christian Life and the Unconscious* holds that the degree of conflict modified by inherited characteristics will determine the emotional disease. "It is a law of mind that conflicts tend to be externalized. It depends very much on the inherited disposition of the individual how far this externalization proceeds, and at what level it occurs. With some it goes no further than their conscious emotional states. With others it is projected into their bodies, producing various disturbances of bodily functions. With others again, their conflicts are projected on to the outside world, and delusions are the result of this externalization" (59, p. 18).

It should be emphasized, however, that it is not tension, stress of conflict per se which causes mental illness. Stress that is not intrapersonal may mobilize the dimensions of personality and tend to unify and integrate it. Frankl presses this point in his writings, for he observed numerous instances in the Nazi concentration camps where persons stood up under the pressure of all manner of stress and then broke down when liberated. Just as an old structure may be reinforced by adding weight, so may the burdens of life reinforce the unity of the personality.

As White mentions in the previous quotations, the disruptive forces may externalize in personality deterioration at any level. In my dimensional view of personality, this statement means that the primary symptoms of mental illness may be released through any of the four dimensions of personality (physical, emotional, intellectual, and spiritual), but that all dimensions are involved.

Support has been cited for the etiological significance of the first three dimensions, and it remains to be investigated whether the spiritual, or pneumatic, dimension is also causally involved in mental illness. There is an increasing acceptance in evangelical and humanistic circles of the spiritual dimension as a factor in understanding mental illness (of course, a majority of psychologists would not admit the existence of a spiritual dimension at all, and the humanists have a much different conception than the evangelical Christians). Viktor Frankl, the noted Viennese psychiatrist, has insisted (8) that an adequate understanding of mental and emotional disorder involves this spiritual dimension, but he is equally adamant in his assertion that the spiritual factor of personality could not be itself involved in the pathology. His reasons are philosophical and based upon the fact that then there would be no core of personal integrity to which to appeal in times of illness. His logotherapy rests upon such a foundation. Progoff, another of a growing number becoming sensitive to the spiritual needs of man, asserts, "I have found the evidence accumulating that modern man is suffering much more from the repression of his spirit than from the repression of sexuality as Freud once said. It is because traditional beliefs and symbols have lost their inner content that it has become commonplace for modern persons to feel ashamed of their spiritual feelings and spiritual language. They treat the religious strivings within themselves as throwbacks to primitive times, as superstitions unbecoming to a scientific age" (36, p. 47).

Runestam, a Christian, suggested the same possibility several decades ago: "Is it not conceivable that the subdued murmur which emerges from the innermost recesses of the souls of men, distorted in every manner, and which in our day especially expresses itself in the much publicized general nervousness and anxiety, finally, however muffled, becomes the threatening language of the enclosed, forgotten, and suppressed religio-moral needs?" (37, p. 42).

Thus we note that the spiritual dimension as critically related to mental health is accepted by many, both in and outside the Christian camp. Whether the spiritual dimension itself is directly and causally involved in mental illness is another matter. Jacob Mulder, long-time superintendent of a Christian neuropsychiatric hospital in Grand Rapids, concludes, "My own view is that mental disturbance is due to disease of the body . . . In what manner and in how far is this spirit of man affected in mental disease? It is my own view that this spirit is not affected in a destructive sense. When we speak of sickness of the spirit we are using a figurative language. The spirit's disease is of an ethical nature and concerns men's relation to God. The Spirit or psyche requires perfect functioning organs, however, to obtain knowledge and understanding and to perform that most intricate function, rational self-expression" (28, p. 153).

The relationship of the spirit of man and psychopathology, or mental illness, brings us back to the question of religion and mental illness. Most Christian psychologists do not worry about the now nearly passé theory that religious experiences cause mental disorders—"the fact that the mentally disturbed so frequently demonstrate a religious content merely proves that man is fundamentally religious" (28, p. 170)—but they like to keep, if possible, religion and psychopathology in separate categories. Orville Walters (54) holds that the association of the two is unwelcome, for it tends: (1) to blur the boundary between the normal and the abnormal in religious expression, (2) to derive religious generalizations and universals from the pathological, (3) to become judgmental too hastily about deviant forms of religious expression. and (4) to equate sin with psychopathology. That these may be significant dangers if carried to an extreme seems obvious, but equally dangerous is the ignoring of the spiritual nature of man and his illnesses.

To this point we have discussed the nature of mental illness and the fact that primary symptoms can stem from any of the dimensions of personality. The etiology of emotional disorders is but little known except in terms of obvious, though nonetheless mysterious, connections between the illness and physical injury or invasion, and disintegrating developmental stress. In contemporary psychological circles, the tendency is to find causal factors, at least for the functional disorders, in two conflict experiences. These factors are easily related to the spiritual dimension of personality (and not easily understood apart from it). I refer to anxiety and guilt. For some they are identical; others conceive them as entirely distinct. Most see them as intimately related to psychopathology.

ANXIETY

Rollo May, who has written a monograph on the subject, defines anxiety as "the apprehension cued off by a threat to some value which the individual holds essential to his existence" (22, p. 191). Anxiety is usually considered an essentially human experience which is a necessary function of being human. Kierkegaard and Heidegger have brought it to the contemporary scene with their intense, often inscrutable, and influential works (46). Anxiety is an objectless fear, a nameless dread that a future decision may be disastrous, a felt imminence of destruction, a paralyzing uncertainty about the not yet unveiled future.

Although anxiety is almost universally accepted as a pathological factor in mental health, there is some difference of opinion as to whether it is not also a possible asset. Marquart, a Christian psychiatrist, apparently thinks not. "The real cause of Basic Anxiety is the Fall of Man, whereby he sinned against God, and has transmitted to us in some way, the sin nature with its inevitable accumulation of sin acts. Guilt and fear and overcompensatory strivings are all involved in its origin and inevitable continuance" (21, p. 2). On the other hand, Walters considers it a valuable asset in the advancement of the Kingdom:

> There is an irreducible minimum of anxiety for every person. A part is the residual anxiety written into the nervous system by the events of his past life. Another part is the by-product of day-to-day living, as heat is generated by friction in a machine. Anxiety accrues for the Christian when ventures are taken in the name of faith, as when a chastened Saul made himself available on the Damascus road for a life-time of uncertainty and hardship. Anxiety accrues when compassion outruns one's reach, as when John Knox cried, "Give me Scotland or I die." Anxiety accrues in a world where there is perpetual tension between the holiness of God and the selfishness of man, and realization is always short of aspiration. . . . Such anxiety is creative and leads to growth . . . thus Christian faith, far from being a ticket to security, as Freud and Marx both contended, has always produced insecurity. . . . Mature Christian faith offers courage to master the anxiety of spiritual emptiness, of moral guilt and even the anxiety of fate and death in an era of atomic threat. But faith also generates an anxiety of discontent that has moved and continues to move a daring and creative minority in a world that is largely preoccupied with a search for security (51, p. 9).

In spite of this rather optimistic assessment of anxiety, analysis of the anxiety experience reveals the seeds of paralysis rather than of progress. Fear and trembling may point up a crisis situation, but only hope and confidence can resolve it.

Robert White (61) in his classic text in abnormal psychology, *The Abnormal Personality,* uses the concept of anxiety as the basic causal factor in psychopathology. The increase of anxiety is an increase of disintegrating stress and pathological pressures. The circumstances which will stimulate anxiety are relative to the personality development of the individual and his genetic inheritance. Whether anxiety is the exclusive pathological agent in functional disorders is another matter.

GUILT

Another pervasive and universal human experience is that of guilt. It has the same crippling effect as anxiety and has always been considered a factor in psychopathology. "There is no worse suffering than a guilty conscience, and certainly none more harmful. It has not only psychological effects—it acts as a clog upon vitality, and has far-reaching repercussions on general health" (42, p. 210). "Guilt is fundamental to almost every problem of the human personality; it begets anxiety, is manifested in the inferiority complex and follows resentment. Any counseling—whether it is religious or secular—that is going to succeed in helping people with their problems must know what to do with the problem of guilt" (12, p. 156). "A sense of guilt has a peculiarly damaging effect upon the personality. It may best be described as a wound. Guilt cuts deeply into the emotional and spiritual nature. At first this personality cut may not cause suffering and one may feel that 'he has got away with it.' However, if, like the history of some physical diseases, the development is slow, nevertheless the time comes when this guilt malady begins to cause trouble; all of a sudden it may 'break out'. . . . Guilt is an unclean wound. Sorrow, for example, is a clean wound. It pains deeply but being clean the wound heals according to the process of nature. . . . Guilt festers and becomes an infection center; as in the body, so in the mind and the spirit" (33, p. 37). "It is a fact that the psyche is much less indulgent to the unconscious breaches of its own laws and demands (which also are an expression of the 'eternal law' of God) than is the instructed confessor; it will revenge itself for their disregard no less than will the stomach for the consumption of indigestible food stuffs, whether that consumption be conscious and deliberate or ignorant and compelled. For the psyche has its own pattern and laws of origin and growth of functional compensation and order, which cannot be flouted without producing psychopathological symptoms, of which the guilt-sense is the most common" (62, p. 165).

Anxiety is a dread of the future; guilt is a dread of the past. In the former the wrong decision might be made; in the latter despair is experienced because the wrong decision has already been made. The clock of reality cannot be turned back. There is no undoing of the deed.

Freud posited guilt as being due to a violation of the superego. This superego, originating from the restraints and condemnations of authority figures in the life of a child, tends to be oppressive if the social environment was too condemning. Christians tend to waver between this naturalistic concept and the Biblical concept of guilt as a result of sin against the moral law of God. The result is the difficult eclectic idea that guilt is either false, coming from the superego, built up by the traditions of the elders, or true, coming from a violation of God's law. The former is neurotic guilt and is to be analyzed away, whereas the latter must be dealt with theologically. One is potential sickness; the other is sin. One calls for the psychotherapist; the other for the pastor. A complicating factor enters, however, when one tries to separate the two kinds of guilt. "It is absolutely impossible by intellectual processes to separate that of which we are victims from that for which we are to blame. It is not a matter of analysis; it is beyond all analysis" (42, p. 190).

A surprising voice in the affirmation of guilt as a psychopathological force is that of O. H. Mowrer, internationally known psychologist and, heretofore, much more noted for his behavioristic studies of learning theory than for a theoretical foray into the existential realm of sin and guilt. Mowrer (26) sees the difficulty of the dichotomy of guilt into false and true guilt not so much in the inextricability of neurotic and true guilt, but rather in the conviction that false guilt does not exist at all. False guilt is a fantasy of Freud! The mentally ill person in the view of Mowrer has a problem of guilt, not because he is sinned against, but rather because he is a sinner. "The Freudians, of course, recognize that guilt is central to neurosis, but it is always a guilt of the *future*. It is not what a person has *done* that makes him 'ill' but rather what he *wishes* to do but dares not. In contrast, the emerging alternative—or, more accurately, the *re*-emerging one—is that the so-called neurotic is a *bona fide* sinner, that his guilt is from the past and real, and that his difficulties arise not from *inhibitions* but from actions which are clearly proscribed, socially and morally, and which have been kept carefully concealed, unconfessed, and unredeemed" (26, p. 126).

To a lesser degree this "guilt theory" of mental illness has been posited by at least some Christians for generations. There is a recurring conviction that the Biblical emphasis upon sin and guilt as crucial in human problems must be realistically considered. Closing one's eyes to the potentially significant data is unjustifiable, even if done in the name of science. The following pair of citations reflect the attitudes of many Christians professionally involved in the mental health problem. "A sense of guilt plays a surprisingly large part in the mental life of many people suffering from mental ill-health" (58, p. 112). "When the counselor reaches the bases of varied neuroses of the human personality he usually finds the presence of guilt. . . . The feeling of guilt may be focused upon one particular area of life and be known as the guilty conscience; it may also spread itself thinly over life as a whole and be known as the inferiority complex. Inwardly we know that we have failed to live up to expectations—our own, other people's, and ultimately God's. We also know from both internal and external witness that we live in a moral world and that there are consequences of our failures" (12, pp. 175–176).

SIN AND PSYCHOPATHOLOGY

Since the concept of sin is so central to a Christian philosophy of life, it is of paramount importance for our study that we carefully consider its relationship to mental health. One great theme of the Christian evangel has been its proclamation of the cure for sin. If in some way this proclamation involves a cure for psychopathology, then it certainly deserves a hearing. E. White (60, p. 9) points up this crucial relationship in the following quotation: "We see then that guilt is a widespread and deeply rooted emotion, producing much discomfort and anxiety. Although psychiatry may be of great assistance in modifying or removing abnormal or pathological guilt, it does not, in my judgment provide a final answer and satisfactory solution. Christianity, and Christianity alone, provides a complete answer to this problem."

Inasmuch as Mowrer's thesis (26) is the focal point of our discussion, it will be well to reiterate it in his own words. "In psychopathology the trouble arises not from what is being repressed, but rather from what, in the form of a wrathful conscience, is being expressed. *Past* disregard, denial, or 'repression' of conscience may, to be sure, account for the present outbreak or 'attack'; but the very presence of disturbance means that the repression has broken down. And the psychotherapeutic task, it would seem, is much less the releasing of the repressed than of helping the individual to *understand* what is happening to him and how he can help make the final outcome constructive rather than destructive" (26, p. 35). There are those who believe that Mowrer is entirely unrealistic and cite the fact that many people live in gross violation of social and personal morality and are not psychologically ill. Mowrer does not make the error of fallaciously converting his "A" proposition, all psychopathology is (due to) sin, to the generalization that all sin is psychopathology; however, he carefully points out that only particular kinds of moral lapses are necessarily psychologically negative. "Personal sin occurs, as I see it, and sows the seed of psychological destruction when and only when the individual violates a social injunction or regulation but *pretends that he has not"* (26, p. 147). Victor White (62, p. 164), a Roman Catholic priest-psychotherapist, expresses this same point: "Indeed, it may happen that while external nonconformity with accepted morality brings no accompanying moral anxiety, external conformity with it may bring serious breakdown with strong guilt-sense."

The reaction to Mowrer from his erstwhile theoretical colleagues (behavioristically and psychoanalytically oriented psychologists) has been sudden and sharp. His symposium on "Sin as a Concept in Psychopathology" at the annual meeting of the American Psychological Association in Cincinnati in 1958 raised a furor and made *Time* magazine (24, p. 35). This symposium was followed by "Sin, the Lesser of Two Evils" in the *American Psychologist* (25, pp. 301–304), the basic journal of the American Psychological Association. Mowrer set forth the challenge of disinterring sin from the graveyard of liberal theology and reestablishing it as a meaningful psychological concept. He argued that this step is necessary both on theoretical and on empirical grounds. Typical of the reaction, though perhaps a trifle extreme, is that of Albert Ellis (6, p. 192): "If, in this thoroughly objective, non-guilty manner, we can teach our patients (as well as the billions of people in the world who, for better or for worse, will never become patients) that even though human beings can be held quite accountable or responsible for their misdeeds, no one is ever to blame for anything, human morality, I am sure, will be significantly improved and for the first time in human history civilized people will have a real possibility of achieving sound mental health. The concept of sin is the direct and indirect cause of virtually all neurotic disturbance. The sooner psychotherapists forthrightly begin to attack it the better their patients will be." Here is an interesting turn of events! Instead of sin being the basis of psychopathology, *the belief that this is true* is the basis of psychopathology.

There is some support for Mowrer's viewpoint both in the present and in the past. Shoben (38) attempts to modify the brunt of the attack in an article accompanying Ellis' and to set the hypothesis as one to be empirically supported or dropped. Some of Mowrer's associates at the University of Illinois have presented experimental confirmation of his thesis (34). In addition, there are important prior writings from which Mowrer claims to have gained insight, though he learned of these after he had independently arrived at his conclusions. He is particularly impressed with Anton Boisen, a rather humanistically oriented theologian who has been a primary mover in the development of clinical training for ministers and institutional chaplains. Says Boisen (4, p. 568), "Psychological conflict, even in its schizophrenic manifestations, has religious significance." Orville Walters (51, p. 4), a Christian psychia-trist who is in charge of student health services on the same campus at which Mowrer serves, also gives some historical support. "Stekel, a pupil of Freud's, called neurosis 'the disease of a bad conscience' and believed that the remedy lay not in relaxing the demands of conscience but in restoring ethical ideals. Pfister, a Swiss clergyman, and one of the early pupils of Freud, believed that restoring the voice of conscience was a most important step in treating neurosis. O. H. Mowrer, of this campus, has convincingly elaborated this theory of neurosis."

Many Christian therapists, who have an essential interest in, and commitment to, the theme of sin and redemption, do not see such a theory as Mowrer's as a light breaking through the darkness. Vander Linde (49, pp. 100–101), before Mowrer aired his views, spoke rather sharply in an article in the *Gordon Review* against the point of view that sin is the basis of psychopathology. "Those who see faith as the complete answer to the achieving of mental health often have as a basic assumption the equation: illness equals sin. Thus, in the case of mal-adjustment or more severe mental problems such people attribute the cause to bad thinking or bad feelings, which are regarded as sinful processes . . . while mental illness may be a part of the consequences of sin, each individual case is certainly not to be attributed to a par-ticular sin of the people in question. Jesus took the trouble in His day to correct the people concerning the naivete and oversimplification in-volved in such an idea. The psychological tendency in all of us to con-sider any illness, misfortune, or unpleasant event as a punishment is an easily observed phenomenon. Such attitudes are emphasized in the training of children, especially in the homes of the more pious. But, if the relationship were such a direct chain of cause and effect, then ob-viously the more seriously ill would be those with the greatest sin or least faith. On a common sense level we would and do reject this notion as absurd or nonsense." It may be noted, parenthetically, that Vander Linde does not avoid the fallacy of illicit conversion (as Mowrer does) in moving from the thesis that "Illness equals sin" to his concluding remarks.

Another Christian psychologist says of Mowrer, "His reaction to Freud's psychologism carries Mowrer to an exclusively moralistic eval-uation of mental illness, which I think will turn out theoretically as well as practically to be untenable" (3, p. 27).

Many who hold to the Biblical view of sin would see weight in Mowrer's hypothesis but would hesitate to go all the way. They do not want to commit themselves to accepting sin as an exclusive cause for psychopathology though they readily admit a frequent causal relationship. The last of the following supporting quotations, in particular, graphically portrays emotional symptoms as foolish attempts at self-atonement for sin. "Repression of conscience, as well as repression of sexuality, engenders a disturbance in the person. In an endogenous depression guilt feelings and delusions of sin can arise, but conversely we are acquainted with depressions which arise from a realistic guilt" (16, p. 13). "Twenty years of study and nearly that time in actual treatment of psychoneuroses have convinced us that we shall not make progress in the treatment of mental conflicts until we have taken full cognizance of the fact that there is a factor involved in all conflict in the moral and spiritual spheres" (23, p. 15). "A bad conscience can, over a period of years, so strangle a person's life that his physical and psychical powers of resistance are thereby impaired. It can be the root cause of certain psychosomatic affections. It is like a stopper which can be pulled out by confession, so that life begins at once to flow again" (45, p. 15). "Many of the symptoms of neuroses and psychoses are attempts to satisfy the demand of conscience for atonement. Though the animal sacrifice was primitive it was a far more therapeutic form of atonement than our modern forms of self-atonement. There are people who because of feelings of unworthiness are subconsciously bringing on their own failures; others who are torturing themselves with anxieties and worries; others who enslave themselves to a rigid and compulsive pattern of self-denial, not for any altruistic purpose but to obtain a semblance of mental peace. In all these forms of self-atonement—often stimulated by a pusillanimous religion—there is a self-inflicted suffering which becomes meritorious in balancing the budget of just deserts. They are, figuratively speaking, crosses which these individuals erect for themselves on which they can regulate their suffering to the extent that they can tolerate their right to existence. The doctrine of justification is the glad tidings to these sufferers that atonement has been made and that God accepts them as they are. When an individual is convinced that God accepts him as he is, he is encouraged to accept himself. Those whose consciences demand punishments can see that justice has been satisfied: the love of God is demonstrated in sacrifice and in suffering" (12, p. 158).

Unfortunately, Mowrer repudiates the latter part of Hulme's statement as "cheap grace" and pursues his research in the hope of establishing self-atonement as the answer to the psychopathological effects of sin. Even the Christians who are influenced by Mowrer's theory will repudiate his hope for a humanistic resolution to the problem of sin.

Anyone who has been psychotherapeutically related to persons suffering from mental illness needs no convincing that at the root of every problem lies a significant amount of sinful action. The anxiety and guilt which have disorganized the personality are results of decisions and actions which were made for selfish goals. Usually this is the irresponsible action of the sufferer; sometimes he is more victim than villain. In every case, sin is at the door. Every emotional problem is basically a spiritual problem. Problems can always be projected into such secondary components as the physical, emotional, and intellectual dimensions, or to the environment; but resolution of them comes only when personal responsibility is borne. This is a hard saying, but I believe that progress in mental health will be proportional to the number who can hear it.

The functional disorders are those in which anxiety, the threat of the future, and guilt, the threat of the past, have broken down the positive functioning of the individual. Both Biblical and empirical evidence support the view that both guilt and anxiety can best be understood in terms of sin and its consequences in the executive function of the spiritual dimension of personality. If this view be true, then it also involves the factor of personal responsibility which is necessary for the successful psychotherapeutic treatment of these disorders. It also follows that treatment is a significant challenge for the Christian psychotherapist, for he may be especially equipped to share in this healing process.

PSYCHOTHERAPY OR CHRIST?

Christianity and healing are essentially related. The term "salvation" itself is rooted in the concept of healing and making whole. Christ is often referred to as the Great Physician. These factors have a bearing upon our study in two ways. The first is the question as to whether any illness, physical or emotional, can be treated legitimately in any manner apart from the "prayer of faith" in the light of the Biblical teaching. The second relates to the application of Christian faith as a psychotherapeutic measure to mental illness.

Concerning the first item, my own attitude about divine healing is as follows: God can heal any manner or mode of human defect; He is sovereign over His creation. He has done so in the past according to Biblical records. He is apparently doing so in the present, according to reports from many reliable sources, and He will, presumably, continue in the future, extraordinary words of grace in the lives of broken human beings. He has left a prescription for the prayerful request of just such assistance (James 5).

At the same time, there is a natural (though no less divine) means of healing which has been made more efficient through such means of grace as modern medicine and psychological research. It is, in my opinion, gross presumption to ignore them. On the other hand, in the area of psychotherapy one must exercise special caution, for the changes in attitudes involved may have implications much farther reaching than the change of tissue in some physiological process.

The problem of the relationship of the Christian faith to psychotherapy will be the burden of this section. At first glance it seems to be as clear as the title of an unpublished manuscript written by P. B. Marquart (21) entitled Psychotherapy or Christ?

This mimeographed pamphlet consists of a number of case studies reported by Marquart from his experiences as a military psychiatrist during World War II. He presents several instances of the futility of secular psychiatric procedures and, conversely, the healing force of Christianity in the life of the emotionally disordered individual. The symptoms are traced to sources of guilt and anxiety, and then these roots are destroyed by the healing force of "grace through faith." "Psychology and psychiatry ought to be taught right out of the pages of the Bible— for there is a psychology there which needs to be gathered and worked up into a course of its own, separate from the rudiments of men." The method of treatment is not unlike that of an evangelistic counselor—"I don't ever use the nondirective kind exclusively, because a Christian has to be directive in his method—at least in his ultimate objective. Whenever it becomes apparent that a man needs Christ, I insist on pointing him the Way" (21, p. 25). There seems to be little doubt that Marquart chooses the second part of his title for his psychiatric approach.

This attitude is not exclusive to Marquart, though it is a distinct minority group among Christians professionally related to this field. Clyde Narramore (30, 31) seems to support this point of view in both his periodical *Psychology for Living* and his recent volume *The Psychology of Counseling*.

Paul Adolph in *Health Shall Spring Forth* (1) also evinces a similar point of view. "It is the author's conviction on the basis of experience that Christianity, conscientiously applied to the emotional tension problems of our era, offers complete and satisfactory solution, not only to these tensions, but also to the disease symptoms which they so often produce" (p. 11).

The opposite tack is taken by N. L. Peterson, a Christian psychiatrist prominent in the Christian Association for Psychological Studies and the American Scientific Affiliation. He distinguishes psychiatric problems from spiritual or physical problems. For him, Christianity has no more bearing upon his psychiatric practice per se than does it have upon the practice of a plumber who is a Christian. "That we have a physical body which relates to a physical world is certainly a reality, and this part of us is the province of the physician. But that there is a corresponding component, the spirit, which must be related to God, is also reality. This is the minister's province. The sector of the spectrum between these two realities, the physical and the spiritual, is the sphere of the psychiatrist. There is so much to be done by these three professions that there should never be any conflict or competition" (35, p. 10). Thus Peterson would change Marquart's title to *Psychotherapy and Christ* but would tend to keep the components in separate spheres. Paul Tournier (41) would be somewhat adverse to this approach—"A human being is a unity, body-soul-spirit, with reference to somatic medicine, psychological medicine, and soul-healing. Medical science is, in my opinion, all three and it is only a doctrinaire prejudice to erect boundaries within this unity."[2]

Runestam seems to support the viewpoint of the distinction between psychotherapy and Christianity, while providing a closer cooperation than Peterson apparently affords, and at the same time recommending caution: "One must bear in mind that just as analysis can prepare and otherwise set the stage for a richer spiritual life, just as easily can it set up insurmountable barriers against its coming into being. As a matter of course, this applies somewhat to spiritual ailments. The closer these approach the nature of religio-moral conflicts, the more indeed must one be cautioned against seeking to alleviate them by mental release of energy in terms of psychoanalysis. But where the conflicts have so completely eclipsed the soul that the sun rays of grace cannot penetrate the darkness, there a psychic preparatory function is needed" (37, p. 170).

Rather than choosing either horn of the dilemma: psychotherapy *or* Christ (or in the case of Christians who choose the former, converting the phrase to psychotherapy *and* Christ), there is a *tertium quid,* a third viewpoint, which attempts to transcend the dilemma and, in the words of T. Jansma, to "Kill the Conjunctions." He asserts that the situation calls not for a critical choice between psychotherapy and Christianity, or a questionable alliance of the two, but rather the application of a

---

[2] This and other quotations from German editions of Tournier's books were translated by me. My introduction to Tournier was through his German works, and several of these citations were collected before I came in contact with later English translations.

psychology that is basically Christian. "We are engaged in Christian Psychiatry, not pagan-rooted psychiatry. The person we treat is the image bearer of God. His functional sickness is related to the sickness of us all: our fundamental alienation from God, our promises to hate God and our fellow man, the disintegration of the personal self, the tension of the fallen world of nature and man. We must be more bold, nay more godly, in applying clinically what we profess creedally" (15, p. 7). William Goulooze (10, p. 86) expresses a similar sentiment in his *Pastoral Psychology:* "We need to have the aid of psychology for an effective ministry, but it must be a psychology that will recognize the place of the Bible as God's revelation and the place of Christianity as God's work of redemption." J. A. C. Murray also echoes such a thesis throughout his *Introduction to Christian Psychotherapy:* "Modern medical psychology can indeed unveil the shadow side of life, and explicate the complex, but only a religious psychology can give meaning and unity to life and explain man's deepest desires to himself" (29, p. 8).

Only from such an approach can we be realistic concerning an adequate view of man and mental illness. Only through a Hegelian-like synthesis of transmuting the data of psychology into a Christian world view can we avoid the subtle hypocrisy of divorcing belief and action in a psychological vocation, and the irony of offering the hungry stones instead of bread.

PSYCHOTHERAPISTS: THE NEW CLERGY

A widespread phenomenon in the twentieth century has been the transfer of pastoral functions to the psychotherapist. Personal problems which formerly would have been discussed in the pastor's study are now the topic of psychiatric consultation. A recent article by P. London and C. Wallace in *Christian Century* with the intriguing title: "Psychotherapists: the New Clergy" discusses this rather well-established modern practice, coming to the following conclusion: "We do not wish to argue whether therapist or pastor is the more appropriate agent for such ministration, nor for that matter to assess where actual competence might lie. . . . Our purpose is rather to emphasize the fact that churchmen have been rather uncritical in their championing of the psychotherapeutic priesthood" (17, p. 516).

It is true that some ministers have made psychotherapeutic referrals to avoid responsibility, but more often, I believe, it is due to a felt incompetence to deal with the problem. Occasionally catastrophes have given impetus to this movement. "One lesson we must draw from at least one of the tragedies (two prominent British churchmen had committed suicide) is that more often than we thought technical psychiatric treatment is indispensable. Earnestness in personal prayer, sacramental grace, and counseling by richly experienced pastors—all, no doubt, have their place in the Christian cure for mental illness, but the Christian who believes that these means of grace leave little or nothing else to be desired lays himself open to disaster. Too often it is assumed that Christian faith renders it unnecessary, perhaps indeed disgraceful to turn to a psychiatrist for systematic treatment" (5, p. 38).

McKenzie believes that modern psychology has taken the steps to research and to gain experience in areas where the minister had the theoretical equipment but did not think it a vocational obligation to carry it through. "We must confess that modern psychology and psychotherapy tell us no more about the incompatible motives that tear the human soul asunder than was already in the Scriptures for all to read; but we lacked the perceiving eye and the understanding mind and the believing heart. Modern psychology has elucidated how human motives work, how they become perverted, how they 'split' our personality into flesh warring against the spirit and spirit against the flesh. It has added no knowledge of new motives; albeit, it has helped us tremendously to realize how motives in the unconscious may work their havoc in our spiritual life" (23, p. 218).

Mowrer seems to see the inroads of the contemporary psychotherapist into human affairs as being mostly negative. He believes that this has transformed "sin" into "sickness," missed the point of diagnosis, and has engaged in making both individuals and society sicker. The following quotations will make clear his objections to the passing over of spiritual problems into the hands of secularists. This objection is of particular interest coming from a famous scientist hitherto identified with the secularist. "In the past we had, it seems, a sort of tacit understanding: the theologians would leave the question of facts to the scientists if the scientists would leave the question of values to them. This won't do, because it results in unconcerned scientists and uninformed theologians" (27, p. 10). "Most pastoral counseling, as we know it today, therefore falls short, as does secular psychotherapy, of the crucial and ultimate step in the quest for salvation and personal wholeness. If one takes the neurotic's guilt seriously, that is, if (as now seems likely) 'neurosis' is just a medical euphemism for a 'state of sin' and social alienation, therapy must obviously go beyond mere 'counseling' to self-disclosure, not just to a therapist or counselor, but to the 'significant others' in one's life, and then on to an active redemption in the sense of the patient's making every effort within his power to undo the evil for which he has previously been responsible" (26, p. 168).

Most of Mowrer's criticism is devoted to the psychoanalytic movement, with which he is intimately familiar both theoretically and experientially. "Psychoanalysis as a movement is in trouble. Church attendance in this country, by contrast, is rapidly increasing, well beyond population growth. In other words, Freud's 'reality principle' appears to be doing less well than the 'illusion' with such an unpromising future. Perhaps Freud was still, in one sense, right; maybe he was only wrong in his estimate of man's growing capacity to live *without* illusion. Or, can it be that he himself misperceived 'reality' " (26, p. 10). "From testimony now available from both the friends and the foes of analysis, it is clear that, at best analysis casts a spell but does not cure. By aligning himself with the patient's id, the analyst (devil?) may indeed succeed, as Bakan puts it in *suspending* the superego; but the superego (or conscience), more commonly than we might wish to believe, is a reflection of enduring social realities; and the advantage we gain by overcoming it in analysis is dearly paid for later, many times over. Man's salvation must surely come, not from his looking and moving downward, but from an upward reach, toward reconciliation and community, made by means of confession and manifest restitution" (26, pp. 121–122). "I don't know how often, when I have criticized psychoanalysis, the protest has come back: 'But isn't it true that the superego *is* overly severe in the neurotic individual and needs to be softened, made less harsh and demanding?' It is true that this is what Freud *said,* and a lot of people have tried to believe and apply this doctrine. But it is public knowledge that both therapy and prevention which are based on this premise lead only to the most dismal consequences; and one might suppose that it was time that we stopped, for purely pragmatic reasons, accepting the premise itself. If it doesn't *work,* what is to make us think it is *true,* especially when it contradicts some of the most basic principles of the Judeo-Christian ethic?" (26, p. 158).

Mowrer's negative criticism of contemporary psychotherapy is not exclusively reserved for Freud, however, and the approach of Carl Rogers gets some attention. "The non-directive or client-centered type of therapy which is associated with the name of Carl Rogers will, of course, be immediately thought of by many as 'non-Freudian.' But as I am using the term, I would say that Roger's approach is deeply 'Freudian.' Like classical psychoanalysis, it begins by not holding the individual personally responsible for his difficulties and gives him no prescription for dealing with them on his own initiative. Rogers views the individual as inherently good and holds that he is corrupted and diverted from his indigenous growth tendencies along normal and healthy lines by the untoward actions and attitudes of those around him. Here the encouragement of self-pitying and hostile tendencies within the client is hardly less direct than it is in psychoanalysis" (26, pp. 164–165).

Thus Mowrer sees the root of mental disorder to be in sin, and the pastor as the person with the best potential for treating the problem. The modern movement from the priest to the psychotherapist is motivated by the unwillingness of the patient to confess his responsibility and to reveal his sinful action, as well as the readiness of the minister to "pass the buck" of responsibility to the therapist, even though the latter may undermine the principles which the minister professes to hold dear. Mowrer believes that the answer lies in a clinically trained ministry, whose clinical training is oriented to the application of a religious view of man. Evangelicals will, perhaps, tend to become enthusiastic about Mowrer's thesis, but they had better be cautious in judgment for they are held to be equal, or nearly so, in ineptitude along with the contemporary psychotherapist. Of the neurotic personality, Mowrer says, "what, now, can a person in such a predicament do to be 'saved'? It would appear that two equally misleading answers have been given to this question in our time. Protestant theology has preached a doctrine of 'justification by faith.' Place your *trust* in God and *believe* in Jesus Christ, we have been urged, and your sins will be immediately *forgiven*. And for those who prefer a 'scientific' rather than a 'religious' approach, there has been the doctrine of 'justification by insight.' In the latter approach, one comes to see that his sins are not real and that he doesn't really *need* forgiveness. It is hard to determine which of these doctrines has been the more pernicious" (26, p. 232).

In any case, Mowrer's revolt against the "priesthood of therapists" has a strong argument for Christian psychotherapy in spite of the fact that he obviously repudiates such a perspective. It is clear that he does not know of the potential personal power that is inherent in what he terms the "cheap grace" of reformation theology.

CHRISTIAN PSYCHOTHERAPISTS

We have asserted that it is not a matter of choosing between Christianity and psychotherapy to meet the pressing needs of mental health; nor is it one of making an uneasy alliance between faith and secular psychology. A Biblically oriented psychology, a Christian psychotherapy, appears to be the theoretical and practical answer. I would like to present three men who have attempted such a program and give the reader insight into their attitudes and aims.

Paul Tournier

Paul Tournier, a Swiss psychiatrist-internist is a prolific author relating Christianity and psychotherapy. Recently translated and printed in this country by Harper's are *The Meaning of Persons, A Doctor's Casebook in the Light of the Bible,* and *Guilt and Grace.* All reflect a Biblically based approach to personal problems, carried out with no artificial dichotomy as to the roles of a therapist and a Christian. In short, they present Tournier's attempt to formulate a Christian psychotherapy.

"The analysts really practice soul-healing when they bring more clearly to the attention of a person the past events which influence his psyche, the drives of impurity and self-seeking, which are basic to their therapy; for they help him to be more honest with himself. Therein consists, from my standpoint, the secret of their successful treatment. For to help a man to be more honest with himself is to bring him nearer to God" (41, p. 250). "To treat the sick person and not the sickness is to help our patients solve their life problems. This solution lies, for the most part, in the spiritual sphere" (41, p. 16). "I have sometimes been accused of not recognizing the frontier between these two (psychotherapy and soul-healing), and of being in danger of confusing them. It seems to me that the real danger is that of mixing them without realizing it, and not in intermingling them openly and consciously as I do. For in practice all psychotherapists do intermingle them. The one who does not recognize the frontier is in fact one who sincerely believes himself to be still a psychotherapist, and who claims to confine himself to the scientific realm of psychology, when actually he has entered the field of soul-healing" (44).

"Every psychotherapist sooner or later goes beyond the strictly psychological sphere—even the Freudians, in spite of their principles. The recounting of a life story, a mind thinking aloud, freed from the bonds of formalism, leads one inevitably to the consideration of problems which are no longer psychological but spiritual problems such as the meaning of life and of the world, of desire and of death, of sin and of faith, or one's own scale of values" (45, p. 109). "Further, I have a threefold vocation: medical, psychological and spiritual. It is bad enough to fall into a technical routine as a doctor or as a psychologist; it is much worse to turn soul-healing into a matter of routine. I confess that it is the spiritual vocation which interests me most, for the very reason that all my experience has taught me the limitations of medicine and psychology, and because the supreme and universal need of man is to find God" (45, p. 37). "Soul-healing consists in putting men in touch with Christ" (41, p. 232).

Ernest White

Ernest White, a British psychiatrist, has made a significant impact upon the Christian public through his various writings, especially his *Christian Life and the Unconscious* (59). His reliance upon a Biblical foundation for his vocation as well as in his personal life seems to identify him as a Christian psychotherapist rather than as a Christian who is a psychotherapist.

"The experience nearest to Christian conversion in its effect on life and character which I myself have observed is the striking change which sometimes occurs in people as the result of psychotherapy. It is really remarkable to see the liberation which follows treatment in some cases. People are literally transformed in character and outlook. But however great and radical the change, psychotherapy does not create saints. Christian conversion is, in essence, turning to God. Psychotherapy, as such, knows nothing of this, and neither does nor can effect it. It may enable a patient to adjust himself successfully to the main tasks of life on a material plane, but it cannot from its very nature, satisfy the deeper spiritual needs of the questing spirit. The non-Christian psychiatrist may lead his patients along the road to health and enable them to lose their neurotic symptoms, but cannot deal with the sick and hungry spirit" (59, p. 60).

"No one who has intimate dealings with men and women such as occur in psychological analysis can fail to discover the important part played by religious questions in the minds of those who consult him. Spiritual factors, that is, factors concerned with morals and religion, and ultimately with a man's relationship to God, must be taken into consideration if we are to deal adequately with any individual who is sick in mind" (58, p. 109). "We are all sinners in one way or another, and it is not the function of a psychologist either to condemn or to absolve the sinner. His purpose is to seek to understand the sinner, and to show him the path to a better way of life" (59, p. 152).

Orville Walters

An American psychiatrist who shares the same campus with Mowrer (University of Illinois) and also has a voice in formulating a Christian psychotherapy is Orville Walters. A frequent conference speaker, he has published numerous significant articles that support and promote a Christian point of view.

"To ignore or minimize the field of metaphysical concern in favor of sexual conflict or any other predetermined framework may leave untouched the most important cause of difficulty. . . . The frequent concern of the religious-minded patient and his family over the therapists's attitude toward religion is not without relevance. The naturalistic orientation not only includes certain beliefs, but excludes others" (52, pp. 249–50). "Ethical neutrality is an abstraction that does not exist in fact. Every man has his own hierarchy of values and in the process of psychotherapy, where understanding of deep motivation is sought and where issues of ultimate consequence are faced, the value systems of both therapist and patient are inevitably implicated. When the psychiatrist offers to pit his professional knowledge, skill, and time against the patient's illness for a fee, his activity is no longer heuristic, but therapeutic. He may try to preserve the objectivity of a scientist, but he now has an interest in the outcome" (55). "The hidden hungers of the human spirit can never be satisfied by psychotherapy as long as it tries to maintain ethical neutrality. The stability that Freud and others have observed in Christian people can never be fully understood in scientific terms" (53).

"But even psychotherapy cannot bring peace of mind until there is first peace of soul. As Gordon Allport has asked, 'Can a person ever really attain integration until he has signed and sealed a treaty of peace with the cosmos?' Religion and experience both answer, No" (51, p. 8). "Jung is neither correct nor realistic when he says, 'We cannot expect the doctor to have anything to say about the ultimate questions of the soul. It is from the clergyman, not the doctor, that the sufferer should expect such help.' The statement is unrealistic because there are few psychiatrists who do not directly or indirectly influence their patients' choice of life philosophy. . . . Jung's pronouncement is wrong because it is inconsistent with the Protestant tenet that every man is a priest. Theology may have its technical aspects, just as medicine does, which would make unwise any indiscriminate trespass upon another's professional field. There is no such restriction upon the essentials of victorious Christian living, which the wayfaring man may share and to which he may bear glad witness" (50, p. 8).

These three men set forth lucidly, both from an experiential understanding of the Scriptures and a wealth of practical psychotherapeutic experience, the conviction that a Christian psychotherapy is the answer to the question of relating Christianity and psychotherapy, and to the needs of modern man in his illness.

"CHRISTIAN" PSYCHOTHERAPY

Many would object to using the term "Christian" as an adjectival modifier for psychotherapy, on the grounds that it leads to the reduction of this science to an absurdity (14). This objection would imply that there is a special kind of procedure that a Christian should employ for every action: Christian surgery, Christian transfusions, Christian anesthesia, etc. It also leads to the inference that there is a Buddhist psychotherapy, a Mohammedan psychotherapy, etc.

If this be absurd, then I suppose that we must make the most of it, for it is certainly to the point. This radical approach is a central component of Christianity. Christianity is radical; it penetrates to the radix, or root, of everything. It maintains that the God and Father of Jesus Christ is the sovereign Creator and Controller of heaven and earth. Therefore, no vocation or vocational art is exempt from His jurisdiction. Every hypothesis and each instance of hypothesis testing flows from a basic philosophy of life. Each scientific observation is affected by the subjective experience and frame of reference of the observer. Each subject taught is modified by the philosophical perspective, whether conscious or unconscious, of the teacher. Every field of science is relative to the philosophical foundation of the one who articulates that field. We must be careful that we do not let "science" become a sacred cow; as every scientist knows well, the absolute certainty of his discipline exists only in the mind of the layman.

According to the Christian *Weltanschauung,* or world view, objectivity and stability in the world is in Christ. This implies the validity of using the term Christian psychotherapy. Inasmuch as every datum finds its significance in the personal values of the observer, the term Christian psychotherapy is not only not absurd, but a direct implication, if Christ really is the Way, the Truth, and the Life.

I do not wish to argue further for the nonexistence of scientific neutrality. The philosophical apologetic for such a viewpoint is easy to discover. The works of Cornelius Van Til, Edward John Carnell, and Gordon Clark are profound analyses of this point from the perspective of evangelical Christianity. Non-Christian sources which support this argument also abound (39).

It is, of course, not only non-Christians who would oppose the concept of "Christian psychotherapy," for there are many evangelicals who maintain the validity of scientific neutrality. S. Norborg, in his interesting answer to William James' classic work *The Varieties of Religious Experience* strongly supported this—"We are not seeking any 'Christian' psychology. Psychology is psychology just as geology is geology or medicine is medicine. Psychology can never become 'Christian' or 'Buddhistic' or 'Mohammedan,' as long as we cling to an objective, scientific conception of psychology" (32, p. 9). The evidence underlying the following comment from Runestam, a contemporary of Norborg, points out what I believe to be the dubious vantage point upon which Norborg would encourage us to cling—"Christian theology has its own psychology, and its own conception of man's essence and basic constitution. Psychoanalysis and Christianity: this is not only psychology versus theology; it is also psychology versus *psychology*" (37, p. 7). Christian psychotherapy is not merely a possibility but rather a necessity if there is validity in a Scriptural view of man and his motives.

PSYCHOTHERAPY AND VALUES

This myth of neutralism and objectivity has been a common belief of psychotherapists. The purpose has been to elevate their art to the lofty plane of science, understood as an objective description of physical processes, and to avoid any hint of value judgments with their patients. To the uninitiated, who is not aware of the surging drive for scientific status in this field, this seems to be a strange situation, for nothing would seem more obvious than that the individual with a mental disorder is having a serious value problem. His value system, his ethical ideals, his moral standards, and his world view are all involved in his personal problem, and they threaten to totter and to fall. There is much evidence to suppose that an unstable set of values is the root of his illness.

Many psychologists, both secular and Christian, are now recognizing the necessity of reevaluating the whole concept of values in psychotherapy. The recognition that value neutrality is an impossibility, and that value change in the life of the person is a positive goal, is becoming increasingly defended in the literature. "The therapist, whatever his pretenses, is not exclusively a scientist—in practice he is an active moral agent" (17, p. 516). "There are other psychologists, however, who feel that this quest for objectivity represents a spurious goal, that there is no such thing as a psychotherapy unconcerned with values and the role they play in the therapeutic work. As Sol Ginsburg has pointed out 'In the last analysis, adjustment is a name for the process of living up to a set of values.' " (7, p. 566).

"An amoral therapy is a contradiction in terms. What therapist of any school is prepared to accept with complacence the decision of an alcoholic patient to go back to the bottle, of a male homosexual to seduce a small nephew, or of the apocryphal Rogerian patient to jump out of a skyscraper window?" (57, p. 575). "In helping the patient to reformulate his personal philosophy, the therapist encourages him to think of other postulates that he could substitute for his unfunctional ones, and to discover new ways of thinking and acting to sustain his new, more functional philosophy. This must grow out of his own unique personality and experiences rather than being imposed upon him by the therapist. If the patient cannot be encouraged to take the lead in reformulating his personal philosophy, the therapist makes suggestions, but keeps these to the minimum necessary to stimulate the patient" (19, p. 53).

Likewise does the Christian psychotherapist have a specific set of values which can give meaning to living and dying. It is folly to try to carry out an interview in an atmosphere of value neutrality or complete scientific objectivity; it is double folly for the Christian to try so hard to do so that he manifests a subtle secularism which is foreign to his faith. This is just what the attempt to relate to others without significant values is, a secular and vain value.

A Christian psychotherapy embodies a positive set of values capable of dealing constructively with that great disvalue, sin, so central in the problems of the emotionally disturbed. Here lies the solution to the negative stimulus directing the hopeless down the road to mental illness and the positive stimulus that can redirect and motivate him toward the goal of mental health. We would beguile ourselves if we supposed that the whole psychotherapeutic movement is coming to this or to a similar point, however, for there are many, like Ellis, who think that such a trend would be catastrophic. "Because of these most serious disadvantages of giving individuals a serious sense of sin and because any deity-positing religion almost by necessity involves endowing those members who violate its god's laws with a distinct concept of blameworthiness or sin, I am inclined to reverse Voltaire's famous dictum and to say that, from a mental health standpoint, if there were a God it would be necessary to uninvent Him" (61, p. 191). The Christian therapist must have the courage of his convictions and stand firm in the authority of the

Scriptures, in his diagnosis and in his prescription for those in distress and despair.

DIRECTIVENESS AND VALUES

Much of the discussion in contemporary psychotherapeutic circles concerning nondirective versus directive counseling is due largely to the influence and impact of Carl Rogers, whose theory is known popularly as nondirective psychotherapy. Rogers himself refers to his therapy as "client-centered," which is a more realistic description. The reaction of permissiveness to the doctrinaire authoritarian counselor role is justifiable if not carried to an extreme. Nondirective therapy, just as value neutrality, is actually an impossible ideal. The personality of the therapist, as well as his technical methods, will influence the direction of therapy in many ways. The point is not to close one's eyes to this influence but to make it positive and supporting of the therapeutic goals. The Christian therapist is neither exclusively passive nor authoritarian, but he moves, as does every other therapist, in the dialectic of these two extremes.

The subtle and significant difference between presenting values to the patient and imposing them upon him is extremely important. Critics of a self-consciously value-oriented psychotherapy frequently pose the accusation of value imposition. They are quite right in pointing out the dangers involved—an increased immaturity in the patient and a deepening of his neurotic dependency. This may be a straw man argument, however, for it is doubtful whether it is really possible to impose values and basic decisions upon another person. It is possible to try to do so, but the attempt invariably breaks rapport and generates an increase of conflict. The Christian therapist, in suggesting value options, does not take away the patient's freedom but rather encourages him to exercise his freedom more responsibly. The patient's problem often is that he has never learned to live satisfactorily in the dialectic of freedom and responsibility. The Christian therapist believes this situation can only be accomplished in Christ. He also knows that this choice must be a free one of the person in distress.

"We are not called upon to impose our scale of values on our patients. But if we help them to recover this fundamental function of life, namely choice, sooner or later they will raise the question of values—the dialogue will become spiritual. I cannot at this point break off the dialogue on the grounds that I am neither a philosopher nor a theologian, but merely a doctor. What I must do then is to know what my own convictions are, and take responsibility for them, without attempting to impose them on others" (45, p. 209).

It seems to me that at a certain point in the therapeutic program it becomes not only an opportunity but also an obligation to present value options to the patient. In any case it will be done either with one's eyes open or blindly, either as a fundamental to therapeutic goals or inexorably out of the sheer fact that the therapist is also a human being. Christian therapy, in fact, entails an exposition rather than an imposition of values.

At this point it is, perhaps, appropriate to mention the problem of the counselor bringing his own personal history into the counseling process. Many are adamant in the conviction that this is absolutely contraindicated. This attitude appears, however, to be an artificial and arbitrary denial of the personality of the therapist. My own observation and experience lead me to agree with Tournier—"I believe that nothing is more fruitful than to speak to the patient about our experiences" (43, p. 267).

The Christian therapist attempts to effect a careful compromise between the extremes of nondirective counseling in which the counselor endeavors to portray an amoral, objective, impersonal person, and the fallacy of authoritative directiveness which tends to usurp both the freedom and the responsibility of the patient. The Christian counselor interacts in a living dialogue; a mutual enterprise for the achievement of emotional well-being and personal growth.

TECHNIQUES OF THERAPY

Often in therapy there is an overemphasis on techniques. A therapist cannot carry out a therapeutic program without employing some method of treatment or interviewing, but care must be exercised not to make any particular techniques ends in themselves. Our view of man and human personality forbids an attitude toward the patient as though he were an object to be manipulated. The emotionally ill person is not like a broken-down automobile that can be fixed with certain tools and by replacing certain parts. He is, rather, a despairing human being, with potentials of personal power far beyond his fondest dreams, who believes that his present situation of suffering is the best adjustment to life that he can presently make. More basic to his recovery than specific modes of treatment is a therapeutic relationship that communicates love and acceptance, a supra-technique relationship that is the substance of therapeutic success.

However, counseling apart from specific techniques is both a hazard and a haphazard. The counselor must be able to modify his approach to the uniqueness of the patient and the problem in each counseling contact. Nonetheless, experience with as wide a variety of techniques as possible will furnish confidence and a sense of competence to the counselor, which will, in turn, flow to the counselee. The important thing to remember is that a counseling process is not exhausted in its techniques. "Counseling is not simply a technique. It is an art, a specific form of spiritual creativity. We are not satisfied with being a Christian in one aspect of life and being psychologist or counselor in another" (40, p. 95).

Techniques are necessary to the therapist's activity, but they can become, apart from due caution, opportunities of avoiding interpersonal confrontation and the demands of a mutually responsible relationship. On the other hand, apart from a specific therapeutic program, psychotherapeutic counseling may deteriorate into a mystic meandering, frustrating both participants, neither art nor science, nor a composite of the two.

There is a certain sense in which there are no specifically Christian psychotherapeutic techniques. Many methodological approaches are equally well adapted by various theoretical viewpoints. Frequently therapists with a Christian orientation distinguish between psychoanalytic methods and psychoanalytic theory. The latter is held to be counter to Christianity, whereas the former are eminently useful. "Much confusion could be eliminated if people would see more clearly the distinction between psychoanalysis as a technique and as a theory" (13, p. 7).

Such therapeutic activity as prayer or the use of the Bible would be exclusive to a Christian, or at least a religious therapy, though other techniques are somewhat "neutral." On the other hand, the attempted relaxing of some moral attitudes and the encouragement to "live less rigidly" in these areas, though perhaps not widespread, nevertheless occurs and would be opposing to a Christian therapy. Many other faddish techniques that come and go are either so inane or so indiscreet that they would be practically excluded from the repertory of the Christian therapist.

However, neutrality of techniques is an abstraction which never really exists, for techniques only exist in action. They are not stockpiles in some platonic world of ideas, but rather they are found only in therapeutic activity. This activity is always intended to be the means to some therapeutic goal. And every therapeutic goal entails a philosophy of life and a value system which either correlates with the Christian world and life view, or does not.

Thus techniques are therapeutic necessities serving as the content of a therapeutic program. Their significance is found in supporting a personal relationship between therapist and patient, in sustaining a developing context of understanding, confidence, and decision. They are steps that hopefully will lead even the sickest individual toward a life of health.

I will not discuss techniques further other than to say that I use a wide variety of them including psychodiagnostic testing instruments, group therapy, hypnotic relaxation, dream analysis, and various "homework" task demands. The therapeutic program is designed with reference to my perception of the best way to handle the unique situation presented. Sometimes group interaction seems indicated; at other times individual free association fantasy experiences or else behavior modification programmed living seems pertinent.

As a part of preparation for an appointment, I generally engage in personal and intercessory prayer to enable me to "get set." This period of preparation also entails the request and the presumption that God the Holy Spirit will be a "participant observer" in every session.

Other distinctive aspects of my own application of a Christian commitment as a function of therapy may be suggested by my perspective of the therapeutic process.

THE COUNSELING PROCESS

The counseling program may be conveniently divided into four phases: introductory, analytic, synthetic, and terminal. In actual practice the boundaries of these phases are indistinct, and considerable overlapping is the rule rather than the exception. They are frequently clearer in retrospect than in the present. There is no timetable that can be arranged for the various phases of psychotherapy since each program is an unique experience with an unique personality. (I am presently involved in some "timetable" research, however, which may change this foregoing statement.) An interesting observation of every therapist is the experience after a successful therapeutic program, when he becomes confident that his procedure is the indicated one for any such cases. Then when confronted with what at first seem almost identical symptoms, he rediscovers that the previous procedure has little or no relevance, for each individual presents a special case.

The Introductory Phase

This phase of the counseling process has a fourfold function. It is the period of sizing up each other by counselor and counselee. Here first impressions develop into a relationship of rapport (or not.) This mutual trust and confidence is necessary for effective counseling. The introductory phase is an opportunity for the client to recite his symptoms, as he explains his reason for requesting an appointment. The level of emotional control, the severity of symptoms, and the duration of the illness are important observations to obtain.

A brief life history also is involved in the introductory phase. The important factors are the significant people in the patient's life, as well as the significant incidents, especially those which were traumatic. I do not use a formal outline but rather suggest that the individual tell me about himself and his family. At any point digressions relating to the emotional disturbance are permitted. It is important to try to see the patient as he sees himself.

The final aspect of the introduction might well be termed the diagnostic decision. A psychodiagnostic test battery may preface this decision. This decision is not to be construed in the sense of giving some technical name to the patient's problem (though he often requests it), but rather as a time to decide whether a counseling program is indicated and would, presumably, be beneficial. Economic factors, available time, and severity of illness are considerations of the decision. Occasionally the presence of uncontrollable psychotic symptoms, or physiological factors, indicate a medical referral for hospitalization and chemotherapy. It is important for the nonmedical therapist to work closely with the medical profession to fulfill the best interests of the patient.

When a decision is made to begin a psychotherapeutic program, it is well to avoid any promise of success or of shortness of time involved. My own practice is to indicate that these factors are impossible to predict and that the decision of a person to do something constructively about his problem is in itself a significant element of a good prognosis. If he feels that he can trust me, and is willing to reveal himself and his private world to me, then there is ground for optimism that, working together, we can both experience personal growth and emotional maturity. It seems to me advisable at this point to set specific goals of therapy. The patient is requested to do so, and I also supplement his hopes for the future with the goal of a "man of God, thoroughly furnished unto all good works." The degree of specificity must, of course, be carefully correlated with the religious insight and experience of the client.

The Analytic Phase

The analytic phase is a series of interviews that attempt to analyze the symptoms and their development as well as basic factors in the development of the personality. It is an endeavor to bring to light the underlying experiences which have made the individual's world one of sustained fear and anger rather than love and confidence, a threatening world rather than a challenging one. Since I hypothesize much of this "material" to be unconscious, either repressed or forgotten, the analysis is usually carried out as an analysis of dreams, fantasies, or recent moods of stress or elation, and often under hypnotic relaxation. The time of analysis is so variable in my practice as to make impossible even vague time limits. It has varied from one interview to several interviews weekly over a period of ten months. A successful analysis usually involves the nonrecurrence of acute symptoms, the feeling of the patient that he "understands himself," and the feeling of the therapist that he knows how the personality of the patient developed and how the person felt in his symptom-sickened world.

The Synthetic Phase

This phase of therapy is directly related to the goals of therapy. The analysis of personality may be in itself depressing apart from a transforming synthesis. I do not view this change in which the person becomes confident and decisive in his life experiences as a reconstruction of personality factors or a redirection of basic attitudes but rather as a transformation of the personality. For the Christian it involves the discovery that "all things work together for good for those who love God" and that there is power in positive action. The non-Christian learns that the transformation of personality is dependent upon a transformation of the person.

In the synthetic phase it is of particular importance for the client to face, and to bear, the responsibility of his condition. Others have entered significantly into the experiences that have formed the malfunctioning of the personality, but only the patient can make rectifying decisions and attitudinal changes. Many analyses are unsuccessful because the patient is encouraged to see his problems as arising from the actions of emotionally significant persons in his life. Although this occurrence is frequently, too frequently, true and invariably partially true, anything short of shouldering the responsibility by the patient will obviate any attempted synthesis.

In the synthesis the therapist often makes suggestions concerning the grounds upon which an effective personal adjustment can be made and sustained. It is in this phase, as the patient seeks meaning for his existence, that the Christian world view and Christian faith become pertinent. The personal fragments derived from analysis are poor building bricks for personality reconstruction. New materials and a new architect are needed. Murray lucidly describes the goal of synthesis in Christian therapy as it is related to analysis. "Unlike other systems, a Christian psychotherapy has a twofold aim. In the first place, it shares with materialist psychology the technique of tidying up the mind. It, too, uses every discovered probe and pointer to the sub-conscious—analysis, dream-analysis, association, suggestion, and the like—but it uses them with a greater purpose in view, and its special function only begins where other psychologies stop. Even while fulfilling this first purpose, it never loses sight of its greater purpose, which is, to make health and salvation synonymous" (29, p. 177).

The Christian therapist forthrightly suggests the healing force that enables unity and maturity of personality, the power of God. Rather than being professionally unethical and therapeutically unwise, this responsible action may lead to a positive, constructive goal, and it avoids the onus of precipitating and perpetuating an "analytic wreck." "For a humanistically-minded therapist or counselor to prolong the wallowing and floundering of a confused soul in the morass of his own frustrations and conflicts—when he needs the regenerating grace of God—is like unto a physician stubbornly withholding a proven remedy because of his own prejudice or ignorance, while the patient suffers or dies" (50, p. 8).

The synthesis gradually emerges from the analytic phase. Sessions become more future oriented. Plans and hopes are discussed. Termination becomes an imminent possibility, often through the content of dreams and fantasies as well as the waking, directed thought of the client.

The Termination Phase

Termination of therapy should be a mutual decision, just as are the other decisions in therapy. The topic of termination will grow out of the synthetic phase in the counseling context. This phase ordinarily involves less-frequent interviews so that a period of personal growth, under conditions of increasing independence from the therapist, may be observed and reinforced. Sometimes termination is a unilateral decision of the patient before the therapist deems it a wise decision. I do not resist such a choice for at least it is a significant decision which the client is making. He will likely return if his symptoms return or else seek help elsewhere. In any case, therapy with an unwilling client is largely wasted effort.

The Christian therapeutic process is a process in which an ill and confused person, living in a threatening restricted world is transformed into a healthy and confident individual with challenging tasks to perform in an open and ever-widening world of opportunity. This model is the ideal. This process is made possible through the future directedness of the Christian faith, which gives significance to the present and makes assets out of the crippling liabilities of the past. The mysterious grace of God, working through a well-trained and dedicated Christian therapist, enables the ministry of psychotherapeutic healing.

Perry London, in his perceptive analysis of the psychotherapeutic state of affairs, asserts that every system of psychotherapy has three basic components: a theory of personality, a moral code, and a repertoire of techniques. This paper suggests that essentially aspects of a biblical anthropology and a Christian system of values—a Christian *Weltanschauung*—coupled with an appropriate therapeutic methodology are important considerations for this "state of affairs." A more detailed account, both in theory and application, has been presented elsewhere (48).

Rather emphatic claims have been presented concerning the possibility and desirability of a Christian psychotherapy. There is also an attendant presumption of superior efficacy and validity for this approach, in the highly competitive therapeutic arena. Supporting data are largely of the order of clinically anecdotal case comments and statements of personal satisfaction by Christian clinicians. Such a presentation is justifiable in its own right, but if a Christian psychotherapy is to have a place in the psychotherapeutic sun, it is incumbent upon those of us who are identified with it to substantiate these claims with significant reports of controlled research and observations. I can only report at present that such is our intention. A hopeful factor is the growing number of psychotherapists who are becoming significantly involved in the discharge of this incumbency.

REFERENCES

1. Adolph, P. *Health shall spring forth.* Chicago: Moody Press, 1956.
2. Allers, R. Psychiatry and the role of personal belief. In F. Braceland (Ed.), *Faith, reason and modern psychiatry.* New York: P. J. Kennedy, 1955.
3. Bijkerk, R. J. Reactions of a psychologist. *Proc. Christian Ass. Psychol. Stud.,* 1960.
4. Boisen, A. Religious experience and psychological conflict. *Amer. Psychol.,* 1958, **13**, 568.
5. Edwards, D. L. The twentieth century sickness. *Frontier,* Spring, 1960, 38.
6. Ellis, A. There is no place for the concept of sin in psychotherapy. *J. Counsel. Psychol.,* 1960, **7**, 192.
7. Feifel, H. Symposium on the relationship between religion and mental health. *Amer. Psychol.,* 1958, **13**, 566.
8. Frankl, V. *Der unbedingte Mensch.* Vienna: Deuticke, 1949.
9. Frankl, V. *Theorie und Therapie der Neurosen.* Vienna: Urban & Schwartzenberg, 1956.
10. Goulooze, W. *Pastoral psychology.* Grand Rapids: Baker Books, 1950.
11. Heerema, E. *Christian faith and the healthy personality.* Unpublished lecture series delivered at the Reformed Episcopal Seminary, Philadelphia, no date available.
12. Hulme, W. *Counseling and theology.* Muhlenberg Press, 1956.
13. Jaazsma, R. Psychoanalytic theory: misunderstood or resisted? *Proc. Christian Ass. Psychol. Stud.,* 1955, 7.
14. Jansma, T. Christian psychotherapy. *Christianity Today,* 1960, June 20, 9–10.
15. Jansma, T. *Kill the conjunctions.* Address given at the 50th anniversary of Bethesda Hospital, Denver, Colo., Aug. 24, 1960.
16. Kingma, J. The anthropological approach to the problem of the ego. *Proc. Christian Ass. Psychol. Stud.,* 1956, 13.
17. London, P., & Wallace, C. Psychotherapists: the new clergy. *Christian Century,* 1961, April 26.
18. London, P. *The modes and morals of psychotherapy.* New York: Holt, Rinehart & Winston, 1964.
19. Lynn, D. Personal philosophies in psychotherapy. *J. Indiv. Psychol.,* 1961, **17**, 53.
20. Marquart, P. B. Basic anxiety and adamic motivation. *J. Amer. Scient. Affil.* 1950, **2**, 2.
21. Marquart, P. *Psychotherapy or Christ.* Unpublished manuscript, Wheaton College, no date available.
22. May, R. *The meaning of anxiety.* New York: Ronald Press, 1950.
23. McKenzie, J. *Psychology, psychotherapy and evangelicalism.* London: Macmillan, 1940.
24. Mowrer, O. H. *Time,* Sept. 14, 1959, 35.
25. Mowrer, O. H. "Sin," the lesser of two evils. *Amer. Psychol.,* 1960, **15**, 301.

26. Mowrer, O. H. *The crisis in psychiatry and religion.* New York: Van Nostrand, 1961.
27. Mowrer, O. H. Even there, Thy hand. *Chicago Theol. Sem. Register,* 1962, **52**, 1–17.
28. Mulder, J. *Psychiatry for pastors, students, and nurses.* Grand Rapids: Eerdmans, 1939.
29. Murray, J. A. C. *Introduction to Christian psychotherapy.* Edinburgh: T & T Clark, 1941.
30. Narramore, C. This way to happiness. *Psychology for living.* Grand Rapids: Zondervan, 1958.
31. Narramore, C. *The psychology of counseling.* Grand Rapids: Zondervan, 1961.
32. Norborg, S. *The varieties of Christian experience.* Augsburg Publ. Co., 1937.
33. Peale, N. *A guide to confident living.* New York: Prentice-Hall, 1948.
34. Peterson, D. *The insecure child: oversocialized or undersocialized.* Urbana: University of Illinois Press, 1962.
35. Peterson, N. L. Psychiatry and Christianity. *Christianity Today,* Nov. 9, 1959, 10.
36. Progoff, I. Psychology as a road to personal philosophy. *J. Indiv. Psychol.,* 1961, **17**, 47.
37. Runestam, A. *Psychoanalysis and Christianity.* Rock Island, Ill.: Augustana, 1958.
38. Shoben, J. Sin and guilt in psychotherapy: some research implications. *J. Counsel. Psychol.,* 1960, **7**, 198.
39. Straus, E. *Vom Sinn der Sinne.* Zürich: Springer, 1956.
40. Thienemann, T. The art of counseling. *Gordon Rev.,* Sept. 1957, 95.
41. Tournier, P. *Krankheit und Lebensprobleme.* Basel: Benno Schwabe, 1941.
42. Tournier, P. *A doctor's casebook in the light of the Bible.* New York: Harpers, 1950.
43. Tournier, P. *Bibel und Medizin.* Zürich: Rascher, 1953.
44. Tournier, P. The frontier between psychotherapy and soul healing. *J. Psychother. Relig. Process,* 1954, **1**, 12–21.
45. Tournier, P. *The meaning of persons.* New York: Harpers, 1957.
46. Tweedie, D. *The significance of dread in the thought of Kierkegaard and Heidegger.* Unpublished doctoral dissertation, Boston University, 1954.
47. Tweedie, D. *Logotherapy and the Christian faith.* Grand Rapids: Baker Books, 1961.
48. Tweedie, D. *The Christian and the couch.* Grand Rapids: Baker Books, 1963.
49. Vander Linde, L. Christian faith and mental health. *Gordon Rev.,* September 1956.
50. Walters, O. Spiritual malpractice. *Action,* 1954, May 1.
51. Walters, O. Christian faith in an age of anxiety. Unpublished radio lectures, University of Illinois, Sept. 20, 1958.
52. Walters, O. Metaphysics, religion, and psychotherapy. *J. Counsel. Psychol.,* 1958, **5**, 249–250.

53. Walters, O. Faith: A built in psychotherapy. *Christian Herald,* January 1959.
54. Walters, O. Religion and psychopathology. *Acad. Reporter,* Academy of Religion and Mental Health, March 1959.
55. Walters, O. The psychiatrist and the Christian faith. *Christian Century,* July 20, 1960, 847.
56. Waterink, J. Man as a religious being and modern psychology. *Free Univ. Quart.,* 1959, **6,** 59.
57. Watson, G. Moral issues in psychotherapy. *Amer. Psychol.,* 1958, **13,** 575.
58. White, E. Spiritual factors in mental disorders. *J. Transactions Victoria Inst.,* 1949, **81,** 112.
59. White, E. *Christian life and the unconscious.* New York: Harpers, 1955.
60. White, E. *Guilt. HIS,* April 1959, 9.
61. White, R. *The abnormal personality.* New York: Ronald Press, 1956.
62. White, V. Guilt: theological and psychological. In P. Mairet (Ed.), *Christian essays in psychiatry.* New York: Philosophical Library, 1956.

Chapter 23

Behavioral Pastoral Counseling

JOHN M. VAYHINGER

John M. Vayhinger: b. 1916, Upland, Indiana.
A.B., Taylor University, 1937. B.D., in theology, Drew Theological Seminary,
1940. M.A., in philosophy, Drew University, 1951. M.A., 1948, Ph.D.,
1956, in experimental and clinical psychology, Columbia University.
Chairman, Department of Psychology and Pastoral Care, Anderson College
School of Theology, Anderson, Indiana, 1968–date. Professor of
Psychology of Religion and Pastoral Counseling, the Iliff School of
Theology, Denver, Colorado, 1964–1968. Professor, Pastoral
Psychology and Counseling, Garrett Theological Seminary, North-
western University Campus, 1958–1964. Joseph P. Kennedy, Jr., Foun-
dation, Research and Religion, 1966. Project Director, Garrett Psy-
chological Research Project on Seminary Students, Lilly Foundation,
Inc., supported 1958–1962; NIMH supported, 1962–1964. Chief, Clinical
Psychologist, Adult and Child Guidance Clinic, South Bend, Indiana,
1951–1958. Pastor of several Methodist churches, 1938–1944, 1951–1958.
Chaplain U. S. Army, 1944–1947.
Diplomate in Clinical Psychology, American Board of Examiners in Profes-
sional Psychology. Fellow, American Orthopsychiatric Association.
Life member: Academy of Religion and Mental Health; National
Congress of Parents and Teachers.
Books: (Co-author) Casebook of Pastoral Counseling (1962).
Articles: Awareness, goodness. Review of Erich Fromm, The heart of man.
Contemp. Psychol., 1966, 11, 24–26. Christianity and psychotherapy.
Taylor University Bulletin, 1962, 54, 4–7. First steps to maturity, Cross-
roads, 1961, 12, 78–81. The role of the church in the lives of the aging.
Kirkpatrick Memorial Programs on Gerontology, 1957, Ball State Uni-
versity. Psychological counseling with college students. Proceedings
of the West Virginia Academy of Science, 1951, 1–3.

For nearly 2,000 years the Christian Church has been drawing attention to the fact that resources of a sound mind, i.e., love, joy,
peace, may be found within her fellowship through her worship,
prayer, and sacraments, and through what the church calls the work
of the Spirit. For well over a thousand years before this the priests
and prophets of the Jewish religion found communal stability and

678

personal integrity through the worship of one God and a theocratic view of the nation.

If one can avoid certain perceptual distortions, a reductionist attitude, an irrational prejudice against theological reasoning, a need for excessive simplification, perhaps a prejudice of the laboratory, against the "more-than-natural" thought patterns, one may find that practical, parish-centered counseling by clergy has always been deeply involved in behavior or reality therapy. Using the real situations of daily living, individual and group involvement, a common-sense description of behavior shed of the myths of behavior determinism (though often with its own sets of "myths"), the parish has for centuries been the scene of real people facing real problems and solving them by real methods.

As an English psychiatrist says, "What of the clergy and the cure of souls entrusted to them for many generations? They are not new boys as we psychiatrists are, in this business. A.D. 30, not A.D. 1930, marks their entry into this profession" (14, pp. 7–8).

Indeed, the resources of the religious institution, church, or synagogue are considerable. Regular services (the Mass, worship services, small groups, religious education, etc.) characterize the regular involvement of many millions of persons all over the world. Personal pastoral services continuously involve many of these millions through, in the United States alone, more than 300,000 ordained and professionally trained religious leaders. Personal devotional acts, solitary or in groups, involve uncounted millions of persons daily.

These large amounts of expectation and actual activity have considerable effect on the emotional stability and the social adjustment of the persons involved, plus the reinforcing effects on the social and cultural and educational customs of their groups. Some of this already involved and potential behavior, for therapeutic results, has been neglected through the slanted attitudes of those who would define any religious beliefs and behavior as resulting from cultural neuroses, anthropomorphic projections, or authoritarian attitudes, and would then neglect or attack religion.

Though the naturalistic reductionists have retained some of the flavor of "religious belief," i.e., Carl Jung, etc., they have often so defined its sources, content, and effects as to separate themselves, by and large, from the significant forces of the religious faiths in this world.

It would be easy to oversimplify here, to attack or defend, either the supporters or detractors of any or all religious institutions. However, this paper is neither defense nor attack, nor even the description of a profound alliance of religion and psychotherapy, but rather a common-sense, reality-oriented description of one use in direct or reality therapy of religious beliefs and institutions and professional leaders, all already established in the lives of individuals, to solve and re-solve the real problems of living.

Most "dynamic therapists," including me, will be well aware of further needs of persons, both psychologically in terms of insight getting and interpersonal relations improvement, or theologically, in terms of salvation and holiness, or health and wholeness. In the cases referred to later, the further needs of the persons are an illustration of this point, but these further insights and needs do not undermine the effectiveness of these pastoral counselors' actions in meeting in behavior the personal and marital conflicts in these cases.

The term "religion" is such an all-inclusive term, so indefinite of limits (mysticism and LSD, institution and service, a Supreme Being and human response, etc.) and yet so necessary in delineating the "pastoral" from other kinds of "counselors," that we must speak a word. Sociologically, it may be defined as "religion, or what societies hold to be sacred, comprises an institutionalized system of symbols, beliefs, values, and practices focused on questions of ultimate meaning . . . value orientation . . . those overarching and sacred systems of symbols and beliefs, values, and practices concerning ultimate meaning which men shape to interpret their world" (7, pp. 4, 9). Religion might be defined psychologically as "the inner experience of the individual when he senses a Beyond, especially as evidenced by the effect of this experience on his behavior when he actively attempts to harmonize his life with the Beyond" (4, p. 22). Allport would insist that the individual, struggling for validation in religious experience, would find individual assurance if "he is persuaded that God of His free generosity has chosen to give dependable, if partial, knowledge of Himself through the devices of the intelligible universe that affects our senses . . . to assume that God chooses to declare Himself to us in our own language . . . Faith, based on this premise, is enjoined by the historic church, and is for millions the decisive consideration" (1, pp. 138, 139).

For purposes of describing religion as phenomenon, and more accurately describing psychological response to its symbols and experiences, we should also further define religious experience as either extrinsic or intrinsic or as a combination of both.

Extrinsic religion is an assumed religious sentiment, "the extrinsically religious person turns to God, but does not turn away from self" (2, p. 195). Research criteria define him as one who uses religion and religious membership primarily as a shield for self-centeredness, as a defense against anxiety and to serve personal advantage. It arises out of a need for security, status, self-esteem, and the formation of extrinsic religion as an immature form of faith. This is the kind of religion that Freud, had he been more perceptive, would have seen resembling the infantile illusion, a social neurosis.

Intrinsic religion, on the contrary, is fundamentally motivational, though partially intelligent and logically determined, and is a generic and embracing and guiding religious motive, homogeneous and harmonious in its structure. To the intrinsically religious individual, his faith is the center of his life, his skills and possessions are for its use. By research criteria one finds him by regular attendance at his place of worship, a personal devotional life, a high belief index on religious information, a devotion to the service of his brother, and a willingness to identify himself with religious institutions. Allport's prediction is that "mental health will vary according to the degree to which adherents of any faith are intrinsic in their interpretation and living of their faith" (2, p. 195).

Though well-defined research is sparse yet concerning the relation between mental and emotional adjustment and the religious experience of any given person, we must admit it is also a fact that there is little proof that psychotherapy makes a determining difference with persons emotionally disturbed, as Eysenck is quick to point out. Yet, just as psychotherapy of some sorts is helpful to some types of patients under certain conditions (12), so religious experience and congregational belonging are functionally helpful to many persons under certain conditions of living. Certainly in times of crisis, such as at the death of a loved one, the uniting in marriage of two people, etc., pastors and religious experience are reported by the persons involved as very helpful. This all, of course, begs the question of what religion itself sees as also of primary importance, i.e. salvation, holiness, eternal life, etc. The psychologist is indeed an intruder for theologians and philosophers; religious workers and pastors have long had prior rights in this territory. However, as Leslie says, a joint endeavor turns up the best results, "as alert minds move together in the pursuit of a clearer formulation of truth" (15, p. 91).

This will not resolve all tensions between psychologists and religious persons. In fact, as Joseph Havens points out, there will be inevitable tensions. "For most Christians, God in His inmost Being still acts from a center beyond the natural world as we know it. And for most psychologists their science shares the same philosophical assumptions as physics, chemistry and biology. It is evident that (anyone's) life cannot be viewed through both perspectives simultaneously without contradiction" (8, p. 143).

In this paper we are simply able to live with both sets of assumptions. Just as during the fifteenth through the eighteenth centuries it was simpler to live within the theological framework and place the scientific assumptions outside the "real world" for most people, so in the twentieth century it is easier in our society to place the theological assumptions outside and the scientific assumptions centrally to our point of view, even for religious people. But for purposes of this paper, we will simply assume that both are practical and possible, and that the "warfare between theology and science" is relegated to its day, and that we can indeed develop a "rich bilingualism," which, as Allport would say, "requires both the poetic and prophetic *metaphores* of religion and the precise, hard grammar of science" (2, p. 187).

HEALTHY AND 'SICK' RELIGIOUS EXPERIENCE

Not all religious behavior is contributory to emotional and mental health. We must distinguish between those religious beliefs and acts which, when a part of an individual's natural response to real life situations, increase his healthy condition and those religious phenomena which contribute to emotional and intellectual disturbance.

Clinebell has constructed some realistically determined criteria for distinguishing sick and healthy religious experiences which we shall summarize here. Certainly any human experience may be interpreted to include both healthy and 'sick' elements, but we shall ask of any religious experience if, in the main, it provides these behavioral and attitudinal results (5, pp. 30–50):

1. Does it bring the participants together or does it build barriers between persons?
2. Does it strengthen or weaken the basic sense of trust and relatedness within the universe?
3. Does it stimulate or hamper the growth of inner freedom and personal responsibility or does it encourage unhealthy dependence relationships and immature relationships with authority?
4. Does it create healthy consciences?

5. Does it help persons to move from shame and guilt to forgiveness, given and received, and does it provide well-defined, ethical guidelines, which contribute to the underlying health of the individual?
6. Does the religious thought and practice increase the enjoyment of living and enable individuals to handle the vital energies of aggressiveness and sex in positive and constructive ways?
7. Does it encourage the acceptance of reality and mature religious beliefs, or does it oversimplify or make unnecessarily more complex the human situation?
8. Does it emphasize love or fear, and does it instill in its believers a frame of orientation and object devotion that is efficient in handling existential anxiety constructively?
9. Does it strengthen realistic self-evaluation and endeavor to change the neurotic patterns of society?

In essence, we are asking for a value evaluation for any religious experience or psychotherapeutic involvement: Is it able to report that the human individual is better equipped to face life realistically? That is, by what criteria does the therapist report "improved" or "cured" for his patient? The pastoral counselor constantly asks himself in counseling is this person's religion a constructive, creative, healing, life-affirming force, or is it a dark, repressive, life-crippling force, for its effect depends on the way it is understood. Reality-oriented pastoral counseling encounters many situations where the Judeo-Christian faith enables persons to handle crises and conflicts with realistic courage, strength, and fortitude and to survive destructive situations of almost unfathomable dimensions. But at other times religion has been a crippling and distorting force, separating persons and damaging personalities [this latter occurrence is discussed at some length in reference 6].

PSYCHOTHERAPY CARRIED OUT BY PASTORAL AND OTHER PROFESSIONAL COUNSELORS

Practically, however, clergymen and psychotherapists do work together in the care and treatment of persons. Clinics and hospitals and family counseling centers are increasingly using teams that often include not only the conventional psychiatrists, clinical psychologists, and psychiatric social workers but "often include work associates and other professional people in the community, such as clergymen, physicians, lawyers, and social case workers" (17, p. 1). In the graduate school where I was on the faculty, doctoral candidates work as staff members in a Division of Alcoholism in a state mental health center hospital and on the staff of a family service center.

Since values and goals may well be as important a part of personality and its disturbances as emotional and intellectual and social factors, they must be a part of the treatment also. "Even though," writes Vaughn, "the therapist makes every effort to exclude his religious position from therapy to some degree, his religious and moral values will influence the patient. This fact favors the therapist having the same religious affiliation as the patient, whenever this is possible" (19, p. 207). Religious affiliation here refers not to denomination but to the same broad and basic religious attitudes toward the universe and man.

Or to make the point more concrete, many patients in therapy complain that their therapists seldom or never involve their religious beliefs in the treatment except in a negative and reductionist manner. Allport reports that the patients he has studied often insist that their religious faith is exceedingly important in their lives and feel its neglect interferes with their therapy. It may well be that some psychotherapists' customary neglect of this factor is, in part, due to their own lack of or antagonism toward personal religious faith. In part, it may also be due to their habituation to the grammar of science. In either case, unlike the pastoral counselors, they may fail to recognize the power of healing that lies in generic faith (2, p. 191).

In their relationships with many professional psychotherapists, however, pastoral counselors find that many of the older boundaries are melting away. Thornton (18) presents two therapy treatment cases in which the dynamics are similar, the depth of pathology somewhat equal, and he describes the diagnosis and treatment. He then reveals that one was treated (in two therapy hours) by a psychoanalyst, and the other (in fifteen therapy hours) by a minister of the United Church of Canada, the psychoanalyst, Alphonse Maeder, M.D., and the pastoral counselor, The Rev. Murray Thompson. Thornton then discusses criteria for differentiating the two professional roles. Psychiatric care usually covers many more hours whereas pastoral counseling is thought of as short-term, but any pastor knows of parishioners to whom are given hundreds of hours, when the clergyman must, as it were, leave the "ninety-and-nine" to go on a time-consuming search for the one who is lost.

Another criterion has to do with the content of the therapeutic conversations, probing into unconscious material contrasted with meeting the real crises of daily living. In reality therapy, however, both pastoral and psychiatric treatment often deal mainly with the conscious or "real" factors in the patient-parishioner's experience. Both deal with man at the point of his existential anxieties, anxiety over his finiteness, death, guilt, and the meaninglessness of many persons, "the empty heads stuffed with straw," of T.S. Eliot's "Cocktail Party." While in some settings the pastoral counselors might be expected to use a directive-advice-giving technique while the psychological therapist uses specialized, interpretive or reflective techniques, certainly most of the techniques used in direct or reality therapy lie within the pastoral specialist's skill also. Perhaps the pastoral counselor is supposed to use religious language and theological or ecclesiastical resources (prayer, the Sacraments, worship, Scripture, etc.) and obviously does so, but no competent pastor feels the need to compulsively apply these very real helps indiscriminately any more than a psychiatrist uses drugs, hospitalization, or group therapy indiscriminately (18).

Choosing a style of life, or changing the current one, is the prerogative of the patient-parishioner. Therapy simply gives him the inner freedom to choose. This choice would seem to include the therapist's being acquainted with the patient-parishioner's religious attitudes at least to the degree where the therapist may handle realistically whatever conflicts come from the religious dimensions of the patient's self. Margaretta Bowers insists that any therapist who works with people with religious sectors in their problems should have come to an understanding of their own religious attitudes, have had training in the techniques of therapy with religious conflicts, have some orientation in the theology of his patient's religious group, and "he must regard the patient's religious conflict as a core problem and respect the patient as a religious person" (3, p. 74).

Particularly damaging might be the therapist's inadvertently indicated contempt for the patient's religious values, be they Jewish, Catholic, or Protestant, which would create greater emotional confusion and "wild" transference. There seems to be a growing awareness among psychotherapists of this problem so that an increasing number (though small in its total count) of counselors are beginning to refer a patient to a clergyman, priest, minister or rabbi, who may help resolve conflicts with religious symbols or inadequate and infantile religious beliefs or interpersonal denominational or congregational relationships, and who then refers the patient back to the psychiatric psychotherapist.

A case in point here is Susan, a 33-year-old divorcee, Protestant, school teacher. The psychiatrist responsible for the treatment of her anxiety reaction referred her to a pastoral counselor when a tentative return to the Church of her childhood and youth brought on a panic of tears during the service. Exploration of her attitudes toward religion quickly uncovered a formally church-oriented set of parents who possessed only extrinsic religion. Two unfortunate experiences during childhood, one at nine and the other at fourteen with clergymen who betrayed their responsibilities, one in the handling of money and one sexually with a woman in the community, had catastrophically destroyed a strong identification with them as heroes and friends. While the patient explored her feelings from the past with the pastoral counselor, he set up an involvement in a nearby church of her denomination whose minister possessed unusual pastoral capabilities, preaching skills, and a real concern for persons. She began attending the church every Sunday, participating in a young adults group during the week, and repeating in considerable detail with her counselor her experiences, the feelings that went with them, and how she planned to handle them in the coming week.

Positive identification (reinforcement) with these positive and constructive present-day experiences restored her involvement in her church and her psychiatrist was able to resume his treatment with her, now with a positive resource in her church that reintegrated her into a caring group of her peers who involved her in constructive experiences, adequate and appropriate for her situation and age.

THE ROLE OF ANXIETY, COMMUNICATION, AND CONFRONTATION

Constructive anxiety has some similarities to religious anxiety (11). The first is an anxious striving to be a mature and responsible individual, a searching for personal values by which to guide one's life. The second is an anxious longing for lasting security, a desire to relate to and to know God, and to mature as a religious person. The relationship between therapist and patient is similar, in some ways, to the worshiper and his God, though also with some real differences. As Charles Curran would insist, the Judeo-Christian tradition can go beyond the naturalistic limits of professionial psychotherapeutic skills. Psychotherapy and religious experience have often been used interchangeably, that is, for the alleviation of psychic suffering, when religious faith or dependence has been used to tranquilize or to alleviate neurotic hurt, and often efficiently. Psychology has offered, on the other hand, a way of life to many individuals.

Functionally both serve to relieve conflicts, to increase abilities to relate between persons, and to help individuals adjust to their societies. As with Susan, there are many recorded instances when clergymen have been identified with frightening or destructive experiences from childhood in the minds of patients. On the other hand, pseudo-scientific rationalisms may substitute for a healthier religious symbolism. Or primitive, prelogical thought processes may interfere with reality adjustment in other individuals, and religious experience may be ineffective in helping. But in other situations, religious experience and understanding may bring relief from experienced guilt, or give direction and meaning to the individual's relationship to the universe as well as within the individual life, or provide the loving experience that makes it possible for an individual to forgive and relate kindly to other persons. Neither kind of "treatment" should suppress the other, rather both should be used when the situation calls for appropriate help.

In reality oriented pastoral counseling, one of the chief mediums for psychotherapy is communication, that is, the description of one's situation and one's feelings about himself with and among other people. A basic requirement for communication is mutual understanding of the content of what is being communicated. When one person learns the language of another, barriers may be broken down and relationship established. And the more complete the new language is, the more likely the development of a relationship. This principle applies in the therapeutic relationship also. For progress in treatment to occur there must be understanding on some level, that is, both the therapist and patient must be able to grasp the other's meaning regarding the relationship to the patient's behavior, its meaning, his goal in life, and his desire to make changes in his present perception of his behavior. In regard to religious convictions, it is essential for therapeutic progress that the therapist comprehend both the material and the feelings the patient brings to the therapy hour. For instance, as Vaughn describes such a situation, if a Catholic patient in a state of anxiety complains that he must make his Easter duty but is unable to take himself to church and, after confession, still feels guilty, his lack of relief must be set against the meaning his religion has for him. To understand this pathological condition, the therapist would have to understand values and conviction on a fairly technical level. If these are foreign or nonsense to the therapist, he cannot but communicate this to the patient, likely with unfortunate results for progress. "At times, therefore, an understanding of the patient's religious convictions is essential for success in treatment. At other times, it may not be essential, but it is most certainly conducive to the development of rapport" (19, p. 205).

An illustration of such understanding by a person whose training included the skills and techniques of religious counseling follows. A local pastor had been in his parish for some five years. He reports on a counseling situation.

It was 11 o'clock in the evening when the doorbell rang. Slipping a robe over my pajamas, I opened the door to find Bob standing there, in some distress, asking if we might talk for awhile. He refused to come into the house, suggesting the car instead.

Bob: "Pastor, I think I had better give up my membership in the church."

Pastor: "Oh."

Bob: "Yes, I am in bad trouble. I'm too bad to be a member. I hate to bother you with all this, but I don't know what to do. I don't think I can even go home." (There were pauses and sobs between each phrase).

Pastor: "Can we talk about it?"

Bob: "I don't know. June said the next time would be my last. I guess this is it. That's why we left Columbus. I was out with another girl. Now, I can't go home."

We talked about an hour. I found that he and June had been married eleven years. She was only seventeen at the time of their marriage; he was twenty-two and a veteran of Korea. They were married in a compromising situation, June in the firm belief she was pregnant. Their premarital relations hung like a cloud between them and both suffered considerable guilt. Subsequent talks with June revealed that she had always felt Bob married her only out of pity and pressure rather than love. Finally, Bob came to the end of his story.

Bob: Pastor, what can I do?"

Pastor: "Well, there are several things you can do. Perhaps the first thing is to discover what are the factors important to June and what the possibilities are that are open."

Bob: "Yes."

Pastor: "You could spend the night here in the parsonage. We could pick up clothes in the morning and figure out things from there. Or do you feel we should go talk with June tonight?"

Bob: "You think I ought to go home, make a clean breast of the whole thing, and let the chips fall where they may?"

Pastor: "This came from you, Bob, certainly it's one of the possibilities, but we need to face the facts that June may not see you."

Bob: (After considerable silence) "Will you go with me?" (I indicated that I would and I was soon ready and back in the car.)

Bob: (Along the way) "Pastor, I'd rather step in front of a fast-moving truck than do this."

Pastor: "That is something you can still do. But in any case, we're committed to this first."

June was up and waiting for Bob's return. She made coffee and invited us to be seated at the kitchen table. Bob made his confession like a man, prefacing it with, "June, I remember what you told me, and when I'm through whatever you want to do with me is what we will do." This was the raw drama, and it continued for nearly an hour. All three of us were frightened. Bob was afraid he had finally destroyed his home. June's worst fears were realized. I was awed by the position in which I found myself. June reacted with super-charged emotions. She swore she could not go on being terrified every time Bob left the house after dark and that this time she couldn't forgive with any hope of the future. She recalled how she had left Bob once before and returned only because she loved him. She approached hysteria several times. Only after the storm had blown itself out and both had calmed to silence did I enter the discussion verbally, aware of the awesome responsibility of my words.

Pastor: "June, could this time be different?"

June: "Why? It has always been like this. He's like an alcoholic swearing off after a binge. I have seen him just as remorseful at least seven times in eleven years."

Pastor: "Has anyone else besides yourselves been in on it before?"

June: "No, we have handled it by ourselves, and I am tired of running from it."

Pastor: "But this time he brought his confession to God. The living Lord is a third party this time. I can't defend him, or urge you, but you've both shared your hurt, and he his sin. Jesus told us not to **stop forgiving at seven times but to go on forgiving as long as any love remains.**"

This was the turning point. At the time I spoke, I had a firm hand on each of their shoulders, praying that the quivering in my knees did not transmit itself through my hands. But reconciliation did not come immediately. It seemed necessary that accumulated antagonisms have their expression. But it finally did come. I asked Bob if I could use his car, stating that it looked as if a wedding were in order and that I would return soon.

I left and went to the church study. There I gathered up a small cross and candle set, my old Marine communion set, and the Book of Worship. Then I went to the parsonage and changed clothes. I did not hesitate to don a rabat and collar, even though these were not my usual garb. I felt that no symbol of spiritual authority should be overlooked if it might be helpful. And I sensed in them the **need to be able to start over fresh with a minimum of doubts concerning** the involvement of God in their affairs.

When I returned I saw that all was not well. Without stopping, I hurried through the kitchen and went into the living room where I prepared a coffee table as an altar. Amid great sobs, June called me to the kitchen.

June: "He told me who it was. We have had her in the home here any number of times. We've played cards and Scrabble together. She was my friend. And all the time . . . ." (Her voice trailed off under the sobs)

Pastor: "Well, June, I guess it had to be someone." (After a pause as her sobs died down) "I am prepared either to perform a wedding or to take one of you back to the parsonage to spend the rest of the night. I'll be in the living room waiting."

As I waited, I could hear some of the conversation between June and Bob. June was worried about her future relation with the other woman involved and deeply wounded by such a betrayal of her friendship. At one point June told Bob he had always treated her like a child and had never realized she was a woman, and Bob, half-crying, claimed June made him feel like a little boy, "just another of the kids." This mutual belittling came through in subsequent talks with both June and Bob. It became of some significance in their rehabilitation. Once during that long night they called me back to the kitchen to ask about what was right in a religious way and once to ask about why they felt the way they did about each other, June wondering if she needed to be punished, and Bob if he sought her disapproval. I confined myself to the questions. Finally, they called me a third time and reported how they had worked their way around their obstacles. It sounded authentic to me, and I added nothing to it. Leading them into the living room, I asked them to kneel at the altar. On the spot I combined the two services of Communion and marriage. I led them through the prayer of confession, phrase by phrase. With nearly three thousand years of experience behind it, it seemed to be as much a part of their own experiences as their essential human nature. Then I asked them one at a time to make their own detailed confessions, either in their hearts or aloud, not of what they had *done,* but what they had *been.* Bob prayed aloud —simply and, I believe, sincerely. June seized the phrase, "A broken and contrite heart, O Lord, thou wilt not despise," and whether on her behalf or his, I don't know. I served Bob first with communion, then June, though I had not planned it one way or the other. It was a moving experience and voice control was difficult all the way around.

It was only a short time until I pronounced them "man and wife" in the ancient marriage ceremony, indicated my love for them both, and lost no time in leaving.

In the months and years following before I was transferred to another parish, we had many sessions together. In each I tried to step further and further out of the picture and return to my role as pastor. I often suggested good reading materials and suggested, with some success, that they develop the practice of reading aloud to each other.

Bob remained in the church and became one of its most responsible members. With only slight encouragement on my part, he became a teacher of a junior boys class. He began to learn how to express his love within his family as well as his thought, and along with it he began to experience for the first time some of the joys of home life and its fulfillments. At an earlier time June had described him as a "caged tiger," now it was all different. June described her husband as a "model husband," a year later. They began to talk things over together, equally sharing business and domestic decisions. True, Bob had changed to make it possible. But it would not have been possible without a different June, either. She was encouragd to participate in the church's women's work and after a while became president. She began to read for the first time and became interested in the Parent-Teacher Association and the community. She took over the chancel choir and became its director. Training herself and exercising forgotten talent, she soon won the gratitude and heart of the congregation. She became a woman of confidence and poise and the hallmark of Bob's pride.

Of course, there were many problems, and we dealt with them as they came. The older children showed the insecurity of their early years, but they also began to show a new and more secure home life. And, as far as I could know, Bob never again was untrue to his wife. When I came to June's house that fateful night, she knew I was representing responsibility toward them both. I avoided taking sides, and I feel she understood before it was over that I was attempting to represent, not Bob's side against hers or her side against Bob's, but God's side toward them and for them both. When I returned to the home I "took charge," so to speak, freely using the living room, raiding the kitchen for bread and water, and so on. But my demeanor conveyed the idea that I considered their home in grave danger and needing some pretty realistic help both from themselves and from One beyond themselves.

An illustration of reality therapy in pastoral counseling might come from another faith, the Jewish tradition, with mourning. If grief occurs when an individual loses a love object and the investment of affection is suddenly cut off, then three things are, realistically, present. First, an emptiness occurs in the mourner's relationship with the dead person, and an ambivalence is revealed within the relationship in which the mourner likely both loves and at times dislikes the loved person, and finally, there is a tendency to blame oneself for having failed to help, please, or fulfill the relationship with guilt feelings resulting. Especially would these things be accurate in the relationships with the mourner's parents.

In the Jewish traditions, death is eulogized, since at its time the individual's life, with its dignity, its successes, and its achievements, may be described, especially if the person has died with a good name. This is contrasted with an infant's birth, with its unknown quality, "better the day of death than the day of one's birth." (Eccles. 7:1). Judaism insists on a simple and plain funeral, a pine box, a body dressed in shrouds, and insists on the family remaining at the cemetery until the actual burial is completed. At Jewish funerals the departed is eulogized, with several speakers (including members of the family) addressing themselves both to the departed and to the remaining family. Nothing is done to camouflage death's reality. Kidorf (9) describes the mourning rites in detail. They include seven days during which the mourner deprives himself of his usual daily comforts. It is likely that this practice psychologically reduces the guilt feelings the mourner might feel toward the dead love object. Then eleven months are passed in semimourning in which one carries on most of the usual pattern of life but abstains from some form of recreation. The Hebrew prayer for the dead, the Kadish, is recited three times daily in the faithful congregation but with a minimum observance of once a day. Even after this year, semimourning is resumed on anniversaries of the death and specified holidays.

It may thus be seen that the grief is spread out over a long period of time, reducing its overwhelmingness for most mourners. The tradition also makes it possible for the mourner to express otherwise forbidden behavior, such as tears, sadness, periods of inefficient productivity, or simply being by oneself in isolation.

The prayer, the Kadish, itself says in essence, "it was God who gave this person to us; it is God who has taken him from us to Himself. We will not wail, nor murmur, nor complain. Instead, we will exclaim, Blessed is the name of the Lord" (9, p. 250).

The recitation of such a prayer elicits an enormous amount of faith in the faithful Jew at a conscious level and projects outwardly the responsibility for the death of the departed perhaps to the relief of the mourner. One does not have to accept the Freudian postulates of Kidorf to see how practical and reality oriented such a religious tradition might be for mourners and how such religious customs would make for relief of grief.

CONFRONTATIONAL AND CONTINUING RELATIONSHIP IN PASTORAL COUNSELING

Clinebell describes confrontational counseling when he structures within the Christian heritage the ministry of reconciliation, the bringing together of persons into a right relationship with their neighbors and with their God. While this has suffered in Protestant churches recently when psychoanalytic and permissive counseling has formed the bulk of what is taught in Protestant seminaries, historically pastoral counseling has had two primary resources with which to confront persons: discipline (a fraternal word of correction, pastoral admonition) and forgiveness (confession, penance, and absolution). Church discipline is thus described by Seward Hiltner when he writes, that "the original intention of Christian discipline was equally to bring back the offender and to preserve the church" (10, p. 65). This discipline is brought to actual experience by a five-stage process: confrontation, confession, forgiveness, restitution, and reconciliation (6, p. 225).

Equally important in pastoral counseling is the established relationship in which trust and honest openness is possible. Since the pastor "sees" his people weekly if not daily, is instantly available without finances intervening, and is "seen" by his people as the one who is there to help, continuing care is possible in a way the secular therapist cannot have except in the hospital setting. Confrontation and self-confrontation come particularly in the pastor's counseling since the clergyman is inescapably a symbol of the church's and community's values.

Many people come to him specifically because of this symbolic presence, for instance, the young business man with a wife and three small children and a respected place in the community. One morning he called for an appointment with his pastor after missing church and other congregational activities for half a year. That morning he revealed to his pastor that he had been carrying on an "incidental affair" with an efficient secretary who traveled with him sometimes on business trips. After the business man confessed the situation, the pastor replied, "Of course, you know the church and I stand against adultery," to which the man replied, "I know that, pastor, in fact, that's why I came to you. If I had only wanted to relieve my guilt so I could carry on the affair, I'd have gone to a psychiatrist, but I honestly want to break off the involvement and reestablish my relationship with my wife and children." At this the minister was in a position to aid him in facing honestly his responsibility in the unethical affair and to make a clean confession and earnest change in his relationship with his family.

CONCLUSION

Though the professionals in religion must, by definition, keep their "eyes on the eternal verities" (2, p. 188), they have little difficulty in relating their beliefs to more modern conceptions of psychopathology and psychotherapy if we, like Allport, describe the disturbed patient as "one who regrets his past, abhors his present, and dreads his future" (2, p. 188).

Religion, through pastoral counseling as well as the traditional services of the church, may deepen the issue by providing "forgiveness for the past, acceptable meaning for the present, and hope for the future" (2, p. 188). Psychiatry, through its Erik Eriksons, its Erich Fromms, its Menninger brothers, its Bernard Greenes, its Smiley Blantons, and others, is discovering what religious faith has long claimed, that there is "no cure apart from love." Here Allport would say, "the concepts of therapy and of redemption fuse. Healing follows the path of redemptive love, whether human or divine" (2, p. 188).

The therapists, secular or pastoral, must be sensitive enough to refrain from wiping out distinctions between religion and psychiatry, the church-synagogue and clinic, for religion is not merely the servant of hygiene; religion's purpose is salvation, not just psychic health. Religion's goal is the fostering of wholeness of personality. Christ himself healed the sick and "cast out demons," and here religious experience, through the pastoral counselor, is the potential integrator of all of life.

Even as Dietrich Bonhoeffer insists there is no "cheap grace," the pastoral counselor is in a crucial place to insist that "the only form of love that is genuinely redemptive and therapeutic (two terms for substantially the *same* reality) is one that is demanding, expectant" (16, p. 31).

Rabbi Robert L. Katz describes

> in religious tradition an emphasis on the value of unconditional love, of support and of consolation. These values, which might be called *maternal,* are closely linked with the care of the sick, the protection of the weak and the indulgence of the dependent. But religion speaks also of a parallel set of values which might be called *paternal.* These deal with the life of the individual in the community, with his responsibilities, his relationships and his commitments. There is a danger these days of identifying religion exclusively with healing and with consolation. Material values are over-emphasized and frequently misrepresented. Religion tends to be divorced from the paternal and the more prophetic values. No more is asked of it except that it tranquilize man's anxieties. (13)

With religion's real values and high goals, continuous involvement in the lives of its people, its offer of confession and restitution and acceptance and forgiveness and group inclusion, the Church offers reality and behavior therapy at its highest level, when pastors are trained to practice it and the congregation is motivated to experience it. Like Alcoholics Anonymous, which found its head in psychology and its heart and viscera in religion, the pastoral counselor relates to a seeking, hurting person in need, "in a moment of broken-ness" and shares with him the experience of relating to a Power higher than his own and to a sharing fellowship which, ideally, accepts him as God accepts them, focuses on the here and now, and shares as a fellow "sinner-saved-by-grace" but still with his own temptations, the person's human situation.

REFERENCES

1. Allport, G. W. *The individual and his religion.* New York: Macmillan, 1950.
2. Allport, G. W. Behavioral science, religion, and mental health. *J. Relig. Health,* 1963, **2,** 187–197.
3. Bowers, M. K. *Conflicts of the clergy.* New York: Nelson & Sons, 1963.
4. Clark, W. M. *The psychology of religion.* New York: Macmillan, 1958.
5. Clinebell, H. J., Jr. *Mental health through Christian community.* Nashville: Abingdon Press, 1965.
6. Clinebell, H. J., Jr. *Basic types of pastoral counseling.* Nashville: Abingdon Press, 1966.
7. Glock, C. Y., & Stark, R. *Religion and society in tension.* Chicago: Rand McNally, 1965.
8. Havens, J. Notes on Augustine's confessions. *J. Scient. Study Relig.,* 1965, **5,** 141–143.
9. Hertz, J. H. *Daily prayer book.* New York: Bloch, 1958, p. 269. Cited by I. W. Kidorf, Jewish tradition and the Freudian theory of mourning. *J. Relig. Health,* 1963, **2,** 248–252.
10. Hiltner, S. *Preface to pastoral theology.* Nashville: Abingdon Press, 1958.
11. Hiltner, S. & Menninger, K. (Eds.) *Constructive aspects of anxiety.* Nashville: Abingdon Press, 1963.
12. Jones, M. *The therapeutic community.* New York: Basic Books, 1953. Chapters VII and VIII, Follow-up Inquiry, pp. 96–146.
13. Katz, R. L. The meaning of religion in healthy people. *The Cent. Conf. Amer. Rabbis J.,* 1960, pp. 46–50, Quoted by Mowrer (16).
14. Lake, F., Foreword. In E. N. Ducker, *A Christian therapy for a neurotic world.* New York: Taplinger, 1963.
15. Leslie, R. C. *Jesus and logotherapy.* Nashville: Abingdon Press, 1965.
16. Mowrer, O. H. *The new group therapy.* Princeton, N.J.: Van Nostrand, 1964.
17. Parlour, R. R., Cole, P. A., & Van Vorst, R. B. Treatment teams and written contracts as tools for behavior rehabilitation. *The Discoverer,* 1967, **4,** 1.
18. Thornton, E. E. Health and salvation. *J. Relig. Health,* 1963, **2,** 210–235.
19. Vaughn, R. Religious beliefs, values, and psychotherapy. *J. Relig. Health,* 1963, **2,** 198–209.

Chapter 24

Essential Therapies
and Catholic Practice
VINCENT V. HERR, S.J.

Vincent V. Herr, S.J.: b. 1901, Swanton, Ohio. d. Chicago, Illinois, 1970.
A.B., 1925, and M.A., 1926, St. Louis University. Ph.D., University of Bonn,
Germany, in social psychology, 1939. Licentiate in Theology, Uni-
versity of Gregoriana, Rome, Italy, 1934.
Professor and Chairman, Department of Psychology, Loyola University,
1945–1965. Assistant Professor of Biology, Xavier University, Cin-
cinnati, Ohio, 1926/1929.
President, American Catholic Psychological Association, 1954. Chairman,
Chicago Branch, Academy of Religion and Mental Health. Consultant,
Vatican Council II, Commission on Seminaries, 1965.
Books: *Religious Psychology* (1964). (Co-author) *Psychodynamics of
Personality Development* (1964). *Screening Candidates for Priest-
hood and Religious Life* (1962). *Social Psychology* (1945).
Articles: Mental health training in Catholic seminaries. *J. Rel. Health,* 1962,
2, 127–152; and 1966, **5,** 27–34. The Loyola NIMH Seminary Project:
progress report. *Amer. Cath. Soc. Rev.,* 1960, **21,** 331–336. Comments
in Standahl & Corsini (Eds.), *Critical incidents in psychotherapy,* 1959.
(Co-author) The Loyola NIMH Project on Religion and Mental Health.
Past. Psychol., February 1959. Case reports. *J. Rel. Ment. Health,* 1964,
3, 184–189.

I have chosen this title in order to bring to the reader's attention
some basic concepts regarding human nature. I take nature to mean
simply the source of action in a man. Whatever activities appear in
his behavior at any given time flow from and manifest this deeper
nature. They never quite represent the total because man, both individually and as a race, is constantly evolving in certain respects.
Moreover, tools are not yet available for glimpsing the deepest elements of his being, whether that be considered chemical, biological,
physical, or a composite of all these. Whatever classes of behavior do
show up derive, like physiochemical activities, from a source, a
cause, an energy or dynamic that makes them persist in their behavior as long as they do. Just as all bodies have potential energy

that is not yet activated, as well as kinetic energy (that exists because of movement or change), so man's body has a potential in addition to what Hans Driesch calls life potential. This potential embraces what has not yet been activated, nor probably would ever be activated, but is not the less real in potential, along with the kinetic energy arising out of the "flow" or drift or active push-pull, get-up-and-go style of living. The somewhat blasé, quiescent, passive type of energy betokens the passive person. The dynamic, fiery, go-go-go, do-it-yourself sort of energy belongs to a different type of person. All acts such as these crop out of and give glimpses of that evolving, ever-striving thing called man.

Thus man's nature is never totally known, but whatever of it man knows at any given time earns the right to be called objective knowledge always and only through studying his actions. What he has done depicts some part of his potential for action. The kinds of things he has done, he obviously could have done, or he has had the potential to do. Because man could never activate all his potential at any one instant, scientists and philosophers alike extrapolate by saying: from past acts we infer potential of that same level at least; from his personal history (just as from animal and geological history) we may make best guesses (hypotheses) and test their validity. In this way scientists and philosophers come to a practical working knowledge of what a healthy striving interacting human being should be like by nature or essence.

This digression is intended merely to clear up the confusion that easily arises from the numerous ways in which people use words like essential, existential, natural. I repeat, essence here means no more than nature viewed, not as source of actions, but as root matrix of being-in-itself, that is, in its changeable aspects. If we have arrived at a concept or a certain image of classes of beings who do certain things, who show certain fundamental basic properties, we know something of their nature or essence.

Let us contrast this notion of nature-essence with that of existence, so as to clear away some of the cloudiness surrounding existentialism in the United States and abroad today. We may start by considering that we are embedded in a stream of ongoing life. Every second about four human beings die and about five others come into being. This means approximately 18,000 new human beings come into existence every hour. The result? A population explosion. This is the change of existence. A statement of the fact that a certain object, say Plato, was not, then was, and now is not, tells pointedly what is meant by existence. The root meaning from *ex* and *stare* connotes a coming, a standing off from another, a being-other-than the cause or parent or producer. In contrast, *esse*(nce) is from *ens, being,* whether actual or possible. So computer experts, extrapolating processes with which we are all familiar, readily calculate the number of real, actual, striving-to-be-fed human beings by the year A.D. 1999, giving data about present realities and projecting them into future human beings, the number of them possible per so-and-so much time and space.

Keeping to this simple notion of existence as differing from essence enables us to escape the dilemma of some existentialists who say earthly life alone has meaning, death is annihilation, there is no after, and who also say that death has meaning only when viewed as a reality for which man must prepare and strengthen himself from the first moment of his existence. The being-not-another or the being-the-self concept of Heidegger, Allport (1, 2) and others, expresses what we mean simply. When self-being ends—say that of Aristotle—what was then now no longer is; but it was actual and remains *post factum* the same essentially for all future generations to contemplate.

Trained by a teacher in Bonn who was trained by Martin Heidegger, I naturally draw heavily now upon European writers. As is well known, Heidegger studied under Husserl and admired Kierkegaard's work, combining their two views in his famous *Sein und Zeit* (*Being and Time,* 1962). The Swiss psychiatrist Ludwig Binswanger (4), Rollo May in America (10, 11), and the Viennese Viktor Frankl (5, 6), well interpreted by Magda Arnold (3), have done most to bring these two views to America. Since the major emphasis and approaches of these writers follow my own so closely, I shall give a quick sketchy account of them before beginning the study of a typical case treated by applying the principles of essential therapy.

Actually the least common denominator of all existentialist assumptions can be stated quite briefly. First, the existentialists assume that man has by nature the ability to be aware of himself, of what he is doing, and of what is happening to him. The consequences are his ability to make decisions about all these things and to take responsibility for himself—to see the self as a causative factor. He can also think of the possibility of becoming totally isolated and alone, nothing, and this state is innately feared and is symbolized by death. Man is always becoming, never passive or static; he changes continuously in his way of relating to self and other. His real worth and meaning, as perceived by himself, derive not from his past but from what he is now and how he is developing toward fulfillment of his potentialities.

Man's behavior always occurs within a situation and can never be considered apart from this. For example, a sad cry has no objectively observable meaning unless the observer considers the situation toward which it is directed (a call for help), as well as the conscious inner intents and purpose which guide it. Without these it cannot be understood. One must consider as a unit subjectively and objectively observable responses and situational events.

When we say of a man: "He was then, he is now, and then the end," that is the language of human existence and of most of the existentialists by implication at least. When we say, however: "Man is an object of thought in the mind of his creator who cares for him as He always did; man now is and always was, but at some point of time came into actual existence and at another point of time ceases to have this earthly existence," we speak the language of the essentialist. We, thus, also imply that it is man's nature to believe that he carries on while on earth, with the help of his Creator, in such a way as to plan and deliberately to decide, somehow to determine personally how he shall live in that great timeless future beyond the gate of death. We imply that he sincerely believes death is not a horrible nothing but only a precise cutting point between earthly existence and some other more desirable one, and again we speak a language that is understandable to all. We need to spell out this position, or our analysis of the treatment of our case cannot be grasped as it was intended. We repeat most emphatically: Man honestly believes, in his deeper moods and self-reflections, that when he is at death's door he is but bringing to a close a mode of existence; he has experienced an amalgamation between the *then* of the past and the *now* and that great *beyond* wherein the *then* will always be more grandiose, gratifying, delightful, and rewarding than any other *then* of human experience.

Lastly, in order to understand a person fully we must empathize, seek to get at the reality underlying both the inner awareness and the outer observable total situation. We must try to live ourselves into the other's innerly immediately experienced reality, the ultimately real personal character of his experience (which basically is love) and to grasp the whole phenomenon. This task is indeed hard for a therapist, and in the course of our anamnesis of our applied case we shall combine Rollo May and Viktor Frankl with the Catholics' overall philosophy and try to evaluate the result.

We have chosen this particular case because it lends itself so well to a demonstration of the proper attitude the therapist should take toward the client. On the other hand, it shows what can happen to a patient after he has been subjected to a variety of analyses and treatments including the client-centered technique.

A twenty-six-year-old man approached his pastor with the following complaint:

> I feel tense and anxious all the time and sort of tired, even upon rising in the morning. I began to notice it when I was in the seminary. It's affecting my memory now. And at times I feel as if my heart were out of order; it feels so jerky. Or maybe it is my stomach; I cannot tell for sure. What I do know is that some other symptoms have been appearing which worry me a lot more. It's connected with losing my memory so I cannot apply myself to my work. I have to keep reassuring myself that I am not crazy. I know I am not crazy; yet I do know I am a bit off. I go around making sure all doors are locked when I leave home and put out all the ashtrays when I am the last one to leave the office. This does not seem good to me. Worst of all, whenever I unpark my car, I have an urge to drive clear around the block to where I had been parked, to see that I did not bump or scratch somebody's car or hurt somebody.

Here we see a patient who has already developed psychosomatic symptoms. Being a college graduate of high intelligence, he had done extensive reading in the field of psychology and psychiatry and was inclined to look askance at much of the "wild" theorizing of these two disciplines. He was definitely not the accepting type; everything had to be proved to him scientifically.

The counselor asked if he had seen a physician or done anything else about his problem. The man replied:

> I talked to the counselor in the seminary; he thought I was just a bit scrupulous and that it would wear off in time. He also thought I might need a psychiatrist, but I was against this.

Asked if he had any idea how these things had started, he said:

> Oh, yes. My whole trouble began when I was in the service. I had a terrible shock when my two buddies were just bombed all to hell and I was spared. I sure got religion, but good! I took an oath that if I got out of that hell-hole alive, I would become a priest. That's how I came to go to the seminary in the first place. Well, I had thought of it as a boy, feeling that my father was no good for me. He never would answer my personal questions and seemed to take such a distant, cold attitude toward us kids. All he ever did was punish. Mother had to give all the affection. When she died—I was six, and my two sisters were nine and twelve—we were totally in the hands of priests

and nuns. I just hated my dad, and the nuns for agreeing with him. The priests impressed me with their sanctity and heroic virtues, and I felt that if I did become a priest, it would be to set all people like my dad on the right track. I guess I was too good for any of them. I hated them all, yet felt guilty for this and wanted to make amends. That's why I made the promise to be a priest, I guess.

The counselor then asked the client why he had left the seminary after so short a time. He replied:

> I could not stand the tension and anxiety. The boss said I would do well to leave for a while, and to recuperate my strength. He practically expelled me, but he kept insisting that I go for some help. But I could not stand the thought of a psychiatrist or psychoanalyst after what I had experienced in the army. All I knew about them was that they kept probing and digging into the unconscious and the experiences of your early childhood and trying to trace all your troubles to sex. Of course, when I left, I asked the boss about my promise to become a priest. He said, and I tried to believe him, that I did not have to worry, that if I couldn't be a priest, I couldn't, which was precious little consolation. It did nothing to alleviate my anxiety or to relieve my confusion and doubts.
>
> Another thing I now recall probably added to my dislike of my father. He allowed my sister to go out in a boat on a big lake with her fiancé for a whole afternoon. The boat capsized, and my sister was drowned; her fiancé, who was unable to save her, was rescued and came home to report the incident. This was more than I could take, and I blamed both my father and this man for losing my sister. I must have been about eleven or twelve at the time. I think the accident also helped me turn to God in a new way.
>
> But now I can't seem to do anything right, even on the job. I thought that since you were a religious person, as well as a trained counselor, you could help me. I liked you from the start; but all I wanted, I guess, was reassurance that I was all right. I still mean to go back to the seminary if I can get over these terrible fears. It's so bad now I can hardly go to church. And when I do go, I cannot receive the sacraments as I would like. At times, I manage to go to confession, but it never quite gets me the forgiveness I need. Maybe I ought to do more penance.

This long summary is intended to show that although the client had been reared in a very Catholic home where many means were available for developing a strong character (self or ego with high frustration tolerance), he had actually acquired little or none. The particular circumstances and causal events of childhood are perhaps accountable for this. The religious situation may have had something to do with it, not to speak of the peculiar characteristics of his father.

The client held a good job in a management consultant firm at the time, owned a car, lived in bachelor's quarters, and often visited his former seminary classmates and his surviving sister and her family. He drank slightly and only socially, but admitted that "a nip or two" would help him to get the church matters settled better. He dated but not steadily, and he found that "parties" only increased his anxiety after they were over. He swore he would never see a psychiatrist, but as he began to feel somewhat more calm and effective on his job, he began to push the counselor for permission to rejoin the seminary group in order to keep his promise and make amends to God. He felt this would be the only way to regain peace of mind.

Psychoanalysts will see in this patient a clear example of repressed guilt feelings, self-condemnation, and recurrent "reparatory needs." Although the patient did later subject himself to psychoanalysis, he never quite rid himself of the deep-seated need for repentance and making reparation. What seems to have helped him more than anything during these earlier counseling sessions was the support of his religious counselor who gradually led him to see new purposes in life, to undertake and successfully complete tasks in which his own self-worth and self-respect were enhanced to a considerable degree.

The young man actually did get rid of his obsessive compulsive symptoms, but he did not radically resolve his guilt feelings about his father and sisters. Obviously, the religious counselor could never approve of his return to seminary life; he did, however, help him secure a position that satisfied the client's religious needs: teaching in a religious setting. Meanwhile, after six or seven months of weekly counseling, the patient gave up teaching and was promoted to a responsible position in his firm as a management consultant. But his health became noticeably worse. New symptoms began to replace the old ones at the thought of leaving home and his counselor. Memory lapses, although barely noticeable to others, became more troublesome. The young man became almost obsessed with the fear of "going batty" and grew more and more determined to keep his promise to be a priest.

> Many of my other symptoms are better, but my heart suddenly flares up so violently at times that I just have to leave work and call you for an appointment. I saw the family physician, and he says I'm O.K. He suggests a week at my sister's cottage, but I can't leave work. Do you really think my self-concept is a healthy one? Do you think one can actually recognize a big sin when he commits one? I never

know for sure about my thoughts—did I or did I not consent? Why can't I do as I know I ought—just realize my self-worth as a human being and forget this self-torture and doing penance? But then not to do penance would surely not make me any more worthwhile in my own eyes. I think I need a better father figure than my dad, or even you. And perhaps I never will live down the loss of my mother. I am following the plan we drew up: when the doubts arise, I picture myself doing something really good, like being a missionary in Africa. Sometimes it helps; sometimes it makes it worse. I do profit a good deal from reading about mental illness and trying to help others. I think I would make a good psychiatrist if I cannot be a priest.

Notice his more frequent reference to his increased self-worth as decreasing his need for doing penance. His analysis of the "consent" act to a big sin or a little one is typical of religiously misguided souls who try to divide sharply in their own minds the status of a person in a state of mortal sin (*Todtsuende*) from that of one with minor imperfections. The case also clearly reveals the oddity whereby neurotics can magnify minutiae out of all proportions: They strain at a gnat and swallow a camel and can't see the forest for the trees!

After a year of maintaining this condition, his work required him to move to another city; he could barely bring himself to accept his advancement to a higher position as instructor in management with a good salary. The counselor moved him practically bodily to the distant city and arranged a joint counselor situation for him with a trusted priest (not yet fully trained) and a psychiatrist with analytical orientation. Weeks passed with nothing but favorable reports from the client. One remark in a letter is significant: "What I like about this therapist is that he does not try to reduce everything to sex. He does want me to date, though, and finally convinced me I can find my vocation in works similar to religion rather than in the actual priesthood."

This case was a difficult one for a nonmedical counselor to handle. It is doubtful, however, whether a medical man could have done much for the client without the collaboration of the religious counselor. The case presents some typical instances of failure to adjust to home and school situations, with a corresponding trend toward symptoms (defense mechanisms) that would enable the client to keep up his appearance of being the large, healthy, young intellectual that he is. The reader will have noticed also that the client shifted from a stage in which symptoms were his main problem to one in which deeper life problems were his main concern—mainly his doubt about his worth as a person. In the earlier stage, he was inclined to attempt a purely intellectual solution to his problems, paying only a sort of lip service to the deeper emotional needs of his nature. As he grew older and had to face new and more complicated work problems and to take his place as a "leader" of men in the industrial field, his inner states of anxiety and inadequacy came to the fore. Periodically he was carried along by supportive therapy, both by his religious counselors and later by his psychiatrist.

Approximately three years after the client had left his home for the East, he moved again, to become Dean of the Business School of a midwestern university. He had been seen once a week by a psychiatrist during this period. On his return to the Midwest, he visited his former priest-counselor for an interview, from which the following is quoted:

> The real reason for seeing you at this time is that I believe I have come to a sort of crisis or turning point. You seem to be the only one I can really talk to. I do not want to re-establish a therapeutic dependency, but I wanted to tell you about a dream. For months I had been feeling guilty for never having prepared the teaching materials on scrupulosity for your project. I didn't want to face you and admit this. My dream has repeated itself on several occasions. In it, I always came to see you, but all I could see was the back of your black coat, collar, and head. Then there was something about a transfusion. You turned around, and it wasn't you as you are now, but a much younger man. Then I awoke and asked myself what it meant. The immediate answer was: "from father to brother." Then there was a sense of relaxation and the fear was gone. I guess this means I have changed from a state of total neurotic dependency on you to one of mature dependency.

The technical teaching material he promised to send the counselor was merely notes and dialogues the client had recorded during his own brief teaching experiences at the university.

The dream here recorded is only one of many that this man related, not at the request of the counselor, but merely by reason of the fact that this morbid, intellectual, isolated neurotic was obsessed by the idea that dreams had a meaning. We see here some consequences of the three years of psychotherapy. The young man now knew what some of the items in his dreams meant. He was striving mightily to live down his "childish dependency" on father figures.

The patient then enumerated a whole series of religious difficulties, such as worry about sorrow for sin, certainty of state of grace, and repentance. His enumeration suggested a thoroughly confused and anxious person who could scarcely judge his mental acts sufficiently well to be capable of a serious sin. Yet it would do no good to tell him this. It did seem, at this time, that he had made some progress with the psychiatrist over the three years. The man now felt somewhat strong, daring enough to admit his own confusion and dependency. Before he had been more despairingly self-assertive, saying in effect: "God cannot do this to me."

The patient recalled his doubts about faith from the time when they had centered chiefly around the genuineness and truth of Christianity. His theoretical doubts spilled over into the practical order. He would reason with himself about the futility and stupidity of attending church services, of abstaining and fasting as prescribed, of bothering about the commandments. It seemed equally meaningless to deny the senses, to practice mortification, to make reparation, or to strive for union with God. This whole business was, to use his expression, "cold, austere, and uninviting," and did not seem to square with the facts.

Fortunately the psychiatrist never thought it practical to argue with this client about values and the like. He allowed and even urged the client to abide by the decisions of his religious counselor. Though not of the same faith as his client, the therapist kept an attitude of calm indifference to all the religious issues raised. Had he done otherwise, no one can say what the outcome might have been. Our patient ran across the kind of writers who fortunately supplemented the work of counselor and therapist.

Next, he described in telling terms the sad but revealing story of his turn for the better he had mentioned in his previous interview:

> Where to begin? I don't remember when I began doing this, but for several years, whenever the anxiety used to get bad or some problem was bothering me and I thought I was losing perspective, I would go through a little formula. God created me; God created man; man sinned and the gates of heaven were closed; Christ came as a Redeemer with the Gospel. What is this "good news"? It seemed to help to put my little problem into perspective and to reduce the anxiety. It was also a new way of asking my question of nineteen (eight years before) or a little after: What is Christianity? At that time, I sensed that it must be something more than what it meant for me and what it seemed to so many of those around me.
>
> As time went on, I would think about each section in *Love or Constraint* by Marc Oraison in which in a few pages he made clear for me something all of us have heard a thousand times: That we should be sorry for and avoid sin because it breaks the bond with God, rather than because of the fear of hell. In this section he wrote of God's love for man. Well, every night for some time—and it's

difficult to put dates on this—before going to sleep I would think about this fact. Then gradually—or I suppose rather abruptly—one day it all made sense. Out of his Love, God did create man.

The patient seemed to want to keep on repeating the fact that the experience just related was critical, of the nature of a basic insight. From it came a whole series of reflections regarding the past, present, and future. The fragments, he said, seemed to be coming together.

In the next interview he discussed briefly the girl he occasionally dated, then immediately said that his old friends, the neurotic symptoms, kept coming back, but mildly now. (Notice he called them "friends," as if he loved them). He felt now that he was in the command of the symptoms, rather than the opposite. "If they go away, fine," he said, "if not, all right, too."

Many weeks were required to accomplish these changes. He had felt impelled to go into "a desert place" and do penance. Now he felt only a need to "help people" and even to share "communion" with them. His job had always been "only anxiety producing," but now "to use one's skills and knowledge seems like fun." Frankly he admitted his occasional confusion when engaged in unfamiliar tasks (the old fear of loss of memory). Then he again would become bothered by doubts about God. How can He sustain the world? Why does so perfect a being bother Himself about us? Finally, he had begun to get a wee bit outside himself. He summarized:

> Out of the above skeleton I can spin in my mind the ideas on which to base the patterns of the "new world," the ways to go about it, the redefinitions, etc. Of course, I have ideas about almost everything! The bits and pieces of things I've read over the past several years come back, and I want to relate them to the things I learned earlier. I get excited when I read Guardini, Oraison, and de Chardin. I get the feeling I want just to walk out of my apartment some morning, lock the door, and seek the new life (imitation of Christ, the perfect self-immolation).
>
> But even as I let myself go and write like that, I know that it's the easy way. People today just don't think like that and do these things. The above is the "stranger" speaking, that I mentioned earlier. And the record—my record—offers little foundation for the aspirations. My academic record doesn't bespeak a good mind; my working life is somewhat mediocre; I'm only a few drinks away from all the old ways; no publications, poor memory, scruples, some emotional malfunctioning, etc. This is the person I am. Even when I recently "found" these new thoughts, I felt I should do something, just to prove their reality. I thought of giving up liquor, but told myself it

now didn't play a big part in my life and wouldn't really be a sacrifice. Then cigarettes—but I discarded that because I'd be giving these up for fear of cancer. I hit upon the idea—bright, ain't I?—of going to church in the morning, not so much for the difficulty involved in getting up, but for the spiritual benefits. You know how many times I've gone the 250 feet to do this? Zero times.

Actually he was never more than a social drinker, and he was quite capable of teaching a college class successfully.

Now the interviews turned again to his phantasms, daydreams most probably, but also night dreams. He said:

> So I keep asking myself, what is the best route for me? At times I feel it is only by making a clean break with the present way. I have never mentioned to you, I believe, a kind of phantasm I've had for a number of years. I don't know whether it was a dream originally or not, or how it came about. I see myself in kind of a bleak desert, writhing in dust, trying to rid myself, I guess, of the past and the guilt. It always seems to be in the southwest U.S., and I say: "See"— but I don't mean see, really—because it is too closely attached to some feeling.

Though still guilt ridden, he now sees himself actively doing something about it while yet expressing a healthy kind of helplessness, writhing in the dust of his felt inadequacy. Truly he is an ill person; yet, no one on earth seemed to be able to help him until he was able to learn how to help himself grow. He had to grow out of years of devastating and desolate experience and grow into a new and more acceptable pattern of living, one that to him was the real self.

We may say that our client had made steady progress toward removing the sad effects of his unhappy childhood and of the terrific shock experienced in the war. He had promised to devote himself to religion if he got out of that mess alive. He had then, as now, felt irrational guilt for childhood remissness, as well as for unkindness toward his buddies who were killed; as a result, he felt a deep need to make amends.

His fear of accepting adult responsibility remained until he was thirty. This fear was accompanied by a nagging self-blame for not carrying out his better resolutions, not devoting himself to the salvation of others. When the demands of his new job became unbearable, he almost suffered a complete break with reality, and a complete change of environment was needed to rehabilitate him. Fortunately this change proved successful, but the patient keeps up a continuing relationship with both the pastoral counselor and the psychotherapist, and only God can tell which is more effective.

It would seem that the aids which religion supplied were minimal. But the need for them was precipitated by the early and prolonged stress states that he endured precisely by reason of his peculiar use of such aids. It will help to go back over this diary to highlight the main points of method used in this and countless other cases treated by means of essential therapy. It was emphasized earlier that this method is based on a particular set of philosophical principles concerning the nature and destiny of man. It was also stressed that each individual man uses or can use reflection and comparison as tools for arriving at these principles; and, once he has arrived at the notion that he has a unique dignity and a place in the world of men which no one on earth can deprive him of and in which he can learn to tolerate stress as a means for ego strength, then he derives new meaning out of existence and strives to fulfill his destiny, to play his role, to activate his capacities for other motives besides passing pleasures. He gets real existential gratifications and even earthly rewards precisely out of working hourly toward an end or goal that defies temporal analysis, which is in the true sense out of this world or timeless.

In the case that we are presently considering, the counselor had been approaching the counselee as a creature of God, struggling with various existential stresses and misdevelopments in his personality reactions, to help him to live out and finally realize the essential, eternal purpose, namely, the alignment with God's will for him. The counselor was congruous in his contacts with the client as both of them were embedded in the same essential condition, that is, they were both carried in the ongoing stream of reality both in its existential and its essential aspects. In this respect, psychotherapy is considered basically a function of neither counselor nor the client but of the Creator working through both the client and the counselor. The counselor and the client are co-workers, while the prompting of the Creator within them is among the chief factors acting therapeutically. The technique itself becomes unimportant; what matters most is the religious awareness and the existential trust and patience in both counselor and client, to let the Creator work in both of them.

The client was burdened from earliest childhood with fears of losing his mind, with anger and hostility to parents and God alike, as well as toward their substitutes and psychiatrists; he was perhaps overly attached to his sister who was drowned; he could himself never quite be sure he had not committed the "unpardonable sin"; he could not face the reality of sex and set up very rigid defenses against it. But he could never quite come to feel that his own failures had been forgiven. Hence, one of the best remedies for guilt in the healthy man, namely, repentance with forgiveness as a consequence, was denied him. In essential therapy we are absolutely convinced that man will never face his normal amount of trials and tribulations unless he somehow accepts them as the lot of every normal, healthy individual; unless he in all humility admits he has somehow failed in duties to himself, God, and his fellow man, but that he can by his own will and intention be freed of the guilt before God, that he can repent and will be truly forgiven. This gift is the greatest of all the gifts of religion to all men of all times. And this seems to be the one that is most often rejected by the obsessive–compulsive neurotic.

This perfectionistic young man always seemed to want to be or become more Catholic than the Catholic Church. Many neurotic religious persons develop patterns of behavior similar to his. The compulsion to self-blame characterizes scrupulous persons of many faiths, but such morbid guilt feelings as this man experienced certainly could not have been derived from a proper training in the principles of his own belief. Persons like this seem to wish to make over entirely the human natures with which they were born. Their religion teaches them instead to try to develop their own potential to its fullest. The nature of man, according to Catholic doctrine, is essentially good in itself, though limited in countless ways by reason of the behavior of human beings in general and by reason of the environments in which a human being finds himself.

THE RELIGIOUS MATRIX OF ESSENTIAL THERAPIES

We shall sketch the Catholic position on morals and education in order to demonstrate that it could not be interpreted as fostering the type of compulsive scrupulosity found in the present case. In fact, if its doctrines were adequately comprehended and applied from childhood to maturity, the human being should develop a great, nay, an unlimited, backlog of peace and calm. This calm would be the natural accompaniment of that limitless confidence in the aids that religion can give him. There will be a self-assurance and ego strength that will bolster him up in times of stress and strain, that will push him forward in his endeavors to cope with the disappointments of life. It will enable him to renew his resolutions to work toward fulfilling his destiny, in a period of enlightened existence, which makes very serious demands on him at every turn. Part of the demand arises from the fact of life itself, which is a striving ever and anon with the forces that would tend to destroy it. Man lives only by resisting such forces. In addition, he must cope with social forces in order to adjust to the changing times and situations in which he finds himself. Lastly, he must carry out his existence in a continual kind of inner environment loosely called psychological.

Man could, theoretically, derive much joy and satisfaction from meeting his various socio-psycho-biological needs. But as a matter of cold fact, there is usually a good deal of stress and conflict in the process. Every Catholic knows, and is continually being taught, that he can cope with these conditions in a way that will bring about his ultimate happiness and conduce to the common good of humanity. This doctrine, which Catholics are taught by their church from their earliest days, is the same one which Jesus Christ came on earth to teach by his words and example. He emphasized the need for self-denial and suffering. Many of our contemporaries have not understood that the ego strength that one develops through suffering enables man to keep his sanity and sense of security under stresses of all sorts.

Thus religion is not a mere series of don'ts and restrictions, but a secret source of support for the Catholic. Through it he gains feelings of self-worth based upon his newly gained ego strength. He understands that growing in Christian perfection implies both removal of faults and acquisition of virtues. Virtues imply rather permanent modification of his inner powers and dispositions, and actualization of his latent potential. He knows that one way of acquiring these virtues is to strive to share deeply the experiences of his brethren, to communicate his secret self to them, to show these inner dispositions by means of charitable deeds and corporate worship; all this in the service of the Divine Majesty.

Christian asceticism, as practiced by Catholics, carries the application of these principles in regard to healthy development and perfect dedication to God in this life to their logical conclusions. This is achieved by man in a life of total self-surrender, of complete self-annihilation, in an endless immersion of the self in the divine. He does all this for the sake of carrying out the total plan that God had in creating man. This plan is the spreading of the kingdom of God among men, thus to give glory to God their Father, in heaven, for ever and ever.

After being accepted into the Church of Christ through the purifying waters of baptism, the human being becomes entitled to receive all the other sacraments. Each of these was instituted by Christ for a special purpose, and all for the benefit of man. Each one gives strength and support for very special conditions of living. Confession and communion are the first to be taught the child. In the first, the child learns that his failures to do the good thing can be forgiven, provided certain conditions are fulfilled. He, the sinner, must do something in order to gain forgiveness. He must first of all change his mind, and after admitting that he has done wrong, promise to try to do better in the future. In case some other person has been injured by his fault, he must try to undo the wrong in so far as he is able. This is the notion of repentance, which the small child easily grasps. Far from being a source of self-torture, the acts of reparation that he performs give real internal satisfaction—as every pastor of souls realizes—particularly to small children.

Yet as the child grows older he also realizes that it will be difficult to be sure that he has sufficiently repaired the wrongs he may have done to others. He will also arrive at the great truth of Christianity, that man, if left to himself, could never adequately repair the injury done to God by a deliberate, serious, human fault. He will have to rely upon the infinite merits of our Lord and Savior Jesus Christ. Thus the child grows in the knowledge of two things: first, man is helpless by himself; second, with the aid and intercession of Christ he can do all this and more. Thus we see that altogether apart from the consolation in the natural order, which a sinner may receive by declaring his faults to another ordained human being in the sacrament of confession, there is the notion of divine forgiveness. The confessor, acting in the name of Christ, forgives man his fault, provided he is properly disposed; that is, provided he is earnest and sincere in his desire to improve himself.

Along with the teaching of confession, the child is given instruction on the meaning of the sacrament of love called Holy Communion. Usually he will wait some time before being admitted to this heavenly banquet. This sacrament is the sharing of the boundless love of God by receiving the Eucharist, or the banquet of love. This commemorative banquet is really a continuation of the supreme act of redemption Christ performed on the cross. The early reception of this heavenly banquet gives the budding Christian his first sense of being a true Christian by participation and sharing, of becoming one with Christ and the whole mystical body of the church, of communicating with

God and fellow man in a most real sense. In a mysterious but very real sense man is taking on a nature higher than his own could ever be; yet, the frequent reception of the Sacrament of Love, the agape of the early Christians, the caritas of the modern theologian, helps man to fulfill his need for constant colloquy with God, with his fellow man, and for confrontation with his inner self. This communion—union with—God, man, and all creatures through the gifts of altar bread and wine, this sublime act gives the Catholic and Christian his power to go on striving against the forces of evil in the world and in himself, to continue to live and labor for God and his fellow man. Such psychological orientation is therapeutic, as many lay psychotherapists have recognized. The real presence of Christ on our altars, through the consecration of the mass, gives the communion a heightened relevance. Its efficacy for Christians can never be overestimated, for the blessed sacrament of the altar helps the person to become really at home here on this earth with God his Father, and, by thus closely living with God, he is better able to incorporate the spirit of Christ and the Eucharist into his daily life.

In the sacrament of confirmation, the Christian gets strength to bear up under persecutions and adversities, to resist evil, and to lead a good life in spite of perplexing temptations during the hectic period of puberty and adolescence. Increased resistance to suffering is symbolized by the act of receiving a blow on the cheek from the bishop and the anointing on the forehead with holy oil. Thus the same anointing which in baptism gave the child its first token of cleansing, and his first promise of strength, now becomes an added assurance of solace and of support while the elder adolescent strives to grow in all the virtues that should characterize a Christian in the various walks of life. We can discern the features of both preventive and actual psychotherapy in these practices of the faithful.

The sacrament of matrimony is the one that youth awaits with all the eagerness and anxiety that a modern society can engender. The Church which Christ founded did, and always will, seek to prepare its members for this great sacrament by encouraging diligent self-study and analysis in preparation for the great act. She urges them to reflect on what a great privilege it is to cooperate with God in the creating of a new soul and on the responsibilities connected with this new state in life. To prepare youth, especially today in the age of pragmatism and experimentalism, for undertaking a lifelong vocation of service to God in the married state is never easy. All the aids of prayer and the sacraments will not be too much, for indeed it is a serious thing in the life of a man when he gives himself up to another human being in the closest union possible to human beings for a period of time to be determined only by God himself. This prospect cannot but have its problems and challenges for a modern couple. They will need all the aids of the sacraments and more in order that they may be able to go through their lives in true fidelity to each other and in helping to fulfill the destiny of those around them, in spreading God's kingdom. They are taught that they are being chosen by God in a special way and that they are to cooperate with their creator in continuing the human family in the kingdom of God and the service of His divine majesty. We can expect that such stabilization of marital relationship will have a wholesome effect on the over-all psychological functioning of the faithful.

The sacrament whereby priests become dedicated for life, by their bishops, to the service of humanity in the Catholic Church is called Holy Orders. Again the symbols used to express the meaning of this vocation are oil and chrism. These, together with the imposition of hands upon the candidates by their superiors and equals, signify the help that the candidates will receive in the execution of the duties in their new way of life. Not only are the ministers of God warned of their obligation to serve humanity, by administering the sacraments to every human being whenever they are needed, but especially they are prepared to go to their flock in times of stress, and particularly in their members' final moments on this earth. They are urged to lead lives of self-denial in order that by developing strength of character they may be able to achieve this arduous task and may persevere until death in their chosen vocation. The greatest self-denial of all is, of course, the voluntary relinquishment of the sexual pleasures of married life, which are legitimate for persons in other states of life. In this regard all Christians worthy of the name surely know that priests and bishops are called upon to imitate, as closely as possible, Christ their model, who chose to remain unmarried until death. So, too, the ordained ministers in the Catholic Church must be ready to sacrifice their own personal interests in the service of the faithful, even if their duties should require of them the supreme sacrifice of their very lives.

Lastly, there is the Sacrament of the Afflicted, also called the Sacrament of the Last Anointing or Extreme Unction. In every stage of human existence the pastor of souls will be called upon to live in close union with the members of his flock in order to be easily available to them in administering to their spiritual as well as other needs. He encourages them to bear up under life's burdens and to maintain courage and cheerfulness even under the gravest kinds of afflictions. There is no doubt that he helps them gain a new kind of support, a new type of personal strength and security in struggling through the ordinary difficulties of living, a new solace in enduring illness and affliction in a way that no other person can do. As a matter of simple statistics, research has shown that people take their troubles most frequently to their pastors and only secondly to their physicians and psychiatrists.

People, then, are somehow trained in our day, to expect that their pastors will stand by them in their hours of greatest need when they are coming face to face with their creator and supreme benefactor for all eternity, their God and Master, Jesus Christ. The sacrament of the last anointing is the one in which the beloved pastor is able to give his singular kind of help to the souls of men. Only one who has stood in the role of the minister of this holy sacrament to the person who has been prepared during his life with regard to its meaning and purpose, can appreciate this next remark: afflicted souls literally glory exceedingly and are elated beyond understanding and description in the thought which their religion supplies them, namely, that their Lord and Master awaits them across the borders of death, that He is there always yearning to take them into His own blessed arms and to keep them there forever in a life of ecstatic joys and satiating peace and serenity.

This, then, summarizes the Catholic doctrine on the therapeutic value of prayers and sacraments for the rightly informed Catholic. There is, always has been, and always will be incomparable peace, hope, and security beyond human comprehension in the thought of the eternal bliss of heaven; such hoped-for rewards are not the aftermath or natural accompaniment of any kind of attainment or achievement man arrives at in this temporal form of human existence.

Lest the reader imagine that the above remarks are pure speculations on the part of a Christian, with regard to the role of religion in the developmental process, some empirical justifications will now be provided. At least four sources of this kind of evidence may be given:

1. Several thousand years of experience of priests and ministers, Catholic and Protestant alike, in the application of these principles. The work of the Academy of Religion and Mental Health and the *Journal of Religion and Health* bear witness to our statements. In almost any issue of this journal, one may find objective descriptions of the efficacy of religious training for safeguarding mental health. The

Academy is, as is well-known, multifaith as well as inter-disciplinary.

2. The special kind of service Catholics have been giving to their country in the military, as well as with their conspicuous representation on the Federal Bureau of Investigation (FBI). High-ranking naval officers and selection officers for the FBI have dozens of times told me that they prefer Catholics, with a sense of honesty, decency, and dedication to their religion, for the most responsible positions in these two important organizations of defense. They also give figures showing that Roman Catholics have been represented in the Navy and the FBI in much greater numbers than their general percentage representation in the country would justify.

3. In Belgium a series of empirical studies have been in progress for over a generation, collecting exact information through follow-up studies on the role of religion in maintaining mental health. The studies also stress the efficacy of various forms of the sacred liturgy and various teaching methods toward the same end. They make a strong case for the role that is played by religion in preventing mental disturbance and maladjustments. The work is similar to and corroborative of that of the Center of Character Studies in Schenectady, New York. The latter was founded by the Episcopalian minister, Rev. Dr. Ernest Ligon, who combined his ministry with training in psychology. The staff for the Catholic studies resides in Belgium and is responsible for continuing the existence of the International Center for Religious Education.[1] This organization has carried out numerous empirical studies, projective tests, attitude measurements, and the like, attempting to discern which forms of religious instruction are best suited for healthy spiritual and moral development.

4. The Catholic University of America has sponsored many research programs the purpose of which was to study the effectiveness of religion in preserving mental health and in preventing mental illness.[2]

---

[1] The center has its headquarters in Brussels, Belgium, but its journal, *Lumen Vitae,* has been published bimonthly in English, French, and German. The United States distributor for it is the Newman Bookshop, Westminster, Maryland. The Canadian address is Avenue Papineau, Montreal, 34, and the address for Great Britain is Duckett, 140, Strand, London, W.C. 2.

[2] Thought-provoking research gives the distribution of the various types of mental illnesses of Catholics compared to that of other religious denominations (9). Several other similar studies are in progress there and in various other Mental Health Centers, notably St. Elizabeth's in Washington, D.C. A rather full account of the relationship between religion and mental health may be found in Herr (7, 8) under the title "Sacraments and Sin" and in Zilboorg (12), especially pages 185–189.

REFERENCES

1. Allport, G. W. *Personality: a psychological interpretation.* New York: Holt, 1937.
2. Allport, G. W. *The individual and his religion.* New York: Macmillan, 1950.
3. Arnold, M. B., & Gasson, J. A. Logotherapy and existential analysis. In *The human person.* New York: Ronald Press, 1954. Pp. 462–492.
4. Binswanger, L. Existential analysis and psychotherapy. In Frieda Fromm-Reichman & J. L. Moreno (Eds.), *Progress in psychotherapy.* New York: Grune and Stratton, 1956. Pp. 144–148.
5. Frankl, V. E. *From death camp to existentialism: a psychiatrist's path to a new therapy.* Boston: Beacon Press, 1959.
6. Frankl, V. E. Psychiatry and man's quest for meaning. *J. Relig. Health,* 1962, **1,** 93–103.
7. Herr, V. V. In S. W. Standal & R. J. Corsini (Eds.), *Critical incidents in psychotherapy.* New York: Prentice Hall, 1958.
8. Herr, V. V. *Religious psychology.* Staten Island, New York: Alba House, 1964. Pp. 189–202.
9. Jarreiss, W. D. Some influences of Catholic education and creed upon psychotic reactions. *Diseases Nerv. Sys.,* 1942, **3,** 377–381.
10. May, R. *Existential psychotherapy.* New York: Random House, 1961.
11. May, R., Angle, E., & Ellenberger, V. F. (Eds.) *Existentialism: a new dimension in psychiatry and psychology.* New York: Basic Books, 1958.
12. Zilboorg, G. *Psychoanalysis and religion.* New York: Farrar, Straus and Cudahy, 1962. Pp. 185–189.

Chapter 25

Spiritual Therapy
with "Alcoholics"

GEORGE W. BURROUGHS

George W. Burroughs: b. 1908, Richmond, Virginia.
B.A., history and education, University of Richmond, 1928. M.S., applied
psychology, Richmond Professional Institute, 1964. T. C. Williams
School of Law, 1944. Union Theological Seminary, 1956. Yale Summer
School of Alcohol Studies, 1958.
Founder and Executive Director: Richmond Council on Alcoholism, 1959–
date; Professional Counseling Service, Victoria, Virginia, 1965–date.
Co-founder and Executive Director: Advisory Board, Norfolk Council
on Alcoholism, 1960–1966; Pastor, McGuire United Methodist Church,
Victoria, Virginia, 1967–69; Pastor, First United Methodist Church,
1969–1970, Winchester, Virginia.
Books: *Spiritually Oriented Counseling and Psychotherapy in Problems
of Alcoholism* (1963).

Cured of "alcoholism" through spiritual therapy, I would like to
share with the reader concepts, procedures, methods, and techniques
derived from introspection and fourteen years' practice of spiritual
therapy with "alcoholics." The lives of thousands of cured alcoholics
have been transformed with the effectiveness of spiritual therapy. It
accepts, without qualification, metaphysical concepts and acknowledges Divine participation in the behavior of man.

REALITY OF THE SOUL

The actuality of spiritual illness (soul sickness) necessitates as a
prerequisite the reality of the soul. The postulate of the reality of the
soul is not new to philosophy or psychology. Implicitly or explicitly it
has been in the forefront of philosophy since Aristotle. Descartes, a
great name in the psychology of the Renaissance, not only recognized
the soul as an entity outside of spatial order, but he located the "seat
of the Soul" in the pineal gland. Spinoza believed that the soul and
body were ultimately one, two aspects of one reality.

717

Historical and contemporary scientists as a body reject metaphysical concepts as unsubstantial and thus unsuited for scientific therapy. The physical and the solid, to them these are the real and substantial. We believe that the day will come as a result of research in such new areas as nuclear fission, which demonstrate that "physical matter" is not real and indestructible, when scientists will recognize that only spiritual forces represent "true reality"; recognizable and assessable, and although incapable of scientific weighing and measuring with present-day tools, yet these spiritual forces are not subject to physical destruction. Scientific thinking that the whole of life is a "closed system" (cause and effect process that denies metaphysical interferences) will expand to accept divine intervention in the behavior of man.

SPIRITUAL ILLNESS

Spiritual therapy not only accepts the reality of the soul but postulates a sick soul that needs, seeks, and is amenable to therapeutic therapy. Spiritual illness can best be understood in the light of spiritual health as evidenced in a "fully functioning person," i.e., a person who is in the process of attaining self-actualization. According to the Bible (Gen. 1:27) every person is born with the "image of God" (soul) as the integral part of his Being; the potentiality of "oneness with God and Other." Potentiality embraces self-actualization; a dynamic striving, with compulsion and capacity to effectuate itself, to reach fulfillment. God's revealed desire and will is that every person achieve this potentiality. This achievement can be described as spiritual homeostasis that is vital to the realization of self-actualization. Spiritual homeostasis is the perfect balance in love (agape) relationships between a person and God and between a person and his brother. This concept of spiritual homeostasis is akin to the concept touched upon by Karl Menninger and his co-authors in their 1963 publication, *Vital Balance.*

Spiritual illness is the disruption of spiritual homeostasis. Violation of the laws of God set forth in the Bible concerning human behavior disturb spiritual homeostasis; self-actualization is impeded or blocked; capability of the soul to function as designed is impaired, and the soul in finite language is "sick." The overt manifestation of a sick soul is progressive personality deterioration; covertly it is experienced as excruciating and unbearable pain. This pain varies in intensity from tinges of anxiety to literal "hell on earth." The pains of a sick soul are guilt; remorse; self-abasement; acute anxiety; conflict; estrangement from God, self, and others; hopelessness; meaninglessness of life; and neurotic fear.

When the spiritual homeostasis is disrupted, all physiological and psychological defense mechanisms of the organism are fully mobilized to combat it, but to no avail.

Spiritual illness is self-inflicted. It is the outgrowth of a choice to serve self, with all the attendant suffering, rather than serving God. Why does man make such a choice? Actually he does not, but he attempts to serve both God and man, to have his cake and eat it. He rejects the responsibility of exercising his courage to "Be"—to forget self; to make God central and "self" peripheral in his person. Unfortunately this action does not meet his spiritual needs, neither does an overt professed allegiance to God, with inner self-direction, suffice. He cannot escape the guilt ensuing from his awareness of what he actually is and what is demanded by his self-actualization. He is a spiritually ill person.

A fundamental concept of this paper is that man has "free will," the unique capacity to modify, to redirect his self-actualization within the limits of his finiteness. This capacity carries with it the obligation to make choices; a responsibility that cannot be evaded. If his choice is to serve God, self-actualization will be achieved, and he will be a spiritually healthy and fully functioning person. He will experience a life of "freedom" from guilt and neurotic anxiety, well able to embrace existential anxiety; he will know serenity, peace of mind, and security in all its significance. To attain and maintain such health (spiritual homeostasis) simply requires one to love God and to love one's fellow man. When we use the word love we refer to *"agape,"* not *"eros,"* not *"caritas."* Disintegration of love within man is indicative of his disintegration of love for the divine, resulting in alienation from self, his fellow man, and God, with subsequent guilt, real guilt.

ALCOHOLISM IS SPIRITUAL ILLNESS

Inability to communicate—the lack of a common basic frame of reference—presents unsurmounted barriers to solutions for problems of alcoholism. Definitions show marked variances from discipline to discipline and among individuals in each and are quite often subjectively defined. A striking example is the term "alcoholism" with its galaxy of definitions.

We postulate that alcoholism is an illness: not physiological, not biological, not psychological, but spiritual. Neither medical treatment nor psychotherapy offer surcease unless spiritually oriented. From our perspective alcoholism is basically a "spiritual illness"—the manifestation of a sick soul. The chemical, alcohol, is not the originating factor of the illness; it does enhance the symptoms. Alcohol is the medicine, usually, but not always self-prescribed, that an individual (man or woman) suffering from out-of-balance spiritual homeostasis takes to alleviate the pains of a sick soul. Alcoholism is the condition of an individual who takes the drug alcohol as a remedy for a sick soul. What one might term "excessive consumption" is an indication of the intensity of spiritual homeostatic disorganization.

With due acknowledgment of the sincere and concerned effort of the medical disciplines to isolate and treat the "alcoholic" on the basis of medical etiology, incontrovertible evidence demonstrates that the exclusively medically oriented approach is not effective. The etiology of alcoholism is not in the medical domain but in the spiritual.

We do not recognize the validity of alcoholism as medically defined, thus it follows that we hold that there is no such person as an alcoholic. An individual who turns to alcohol to meet his basic need is labeled an alcoholic and eventually is stigmatized, persecuted, and rejected, becoming the "leper" of modern society. Paradoxically, a person who uses a tranquilizer to fulfill the same basic need is not labeled a tranquilizeric on the basis of the medicine he takes, neither is he persecuted nor rejected. Apparently the concern of society has been met, not when the ill person has recovered, but when the medicine used to treat the symptom does not result in behavior considered to be a threat to social, economic, or physical security or does not create an offensive stench to its nostrils. We identify an alcoholic as "an individual who resorts to alcohol, any type or amount, to meet basic spiritual needs."

SPIRITUAL THERAPY CURES ALCOHOLICS

Background

Alcoholism, today, is considered by competent authorities to be the third-ranking health problem of the country, with the prognosis that it will be in first place in the 1970s. Psychological, medical, and psychiatric treatment have proven to be ineffective in decreasing the incidence of alcoholism, which is growing at the rate of 1,000 new cases a day.

Present-day thinking looks upon alcoholism as the symptom of an underlying personality disorder. The growing concept that the etiology of such "personality disorder" is spiritual is gaining support. Jellinek (7) says that although it is important to stress the medical nature of the alcohol problem it would be a mistake to disregard the moral aspect. Frankl (5) maintains that a man lives in three dimensions: the somatic, the mental, and the spiritual, and that psychotherapy has given too little attention to the reality of the spiritual. Blake (1) proposes a fourth category of personality needs—"a spiritual need." The British Medical Association (2) issued a report stating:

> It is a matter of history and experience that a religious conversion, in which there is a complete upheaval of the emotional life of the patient, is capable not only of reorientating his whole mode of living, but of curing various forms of neurosis, alcoholism and other functional disorders. This corresponds to abreaction in analysis. It appears to do this by removing the causative factors which contribute so largely to the neurotic temperament. The patient loses his self-centeredness and becomes freed from such emotions as fear, guilt and resentment, and from the grip of indulgences. He also acquires a peace of mind and contentment which to a large extent removes the effects of strain and stress. Conversion basically operates through a change in motives and will, and by giving the patient a personal faith that God can satisfy his deepest needs, gives him adequate purpose in life and supports him in adversity.

Seliger sees the philosophy of religion as universal law, and he has observed the curative value of these laws at work and also the tragedy when ignored. He says, "Within the framework of these laws, lies a way of life that we must have, if we live at all, and not merely exist as moral cripples and stretcher cases" (11). In recognition and application of these laws the British Medical Association identifies "vague spiritual desires" as a symptom of chronic alcoholism and "spiritual needs examined" as a basic step in therapy. Clinebell (3) points out that a religious approach offers a "spiritual substitute" for alcohol, and the ability to provide such a substitute is the most important advantage that a religious approach has over a nonreligious one. The Georgia Commission on Alcoholism (6), after seven years of experience, states that the medical, religious, and psychiatric phases of treatment should be closely integrated and given equal emphasis. Alcoholics Anonymous (A.A.) offers indisputable evidence of the reality of the effectiveness of spiritual therapy in problems of alcoholism. To disregard spiritual therapy because its practice does not follow accepted scientific procedure would be a shortsighted waste of data. It can be said, without fear of contradiction, that spiritual therapy is accepted by many who are actively engaged in the rehabilitation phase of alcoholism and that it plays an integral part in many private programs, individual and group. These programs have prepared a tremendous amount of material in articles, studies, and reports. Only meager attention has been paid to the techniques of counseling and psychotherapy in problems of alcoholism. The paucity of such information is puzzling in view of the growing number of Councils on Alcoholism, the increase in the number of clinics, and the magnitude of the problem.

Textbook

The basic authority for spiritual therapy is the Bible. It is the record of man's existence, empirically demonstrating over thousands of years the part played by the soul in man's behavior and health. It has demonstrated an universal applicability and appeal to mankind through the ages. The Bible sets forth basic laws governing human behavior, describes the consequence of violating them, and, also of vital importance, offers relief or pardon from the consequences. Spiritual therapy utilizes, implicitly and explicitly, quotations from the Bible, pointing out the laws violated and correlating them with the consequences that can be specifically identified in the situation of the client, at the same time lifting up forgiveness. Dr. Smiley Blanton, M.D., a well-known psychiatrist, says, "It's the greatest textbook on human behavior ever put together. If people would just absorb its message, a lot of us psychiatrists could close our offices and go fishing."

The Goal

Spiritual conversion, not abstinence, is the goal of spiritual therapy; the attainment of spiritual homeostasis. With the attainment of this goal, the client will be a new creature; a fully integrated, happy individual; an individual who once resorted to alcohol to meet basic needs, but now is able and does meet them through spiritual resources. It could be said, and perhaps should be, that the goal of spiritual therapy is the cure of alcoholism.

Alcohol by its capacity to anesthetize and offer pseudotranscendency offers the mirage of cure on the one hand, but its very nature creates a vicious cycle of personality deterioration. Alcohol stops self-actualization for it puts to sleep all there is of the Divine in man. It is an anesthetic for spiritual pains, similar to other tranquilizers, but it does not cure the illness. It only treats the symptoms, and the individual gets progressively worse. Spiritual therapy is concerned with the illness, the Being, the health, and not the mere comfort of the individual.

It is felt that too little attention has been given by psychotherapists to the spiritual reality of man. Spiritual therapy must aim at bringing out the ultimate potentiality of the alcoholic, not to penetrate his darkest secrets but to help him actualize his latent capacity. The aphorism of Goethe, "If we take people as they are, we make them worse. If we treat them as if they were what they ought to be, we help them to become what they are capable of becoming," describes spiritual therapy with alcoholics.

The Therapist

"I can't give you the pearl of truth, I can only tell you where to dig," John Ruskin said. This succinct statement aptly describes the spiritual therapist, who does not embody but only channels the spiritual therapeutic power that flows through him. Far and beyond the intellectual capacity and formal training essential to all effective therapy, the therapist must have a faith based on a personal spiritual experience. Truly he must be a converted man, in its fullest meaning, secure in the belief of divine participation of the spirit in man's behavior, with the capacity to communicate the fruits of such conversion. His personal witness must exemplify the fullness of self-actualization toward which his client is striving. Unless the therapist himself has the spiritual orientation he should not engage in spiritual therapy. The number of active therapists, so qualified, is limited. This is a paradox since although the vast majority of psychologists and psychiatrists have taken formal vows to some religious organization, affirming such a faith, yet many in their "scientific approach" negate it. The therapist must have an objective understanding of the results of scientific findings in the field of alcoholism, supplemented by specific knowledge of other individuals, agencies, and organizations working with the problem to which referrals may be made.

Although the usual training and techniques used in the therapist counseling situation can be used in working with alcoholics, certain special factors must ever be kept in mind. Although the therapist must be a "born again Christian" with a comprehensive knowledge and understanding of the New Testament, it is not necessary that he be a member of the clergy. As a matter of fact, a dedicated layman has the better prognosis of effective therapeutic relationships with alcoholics, since we believe in the royal priesthood of all believers.

Alcoholics have an abounding guilt, real and neurotic. This is frequently projected toward the minister who, in their mind, is God's "executive officer," or at least His "first sergeant." No matter how much skill the minister may develop, and despite evidence of his deep concern for alcoholics, this feeling will usually remain. Many alcoholics would rather have the sheriff come for an arrest rather than the minister for a visit. The minister must accept the fact that initially he may be the last person who should attempt counseling a particular alcoholic and be willing to let others render this service. This is one area where the concept of the priesthood of all believers is a valid reality.

The alcoholic has two potent weapons that destroy the effectiveness of most persons who deal with him: The first is an ability to make the other person angry and to arouse disgust or criticism. If you become angry or irritated when dealing with him, you are defeated the moment your anger appears. The alcoholic is often so convinced of his own failure and lack of worth (yet desperately wants and needs help but resents needing it), and is so filled with self-hatred, that he seeks confirmation of this hatred in others. If you express anger, this action confirms his self-hatred and increases his guilt. Thus he feels he might as well go out and get drunk again—and he frequently does! Regardless of the circumstances, if you lose your temper, you have lost control of the counseling situation.

The second crippling technique employed by the alcoholic is that of putting the horse collar of his anxiety around your neck and getting you to pull the whole load. Moreover, if you let him, he may get on your back and ride. It is well to remember that, if you ever do for him what he should do for himself, you have not helped him, you have hurt him. The minister who can be manipulated into a position of fulfilling dependency needs, or doing things that the alcoholic must ultimately learn to do for himself, is adding further injury to the alcoholic and postponing his day of sobriety.

Sincerity and honesty are essential in dealing with alcoholics. It is better for a minister who finds that alcoholics anger or disgust him to accept this and not attempt to counsel them but rather to learn how and where to refer them. The same is true for ministers who begin to enjoy the alcoholic's dependency needs or feel uncomfortable because they are unable to meet these needs. With sincerity and honesty, however, the alcoholic can learn a lot in trying to help the minister understand alcoholism and the minister can learn much in exchange (9).

The saying that "only another 'alcoholic' can help an 'alcoholic'" is a myth. This statement, once widely prevalent, was predicated on the fact that up until quite recently only an alcoholic would help. Today there are literally thousands of concerned and compassionate laymen and clergy who give generously of their time and knowledge in working with alcoholics. However, it is quite true that a trained worker, himself cured of alcoholism would ordinarily be more effective than one who had no personal experience with alcoholism.

> Effective counseling on alcoholism begins with an understanding of the illness, and acceptance of the alcoholic as a sick person. This attitude does not remove moral responsibility—in fact, it is the only basis upon which the latter finds sure footing. If we begin with a conception of alcoholism as an illness, then moral responsibility is multiplied for all concerned—alcoholic, family and society. If we begin with an idea that alcoholism is a sin, it is difficult (if not impossible) to deal adequately with the area of moral responsibility. The attitude of sin is frequently an expression of projected hostility as well as an escape mechanism for the one who holds it. A physician who has achieved phenomenal success in treating alcoholics made the following statement: "A Boy Scout with a bottle of aspirin, a pup tent, understanding and compassion can effect better treatment for an alcoholic than a therapist *if he is hostile and prejudiced* against the client." If this is true of the therapist, how much more of the minister! Other assets will be of little avail to a minister in dealing with alcoholics unless he frees himself from prejudice and hostility, learns the factual nature of the disease, and acquires understanding. Objective understanding and subjective compassion form the basic foundation of therapeutic responsibility in the area of alcoholism. (9)

The key role of the therapist is to establish "respect," reciprocal respect in his relationship with the alcoholic. His approach will be eclectic, ranging from indirect to direct depending upon the extent of personality deterioration evident in the situation. Alcoholics evidence strong dependency needs and often require definite statements and prescribed solutions. The proper approach presents little difficulty to the spiritual therapist because he will be guided by the Holy Spirit. In no way can the therapy be conceived of as client centered; it is Christ centered.

Kellerman (8) offers a specific pragmatic list of do's and don'ts for therapists working with alcoholics, some of which are:

> Begin with self. The place to begin helping an alcoholic recover is with self. Learn all you can. Put it into practice, not just words. This will be more effective than anything you attempt to do for the alcoholic.
> 1. Learn all the facts and put them to work in your own life. Don't start with the alcoholic.
> 2. Attend A. A. meetings, Al-Anon meetings, and if possible go to a Mental Health Clinic, Alcoholism Information Center.
> 3. Remember you are emotionally involved. Changing your attitude and approach to the problem can speed up recovery.

4. Encourage all beneficial activities of the alcoholic and cooperate in making them possible.

5. Learn that love cannot exist without compassion, discipline and justice, and to accept it or give it without these qualities is to destroy it eventually.

6. Don't allow the alcoholic to lie to you and accept it for the truth for in so doing you encourage this process. The truth is often painful, but get at it.

7. Don't let the alcoholic outsmart you for this teaches him to avoid responsibility and lose respect for you at the same time.

8. Don't let the alcoholic exploit you or take advantage of you for in so doing you become an accomplice in the evasion of responsibility.

9. Don't lecture, moralize, scold, praise, blame, threaten, or cover up the consequences of drinking. You may feel better but the situation will be worse.

10. Don't accept promises, for this is just a method of postponing pain. In the same way don't keep switching agreements. If an agreement is made stick to it.

11. Don't lose your temper and thereby destroy yourself and any possibility of help.

12. Don't allow your anxiety to compel you to do what the alcoholic must do for himself.

Finally, the effectiveness of spiritual therapy in problems of alcoholism depends upon the artistry of the therapist in "setting-off" the osmosis of love. Osmosis is the dynamic undergirding spiritual therapy. Osmosis is a term borrowed from physics to conceptualize the dynamic pressure of the diffusion of love between the therapist and the alcoholic. Osmosis is a stream of grace, love, forgiveness, acceptance, and power flowing from God through the therapist to the alcoholic. Both immersed in this stream are lifted up, moved, and guided by a transcendent healing force.

The Client

Alcoholism is no respecter of persons. The clientele encompasses every walk of life: rich, poor; scholar, illiterate; black, white; young, old; male, female; jobless, employed; priest, teacher, banker, artist, laborer, etc.

The factor of motivation of the client is greatly emphasized by most therapists and others seeking to work with problems of alcoholism. It is frequently said that "no one can help an alcoholic unless he wants help." The pragmatic significance of such a statement is limited to its comforting effect upon the therapist in facilitating the projection of his own failure and inadequacy to one already stigmatized. Spiritual therapy postulates that there is no such person as an alcoholic who does not want help; such a desire he evidences as he takes alcohol, which is symbolically an overt indication of the inability to exercise courage to be, yet unwillingness to accept non-being, as described by Tillich (13). The axiom that you can lead a horse to water but you can't make him drink is often quoted as a refuge by those who are not capable of effective therapy in this problem. The odds are very good that a thirsty horse in the presence of water, regardless of how he reached it, will quickly drink because he knows that it will quench his thirst. In a like manner, the spiritually sick alcoholic will grab at therapy, which can be communicated to him as effective help.

However, it must be recognized that the alcoholic seldom if ever feels that he needs therapy. His biggest hurdle is to recognize that the problem exists and that he needs professional help. He comes only as a last resort, seldom if ever voluntarily. Coercion, even though disguised, triggers his coming. There is little pragmatic effect whether his involvement in therapy is voluntary or nonvoluntary.

Many attempts have been made to establish a clear and specific picture of the "alcoholic personality." Lists embrace practically every emotion and personality trait known. To date an alcoholic personality has not been isolated and defined. There is a consensus of opinion that the following traits continue to crop up: (1) omnipotence, (2) dependency, (3) self-centeredness, (4) low tolerance threshold, (5) self-abasement, (6) hostility, (7) resentment, and (8) projection of blame.

Finally, although many alcoholics have charming personalities, it must be borne in mind that this charm is one of the most effective defensive mechanisms in his arsenal. Never lose sight of the fact that as a "con" man the alcoholic has no peer; he is an inveterate liar and procrastinator, long on promises and short on performance; a master in flattery, cajolery, and finaglery. He is an expert in changing the subject of discussion; rationalization is his forte. But also remember that he is one of God's children in need of love and worthy of love.

General Procedure

Initially the therapist must understand that the problems of alcoholism do not lie in the bottle but in the alcoholic. Taking his medicine (alcohol) away from him is not the answer. He, himself, must make certain choices and take specific action if recovery is to occur on any permanent basis. He, as previously stated, experiences his problem as pains, foremost among which are guilt, remorse, resentment, low personal worth, anxiety, tension, and hopelessness. Chemicals, even the most miraculous, can anesthetize these pains by putting to sleep the "image of God"; only the love of God and man can cure them.

Specific promises from the Bible should be shared with the client; the promise of forgiveness, freedom from anxiety and fear, inner peace and serenity, purpose in life, power, comfort, fellowship, self-respect, and victory.

The physical setting has an important bearing on the effectiveness of the conference (interview). I recommend a sitting room type setup with two comfortable chairs. The lighting should be subdued with the client's countenance more in the glow and the therapist somewhat in the shadow, but each facing the other in a way conducive to relaxed conversation. Nothing that even suggests an office, such as desk, type-writer, pencil, never a tape recorder, should be in the room. No notes should be taken. Extreme caution should be taken to prevent interruption of any nature. The phone if necessary should be removed from the hook; clocks with audible ticking silenced or removed; coffee, ice water, and cigarettes readily available. Sensed mutual respect must permeate the atmosphere. The client's self-respect, though at a low ebb, must not be extinguished at the crucial first visit. It must be fanned and fostered in order that he may attain the inner love that binds together mind and body and spirit.

The client may be accompanied by another, spouse, friend, parent, or another concerned individual, at the initial interview. Several meetings may be required before he will come alone, but therapy should start at the initial meeting. The procedure for this first contact, and for as many more as necessary, is to listen in order that catharsis and abreaction may occur. Allow the client to identify his problems as he perceives them. Predicated on his evaluation of the situation, the therapist must decide what is the best course to follow. If there is the slightest indication of need for medical or psychiatric care, the client should be referred to the proper resource. Financial and legal problems also should be appropriately referred. The first step, if therapy is to continue, is to lay out the ground rules. The client must fully understand and accept them. Such things as frequency and length of interviews, fees if any, and abstinence requirements. He should not be asked to make a pledge, but he should understand that he must not consume any alcohol for a period of eight hours prior to the meeting.

Abstinence, for a period, all alcoholics seeking help can accept. But the thought of a lifetime without ever taking a social drink is so formidable and forbidding that many will forego therapy when told, "You can recover, but you can never take another drink of alcohol." Clients undergoing spiritual therapy are "cured" and can safely enjoy a future life of temperance rather than complete abstinence if they so choose. Your attention is invited to the study "Controlled Drinking by a Recovered Chronic Alcoholic" in the last section of this paper.

Above all, the client should be told that the orientation of the relationship will be spiritual and that if he does not recognize the reality of the Divine as the possible solution to his problems, it is needless to waste his time and that of the therapist.

Specific Procedure

The following subgoals or plateaus, in the order listed, describe the motivation and direction of the spiritually oriented therapeutic and the progress of the client:

1. Attainment of intellectual insight into the specific nature of his problem(s); the identification of symptoms and their correlation to his consumption of alcohol; and the insidious progressive nature of alcoholism. The list of test questions used by Johns Hopkins University and "A Chart of Alcohol Addiction and Recovery" distributed by the National Council on Alcoholism are excellent tools for this purpose. This step becomes more difficult in proportion to the extent to which his personality deterioration has progressed. This phase is more or less objective; the next subjective.

2. Attainment of emotional insight; recognition of personal responsibility; realization that he is truly a sick person, spiritually sick because he has violated God's laws and purpose for his life. Here specific quotations setting forth God's laws and judgments are shared with the client but at the same time specific promises are pointed out—forgiveness, pardon, relief, a new change, if he, the client wants it. God's plan of salvation and love is thoroughly discussed as specifically related to the client.

3. Surrender and commitment of will and life to God, as we know him in Christ. This is the conversion experience when the client actually "lets go and lets GOD" guide and empower his life. Commitment cannot rest on promises or words but must be translated into specific plans and deeds. The client must put into practice what he has learned; working through his everyday problems; exercising his new found courage to be based on a recognition of his true worth, abilities, and limitations, and all without alcohol.

4. Specific recovery program established:

    a. Daily prayer (may need to be told how to pray)

    b. Daily Bible reading (specific passages)

   c. Restitution to others (willingness, word, act)

   d. Regular attendance at church worship services (with family if possible)

   e. Alcoholics Anonymous meetings if indicated and feasible

   f. Specific schedule of subsequent visit(s)

5. Environmental adjustments if indicated. Change of job, place of residence, new friends or new ways of relating to old friends, separation or divorce, incarceration may be essential.

6. Family adjustments, particularly in the later stages, are always an integral part of the therapeutic process. Often the spouse and others in the family need counseling and therapy as much as the client. The mistakes made by well-meaning family and significant others are almost unbelievable and often make recovery most difficult, if not impossible, for the client.

7. A supportive program of concern, love, and acceptance is usually necessary. The client should be referred in every case to an appropriate church and in some instances to an appropriate A.A. group. Such support does not infer shouldering his burdens, paying his bills, or protecting him from the consequence of his behavior. To the contrary, it is just the opposite, it means suffering with him, not for him, allowing him to stand on his own feet, in his own strength and that of God. Only thus can he achieve the capacity to love in all of its spiritual significance and power.

8. In the process of recovery, it is not possible to expect that all compulsive actions will disappear overnight. The alcoholic may become as engrossed in his treatment and recovery as he was a short time ago in drinking. Recovery from any serious illness may involve considerable time, and on occasions there may be relapses. The world has not come to an end if after a period of sobriety the alcoholic drinks again.

The termination of the formal relationship is very important. It must be final but not abrupt. It may be initiated by either the client or therapist. A final get-together of all intimately concerned should be held, and a complete review and summarization should be presented. Usually the stage of progression of the illness at the time of the first contact will determine the length of duration of the relationship and the approximate time of termination. Ordinarily the relationship lasts from three to six months, with one or more weekly interviews for the first month and weekly thereafter. The interview should be not less than one and one half hours and not more than three.

SUMMARY

A review of current programs of therapy in problems of alcoholism indicates a marked trend toward an approach in which spiritually oriented counseling and psychotherapy are significant and dynamic factors.

Interdisciplinary cooperation is hindered by difficulties of communication. Herein alcoholism is defined as a spiritual illness, the etiology to be found in disorganized spiritual homeostasis.

The following is postulated:

1. Alcohol is an enhancing, not originating, factor.
2. An alcoholic is an individual, spiritually sick, who takes alcohol as a pseudoreligious remedy.
3. Spiritually oriented counseling and psychotherapy are polar, from the depths of man's soul to the Divine. It is communicated love (agape) or love whose alpha and omega is God.
4. The goal of spiritual therapy is the cure of alcoholism through conversion, not abstinence. The attainment of spiritual homeostasis is the only cure for alcoholism. Spiritual homeostasis is defined as "perfect oneness with God and fellowman."
5. Spiritual therapy alleviates the neurotic struggle underlying the psychic malaise.
6. A therapist should not undertake to use this approach unless he is a converted person.
7. Every alcoholic is positively motivated for help.
8. Inability of the therapist and not lack of motivation of the client is the basic factor in lack of progress.
9. A cured alcoholic can control future drinking.
10. The effectiveness of spiritually oriented counseling and psychotherapy in problems of alcoholism depend upon the artistry of the therapist in setting-off the osmosis of love.
11. This paper deals with one category of problems of alcoholism, namely, covert. Supportive data, which follow, discuss typical case histories, and an experimental study on the controlled drinking of a recovered alcoholic is related in the last section of this paper.

It is impossible to crystallize the process of spiritual therapy or to identify and isolate molecular units of its operation. How it works can hardly be verbalized, but the fact that it does is empirically observable.

The following cases, selected at random, are presented as typical of spiritually oriented counseling and therapy in problems involving the use of alcohol. In each instance follow-up was made from two to five years after termination of the therapeutic process. The cases represent the three phases of the progression of alcoholism; initial, crucial, and chronic—the latter being presented in greater detail.

CASE HISTORIES

Case A is an example of an initial-phase alcohol problem in which spiritual therapy was effective.

Background: Mr. and Mrs. A were 38- and 36-years old, respectively. They were married 12 years and had three children aged 6, 9, and 10 years. Both were college graduates. They were in the upper socioeconomic bracket. They owned a $40,000 home and employed a governess for the children. They moved in a social circle that emphasized cocktails as the gracious way of life. As work kept him out of town from Monday to Thursday night, Mrs. A's time was devoted to bridge, golf, club meetings, and similar activities that kept her constantly on the go. When Mr. A returned home, he was met with a full schedule of social activities for each night. Critical incident that led to therapeutic relationship: Mr. A became very abusive to his guests at a cocktail party arranged by his wife and ordered them to leave. He was very intoxicated at the time. The ensuing argument between him and his wife was resolved by his agreeing to seek help for "his drinking problem." Mrs. A phoned for the appointment and came with him.

Brief resume of this and subsequent interviews with the couple: Sometimes they came together, at other times alone as scheduled. Mrs. A was of the opinion that there would be no conflict in the home if Mr. A cut down on his drinking or quit altogether. Mr. A stated that he had been actually concerned for some time by the nature of his drinking. For the first time in his life, he was drinking alone in the hotel during his absence from home and in addition always fortified himself with several drinks on his way home. He explained that he deliberately brought on the incident that led to his wife's call. He had wanted for a long time to "tell that bunch off and be alone just one night with his wife and children" but lacked the nerve while sober. This particular night his wife, supported by their guests, had brought up the need of their building a larger and more pretentious home so that they could entertain on a more lavish scale. He frankly admitted that he could not accept himself in his manner of life, yet lacked the courage to assert himself and change it, so he was turning more and more to alcohol to anesthetize the conflict. To please his wife, he promised at one of the joint interviews to give up drinking. This he did, but not with the favorable results anticipated by his wife. After a few weeks of abstinence, in which his wife made no adjustments in the social schedule, he was still unable to handle the inner conflict, so he told his wife he wanted a divorce and for her to see their lawyer with whom he had already talked. This brought the wife's house tumbling down around her. Mr. A no longer drank but could not accept her and her way of life while sober. The interviews now took a new direction, as both realized that personality and environmental changes must be made by each if the marriage were to be salvaged.

Program: In a joint interview Mr. and Mrs. A drew up a six month's program of activity, as follows:

1. A week's vacation (second honeymoon) to restore communication.

2. Dismissal of governess and the employment of a maid with no responsibility for the supervision of the children.

3. Mrs. A to accept the responsibilities, in the fullest meaning of the word, of being a wife and mother.

4. Each Thursday night to be designated as family night, in which every member of the family would share experiences and jointly enjoy group recreation.

5. Mr. and Mrs. A's social activities would be limited to either Friday or Saturday nights.

6. Each Sunday the entire family was to attend Sunday School and worship service as a family unit, and in addition, Mr. and Mrs. A were to volunteer to teach and work with the youth group of the church.

7. Daily scripture reading and family prayer and devotion would be held after the evening meal.

Termination: After three months, in which time Mr. and Mrs. A were seen together three times and each separately six times, the relationship was terminated by the therapist.

Summary and follow-up: Several times during the past three years the family phoned or wrote the therapist expressing their gratitude for this newfound contentment and family unity. Both continue to indulge in cocktails when so inclined. Both are active in the administration of their church and also in the youth program. They are still living in the original home, and the governess has not been rehired. Spiritual therapy resulted in the acceptance of new standards and new values.

Case B is an example of a crucial-phase alcohol problem in which spiritual therapy was effective.

Background: Mr. and Mrs. B were 31- and 28-years old, respectively. They had been married 13 years and had two children ages

5 and 9. There were no previous marriages, but Mrs. B had taken the children and gone to her parents' home on three occasions in the previous year for stays of two to three weeks each trip. Mr. B was a skilled workman, and Mrs. B was an employed secretary. The children were in school, looked out for by a neighbor in the afternoons. They were in financial difficulties, despite a more than adequate combined income. They were behind in payments on the mortgage on the home and several payments behind on the automobile. There was no social or religious life; they neither entertained nor were entertained. Mr. B spent most of his nonworking hours at the neighborhood beer "joint," arriving home about midnight "soused to the gills."

Drinking history: Mr. B had been drinking since he was 16 years of age according to his statement but only began to drink heavy while he was in the service. He was in difficulty several times while in the service because of drinking. After leaving the service he had been arrested several times for drunk and disorderly conduct, twice for driving while intoxicated. He had been treated at an Alcoholic Rehabilitation Center on two occasions of eight days each. He had also been in and out of A.A. several times. He did not admit that alcohol was a problem and stated that he could take it or leave it. He prided himself on the fact that he was not an alcoholic because he only drank beer. His difficulties on the job were attributed to some of his fellow employees who "ratted" on him.

Critical incident that led to therapeutic relationship: Mrs. B had Mr. B arrested for drunkenness and on his release informed him she had filed for a divorce and unless he sought help for his problem she was going through with it.

Résumé of therapy sessions: Mr. and Mrs. B came together for several meetings and each individually for weekly interviews. Mrs. B was the only child in her family, very ambitious and precise in her dealings with a marked tendency to dominate. She also had more formal education and made more money than Mr. B. Both of these facts she did not hesitate to remind him about with the result that Mr. B's self-concept, already low, was lessened considerably. This was brought out to a marked degree in the joint sessions.

Program: Mr. and Mrs. B after three months in therapy set up the program that follows:

1. Mrs. B was to quit her job, and the family was to live on Mr. B's income.

2. Each creditor was to be personally visited by Mr. B, and arrangements were to be made for reduced, but regular, payments.

3. A schedule of daily devotion, Bible reading, and prayers for the family was fixed.

4. The entire family was to attend Sunday School and church services. Mr. and Mrs. B were to volunteer for service in the youth activities and the scouting program.

5. Each weekend, when possible, would be devoted to family recreation as a group.

Termination and follow-up: The therapeutic relationship extended over a period of twelve months and was terminated by the therapist. Four years have passed since Mr. B's initial visit. The family is a fully functioning healthy interacting group. They have moved to a more comfortable home in a better environment. Last year the family took their first vacation, going to Yellowstone Park in their new car. Mr. B. had been promoted to a foremanship. Both are active in the church and scouting program.

Case C represents an example of the advanced (chronic) phase of alcoholism. It is a prototype of the more than one million alcoholic American women who are hidden beyond the doors of their own homes. They are desperately ill, spiritually, living in a dream world of fantasy and terror, isolated by guilt feelings.

Situation at time of entrance into therapy: Mrs. C, although living under the same roof as her husband, was not a "wife." It could be best described as a brother–sister relationship in the home with the facade of a completely harmonious marriage exhibited to the world outside. A daughter, age seventeen and a senior in high school, unable to accept the situation and overcome by shame and embarrassment, evidenced her anxiety by withdrawal and the development of "tics" but finally unburdened herself to the mother of her school chum. The mother immediately contacted the therapist who made the initial contact.

Background: Mrs. C, a college graduate, was 45 years of age. She has been married to Mr. C for 26 years. They have three daughters aged 24, 20, and 17. There are no prior marriages, and they have never been separated. They own their own home located in an excelent section of a large city. Mr. C is a part owner of a prosperous business, and they moved, prior to the onset of her heavy drinking, in the higher social circles. Mrs. C is a member of a religious denomination that denounces the use of alcohol as a beverage.

Mrs. C began drinking (social) soon after her marriage. In 1951 her drinking pattern changed: no longer did social functions interest her; less and less she accompanied her husband to outside events, not even those of the church. She became more or less a recluse, rarely going out other than daily trips to the ABC liquor store. At the time of the first contact she was drinking a pint of gin daily. She has never experienced medical complications.

She not only refused to admit that alcohol was a problem, but several times when the therapist was talking to her about his work with women who were experiencing such problems, she expressed concern for them but at the same time stated that she never used alcohol in any form.

Critical incident that led to the therapeutic relationship: The therapist, on his third visit, began the conversation by saying, "Mrs. C, when are you going to do something about your drinking?" Mrs. C, "What makes you think that I drink?" The therapist, "Every time I visit your home, you reek of alcohol." It was as if a bomb had exploded in her face. She threw her head back against the divan as if she had been slapped. There was a moment of silence, then with head lowered, she began laughing; then the tears and deep sobs came, deep as all eternity. As if the core of a volcano had been opened, words, phrases, incoherent sentences, poured out; pus coming to the surface from a malignancy of long duration. Long suppressed feelings about herself were vented without chronological patterning. She talked and talked, gradually her speech became more coherent, slower; she raised her head and talked directly to the therapist, becoming more and more relaxed. It was evident that she was making an effort to organize, not restrain, her thoughts. She talked for two hours; however, there were periods of silence. It was as if she were alone, but comfortable and uncensorious of herself. As the therapist was taking his leave, she said, "Today I had a bath; for the first time in years I feel clean. When will you come again?" Her final words were, "Thank God, thank God."

Therapist's evaluation: Mrs. C was unable to face her loneliness, her estrangement from self and family, and the meaninglessness of her life. She was guilt-laden, not by a feeling of guilt, but by actual guilt and personal condemnation, enhanced by her religious heritage.

Therapy: For a period of three weeks, the therapist had breakfast —coffee—each morning at 7:30 A.M. in the home with Mr. and Mrs. C. During this period, the sessions changed and so did Mrs. C. The first morning she sat very quietly, not participating in the conversation except a word or two. She was very preoccupied with her cup and saucer, which she had difficulty in handling because of tremors. By the end of the third week she not only took an active part in the talk but also served as hostess. A more remarkable change was in her personal grooming; the first day her hair was untidy and other personal grooming definitely lacking; by the end of the third week she was attractively groomed. During this period the word alcohol was not mentioned, but the conversation was carefully steered in other directions. The greatest progress was indicated by the restoration of communications in the family, the daughter having joined the group at the beginning of the second week. Individual counseling sessions were held with both the father and daughter, and then the two together. It was pointed out to them that they must reorient their attitude in keeping with scientific facts concerning the nature of alcoholism. Appropriate literature was given them to study. In addition to the morning sessions (30 minutes each), individual afternoon sessions were held with Mrs. C on alternate days, each session lasting about two hours. The first session is reported in detail.

Mrs. C. "Last night, after our talk yesterday, I was unable to sleep. I walked the floor, my stomach tied in knots. I can tell you because you understand. As you noticed, I was hardly able to lift the cup this morning. As soon as the ABC store opened, I was there. I could barely wait to get home and take a drink, but something was different. I didn't gulp it down as I usually do; somehow I didn't want it. I wish I could tell you that I didn't, but I did take a drink, and in a few minutes another—several more. And now you are here and I smell of gin, perhaps I should change to vodka, as they say it doesn't smell. I know I smell terrible, yet you don't look at me with repugnance, as if I were a nauseating object. I don't want to drink. I have tried many times to stop but, without it. I can't face my shame over how I am hurting my husband and child. They never fuss; I wish they would and then I wouldn't feel so guilty. Why do I drink? I have everything a woman could want, yet my life is so empty, so meaningless. I don't know; can you help me to find the answer? Is there any hope for me?"

Six sessions later, Mrs. C greeted the therapist with a smile, excused herself for a moment and returned with a pot of coffee. She seated herself on the divan, lit a cigarette, leaned back and relaxed, waiting for the therapist to speak, but he said nothing. In a few minutes Mrs. C began to talk. as if she was talking to herself, "You know, during the last two weeks, after you would leave, I was overcome with shame, realizing that my dreadful secret was out and the terrible person that I am revealed. Yet you have listened to every word I said as if it were important to you. You haven't lectured, or sermonized, but made me feel that you understood and accepted me, wanted to help me. After your first visit I went up to my dressing room and, for the first time in many months, I really looked at myself in the mirror. My hair was unkempt, my face untidy, and my dress sloppy. It was a familiar picture, but instead of accepting it as I have in the past few years, I began to comb my hair . . . must have spent an hour or more at it, fixing and refixing. I went through my wardrobe and selected an attractive dress. I felt like I did when as a teenager I attended my first party. But when I came downstairs, the ecstasy left me. Once again I felt lonely and unneeded. Why was I fixing up? My husband wouldn't even notice me when he came in; and he didn't. No one was interested in me; I was not wanted or needed. I was dejected and miserable, my guilt an excruciating pain. I couldn't stand it.

My bottle was empty, but I comforted myself that bright and early next day I would get two. But after breakfast, and you had gone, instead of dashing to the store, I fooled around and believe it or not, I didn't go that day, and I haven't been since. I threw myself into cleaning the house and working in the garden. In the afternoon, I bathed and dressed, and believe it or not, my husband took one look at me of amazement, and kissed me."

Practice: Mrs. C was now ready to set up an activity program, to put her new found self-affirmation to work. A tentative program was formulated: an immediate resumption of Sunday School and church activities; attendance with daughter and husband at a soon-to-be-held school function; and the acceptance of an invitation to attend a social function at the Yacht Club, where cocktails would be served. Once initiated, this program was expanded during the weeks to come to include many other activities, particularly visiting and in turn entertaining friends in the home.

Termination: The therapy sessions were reduced to two a week for a period of three weeks; one a week for eight weeks; and finally bimonthly for three months. The final session (26 sessions in all, not including the breakfast get-togethers) was held approximately seven months after the initial contact. The entire family was present—father, mother, and daughter—and each freely participated. The situation prior to accepting help, the progress of each individual and the family unit, and plans for the future were discussed.

Summary and follow-up: At the beginning of therapy the family was completely disorganized, each member functioning in a maladjusted manner. The father had resigned himself to the situation as hopeless but to be tolerated. The daughter was so emotionally disturbed that she had withdrawn within herself, was embarrassed, ashamed, and unable to function with her school peers. Mrs. C, the mother, lived in an alcoholic world of her own, her personality progressively deteriorating.

Through spiritually oriented therapy Mrs. C developed her capacity to love. Love overcame and cast out loneliness, rejection, and meaninglessness. A newfound faith, in herself and in God, cast out all her fears. Through perfect trust she came to a perfect peace of mind. A planned program of day by day practice of fellowship with God, undergirded by prayer and the reliance on God gave her strength to live each day without alcohol.

At the time of the termination of the spiritually oriented relationship, she was well on her way to becoming a fully functioning person. The daughter took on new life and began to participate in school activities and a few months later was elected by her classmates to the May Queen's Court. The husband was beginning to assume the role of a husband in the fullest meaning, and once again he and his wife shared the same bedroom. The family took on unity. The therapeutic relationship began in September of 1955 and was terminated in February of 1957. Yearly follow-ups have been made, and today six years later the daughter graduated from college with honors, scholastic and extracurricular. All are active in church, social, and civic affairs. Mrs. C. can be described as a fully functioning, self-actualized person, living her life without the need of alcohol.

She no longer tries to "live by bread alone." She now lives alone, as the daughter is working in another city. In 1964 Mr. C dropped dead from a heart attack while shoveling snow. Mrs. C's reaction to this crisis was in her own words, "If I had been faced with this great personal loss and grief a few years ago, I would have immediately sought comfort and strength from the bottle. Today this does not enter my mind because I know real comfort and strength in the experience of the love and presence of Jesus Christ."

CONTROLLED DRINKING BY A RECOVERED CHRONIC ALCOHOLIC

There is wide agreement, practically unanimous, among those who work with alcoholics, that an alcoholic can never drink "normally" (controlled) again. Literature dealing with alcoholism and the treatment of the alcoholic expresses this viewpoint (10; U. S. Public Health Service, 1961; Metropolitan Life Insurance Company, 1959). To deny this stand in the face of such unanimity of opinion of competent persons catalogs me as being presumptuous in daring to offer evidence to the contrary. However, the conclusion that no alcoholic can return to controlled drinking does not fit in with the definition, used in this report, of what constitutes an alcoholic. I define alcoholism as follows: Any drinking that has as its purpose relief from dissatisfactions with self or with environment is alcoholic drinking; and the person who continues to engage in this type drinking is an alcoholic. If the purpose of drinking is personality adjustment or the alleviation of situational problems, and the person continues to drink in this pattern, this constitutes alcoholism. The phrase "prealcoholic" has no pragmatic significance. The only difference between the initial stage and chronic alcoholism is one of degree. Uncontrolled drinking is the symptom of underlying personality (spiritual) maladjustment. Thus, if the symptom is adjusted, there should be no reason why a person could not abstain or drink within self-set limits or controls. I have seen the validity of this assumption verified in many individuals, and it is the purpose of this study to report a specific case which authenticates this position.

Method

Subject. A male over 40; weight 150 pounds; of professional status; institutionally diagnosed as an "alcoholic-chronic, prognosis unfavorable"; drinking history extends back over 25 years, but at the time of this experiment he had been an abstainer (100%) for a period of five years. Subject entered spiritual therapy in June of 1955 and remained until March of 1957.

Definitions. For purposes of this study the following terms are defined:

1. "A drink": a beverage; highball; cocktail, or straight, containing three ounces of 100-proof alcohol.

2. "Controlled drinking": drinking which does not result in behavior unacceptable to the group (social, business, or religious) of which the subject is a part at any given moment.

Procedure

1. The following schedule of controls was established for the period December 18, 1960 to January 1, 1962.

   Period from December 18, 1960 to January 1961: The experimenter instructed the subject, who had come to him for counseling during his drinking days, to drink a minimum of two drinks each and every day. No maximum was established, and the subject was told that he could drink as many more as he saw fit.

   Period from January to April 1961: The experimenter instructed the subject not to consume any beverage with an alcoholic content during this period.

   Period from April 1 to April 30, 1961, inclusive: The subject was instructed to alternate 48-hour periods, as follows: During the first 48 hours he was to drink a minimum of two drinks each 24-hour period, but again there was no maximum. The next period of 48 hours was the same as the first except that he was to drink each 24-hour period two drinks—no more, no less. The one restriction for both 48-hour periods was that there were to be no "eye-openers."

   Period from May 1 through May 15, 1961: The subject was to drink one drink just before the evening meal, with the proviso that an interval of five or six hours must have elapsed since the last solid food was taken. No other drinking was allowed.

   Period from May 16 through June 15, 1961: Subject was instructed to attend a minimum of six social functions where drinking was a part of the mores. He was to take one drink, no more, no less, at each. No other drinking was permitted during this period.

   Period from June 16 through December 31, 1961: The experimenter instructed the subject that he was now on his own and could drink or abstain as he desired.

2. The subject was to make a record of any deviation from the

schedule, said record to be submitted with a narrative report covering the drinking aspects of the full period.

Results

The summarization of the subject's report follows and constitutes the results of the experiment:

Period. December 18, 1960 to January 1, 1961. Minimum control, two drinks each day, maintained. Maximum—The period covered was a holiday season when according to tradition there is a tremendous increase in the amount of convivial and social drinking, particularly in our set. There was only a couple of days during this period that I kept to the minimum. This was the first time that I had touched alcohol for more than 5 years, so I really let myself go. On several occasions I drank a great deal, passing out on two of these. I suffered no blackouts during this period, which was quite different from my previous drinking history. When I drank heavy the night before, I started the next day with an eye-opener, and continued to drink the rest of the day. During this entire period I made no effort to control my drinking, and my behavior was compatible with those around me.

Period. January, February, and March 1961. During this period, I did not take a single drink. I exercised the control of abstinence. The first two days, coming right after a period of heavy drinking climaxed by a New Year's Eve binge, were very difficult, and I experienced a gnawing compulsion for a drink.

Period. January, February, and March 1961. During this period, deviation.

Period. May 1 to May 15, 1961. Schedule and controls maintained without deviation.

Period. May 16 to June 15, 1961. I attended eight social functions during the period; two more than called for. They included a weekend with a group at the beach, a poker game, a wedding, a social gathering in a private home, and four dances. Drinking was openly and acceptably a part of each function. I maintained my schedule of one drink at each function and no other drinks during this period.

Period. June 16 to January 1962. No controls, maximum or minimum, were established for this period. However, I controlled my drinking, but according to individual situations. During this

742   GEORGE W. BURROUGHS

period there were many holidays and festivals, including the Thanksgiving and Christmas seasons, which I celebrated (Christmas) last year by drinking. Two or three times during this period I did imbibe, but never exceeding ½ drink at any one event. For the rest of the period I abstained. *I now know that I am completely cured of alcoholism and am able to maintain absolute control (abstinence or moderation) over my consumption of alcoholic beverages.*

Discussion

Although the results are based on the unconfirmed report of the subject, the nature of the experiment was such that violation of the control would have been manifested in overt behavior and the experimenter was close enough to the social circle of the subject to have known. In addition, through casual contacts with family and employer the experimenter was able to verify the veracity of the report. Incidentally, during this period the subject received a $500.00 increase in his salary, and the nature of his work was such that the first indication of uncontrolled drinking would have met with severe consequences. It should be noted that in the last period, with no restrictions, the subject for the most part practiced abstinence, and when he did imbibe, the volume of the drink was reduced.

Although the medical diagnosis classified the subject as a chronic alcoholic, the validity of the findings might be questioned on the basis that this is an individual case and that no generalizations can be drawn. But even granted that this is an individual case, it refutes the hypothesis that NO alcoholic can return to controlled or normal drinking. Added support to the validity of this experiment is presented by Davies (4), who presents a similar study, except the findings were based on observation in social settings of alcoholics who had returned to controlled drinking.

Summary

This experiment was undertaken to test the validity of the statement that an alcoholic can never return to controlled drinking. The subject, a medically diagnosed chronic alcoholic, was instructed to follow a set schedule of rigid controls, ranging from abstinence to minimum to no maximum in the amount of alcohol to be consumed. During the last six months of the experiment, which extended over a year, all controls were abolished and the subject was on his own. During this period, with the exception of a few occasions, he chose to abstain. The times when he did imbibe it was with moderation. This is strong evidence that the subject, a chronic alcoholic, could and did return to controlled drinking. I believe that such cases are more common than has been recognized, thus the view that NO alcoholic can return to controlled drinking is untenable.

REFERENCES

1. Blake, J. A. The fourth category of personality needs. *Ment. Hyg.,* July 1953, **37,** (3), 377–383.
2. British Medical Association. *Divine healing and co-operation between doctors and clergy.* Memorandum of evidence submitted by a special committee of the Council of the British Medical Association to the Archbishops' Commission on Divine Healing. London, England, 1956.
3. Clinebell, H. J., Jr. *Understanding and counseling the alcoholic through religion and psychology.* New York: Abingdon Press, 1956.
4. Davies, D. L. Normal drinking in recovered alcohol addicts. *Quart. J. Studies Alcoholism,* March 1962, **23,** (1), 94–103.
5. Frankl, V. E. *The doctor and the soul.* New York: Knopf, 1957.
6. Georgia Commission on Alcoholism, *Georgia looks at alcoholism.* Atlanta, 1958.
7. Jellinek, E. M. *The disease concept of alcoholism.* New Haven: Hillhouse Press, 1960.
8. Kellermann, J. L. *A guide for the family of the alcoholic.* Charlotte, N. C.: Charlotte Council on Alcoholism, Inc., 1961.
9. Kellermann, J. L. *Alcoholism: A guide for the clergy.* Charlotte, N. C.: Charlotte Council on Alcoholism, Inc., 1963.
10. Mann, M. *New primer on alcoholism.* New York: Rinehart & Co., 1958.
11. Seliger, R. V. *How to help an alcoholic.* Columbus, Ohio: School and College Service, 1951.
12. Symonds, P. M. *Dynamics of psychotherapy,* Vol. 1. New York: Grune & Stratton, 1956.
13. Tillich, P. *The courage to be.* New Haven: Yale University Press, 1952.

Part Five

"LAY" AND SELF-THERAPY

Mowrer (6) foresees these approaches as the psychotherapy of the future. The various myths developed by some medical and professional psychological therapists are clearly debunked by the successes of these unorthodox approaches in dealing with emotional and behavioral imbalances. Kerchner and Goldman describe the positive therapeutic effects of Recovery, Inc., a lay-directed group for psychiatric patients. The ideas of Dr. Low, the founder of Recovery, Inc., are exemplified in the selections from the Manual of the movement he started. Yablonsky's observations on Synanon show a lay approach to therapy of drug addicts which is more successful than treatments conducted by professional therapists. Bellwood reviews the best-known lay psychotherapy movement, Alcoholics Anonymous.

However effective, these psychotherapeutic movements do not always meet with the understanding and support of professionals. Meerloo (5) describes the storm he aroused among his psychiatric colleagues when he expressed the opinion that some patients could profit more from being left alone than from the services of a professional psychotherapist. Like other professionals, psychotherapists apparently suffer from the illusion that they are indispensable. A few psychologists and psychiatrists apparently have been free enough from this illusion to carry

745

out controlled experiments using "lay" therapists. Heine (3) studied the efforts of third-year medical students acting as psychotherapists and found that these young men, although hurried and harried by their academic tasks, were just as effective with neurotics as more highly trained professional therapists or psychoanalysts. Carkhuff and Truax (1) report that psychiatric aides, most of them without a college education, can be trained to achieve results of which any professional psychotherapist would be proud with regressed hospitalized schizophrenics. Rioch and associates (7), in a study at the National Institute of Mental Health, showed that lay people with certain personality qualities can be effective therapists after a relatively short period of training. These and other studies have led one psychiatrist to wonder if highly trained psychotherapists should not abandon therapeutic work and concentrate on training and supervising the lower echelon of workers in the mental health fields.

It may well be that the lay therapeutic movements described in the following chapters are comprised of sensitive and dedicated individuals, trained in the hard school of personal suffering and recovery, who can be highly effective with their fellow sufferers from drugs, alcohol, or schizophrenic confusion and alienation. In his professional conceit, many a psychotherapist may tend to forget that spontaneous remission is one of his best allies, that hope (2) is psychotherapeutically potent, and that curing of souls was carried out for thousands of years before he arrived on the scene (4). These lay movements may teach us that the methods of new group therapy may be using the rational, irrational, and superrational resources neglected by us because of the prejudices inculcated by our training.

REFERENCES

1. Carkhuff, R. R., & Truax, C. B. Lay mental health counseling: the effects of lay group counseling. *J. Consult. Psychol.,* 1965, **29**, 426–431.
2. Frank, J. The role of hope in psychotherapy. *Intern. J. Psychiat.,* 1968, **5**, 383–395.
3. Heine, R. W. (Ed.) *The student physician as psychotherapist.* Chicago: University of Chicago Press, 1962.
4. Kiev, A. *Magic, faith and healing: studies in primitive psychiatry today.* New York: Free Press of Glencoe, 1964.
5. Meerloo, J. A. M. The essence of mental cure: the manifold principles active in psychotherapy. *Amer. J. Psychother.,* 1958, **12**, 42–63.
6. Mowrer, O. H. *The new group therapy.* New York: Van Nostrand, 1964.
7. Rioch, M. J., Elkes, C., Flint, A. A., Udanski, B., Newman, R. G., & Silber, E. National Institute of Mental Health pilot study in training mental health counselors. *Amer. J. Orthopsychiat.,* 1963, **33**, 678–689.

Chapter 26

Synanon

LEWIS YABLONSKY

Lewis Yablonsky: b. 1924, New Jersey.
B.A., in economics, Rutgers University, 1948. M.A., 1952, Ph.D., 1958, in sociology, New York University.
Professor and Chairman, Department of Sociology, San Fernando Valley State College, California, 1960–date. University of Massachusetts, 1956–1959; Columbia University, 1952–1956.
President, American Society of Group Psychotherapy and Psychodrama, 1959. Member Board of Directors, Synanon Foundation, Inc., 1966–date.
Books: *The Tunnel Back: Synanon* (1965). *The Violent Gang* (1962).
Articles: Over forty.

Synanon[1] is a new social movement and approach to life that has helped more than six hundred people overcome a severe past of crime and drug addiction. It was founded in 1958 by Charles E. Dederich, a layman with a genius for understanding and solving human problems. The creation and development of this novel human experiment is a story of courage. It is about people who moved from the gutters, prisons, brothels, and back rooms of our society into a position of moral leadership.

The word "synanon" originated with a newly arrived addict in the early days of the organization. In his attempt to say two foreign words, "symposium" and "seminar," in the same breath, he blurted out "synanon": "I want to get into another one of those—symp . . . sem—*synanons.*" In this way, a new word was introduced into the language to describe a new social phenomenon.

Synanon is more than symposiums and seminars. It is a new kind of group therapy; an effective approach to racial integration; a humane solution to some facts of bureaucratic organization; a different way of being religious; a new method of attack therapy; an unusual kind of

---

[1] The text consists of extracts from Professor Lewis Yablonsky's book *The Tunnel Back: Synanon*, New York: Macmillan, 1965. Reprinted with permission of the publisher and with some changes to comply with the style of this book.

communication; and an exciting, fresh approach to the cultural arts and philosophy. One side effect of intense participation in these diverse human experiences is that people who were criminals and prisoners have found a new existence and now lead constructive lives.

The central organization of Synanon currently comprises more than five hundred people. They use a variety of living quarters, buildings, warehouses, automobiles, and trucks based in Synanon's five locations throughout the country. There are Synanon establishments in Santa Monica; San Francisco; San Diego; Westport, Connecticut; and Reno, Nevada.

Importantly entwined in the Synanon movement is a cross section of citizens who visit and support the work of the Synanon Foundation. Since the beginning, there have been more than fifty thousand separate visits by citizens from all walks of life to Synanon Houses. In reverse, Synanon members have filled more than one thousand educational speaking engagements to college, university, church, high school, civic, and other community groups. This unique pattern of social interaction between Synanon people and the more interested public may very well be one of the important secrets of Synanon's success.

Not everyone has supported Synanon. Many segments of society have balked at the spectacle of criminals and addicts living in "respectable" communities and trying to solve their problems in their own way. Cries of fear and outrage have been followed up by a variety of legal maneuvers. The enemies of Synanon have attempted to drive Synanon people and their families (children included) from their newfound homes and their foothold on a constructive way of life. When Synanon's prejudiced enemies could not find anything illegal in the behavior of Synanon people (and they tried), they invoked irrelevant zoning laws in an effort to destroy Synanon's interracial community. (It is interesting to note a paradox: these people invoked what is generally the most corrupt arm of city government, the housing and zoning divisions, in their attacks on Synanon.) In all cases, the zoning boards (in Santa Monica, Westport, and San Francisco), angrily prodded by the supporters of "lily-white" living and by people concerned with property dollars, jumped onto Synanon's back. On the surface, it was zoning; at the murky bottom, it was prejudice.

EARLY ENCOUNTERS

The first time I heard about Synanon was at the United Nations Congress on Crime and Delinquency in London in the summer of 1960. One evening, at an informal gathering, a new experiment for treating addicts was described to me by the noted criminologist Dr. Donald Cressey.

I found Cressey's remarks exciting. In more than ten years of work with the crime problem on the East Coast, I did not know one so-called ex-addict who had totally quit using drugs. If there were more than thirty addicts and criminals staying "clean" in Synanon, as Cressey had informed me, this was a major breakthrough in treating the problem.

My first look at Synanon surprised me. The immense five-story red brick armory was nothing like the beatnik beach-house pad I was led to expect. The large, respectable black-and-yellow SYNANON HOUSE sign on the front of the building was also a surprise. Somehow I had expected Synanon to have a more clandestine face to the world.

It became increasingly difficult to believe that the place was entirely managed by ex-addicts. Everywhere I looked I saw signs of efficient organization. On my way to the second floor, I passed a sign stating "Business Office." The large room had rows of typewriters, files, and the other accouterments of an office. A small theater marked "Stage One" was at the foot of the stairs. The hall was carpeted with colored rugs, which were well worn but neat and clean.

On the second floor, I saw men and women bustling around in different directions. They all seemed to be on important errands. With the exception of the sight of several jail-scarred faces and a young man going through drug-withdrawal pains in the center of the living room, I found it difficult to believe this was a "drug-addict rehabilitation center." It seemed to be more of a poor man's version of a coed college fraternity house.

Charlie Hamer introduced himself, welcomed me, and introduced me to another "member of Synanon," Jack Hurst.

Before Hamer and I could get any serious conversation underway, I observed that most of the people in the house had gathered in the front room. I was informed that the synanons were about to take place and that we would get to talk further "after they were kicked off." According to Hamer, "The synanon is our form of what you probably call group psychotherapy in your business. People here go to these sessions three evenings a week. In the synanon, people can dump their emotional garbage and learn about themselves. It's a kind of pressure cooker for working out what's bugging you."

There were loud curses and shouts coming from the "synanon room" I had just left. I was somewhat disturbed by the voice pitch. I knew, from my institutional experience, that the type of shouting I was hearing was often a prelude to, or accompanied, physical violence. Hurst sensed my reaction and told me about "the two cardinal rules of Synanon. Two capital offenses in Synanon are physical assault and taking drugs or alcohol. The kids are just normally discussing their problems, and they do get noisy. But that's just fine, it helps them get all the pent-up hostility out of their gut and take a look at it. That's what synanons are for."

Hurst described a variety of synanons: "The ones going on tonight are the standard floor synanon and are mainly catharsis-type sessions. It helps people get a lot of emotion out of their system. They argue and fight over what happens to be bugging them at the time. Like they think they have a rotten job; why someone had a need to "look good" all of the time; why someone can't take orders; self-image problems; why someone never talks at all or talks too much."

My own experience in working with addicts in group therapy compelled me to ask Jack what seemed to me at that time an obvious question: "If the people here are drug addicts, why all this discussion about work habits and 'self-image'? Don't you discuss your compulsion to shoot drugs?"

"We're no longer drug addicts. We were all addicts, and when we were addicts we talked about dope. We are trying to do something else. We are trying to learn how to live like human beings. I shot drugs for nine years. When I crawled in here two years ago, almost on all fours, I was at the end of the line. My problem wasn't drugs, even though drugs made me subhuman. What I needed, and still need, is to learn more about proper living. There really isn't much to be said about drugs or a yen. We try to get to the 'person' here. Probably the reason group therapy and jail or psychiatry never helped me is because most of the therapy dealt with the symptom of drug addiction.

"This is one of the problems with you professionals. You are all involved with drug addiction. You want to know how an addict uses, how much, and all that crap. Around here we are interested in helping ex-dope fiends grow up, by talking about living clean."

As we continued to talk, I became increasingly impressed with the stark honesty and candor of the Synanon people. Never in my professional experience (certainly not in various institutions or in my research on the "street") had I encountered a more direct and honest response to any questions I chose to ask. I said, "You know, I've done a fair amount of research on crime and in particular with violent gangs in New York. I've never had the experience of such frank responses to my questions. After all, none of you know me that well."

Hurst picked up this point: "Around here, we operate on what we laughingly call the truth principle. If you want to look at it that way, part of our therapy is truth and honesty. We have nothing to hide or creep around about. We aren't proud of our past behavior, but at the same time we can't go around paralyzed with guilt. It would just incapacitate us."

Hamer said, "Most people in the world can get by with their little white lies and conning each other. We have found we cannot afford to lie at all. Any slips of truth on our part can be deadly. If we do not level with each other, we add more guilt to our already heavy load. This would fester, and we might split [leave] and go back on dope, get ourselves dead from an overdose, or go back to jail. We have to be honest to stay clean."

I asked, "Is this standard practice in a synanon; are they always this intense?"

Hamer said, "No. In some synanon sessions, we discuss things without dragging in all of our hostility. The longer a person is around here, the more likely he is to have better self-control. Our older members are mixed in with the newcomers and try to get something into the session besides the kind of raw attack you just heard.

"By the way, although we don't make a big thing of it, and profanity is freely allowed in the synanons, we try to keep it to a minimum outside of the synanon sessions. In fact, someone may be pulled up [chastised] for excessive cursing."

ORIGINS

Synanon began within Charles E. Dederich. It seems that Chuck was able to plunge into the development of a new approach to life as completely as he did because of his lack of commitment to any specific system of ideas, yet a limited belief in many. His involvements with philosophy had included the study of Freud, Thoreau, Lao-tse, Buddha, St. Thomas, Catholicism, Plato, and Emerson. At the time that Synanon was founded, Chuck was a man with no firm position, searching for a meaning to his own life.

He had been an alcoholic on and off for twenty years and had been through a variety of jobs and wives. Alcoholics Anonymous (A.A.) had accomplished its mission of symptom removal; however, Chuck's restless urge continued. His life lacked completion and was generally self-defeating. When he felt that he could win or succeed in another man's land, he would smash the track he was on and begin anew. This happened to him when he quit college as a sophomore at Notre Dame; as a junior executive in the Gulf Oil Company; and later as an employee of Douglas Aircraft in California. Immediately before founding Synanon, Chuck had been a devotee of A.A., and although it helped him quit drinking he found it limiting. In retrospect, it seems that any approach not completely developed by Chuck himself was too binding for his roaring ego needs. The development of Synanon confirms this speculation. Chuck appears to need an "empire" based on his own ideas, and Synanon has fulfilled this prescription.

Some professionals became interested in Synanon, and they invited Chuck to talk to a group of Southern California parole officers. For this event he wrote a speech that could be considered "Synanon's Manifesto" (the principles incorporated in this original statement are the backbone of the current larger, more streamlined Synanon organization):

> The Synanon Foundation is a nonprofit corporation which has emerged as part of an over-all phenomenon that is taking place on the beach at Ocean Park, California. At this time it appears that an environment has been created which seems to have a beneficial effect on some narcotic addicts.
>
> We have here a climate consisting of a family structure similar in some areas to a primitive tribal structure, which seems to affect individuals on a subconscious level. The structure also contains overtones of a 19th century family setup of the type that produced inner-directed personalities. It is the feeling of the Synanon Foundation that an undetermined percentage of narcotic addicts are potentially inner-directed people, as differentiated from tradition-directed or other-directed people.
>
> A more or less autocratic family structure appears to be necessary as a preconditioning environment to buy some time for the recovering addict. This time is then used to administer doses of an inner-directed philosophy, such as that outlined in Ralph Waldo Emerson's essay entitled "Self Reliance." If it seems paradoxical that an authoritative environment tends to produce inner direction, it must be remembered that the inner-directed men of the 19th century, viz., Emerson, Thoreau, Oliver Wendell Holmes, Longfellow, were products of an authoritative family structure. It might also be remembered that intellectual, emotional, and spiritual food fed to the recovering addicts while in the climate is rather carefully selected, as previously cited.
>
> The autocratic overtone of the family structure demands that the patients or members of the family perform tasks as part of the group. If a member is able to take direction in such small tasks as helping in the preparation of meals, housecleaning, etc., regardless of his rebellion at being "told what to do," his activity seems to provide exercise of emotions of giving or creating which have lain dormant. As these emotional muscles strengthen, it seems that the resistance to cooperating with the group tends to dissipate. During this time, a con-

certed effort is made by the significant figures of the family structure to implant spiritual concepts and values that will result in self-reliance. Members are urged to read from the classics and from the great teachers of mankind—Jesus, Lao-tse, Buddha, etc. These efforts have been successful to a rather surprising degree. The concept of an open mind is part of a program to help the addict find himself without the use of drugs.

Another device that has seemed to produce beneficial results is the "synanon." The synanon can be defined broadly as a kind or type of group therapy. Synanon, which is a coined word, is used to describe a more or less informal meeting, which ideally consists of three male patients and three female patients plus one Synanist who is himself an addictive personality but who has managed to arrest the symptoms of his addiction for some considerable length of time, or seems to be progressing at a rate somewhat faster than his colleagues in the meeting. The Synanist acts as moderator and, by virtue of an empathy that seems to exist between addictive personalities, is able to detect the patient's conscious or unconscious attempts to evade the truth about himself. The methods employed by a Synanist in a synanon meeting may include devices or weapons that appear to be unorthodox, but such surprisingly beneficial results have occurred in an encouraging number of cases that we feel we must further explore the method.

The Synanist leans heavily on his own insight into his own problems of personality in trying to help the patients to find themselves, and he will use the weapons of ridicule, cross-examination, hostile attack, as they become necessary. These synanon sessions seem to provide an emotional catharsis and seem to trigger an atmosphere of truth-seeking which is reflected in the social life of the family structure. The Synanist does not try to convey to the patient that he himself is a stable personality. In fact, it may very well be the destructive drives of the recovered or recovering addictive personality embodied in a Synanist which make him a good therapeutic tool—fighting fire with fire.

The sharing of emotional experience in synanon sessions seems to encourage in the family structure a tolerance and permissiveness within rather loosely defined limits in which the addict who wants to recover feels sufficiently comfortable to stay and buy himself time. This permissiveness, of course, does not include the taking of any form of addictive substance. It is stressed, for instance, to everyone that no addictive personality can take anything that will have an effect on his mind. The ingestion of alcohol, opiates, barbiturates, tranquilizers, or psychic energizers is strictly forbidden. Permissiveness in the psychic area of verbal resistance or rebellion to authority is rather encouraged than discouraged. The insistence is on performance. For example, if it is suggested that one of the boys or girls help in the kitchen he is free to "gripe," "beef," as loudly as he wishes, but it is required that he comply in the area of action. It has been observed that the verbal rebellion toward authority seems to relieve inner tension and that compliance in the action area seems to exercise the "muscles of giving."

Another device, which in the opinion of the foundation has been successful, and which is paradoxical in the extreme, is the "haircut." The "haircut" is a session attended by relatively new patients and four or five of the significant figures of the family structure during which the patient is "taken apart," and his performance to date, both constructive and destructive, is pointed out to him, together with suggestions for his future behavior. These sessions may even contain tones of the "third degree" and may become quite brutal, on a verbal level, of course. Surprisingly, the patient's reaction has been almost 100% favorable. As one of our members put it, "When the word gets around that 'haircuts' are being given, people seem to get in line."

It might be that this device awakens in the subconscious of the patient a realization that someone cares about him. It may satisfy a desire to be the center of attention. It may help to make him realize that a loving father must also be a firm father. Many of the people who have experienced these "haircuts" reported a change in attitude or a shift in direction almost immediately. There is, of course, no policy as to timing, and many times a "haircut" session will be in no way critical. They seem to be guided only by intuition.

NEW PATTERNS

Some of Synanon's "philosophy" corresponds closely with "square society"; other Synanon viewpoints represent unresolved vestiges of the addict-criminal underworld; and still other ideas are unique human imprints developed in this new community. The common bond of these often disparate social elements is that they collectively reflect Synanon's new way of life. "In front," the Synanon approach has caused many friends and enemies to see Synanon varyingly as excessively brutal, totalitarian, communistic, beautiful, loving, corny, naive, vicious, and constructive.

The process of building a constructive society with the varied "characters," misfits, "boss criminal-addicts," and others who form the Synanon amalgamation has produced many unusual thoughtways. Synanon has not evolved too many completely new positions or postures in life. The social system of Synanon, however, has shifted and modified standard philosophies to fit its own needs.

In Chuck's opinion, because of the criminal-addict's free-floating past, his actions must be completely controlled when he first becomes part of Synanon. This is believed to be necessary until he shows some signs of being able to think for himself in a constructive direction. Therefore, when he moves into Synanon, he must, at first, accept a kind of autocratic government run by Chuck and a select few.

Chuck describes it this way: "We were able to get Synanon off the ground because, basically, most people who come here are apolitical and tend toward some kind of anarchy. Their behavior is anarchistic. This is what they have acted out as criminals and addicts. Because they think anarchistically, they wind up being separate and apart from society. They usually have few ties and are, therefore, quite easy to organize into the autocracy that we have here.

"In over-all organization, we can also be looked at as a corporation that produces 'clean-man days.' Like a corporation, our flow of power comes from the select few. Most corporations are autocracies with a Board of Directors. American corporations are not democratic, and neither are we."

Synanon is most attractive to people who need help and seem at rock bottom. People who have a drug habit but who are more established in the community show a resistance to accepting the "necessity" of placing themselves (at first) totally at Synanon's disposal. When they have something "going for them" outside, this interferes with their desire to accept the total commitment that Synanon demands.

In one case a twenty-eight-year-old physician showed up at the foundation one day "begging for help." He said that he had become hopelessly addicted to drugs and wanted to quit. He was told that he would have to give up his medical practice for a time and his family and move into Synanon. He was informed that he needed the complete program and that this was the only way Synanon could help him.

According to Chuck: "We told him he was, of course, welcome to Synanon and explained how we worked. But when he found out he'd have to live here to get well, he apparently decided his business and family came first. He said he had some things that he had to take care of, and he left. A couple of days later the papers carried the story. He'd gone home and blown his head off with a shotgun."

Chuck was the basic therapeutic agent for the first thirty to forty people with whom Synanon succeeded. He necessarily carried the power, glory, and responsibility of this type of therapeutic leadership role. He said, "The addicts who gravitated around me in the early days wanted a superbeing. I tried as best I could to fill this difficult role for them. You know, the 'all-knowing, all-understanding' bit. That's what they wanted.

"People that submit to this type of leadership not only give you the right to help them, they give you the responsibility for their destiny. You can't really accept one without the other.

"At first, it's fun and ego gratifying to have the power and the feedback of gratitude. Then it becomes commonplace and gets in the way of business. People crawling all over you physically and emotionally becomes tedious. You begin to set up guards. You try to cut them loose. People who go overboard like this become overly dependent, and you have problems like sibling rivalry, and this sprays out into the organization.

"It isn't as much strain in a secondary group organization. The people who have come into Synanon in the last year or two are not in the direct rays of my efforts. They look at me as a big shot and figure I must know what I am doing. 'Look at what he's done and blah, blah.' But I'm not their salvation. The whole organization has helped them. Their growth is not all on my back as it was with the early group. There isn't much jealousy and sibling rivalry among the two-year-old people, but there is still a helluvalot between the four- and five-year-old Synanon people."

Every Saturday night, immediately preceding the evening's events, what is known as the "Synanon Philosophy" is read. It contains some of the elements of Synanon's "religious" position:

> The Synanon philosophy is based on the belief that there comes a time in everyone's life when he arrives at the conviction that envy is ignorance; that imitation is suicide; that he must accept himself for better or for worse as is his portion; that though the wide universe is full of good, no kernel of nourishing corn can come to him but through his toil bestowed on that plot of ground which is given to him to till. The power which resides in him is new in nature, and none but he knows what it is that he can do, nor does he know until he has tried. Bravely let him speak the utmost syllable of his conviction. God will not have his work made manifest by cowards.
>
> A man is relieved and gay when he has put his heart into his work and done his best; but what he has said or done otherwise shall give him no peace. As long as he willingly accepts himself, he will continue to grow and develop his potentialities. As long as he does not accept himself, much of his energies will be used to defend rather than to explore and actualize himself.
>
> No one can force a person toward permanent and creative learning. He will learn only if he wills to. Any other type of learning is temporary and inconsistent with the self and will disappear as soon as the threat is removed. Learning is possible in an environment that provides information, the setting, materials, resources, and by his being there. God helps those who help themselves.

Synanon emphasizes self-help, with a focus on individual self-reliance. This attitude reflects one of the major areas of contrast between Synanon and Alcoholics Anonymous. The latter builds upon man's reliance on a higher being, Synanon's emphasis is upon the individual's self-help and "actualization." This theme is further revealed in the formal Synanon prayer that is read each day at Synanon's morning meeting:

Please let me first and always examine myself.
Let me be honest and truthful.
Let me seek and assume responsibility.
Let me have trust and faith in myself and my fellow man.
Let me love rather than be loved.
Let me give rather than receive.
Let me understand rather than be understood.

Dederich takes religion very seriously, despite his limited practice of any formal, organized religion: "Here at Synanon, we try to practice the Golden Rule. For example, in a synanon session, 'doing unto others what you would have them do unto you' is a major theme."

METHODS

Welcome

In the following talk to a group of ten newcomers (in Synanon less than a week), Chuck attempts to communicate Synanon's basic philosophy. The group members (white and Negro) were fresh from the "streets," various jails, and prisons. They ranged in age from nineteen to fifty. They sat in a circle around Chuck and listened attentively to his statement on Synanon (extracted here).

What we are trying to do here will dawn on you in time, and that's extremely important. We're not going to measure your psyche or find out who your grandfather got mad at. This has been the approach that I guess has failed. The fact that you came here, and have had a narcotics problem, is enough.

All of you are different. I haven't yet found anything in common about drug addicts except that they use drugs. We are not going to examine the broken homes in your background. You are more familiar with this information than I am. I don't know too much about those matters. I would like to give you an idea of where we are heading and what we have to offer you.

I have met hundreds of people in the past years who were exactly as you are today. You sit here at the end point of your thinking, feeling your genetic and cultural backgrounds. This is the end point right here. The values that you have accumulated through life for your own protection, to get what you want, or what you think you want, have brought you here. This is pretty clear, isn't it?

We don't have sitting in this room ten people who have been successful, creative lawyers, ministers, toolmakers, or anything like that. We've got some people that have spent time locked up in various playpens—jails, penitentiaries, nut farms, and things of that nature. In other words, you've landed periodically, or at least once, on your part. We have a starting point if you can concede that the set of values and the things that somehow you've built up, the things you learned and absorbed through your skin from your parents, teachers, friends, siblings, and others, brought you somehow at loggerheads with things as they are.

You are now living in a place with several hundred people who were addicts like you and have not used any drugs for over a year, many for two years, and it goes into the hundreds of those that haven't used any drugs or alcohol for three to five years. In addition to not using drugs, these Synanon people have not been in trouble. They haven't bumped heads with the police, they're not starving to death, and they haven't run out of the things that one needs to live. They managed to get around.

You must have tried to grow up as I tried. I bloodied my head, fouled up my environment, and screwed everything up in a real boss way. I conned people out of more money than all of you put together. It never did me any good. You have tried somehow to go after the things you wanted. When you were a baby, you wanted the red fire engine that the kid next door had. When you got into high school, you wanted the wardrobe or the little Chevrolet roadster that the guy across the aisle had, and you wondered how in the hell you could get it. Possibly, you tried to help yourself to success, but you haven't been too successful. You've gone after things, position, status, more or less directly, and they have all slipped through your fingers. I venture to say that every one of you can think of the time you got right up to the point where you thought you had it. You thought, "If I just had an apartment, that woman, that car, everything in life would be swell," and—boom—there you were back in a tank of some kind. "What the hell happened this time?" you say to yourself. You say, "Well, I made a little mistake," and then you go out and do it again and again and again.

Here we will teach you how to get the things you want constructively. If you can admit that you don't know too much about life—because not knowing got you here, and there has been a lot of psychic pain and nonsense and trouble in your background that you would rather not experience again—then you might accept this intellectually. Don't believe it, accept it intellectually. Say to yourself, "I'm going to act as if he knows what he's talking about."

Look at it this way: you have everything to gain and nothing to lose. In the beginning, because you have no power of decision that's any good, you use somebody else's power of decision. You use the power of decision that pervades the whole Synanon Foundation.

After you've been here for a short time, you will learn how to use the synanons three times a week. You will have one tonight, and you will be able to yell and throw your emotional garbage all over the floor. Everything goes. That is, everything short of physical violence. You can call anyone around here anything you wish in synanon. During the day, when we're trying to have a nice home, this kind of profanity gets in the way. It's a lot of nonsense. Who the hell wants someone to curse and swear, look sour, whine, and throw tantrums in the living room or dining room. It's asinine. We have an emotional bathroom three times a week: synanons—the most powerful form of group therapy that any of you have ever experienced, this I assure you. You will begin to use them pretty soon, and the gang will begin to nudge you a little bit, try to hurt your feelings, stir you up so that you can get this crap out. The rest of the time, do the best you can and try to control yourself.

You'll have a gig [job] pretty soon, but nobody works too hard in Synanon. We don't have time. We have a lot of other things to do. We have seminars, synanons, semantics classes, music classes, bands, choirs, art classes, and photographic studies. We're always doing something. You're only asked, or required, to go to the synanons three times a week, turn up at noon seminars, and do your job. That's all you have to do.

People are going to get mad at you, because the whole house is full of other people just like yourselves. They are going to make all kinds of noises at you. If you're nuts, if you are totally insane, you will run out the door like children do and fall down a manhole or slide merrily back into the penitentiary or whatever nut farm you were enjoying yourself at before you came here. That's what you will do. Remember what I'm trying to tell you. You're going to hear a lot of noises, and noises never hurt anybody. When you were a little kid, you used to stand on the corner and shout out at the kid next door that you were mad at, a very, very deep form of philosophy which you've probably forgotten. You said, "Sticks and stones may break my bones, but names will never hurt me." You see, you understood more about semantics then than you probably do now.

Two of you people must have the same writer. Your reasons for coming here are beautiful. They're good. No criticism intended. It sounds nice, but you've probably sat in a police station or the Lexington narcotics farm and told them the same story. I don't believe it; it's a lot of nonsense. And you and I, one of these days, if you stick around and grow up, will have a good laugh over that kind of nonsense. It might be fun to sit down and listen one day to this tape of what you said.

Right now, though, say to yourself, "I came to Synanon, and I went to considerable trouble to get here. I ran around shooting dope and went to jail and got roughed up and degraded. People said to me, 'Get out of that car; stand over against that wall.' " Guys like you and me, drunks and dope fiends, we're always sitting around saying, "By God, nobody's going to tell me what to do." The paradox is that there is no class of people in the galaxy that get told what to do more than nuts like us! [Laughter] Isn't that true? You go over there and live in San Quentin for two years. When you get to San Quentin, you might say, "By God, did I put it over on that judge! He must be nuts—he only gave me two years" Man, oh, man, isn't this fantastic? [Sarcastically] Nobody is going to tell me what to do!

There it is. From then on, you can do anything you are big enough or smart enough to do. You put your head down and you do what you're told, and pretty soon you find out that nobody is telling you what to do at all any more. You will have already begun to grow up. Nobody has to tell adults what to do, they already know what to do, and they're doing it.

Suppose we assume that our problem as a category of people is that we didn't grow up right in the first place; something is missing. We didn't get the brass ring, there's a piece missing out of the pie. The psychiatrists say that people like you and me have a character disorder. We're not neurotic, but we have a character disorder. This means that we act out our pain and our rebellion to our own detriment and to the detriment of anyone who happens to get in the way. Now, our character disorder, the one that I shared with you until a few years ago, the one you have right now, doesn't really do too much harm to other people in the larger society. There is nothing big time about our problem. We run around loaded, maybe engage in petty thievery, prostitution, or pimping. It's really kind of an annoyance, just like a fly that society has to put up with. The point is that we don't do too much harm to the rest of society—but we do tremendous harm to ourselves. Our behavior is self-destructive.

We go through life in a state of terror most of the time. We rationalize it into resentment or rebellion. We tell people what big guys we are. We even get into aggressive behavior sometimes. We hurt ourselves because we are motivated by an immediate self-interest. We want what we want when we want it. We want other people's property, we want their position, we want relief immediately from any kind of psychic discomfort; so we get drunk or we get loaded on drugs immediately. That's the kind of people we are.

We merely have to develop an enlightened self-interest. We have all these disadvantages and negatives behind us. We have, however, a tremendous advantage that many people do not have. Let me tell you what it is. We have inadvertently put ourselves through the most powerful learning process that is possible. The most powerful, that it, by doing things wrong the first time around.

Expand this experience. You have had thousands of experiences, most of them errors. The basis of the learning process is trial and error and "don't do it again." The trouble with nuts like us is that we keep doing it wrong over and over and over. We won't listen. This is our only sin in the cosmos. Our only sin, as far as I'm concerned (and I've made a rather deep study of sin for damn near fifty years), is stupidity. And there you have it—stupidity! You are at the end point of conscious and unconscious stupidity.

We assumed when you first came in here that you were emotionally a baby. I don't blame a baby because he sits in ashtrays, jams his fingers into light sockets, puts his hand on a hot stove, or walks out of the window instead of going down the stairs. No, one doesn't blame a baby. But when a baby begins to grow up a little bit and has been exposed to a learning process, people are trying to teach him all the time, and then this person becomes responsible for his own actions.

As a result of things that are inside yourself, I would say that out of the ten here, at least two of you will be gone in less than thirty days. You will be strung out on drugs again within six months. Within a year, you will be in another playpen, or you will be dead.

You are reaching for something and shooting for something that you cannot imagine. There is no possible way of anyone communicating to you how it feels to be a grown-up human being with a grown-up body and brain. You don't know about this. You've had no experience with it. We're faced with a problem similar to this one. For instance, trying to explain how a chocolate soda tastes to an Eskimo who's been eating whale blubber for thirty years. There is no possible way this can be done. It is out of the realm of his experience.

You can enjoy the experience of living as a creative adult with a grown-up body and brain. All of you basically have the potential. None of you are congenital idiots, none of you have hydrocephalic heads, none of you are morons. There's one main thing wrong with you. You don't know how it feels to be an adult, and you're scared to death of the responsibility and even the rewards.

You think, way down in your deepest gut, that somehow you're kind of a little kid playing with the big guys. You've got a feeling that all these people know things that you don't know. You feel something like the eighth grader feels in relation to high school boys or the the high school boys feel in relation to college boys. You feel somehow like the nineteen-year old feels when he looks at his friend who is a lawyer with a couple of kids. You've got that feeling buried deep in your gut, that feeling of unworthiness, of inadequacy. It isn't true, but you don't know it yet. We'll teach you all we can about life here in Synanon.

I love to talk about Synanon. The very second somebody comes into our door, at the club, I immediately accept the challenge, and it becomes very personal to me. I am speaking only for myself right now, but it has the same meaning for many other people around here. In some way, we hope to be able to put a crack into that wall of stupidity that surrounds people. We want to help them get living again. There is nothing more charming, nothing more satisfying to me than watching people toss away their blinders and begin to live.

This has been and is one of the greatest experiences of my life. When you get past your childish stage, you will find out that you have a lot of tremendous friends here at Synanon. There are other human beings here with whom you will be able to share many deep emotional and philosophical experiences. You will learn more about this as time goes on. As for now—welcome to Synanon.

Indoctrination

After physical withdrawal, there are a series of indoctrinations and discussions with the newcomer. These are not rigorously formalized sessions (as are interviews in a hospital or jail). Some newcomers go to work and are not talked to for several weeks. Others are subjected to many discussions in the first few days. Informal attention is paid to the newcomer, and this is geared to his needs. The indoctrination is not carried out in the institutionalized, bureaucratic style of a narcotics·hospital or other kind of formal setting. It is adapted to the emotional condition of the newcomer.

No indoctrination is typical. Each is geared to the newcomer's special human situation. The following indoctrination session was administered by Chuck, since the set of talks this newcomer had received from other Synanists did not seem to get through to her. The girl involved had some apparent special problems. She was fat (she weighed more than two hundred pounds) and emotionally disturbed. On top of these problems, she thought she was a lesbian. She had arrived several days earlier from New York (1962) with an addicted "girl friend." Both had made motions toward the door and leaving. Chuck delivered this indoctrination of the "Synanon contract" with the aid of several associates.

Chuck: You apparently are confused about Synanon. This is indicated by your behavior. You do not seem to know where you are. You think you're in jail or something. Maybe you could understand what we are trying to do here if I described it this way. Synanon is a corporation; it's a nonprofit corporation. It's a private enterprise; it is not supported by public funds. It is our business. It is sort of like the Standard Oil Company, owned by the stockholders. All the people in this room except you are directors, and we own this corporation.

Now, here's what we offer an addict, in simple terms. We offer an addict an opportunity to go to work for the Synanon Foundation. When you work for the Synanon Foundation, you get the necessities of life: you get shelter as good as we have, you get all the food you can eat, you get cigarettes, you get a pretty nice place to live; and if you continue to work for the Foundation, a month, two months, four months, or a year, eventually you'll be a pretty well-integrated human being. You've seen quite a few of them around here since you arrived, whether you recognize them or not. The small amount of work that you'll be required to do any adult could do standing on his head in a hammock in about two hours a day. Your job will probably run from four to five hours a day.

You will get the only therapy that works, more often than not, for narcotic addicts. In addition to your work, we demand certain standards of behavior around here for reasons known to us; not to you, yet. Someday you quite possibly will understand it; you will if you get well, and then you'll see why we are insistent on certain standards of behavior. There is no "we–they" situation here like there is in a prison.

The minute you kick your habit, you become part of the staff. You become one of some hundred or so doctors, and then you yourself are a patient and you've got about a hundred doctors around you. This is a new concept.

[Chuck now brings up her bad behavior of the evening before.]

In Synanon, we don't, for instance, permit women to go into the men's john and then, when they're reminded of it by another woman, say, "I ain't afraid of no mother-fucking man." That's not the way to operate here. If you want to operate that way, then you go someplace where they work that way.

We insist that you do your work and that you go to synanons. We insist that you stay clean and that you, to the best of your ability, behave like an adult human being. We provide synanon meetings three times a week, where you can have catharsis sessions.

You can sit there and call somebody a mother-fucker. There you can say to someone, "How do you stand that mother-fucking Chuck who runs the joint?" That's fine. I want you to do that, in that situation; but not in the building or in the men's john. You will behave yourself and you won't throw your weight around in this place, because you're an amateur. You don't know how to throw your weight around yet. Someday you'll learn how to assert yourself in a constructive manner. Now your behavior is quite obviously destructive.

Here you are, you're a mess, aren't you? The end point of your thinking and your attitude. Aren't you kind of a mess?

Chris: Yes.

Chuck: Okay, now we can get you out of this mess, if you do it exactly our way. We insist on this; first, for the Foundation and, secondly (always remember that), secondly, for the salvation of your soul. We only have one foundation—that's why we put it first—but we have tens of thousands of dope fiends out there, so you are more expendable than the Foundation.

Now this ought to make some kind of sense to you. We want you to watch your behavior, watch your language, except in the synanons. Blow off in the synanons, great stuff; but not on the floor. If you decide that you want to run off again, nobody is going to stop you; they're going to get right behind you and say, "Bye-bye," boom,

boom, boom, right out the door. That's the way we operate around here. And it's successful, whether you think so or not.

Your equivocations and all the nonsense about your name and your relationship with this other girl are of no consequence in themselves. But they prove to me what a nut you are. I suppose you came out here because you wanted to stop being a nut; is that true? Or did you come out here for the ride? Why did you come out here; do you know?

Chris: Because I want to straighten out.

Chuck: Very good! See if you can get going in here. You can't have very much of a habit. I'm going to assume you don't, because it really doesn't make a damn bit of difference. I'm going to assume that you told me the truth about your ride out on the bus.

Chris: We didn't use any junk [heroin].

Chuck: Junk, schmunk! You didn't use very much because you're really not in very bad shape. My God almighty, you look like a crowd!

You know, dope fiends, as a general rule, are four or five inches wide and weigh about eighty pounds. You can't be in very bad shape. We don't take a little Mickey-Mouse habit seriously; in fact, we don't take any habit as an excuse for behaving like an animal, not around here.

You're in with the experts; all of these people, every single one of them in this room, were addicts. I watched them kick in the Synanon Foundation. They didn't kick in a nice, beautiful building like this, but in a filthy storefront that we opened up in. While we were working, getting this place ready for nuts like you, you were out using drugs. You will keep a civil tongue in your head when addressing your betters, right! Does it make sense to you?

Chris: Yes.

Chuck: How old are you, by the way?

Chris: Twenty-eight.

Chuck: By the time you're thirty, you can be a grownup. This is what can happen to you if you decide to stick around and do it the way we do it here at Synanon.

This is it! No more nonsense; every person that comes in here doesn't get this kind of attention. I, for instance, don't even know anybody's name, as a general rule, until they've been here two or three weeks. They usually get indoctrinated by coordinators; but your behavior made it necessary for us to get some information out of you.

The people who talked to you yesterday couldn't even get your right name. It's all so asinine. You're behaving like a child. If you behave like an adult, you'll feel better immediately. You don't know how to behave like an adult, so we tell you how to behave like an adult. If someone asks you a question, answer the question! We are deserving of this courtesy because you have no right in here at all, only on our sufferance. This is not a government lockup. That's why I bring this thing up. We're a private foundation; we're in the business of making life smooth out for nuts like you. Do you have anything to say?

The indoctrination attempts to pare the newcomer down to his real emotional size. From Synanon's point of view, as Hurst describes it, "the addict who runs up and down back alleys, goes to jail, lies and cheats is an emotional infant." There is an attempt to get the newcomer to accept himself overtly the way he really thinks of himself inside. The mutual recognition of his low self-image is a first step toward progress. Jack once told me that when he was indoctrinated by Chuck, "his perception of me as a punk made me feel secure. I felt good in the presence of someone who really knew me and the kind of guy I was."

Another characteristic of the indoctrination is to tell the newcomer clearly and forcefully what will be expected of him: that he will have to work (at first on a menial level) and that he will have to follow the rules of Synanon. In addition, he is given some information about the nature of the organization.

He is further informed that he automatically becomes part of the staff. This tends to give him a sense of belonging. Also, as Jack put it, the addict "can achieve any status in the organization." He can see this as a real possibility, because the individuals confronting him (although they may not look like it) were once themselves dope fiends.

Another element of an indoctrination is to anticipate and prevent rationalizations and excuses for failure. The newcomer is vigorously apprised "in front" of the set of rationalizations he might use to go out and shoot drugs. This seems to have the effect of involving the newcomer more quickly. It helps him to become increasingly aware that he is dealing with individuals who know him and anticipate his thoughts and drives. In the indoctrination the assertion is repeatedly made that the newcomer has a limited superego, or ability to control his impulses. He is told that this self-control must initially be handled by the organization. ("You do not know how to say no yet, but you will learn.") After the prospect's low self-image is brought out into the open, he can relax about being found out. The indoctrination has already exposed him, and it is not necessary for him to keep up a front.

Another impression made on the newcomer is that he is in an environment wholly different from any he has known. He is told that he is not in prison or in a hospital, that he is in Synanon. This is repeatedly and forcefully driven home to him. Since the newcomer has probably failed in other settings, Synanon's uniqueness and difference may give him an expectation of hope.

Although tough, the indoctrination is honest. Despite the seemingly harsh quality of the attack method, the newcomer is accepted and explicitly informed that he can change. This technique is a most important part of the indoctrination. It helps the newcomer feel that he has overcome an obstacle "in front." He is encouraged to believe that the tough, honest people who indoctrinate him must think that he can change or they would not waste their time. A successful indoctrination transmits a feeling of hope to the newcomer and a belief in his own ability to succeed.

SMALL-"s" SYNANON

The small-"s" synanon is the group psychotherapy of the total Synanon social structure. In a sense it is the force that drives the wheels of the over-all organization. Information is fed into these intensive group sessions for treatment purposes. Also, the content of a synanon tells a great deal about the Synanon organization at any given point in time. Synanons are run regularly as part of the total therapeutic process. In addition to the basic-problem-oriented synanons, special ones on different topics are held. Among these are synanons on status-seeking, organization, prejudice, education, and work problems.

About three times a week each member of Synanon participates in a synanon in its basic form with ten to fifteen people. The groups proceed to different parts of the house. Everyone in the group settles down, as comfortably as possible, in a circle, facing one another. There is usually a brief silence, a scanning appraisal as to who is present, a kind of sizing one another up, and then the group launches into an intensive emotional discussion of personal and group problems. A key point of the sessions is an emphasis on extreme, uncompromising candor about one another. "No holds or statements are barred from the group effort at truth-seeking about problem situations, feelings, and emotions of each and all members of the group," I have been told.

The synanon is, in some respects, an emotional battlefield. Here an individual's delusions, distorted self-images, and negative behavior are attacked again and again. The verbal-attack method involves exaggerated statements, ridicule, and analogy. The attack, paradoxically, is an expression of love. As one Synanist told a person in a synanon: "If I didn't like you and also feel that you could change, I wouldn't tell you the things I do. It would be foolish to attack a cripple you don't like for limping."

Attack therapy in synanon has the effect of toughening up the person. It helps him to see himself as relevant others do. He gains information and insight into his problems. If, at the conclusion of a synanon segment, an individual who has been under attack is able to hang on to any of his defenses, they are probably, in Synanon terms, valid defenses.

A participant in a synanon is forced to examine positive and negative aspects about himself, as well as some dimensions he would never have considered on his own. This often leaves him with a clearer view and a greater knowledge of his inner and outer world.

The process of a synanon also involves learning something about the norms of the over-all Synanon society. The synanon helps to socialize the person and fosters a learning of interpersonal competence. This set of experiences seems to be useful for interaction situations both in Synanon and in the larger society.

Synanon groupings are constructed by a "Synamaster" (usually an older Synanon member), who draws his lists from the over-all population sheet of the house. The Synamaster puts together a group with a variety of considerations in his mind. He may separate an "employer" and his "employee," or he may put them in the same synanon, with a "therapeutic hypothesis" in mind. He considers time in Synanon and chronological age as factors in constructing synanon groups.

Ideally, a synanon should have a chronological and "Synanon-age" range, a correct male–female balance, and a senior Synanist to spark the session. These are only some of the many possible variables taken into account in constructing a synanon group. The Synamaster makes use of both knowledge and hunches in his consideration of the possibilities of each group's structure.

In some cases, the Synamaster will receive requests from an individual who wants to be in a synanon with a particular person in order to work out a special problem or because he has some data on the other person that he wants to reveal or discuss. Often two or more people, because of a particular situation, will request admission to the same synanon (for example, people who work together and have an interperson problem). These requests are usually granted and tend to have constructive consequences.

Some synanons are rigged in advance. Here a group or some key person is given a preliminary briefing about someone's problem, often with a suggestion as to how it might be worked out. Also, a combination of people with very similar problems may be placed in "fighting range" of one another in the same synanon. Big talkers and screamers may be mixed in with quiet types in order to give balance to the group.

Employer–employee problems and on-the-job problems generally are handled in the synanon. The synanon provides the opportunity to understand better a person's combined official and personal role. When an individual is thrown in with someone with whom he works, he has to relate to the individual's role both as a worker and as a person. The synanon provides an opportunity for an employee to confront his employer (or vice versa) on a personal level three times a week.

An important characteristic of synanon construction is the mathematical probability that no one group will meet intact more than once. This fact helps defeat the problem of the "therapeutic contract" that emerges in many professional therapy groups, where the same people meet regularly in the same group. A "therapeutic contract" involves a conscious and unconscious reciprocal agreement between two or more people not to expose one another's psychological Achilles' heel. The unstated contract might be, for example, "If you don't expose or attack my embarrassing and painful mother problem, I won't bring up your problem with your wife."

Although synanon groups shift, as an individual builds up synanon man-hours his particular emotional problems and weaknesses become well known. This information is consciously exchanged and passed around the organization. A person may get a "jacket" (or personality inventory) that becomes well known. It is standard operating procedure not to maintain confidences expressed in a synanon. Personal data are synanon property. An effort is made to use the information for the benefit of the individual and the group.

This fallout of personal information helps to ensure the continuity of an individual's treatment. In synanons, a well-known tough guy, lazy slob, momma's boy, or other type of personality may be continually attacked on his specific problem until he straightens out. The continuity of treatment is also maintained by proper use of the person's "jacket" and the Synamaster's group arrangements.

The content of a synanon session is not usually predetermined. The group's spontaneity is called upon to bring out a timely and significant problem. An individual's problems may be introduced by the comment, "Hey, Jim, how come you look so guilty?" (or nervous or happy or bored). This question may then trigger an investigation by the total group into the individual's feeling state. The person on the "hot seat" [receiving end] is the primary focus of attention at the time and usually defends or counterattacks. In the interaction process, information about the feelings, attitudes, and his life situation emerges for him and the group.

The following is an oversimplified example of the way a segment of a session begins and unfolds. Jack, age twenty-four, in Synanon for four months, is accused of an excessive dependency on his mother. It is then alleged by the group that this has prevented him from identifying with Synanon and becoming part of the processes that could help him. He counters by saying that the accusations are ridiculous and unfounded. "It's a bum beef." It is pointed out to him that he has been observed to do very little else in Synanon but wait for phone calls and mail from his mother. (The accusation is somewhat exaggerated, since Jack has been working and participating in the program.) After about fifteen minutes of group cross-examination, he admits to an extreme, depressing loneliness and a desire to see his mother. He claims that she is the only one in the world who truly loves and understands him. He has thought of "splitting" to go back to New York to see her.

His claim of his mother's exclusive love for him is scoffed at and ridiculed. In reply, as proof of her love, he points out that "she always gave me money for the commissary when I was in prison." This is ridiculed by the group as "guilt money." Jack cites other examples of her mother love, including the fact that "when I was up tight, she would sometimes even give me money for a fix!" His arguments are battered by the group.

He concludes, "Maybe I am sucking a dry tit and ought to let go." The group advises him to "go through the motions" of forgetting her for a while and "joining synanon." They point out how he can resume his relationship with his mother under better conditions when he straightens out. Jack admits to seeing his relationship with his mother in a somewhat clearer light. He "feels better" now that his feelings are "out" and agrees to "get with Synanon."

This is obviously a highly oversimplified glimpse of a slice of a synanon. However, it illustrates something of the kind of interaction used in an attempt to produce facts about a situation, the types of defenses used, some of the insights into behavior, and some of the suggestions for change. Not all dimensions of a problem are worked out for an individual in any single session. Over a long period of time, however, many Synanon members benefit from the help of a group that is familiar with their difficulty, since others in the group have had similar problems.

Built into the synanon sessions is an awareness of each group member's ability to take a bombardment of truth about himself. The Synanon newcomer is often handled lightly [given a "pass"] until he becomes trained in the method. Old-timers in Synanon and synanons are considered fair game for all-out attack. With them, there is an assumption that the synanon experience has toughened their emotional hides. They can defend more capably and are better prepared to handle the group's biting appraisal of their personal problems.

The senior members of Synanon, who have been through many synanons, are more sophisticated in their ability as Synanists. When they get together in a "senior-members' synanon" (as often occurs), they use less profanity, throw up fewer smoke screens to obscure their problems, and waste less time on irrelevancies. Their synanon fighting style is more like a rapier than a bludgeon. When a point is made, the group does not dwell on it and savor its great success; they move into another problem area. At least one senior Synanist is injected into each basic floor synanon to facilitate the interaction, pace, and productivity of the session.

When newly arrived individuals dominate a group, the synanons are apt to be cathartic sessions that involve excessive "emotional vomiting" and wild verbal fighting. As an individual grows and develops in the Synanon organization, he usually develops better control and has greater insight. Older members tend to be more intellectual and in many respects more productive in a synanon.

One ruse that is counteracted by the use of shifting synanon groups and the senior synanist is the "therapeutic contract" for a "dramatic insight discovery." The dramatic insight discovery is a fake insight that is used by a patient to give the appearance of making therapeutic progress, thus avoiding the pain related to true self-examination.

The phony-insight game (avoided in Synanon) takes the following form in standard group therapy. A group member in a therapy session makes the "remarkable discovery" that he shoots drugs (or acts out other deviances) to rebel against his proper, respectable father. The "insight" occurs as a result of a series of interchanges with the "therapeutic-contract" partner, who may in a later session reveal a remarkable "insight" of his own. The two involved in this kind of reciprocal deception (in some cases, a third person gets a piece of the action) nurture and manipulate each other over several sessions into revealing their smoke screen discoveries. These insights (even when they have some degree of validity) enable the individuals who have revealed them to get the group off their backs, since they are "obviously making progress" in understanding themselves. They can then spend the rest of their therapeutic interaction days feeding each other soothing lines, such as, "Of course, that relates to your admitted rebellion against your father," and therapeutic progress flounders. In synanon, shifting groups and the trained synanists tend to deter the development or continuation of this pattern of psychological masturbation.

Also, in synanon group therapy, pat pseudopsychological answers are viciously attacked when they are used as rationales for bad behavior. As Chuck told a newcomer trying this old game in a synanon, "In one sense, we don't really give a damn if your grandfather was an alcoholic, your mother hustled, and your father slugged you daily. None of it is an excuse for bad behavior in Synanon!"

In the synanon system, good behavior is demanded on the implicit assumption that it affects internal (intrapsychic) processes. Synanon uses an approach that is the reverse of that commonly used in psychotherapy. In most therapies, the starting point for treatment is the internal world of the patient. Generally, in professional therapy, the assumption is made that if a person's inner problems are somehow adjusted he will stop acting out his bad behavior. Synanon starts with an attack on the reality of overt bad behavior.

The synanon makes it difficult for an individual to hide behind a false insight, complicate a simple behavioral situation with pseudoanalysis, or maintain a therapeutic contract for any length of time. Insight discoveries are placed under close scrutiny in a synanon. If they do stand up after a synanon group barrage, they probably have validity; and in the process, every facet of the insight or situation has been tested and examined.

Professionals tend to lean more heavily on the psychological insight. Within the framework of standard professional psychotherapy, insight discoveries (valid or not) are the bread and butter of the trade. The professional may, in fact, encourage insight discoveries to validate their own success. Chuck takes this position on the issue: "These are, of course, the professional stock-in-trade. When someone comes into Synanon loaded with all kinds of psychological mishmash, for a while we have a hell of a time breaking through to the person beneath. Of course, many psychological principles are valid and are useful later on in his growth process. But at first we have to deal with the person and his actual behavior at that time. We cannot permit him to use psychological explanations to rationalize his bad behavior. He might shoot dope behind it."

Synanon sessions operate within a social scheme and under a set of conditions different from those of standard professional group therapy.

First: The sessions are administered by a group of peers who have similar problems. Because of a similarity of life experiences and identifications, a fellow Synanist is more likely to be acceptable as a "therapist" than the usual professional. Also, compared with the usual professional therapist, the synanist is not seen as an authority figure in the usual sense.

Second: Synanists can and do reverse roles as "patient" and "therapist" in synanon sessions. The Synanist who plays the role of a therapeutic agent in a synanon expects, and often does obtain, some insights into his own problems in the process of helping the other person. He often projects his own problems into the situation. This kind of cooperative therapy facilitates the realization of a true total therapeutic community.

Third: Synanon involves a democratic approach to psychological interaction. There is an absence of the usual status differences between patients and doctors. This condition of equality among group members seems to facilitate a deeper intensity and involvement than does standard group therapy.

Fourth: The emotional growth of each person in Synanon is of concern to everyone in the group. Everyone's success and personal growth are part of Synanon's over-all development. An enlightened self-interest in helping the other member is a significant motivating force for all participants. There is a "gut-level" recognition that no man can be an island in Synanon. Involvement with Synanon entails involvement with the success or failure of other members.

Fifth: The session material is timely, pertinent, and important to all members of the group, partly because they live together in the same community. The use of material and events in a synanon that have been experienced firsthand by other members of the group is a most significant element of the synanon. The problems dealt with are vital to all the members.

In contrast, in professional group therapy, the group members usually come from various walks of life, convene for a session, and then return to their private worlds. This kind of treatment can become a therapeutic game, not closely related to basic life situations, since the group members do not live in similar environments. In Synanon, a person locks horns with others who are part of his actual primary group. Everyone is a "significant other" to him in his life space. The "other" confronting in the synanon may be his roommate, employer, lover, or wife. Having them understand or get a correct self-picture of himself is of crucial importance. The synanon encounter is therefore a potent interaction, and the outcome of a session has real meaning for all participants. When a decision is made in a synanon session, the person has, in fact, acted. The synanon is not a game. It is live and meaningful behavior.

ATTACK THERAPY

An important method of attack therapy in Synanon is the "haircut." This form of verbal attack employs ridicule, hyperbole, and direct verbal onslaught. In part, the haircut attack keeps the rug pulled out from under the recovering addict. As Chuck describes it: "If he gets set, begins to feel a little complacent, and feels he's in control of himself—which, of course, he isn't—he may even think he can reward himself with a little dope or a pill. Then, of course, blouie, he's dead again." This, of course, is also the classic pattern of the rise and fall of the alcoholic.

An important goal of the haircut method is to change the criminal-tough-guy pose. The self-image held by newcomers as big-time gangsters is viciously attacked and punctured in the haircut. A case in point is the haircut that was administered, in the wake of bad behavior, to a group of twelve self-styled New York gangsters who had come to Synanon for help.

The group of so-called little gangsters was brought into Chuck's office as a result of "bad behavior" on the beach on a Christmas morning. They were called in for cursing and crime talk within the hearing of an elderly gentleman who was passing by the beach side of the building. (Chuck later told me: "Since Reid and I were already going to give our time to the youngsters who had committed the offense in question, we called in all the New York gangsters for a mass haircut. With the same set of motions, we were able to work on the larger little-gangster symptom we find in most of our young newcomers.") In addition to the relative newcomers on the carpet, a six-month member and some older synanists were in the group to serve as role models. They represented models of the change that could take place in the little gangsters if they straightened out.

The elements of exaggeration and artful ridicule are revealed in this haircut. In addition, the pattern of attack and then support is demonstrated. A typical haircut goes beyond the bad behavior of the moment and into a more serious problem, and this is also revealed in the session. Unlike synanons, it is not interactional. A haircut is usually delivered by several older Synanon members to younger members. Chuck and Reid dominate the following scene:

> Reid: I don't know what you'd call this meeting. I don't think you'd even call it a haircut. I think we're going to make some observations on stupidity—stark, staring, raving stupidity. Think about this: we actually have some guys in this room who are representing themselves to each other and other people as New York gangsters. I have an idea that Legs Diamond or Frank Costello would have never wound up in here even if they became junkies.
>
> These punks sit around here and discuss in the back toilet how you hit a guy with a pipe. I doubt if any of you hit anybody. Maybe you've been slapped a couple of times and you think of this as gang violence.
>
> This group was just out in front of our building talking about

boosting and dope and managed to say something like "I don't give a fuck" as one of our neighbors and taxpayers passed by. These little gangsters, all sent out here on mamma's money, haven't even observed that their little clique is made up of dishwashers and service-crew men who haven't even been here long enough to get any of the treatment they so sorely need. They hit rock bottom, and their mothers got some money together and sent them out here.

Here you are, little punks, representing yourselves as gangsters or hard guys. You get around our pool table downstairs, and I guess you think you sound like Legs Diamond or Kid Weil or something. You sound like one of the cheapest, phoniest poolhall gangs over on the East Side, where they chip in fifteen cents to play a short rack of pool. That's what you sound like.

This is really kind of funny. We always figure we have a disturbed ward. Part of the disturbed ward gets in front of the jukebox, and they stick their ear against it and they snap their fingers. We stand at the doorway and we laugh. It's all right—they're insane. But when it starts messing with our business, we have to knock it off.

When the lunatic fringe stands back in the toilet and tells each other the best way to wield a pipe, because they read some pocketbooks somewhere, or when they get out on the oceanfront with this gangster stuff, it's getting too absurd. It's all a part of the insanity.

For a short period of time, we don't mind if you stand in front of the toilet and signify to each other how bad you were or how much dope you shot. You were all such big shots that your mommas put you in Metropolitan Hospital [New York hospital for addicts] three or four times, then a couple of trips to Lexington, and then shipped you out here. We are not going to permit you standing out in front of our beach and insulting our neighbors. You are all so stupid that you don't even know how funny you are. You tell each other about all the dope, all the big scores, how bad you are, and yell "fuck" out in front of our building. Your stupidity is pathetic. Boy, you're sad. I met a few gangsters. They used guys just like you to go get their sandwiches. And if they were big peddlers, they gave you a cap [capsule of heroin] for delivering something.

I really wonder if they get the message. Here's a bunch of punks whose mommas paid for them to come out here and they're talking tough. It's really fantastic! You're funny until you get out in front and say "fuck" in front of our neighbors. You're really funny. Anytime anyone with brains around here wants to get a laugh, we say watch some of those—they're hip and they're tough and they're sharp.

Chuck: The lunatic fringe, the disturbed ward, the punks from the sidewalks of Azusa, New York, Akron, Ohio—they're all the same. They all read the same books off the magazine stand. When they come out here, some of them get with what we are doing, stay, and finally grow up. Others go back and wind up once again in Lexington or some penitentiary or the county jail or sitting in some filthy saloon. We know that we have to put up with this kind of insanity for a period of time, until you work out of it. That's kind of like growing new hair when we cut all your hair off. It's like getting your teeth fixed or other things we have to do for you, like putting some meat on your bones, but as Reid explained to you, we will not permit it to get in the way of our business.

Reid: Let's consider another angle. If this place was San Quentin or Sing Sing, I might agree with your tough-guy act. In prison, I suppose you have to let it be known that you were a hotshot on the street and that you're a bad guy inside the walls. This is what you do to get status in prison. But think of how ludicrous it is when you come here to this place and you try to be tough guys or gangsters. In this place, if you make progress, you act like an adult. If you are gangsters, let's at least concede this, you're the very dregs of gangsterdom, the very dregs.

Chuck: When this thing hits you and you begin to just get a vague inkling of how absurd your behavior has been, you're liable to get hysterical laughing at yourself. This is the beginning of growing up, when you see how extremely and ludicrously funny you are. This is kind of a young group. The old gangster of course, went out of existence before most of you guys were born. There are very few of them left any more. I'm talking about tough guys that really made scores. I would venture to say that in the last five years, all of you in this room, if you took every dime that all of you scored and put it on the table, it probably wouldn't support Reid's old drug habit for six months. You see, the thing is too absurd if you want to use that frame of reference.

Let's look at some of the hipster's stupid behavior. We have the jukebox syndrome. That applies to people who use the jukebox not for what it's intended, not to listen to music, but to put on an act. The jaw kind of recedes and drops a little bit, and you have this bit (snap, snap). That's the jukebox syndrome. Healthy people listen to jukeboxes to hear music.

Then there's the pool hall syndrome. Men go to a pool-hall table to play a game of pool. Nuts go to the pool table to make shots this way (backwards), when it can be done much better the other way. They use it to give it this cigarette bit. They leave the cigarette there until the eyeball is full of nicotine.

Then you have the toilet syndrome. Now, most people use the toilet to go to the john or wash their hands or face. No, not our lunatic fringe. They use the toilet to cut up jackpots of how tough they are and where to hit a man properly. I don't think you really know how to kill a man with your bare hands. You see, we have people around here who do. If you want to find out, we'll have a class in judo. We'll have a lot of fun and put some mats down in the basement. We can then get into that a healthy way.

Let's not worry too much about these little details. Let's think in terms of an attitude. If you can actually get down through your funny little image and say "Where am I?" Let's list where you are not: you're not on the streets of New York, you're not in some big yard, you're not in the county jail, you're not in a private sanitarium, you're

not in Lexington, you're not in a pool hall. "What am I? I am
twenty-five years old, thirty years old, twenty-two years old." Whatever it happens to be. "I'm not a ten-year-old boy." What am I? Who
am I? When am I? You'll get those questions answered. This involves
growing up. It's a much more comfortable way to live, boys, let me
tell you. It really is.

Reid: Let's look at the phenomenon of drug addiction. All of us,
I think, in here are agreed that we might have had a delusion at one
time that it's pretty hip to be a dope fiend. I think it's pretty lame to
shoot dope now, don't you? In other words, you're kind of a lame
if you're willing for three or four fixes to go sit in a cage for ten
years. You know, real dunces and fools. Think about it. There I shot
three weeks of dope, now I'm in jail for ten years. You're like a
goddam bird sitting in a cage. Okay, if that is stupid and lame, then
you have a little period of perplexity.

Remember that everybody here was just like you, including me. As
an example, I'll guarantee you I'm a hell of a lot further from ever
sitting in a cell for the rest of my life than you are. I'm probably a
hell of a lot more comfortable, and I'll guarantee I was just as
nutty or nuttier than you when I arrived.

Chuck: Let's accelerate this program. Would you rather be like
Reid is today than like you are? [They indicate yes] What's stopping
you? You can beat him in this race for sanity, you know.

Reid: Think about either lining yourself up on the side of sanity
or lining yourself up on the side of insanity. You might say to yourself, even now after our talk, you may come out and say, "Well,
I'm not going for that bullshit." Think about it this way. Here are
the nuts in danger of returning to drugs, the street, and their cells.
When you stand around and you listen and you don't make any
comment when some real dingbat is raving and slavering, I guess
you've got to face the facts that you are on the side of insanity.
There are two camps in here all right. We've always had a bunch of
lunatics at any given time. Are you with them or with the same people who have given up the bullshit and are getting well?

Do you realize how funny it is? Nobody in this room ever again
has to sit in a cell or stand on some cold goddam bald-headed corner
waiting for the man to come back with your bread [money] or your
shit [drugs.] You don't have to go to any more lunatic asylums,
you don't have to go through kicking another habit, you don't have
to do any of these things. Nothing in the world is going to make you
do these things. Nothing in the world is going to make you do these
things if you don't want to. This is true only if you decide to give
up the very actions [criminal image] that keep getting you back into
trouble.

Chuck: We can bring it a lot closer to the moment. Do you realize
that you never even have to have another haircut in Synanon? I don't
mean a physical haircut. You don't even have to have anybody talk
bad to you. This session is business for Reid and me. This is work.
Who wants to work? There are many more pleasant things that we

can do than to pull a kid in and try to teach him how to save his life by cutting his hair or giving him hell. You don't ever have to be on that end of it again. You can keep your mouth shut, do your work, and try to behave like a gentleman. In a very short time, you're in a position of trying to help another guy who comes in here sick. Then you can turn to some other guy and say, "Was I like that? Is that the way I acted? Is that the way I appeared to be?" And they will say, "Yeah, that's right, that's the way you were." You won't be able to believe it. You just won't be able to believe it. None of this stuff has to happen to you.

You know, a little humiliation in here is the highest price you can pay, a little humiliation. There is no punishment; we can't punish you if we wanted to. We can't lock anybody up, we can't strap you to a kitchen chair and knock out your teeth like it happens in police stations. We can't do that, and we don't want to. We can humiliate you in an effort to save your lives. That is all. After you get a few of these haircuts, you'll learn how to do it pretty good yourselves, so that you'll be able to help some other guy. But you really don't have to go through this ever again. Keep your hair if you want to. You can live with a little dignity, you don't have to be degraded, pushed around ever again. I don't mean over a period of time. I mean at this moment, right here, you can walk out the door of this office right now and it can never happen to you again as long as you live.

Several weeks later, the "little-gangster haircut" was analyzed in an interchange with Chuck, Dr. George Bach, and myself. We listened to a playback of the session and then "cut it up," synanon style.

George: Why didn't you let the "little gangsters" speak or talk back?

Chuck: Let me clarify that for you, George. Again, the important point is that this is not a regular synanon. Our people do their talking in a synanon interchange. This is a haircut. They have offended, they cursed on our beach. We don't want them to do this, so we communicate this in a one-way direction. It's from Synanon to them.

In the context of a seminar, a drama class, or a synanon, they can yell back and forth all they want. But when we are to correct bad behavior, we don't want to hear any reasons for it; this could become symptom reinforcement. We don't allow them to talk about or rationalize their bad behavior. We know that it's bad behavior to yell "fuck" on the beach. I don't want to hear any reasons why somebody did it. All we want to do is tell them graphically, clearly, with dramatic imagery, the way we want them to behave in the future. I'm not interested in why they want to behave badly. The way they behave is what brought them here in the first place. We attempt to correct stupid behavior. Call it therapy if you want to. We point out their stupidity in the hope that they will learn how to grow up and function like adults. We stress this education for life.

THE NEWEST PROFESSION

I suppose a professional is someone who is trained and professes to do something. Right? The professionals haven't cured any addicts, and Synanon has. I guess we have as much right to be called professionals as they do. Right?

Reid Kimball

Perhaps the most controversial element of the new Synanon society is its profound belief that people can help themselves without standard professional therapy or therapists. The organization has developed an independent approach to social problems and their solutions. Synanon draws its concepts from many quarters and works in somewhat the reverse fashion of the usual professional approach. Chuck once gave me a summary of Synanon's "professional" position: "We use as much knowledge from as many sources as possible. In Synanon we quote and use the ideas of Freud, Ralph Waldo Emerson, Lao-tse, and many of the pronouncements of Christ. We use any system of ideas that helps us to better understand the human condition.

"We use self-training, you know, 'going through the motions.' We deal with the person's identity in the here and now. We use brainwashing and attack therapy here to peel away those parts of the self that haven't been too effective, in fact, that have put the person in the mess he's in. We make him aware of new ideas and ways of behaving. By getting the person to go through certain behavior motions, he is somehow euchred into constructing his own approach to life.

"We work backwards from psychoanalysis. They begin with the id and the unconscious. We get there, too, but we begin with behavior and the superego.

"We do not reward bad behavior here, and we always try to reward good behavior. We give the people here information about themselves and life, and this seems to equip them to construct their own superego. We just provide the tools for learning and a direction. The person does the rest himself."

Over the past fifty years, the treatment of social problems has been dropped into the professional lap and has been held on to tightly. The propaganda about the professional's exclusive right to treat social problems has reached its high mark. The professionals, the public, and even patients are firmly convinced that the only bona fide treatments and "cures" available come from legitimate professionals with the right set of degrees.

The sheer existence of the Synanon approach is considered by some professionals to be an attack upon the status quo and vested interest of their professional domain. Synanon's position that some of its "patients" can become therapists seems to draw fire from many professional quarters.

To balance the scale, it should, of course, be noted that many professional people have supported Synanon in principle and with direct psychiatric, medical, dental, and other professional services. The more absurd professional enemies of the Synanon movement, however, do slow and impede Synanon's natural thrust and growth. Their unwarranted destructive attacks have helped block aid to untold numbers of addicts. Many more addicts might have availed themselves of the Synanon program if it had been accepted and permitted to grow large enough to accommodate more people.

Beyond the bureaucratic explanation, I find it difficult to assay the professional resistance to Synanon. This opposition is unfortunate not only for the addict who is blocked in his efforts to save himself—the ignorant judgments of some professional enemies slop over into the community and give intelligent potential supporters of Synanon pause. An even more damaging result of irrational professional negativism is that it provides fuel for many elements of the community viciously opposed to all "mental-health" efforts.

Part of the resistance to Synanon may stem from the fact that Synanon has been modestly successful in an area where most professionals have admittedly failed. Moreover, this success, in part, has resulted from the "patient's" reversing roles with the therapist.

The examination and clarification of Synanon's position on a variety of issues that relate to "professional" Synanist work may help to delineate some of the boundary lines that exist between Synanon and orthodox professionalism. In passing, these "assays" may reveal some of the overt and covert professional conflict with and resistance to Synanon.

Synanon is totally opposed to the nonmedical use by Synanon people of any drugs, alcohol, or chemicals that modify a person's emotional, or feeling, state. The reasoning behind it is that the use of drugs or alcohol might affect the person's self-control and propel him into using stronger and stronger drugs, up through heroin. Chuck considers drugs to be exclusively the province of the medical profession: "Drugs are properly used by medical men in the course of their work. We do not believe in the use of any kind of drug outside the realm of proper medical practice. As far as alcohol goes, the great big standard American social lubricant—we do not permit our people to use it in any form. There is a flat-out alcohol prohibition policy in Synanon. One reason for this is the bare possibility that residual proneness to an addictive escape might rear its head if a person starts fooling with a few cocktails every night for dinner or even every few months.

"Another reason for this prohibition throughout the organization is that the leaders of a business based on strict abstinence on the part of its rank-and-file members should also forego this pleasure—if it be pleasure. We in the upper reaches, as part of our job, serve as role models, clean examples to our newcomers. I seriously doubt whether I or some of the directors would get in any trouble if we had a drink now and then, but we just make a policy of not doing this. We insist on Synanon people conforming to this posture.

"We do not care whether our square friends are drinking or not. However, when any have the poor taste to show up at our home loaded, we would have to kick them out. We have enforced this policy with several people, and a few of these were important donors."

Synanon is uncompromising on the issue of drug and alcohol use. This moral position regarding drug and alcohol use seems to disturb many "hip-square" friends of Synanon. (The "hip square" would be a person who has dabbled with drugs or had some association with the criminal-addict world in his experience). Many hip squares are attracted to Synanon and its members because they (mistakenly) believe that there is a kinship between their own beliefs and the viewpoint of Synanon members. The hip squares (and this includes some professionals) who visit Synanon often use such hip talk as the greeting "Hey man, what's happening?" They are somewhat surprised and often chagrined when this talk is, in their own hip language, put down [verbally crushed].

This brand of hipsterism and the Synanon response are illustrated by a hip young couple who visited Synanon. The wife thought they would be real "in" [accepted] by her comment: "Yeah, my old man and I blow some pot [marijuana] occasionally—just for kicks— nothing serious." She and her husband were quickly escorted to the front door with the admonition, "We cannot afford to have any using dope fiends on our premises." (The expression "using dope fiend" is Synanon's standard hyperbolic "putdown.")

The moral attitude of clear opposition to drug and chemical use and accompanying hip talk is an attitude clearly taken by the Synanon professional but not necessarily by the professional professional. Many professionals join the criminal culture, if not behaviorally, at least with subtle approval. Many New York psychotherapists I have known have worked with drug addicts and taken no really negative position on their use of drugs. Their working assumption is that if they can successfully treat the psyche, the addict will eventually abandon the use of drugs. I do not know of one case where this professional position has succeeded. Synanon, in contrast, seems to have an approach with a strong measure of moral fiber built in. Synanon works, "in front." They don't hope that the addict will stop using drugs; they demand and get abstinence.

My own hipsterism, when I first arrived at Synanon, clarified a professional disease that facetiously became known in the Synanon administration as the "Yablonsky effect." In my past research, pre-Synanon, in "working with" and doing research on violent-gang youths, prisoners, and drug addicts both in lockups and in the community, I had acted on my belief that the best way to establish rapport (social-work jargon for "get next to") with subjects was to talk their language.

This I began to do in my early Synanon research days. In particular, I began to "hang out" with Frankie Lago and Jimmy Middleton. (Both Lago and Middleton had, in their pre-Synanon past, been "boss dope fiends." Their combined jail and prison time totaled almost twenty years.) We were "buddies"; and, in fact, the association (in addition to being personally gratifying) produced some useful knowledge about Synanon for me.

At about a six-month point in my association with Synanon, in one of the so-called big-shot synanon sessions that I attended (comprising the executive staff), I was "brought up sharp." In that synanon, my "appalling, atrocious behavior" was pointed out by Chuck. He said that there was a "bare possibility" that my hip talk and manner might very well be reinforcing Middleton's and Lago's criminal components. It was pointed out to me very forcefully that my "buddy approach with the patients" was harmful to them. Chuck and other members of the executive staff gave me a vicious "haircut," and it hurt.

But I began to see something. True, I was gathering some useful information, yet I could see that my response to Lago's and Middleton's revealing to me the details of their criminality was in some ways giving approval to this component—the very dimension of their personality that Synanon was trying to change.

I was asked or, better said, was told, "Why don't you talk to them sometimes about sociology or academic life or world politics?" "Why not indeed," I began to think.

This personal (and somewhat painful) experience caused me to review the over-all professional posture toward criminological research and treatment. In fact, it now seems to me that professionals who glory in hearing crime stories can, by tacit approval, negatively influence individuals attempting to "put down" their past (and future) criminality. The wrong approach seems to reinforce the symptom of criminal behavior.

There exists in many criminologists whom I know an intense interest (and perhaps vicarious satisfaction) in the criminal exploits of their subjects. Many are intrigued voyeurs of the criminal world. This inclination and involvement are in some measure reflected in many professional publications on the subject. For example, in the drug-addiction field, my cursory review of recently published conference reports and papers reveals a tremendous preoccupation with the symptoms and various patterns of destructive drug use and with the hallucinatory effects of drugs. In comparison with the symptomatic destructive aspects of addiction, fewer publications appear to be concerned with the causes and cure of the problem.

There seems to be, among many professionals, almost an admiration of the "interesting, exciting world of crime and addiction." In my past work, I found this to be true among professional gang workers in New York City. They would almost brag about how tough their gangs were. In response to a question I asked of a New York street-gang worker (a professional social worker) about his gang's criminal-addict behavior, he commented, "Oh, man, this is a real down ["sharp"] group of ditties. We have all kinds of weapons, and they'll use them at a moment's notice."

Then, laughingly, about drug use, he said, "All the kids fool with some drugs—not much H [heroin], but, you know, smoking pot and pills. The other day they wanted me to get high with them. Naturally, I wouldn't, but I think I lost status because I acted square." This type of blatant symptom reinforcement is quite prevalent among many professionals, including the objective, nonjudgmental breed of therapist.

Changing the laws to fit the needs of self-destructive behavior patterns seems patently absurd. The so-called British system, which permits medical doctors to give addicts drugs legally, is much more complex than described in the foregoing criticism. There is evidence (and I have corroborated this myself in a visit to London) that England has a more severe drug problem than the American experts who advocate free and legal drug use in the United States know about. (I personally and professionally feel that it is totally absurd to give an addict drugs. It's like giving a person dying of cancer more cancer!)

Synanon does not take a militant position about the so-called British system or the use of drugs for withdrawal in hospitals. However, within its framework, the rigid policy against drug and alcohol use has been developed on the basis of considerable sober thought. According to Chuck Dederich: "We do not have any dope problem in Synanon or any drinkers. We do not raise our eyebrows or judge others. Of course, we have our opinions. We don't think that the so-called British system would work in the United States. I've read about its claims and the contradictions in the British press of arrests for drug peddling. Recently, several Americans were arrested for controlling a large black-market drug-pushing business in London. We do not have the time to address ourselves to this paradox, since we are busy with our own work. The British system has no more to do with Synanon than Chrysler Motors. We can't really get involved with these other approaches. We are too busy strengthening and developing our own, which seems to be rather successful in controlling criminal and addictive behavior.

"In Synanon, we don't violate the law or use social lubricants, and we are opposed to this type of behavior. We are more square than our square friends. Perhaps we have to have a more rigid moral fiber than is believed to be necessary in the larger society."

Mental Health

An issue of disagreement between some professionals and Synanon is what constitutes "mental health." To many professionals, a true "cure" can be accomplished only by a bona fide professional therapist. Some professionals say that Synanon works up to a point. When that "point" is reached, they contend, a "real professional" should be permitted to take over for a "real cure." One psychoanalyst friend of Synanon described it this way: "Synanon is fantastic in bringing the person to the level where he can be reached by psychoanalysis. Because of Synanon, we (professionals) are now in a position to cure the addict."

This covert residual of resistance, even by enthusiastic pro-

Synanon professionals, reflects a generally held belief that, in an "underground" way, blocks Synanon's forward thrust. In my view, on a deep level, many professionals and fund-granting agencies (government and private), and even some Synanon members, firmly accept this sneaky propaganda that mental health can result only from the aid the patient gets from bona fide professional agencies or people. This viewpoint is, I believe, one of the greatest and most persistent blocks to Synanon's acceptance and growth. It is the position that prods the more irrational professionals and lay citizens to attack Synanon.

Despite these overt and covert resistances, Synanon continues to produce, if not bona fide, legal mental health, at least healthy behavior. Synanon maintains a relatively liberal view of what constitutes mental health.

At Synanon, mental health (a term often facetiously used: "He thinks he has 'mental health' ") is associated with rational behavior. Important among the characteristics of mental health in Synanon is a freedom from specification for mental health and freedom from the use of alcohol and drugs. The abstinence is the starting point for the growth and development of Synanon people.

According to Chuck: "If one gives off an aura of enjoying life more than not and has the ability to do his job and conduct his human affairs rationally, we would say here he has 'mental health.'

"We don't subscribe to the idea, which I find so extant among professionals, that everyone is sick. They look at everyone in terms of his personality weakness.

"One of the forces at Synanon which helps our people's growth is that they are judged by their present behavior. They are appraised at Synanon by what they do now, not in the past. The upper half of Synanon people function as well as people in the larger society in the course of their work and relations with others.

"One can only speculate how this group would do in terms of mental health outside of Synanon. We have some bellwethers, of course; there are currently over thirty of our people working and living outside and doing quite well."

One of the dimensions of the Synanon community that may foster mental health is its emphasis on cultural activities. There is an implicit encouragement to participate in a semantics class, a band, a dance class, or almost any other kind of cultural or intellectual activity. There is little boredom at Synanon because of the variety of available "healthy" activities.

"Attack Therapy"

Some professionals who have been exposed to Synanon's verbal-attack approach to therapy find it highly unorthodox. Some consider it destructive; others, supporters, believe that it gets to levels of human problems that have not been reached by other approaches. A first encounter with Synanon's hard-hitting approach to therapy is often shocking. A close appraisal of the method reveals some sound underlying logic.

In a forthright statement on some aspects of this "hard line" Chuck commented: "Dope fiends shoot dope. As long as they are dope fiends, they are not much good; they are slobs and thieves, with the temperaments of nasty little children. When they stop using dope, they're something else again. They need self-respect and then general respect more than they do sympathy.

"This will send them running for a fix. Too much laxness with them—particularly in the early stages—makes them take their adjustment problems too lightly. At Synanon we may seem rough on the newcomer at times, but we have to be their guts, until they develop guts for themselves."

Synanon sessions and verbal haircuts are powerful forms of attack therapy. During my first synanon session (even though I had been exposed to fourteen previous years of work in group psychotherapy), I too was shocked by the brutal treatment of individuals when they were placed on the "hot seat." (The "hot seat" consists in the entire group's vicious cross-examination of a person's behavior. He has to defend himself, since no one else will. In the process, his negative behavior is exaggerated, caricatured, and ridiculed. It seems as if his self is being psychologically damaged.)

My first reaction to the rugged synanon was to conclude that the attackers were after "blood" and that somehow this "fixed" their own emotional sadistic needs. I also feared for the victim of the mob. I could see some of the therapeutic rationale for attacking bad behavior; but at that time, I felt that the group was "rat-packing" a "victim" and was going too far.

However, on the basis of my participation in about a hundred synanon sessions and haircuts, I have revised my early personal opinions about what some professionals have labeled verbal brutality. (I personally was a victim and target in about a dozen sessions.) My recognition of the validity of "attack therapy" was gradual. At first, it surprised me tremendously, after a rough session, to see two or more bitter enemies come out of the session laughing about their synanon experience and discussing it in a jovial, friendly manner. After one session that I attended, I remember an individual who had been on the hot seat (accused of goofing off on his job) telling his antagonist later, "You son-of-a-bitch, you really exaggerated my work out of sight. I did most of that work. . . ." The former antagonist, now friend, said, "What did you expect? We were in a synanon."

I began to learn the rules of the synanon game and that almost any kind of verbal tactic is legitimate if it helps a person to look at his behavioral soft spots. The issue of how far one goes in a session is not precisely spelled out. It varies with the person involved, the time, and place. An old-timer in the Synanon described it this way: "I've known Chuck to give people haircuts for giving haircuts and not knowing when to knock off. Chuck can make a man literally climb walls, but he will never push him over the edge. I mean, Chuck somehow has the sense of timing or understanding or feeling—whatever it is—that all of us needed to be pushed up against the wall when we came here. We needed to be pushed hard and have our thinking turned around. Chuck somehow has the exquisite sense of knowing just how hard to go, when to quit, and, of course, to pick up a man after he's run the man up against a wall. He doesn't leave him depressed after a haircut; he'll give him something to pick himself up with."

The "pickup" after a man has been verbally attacked is crucial to the method. I have observed that this invariably occurs at some point. More often than not, it doesn't occur in the same session in which the person was pushed hard to examine himself. The pickup may occur right after the session, over coffee; or, the victim of a verbal attack may be "fixed" by a compliment at a time when he least expects it. The approval or compliment is given at a time of maximum effectiveness.

Chuck Dederich looks at attack therapy as a necessary approach in Synanon: "Of course, some synanons are brutal. So is surgery or amputation. The process of cutting out an emotional element which might turn into a deadly gangrene tends to be brutal."

In synanons, I have noted that each member, almost in turn, takes the hot-seat position and gives the group the right to hack at his disability. The underlying assumption seems to be, "If I'm strong in that emotional area, no screaming at me can hurt; and if I am supersensitive, then good—point it out. I better examine what you say, even if you grossly exaggerate the problem."

Some people would, not too surreptitiously, draw the group's verbal fire because they wanted and needed attention. For example, El Gato would use his Mexican-style moustache to draw critical attention to himself. The moustache seemed to grow in proportion to his need for help. Another individual would bring up a personal problem he had that he knew would attract the group's attention. As the Greek put it to one member, "You like to be hollered at, don't you? I guess it makes you feel good to know someone cares."

After my first twenty-five sessions, I began to feel that, in many respects, the synanon attack was an act of love. Entwined in an attack was the assumption: "If we did not care about you or have concern for you, we would not bother to point out something that might reduce your psychic pain or clarify something for you that might save your life." In this context, the verbal attack seems to be an expression of great sympathy.

Since Synanon does not permit the use of chemicals or violence, the participants in verbal-attack therapy have to confront their problems in the "raw." They cannot threaten another person, even if he is physically inferior, to "lay off" or else face the consequences of physical retaliation. (In contrast, violence is one of the problems in much professional prison group therapy.) Nor can they avoid the impact of what is being said by making use of the sedative qualities or escape qualities of alcohol or drugs. Brutal truth is the keynote, and it must be candidly faced and examined.

In this manner, people who formerly used violence and drugs to protect themselves are thrown onto their verbal resources for relating to others. They learn to interact with words. This means of interaction facilitates their ability to communicate through this mode of expression rather than with their fists or other possible weaponry.

The power of the individual's attack in a synanon appears to be correlated with the emotional strength of the attacker and his position in the Synanon hierarchy. Old-timers in Synanon have developed more powerful verbal weapons and speak from a more powerful status position in the hierarchy. Their sword has a sharper edge; but at the same time, they have learned to level their attack with more precision. They direct their attack at the person's problems rather than his "self," and seem to know when to pick him up again. (Moreover, they are less apt to be doing it out of their own need to attack another person.)

One of my conclusions about synanon attack therapy is that a skillful Synanist batters the individual's emotional flab rather than his "self." The newcomer is much like a ten-year-old with twenty-three-ounce padded boxing gloves. He cannot hit too hard or hurt too much. The older members have eight-ounce gloves and seem to know when and where to hit at the person's hypocrisy, emotional blindness, and problems.

As Chuck Dederich put it: "There is much truth in the child's 'sticks and-stones' poem, which ends 'but words can never harm me.' Of course words can hurt, but so can the set of delusions a person carries around with him that formerly required drugs to control."

The question of whether verbal attack is valid is confirmed, according to Chuck, by Synanon's positive experience: "Look at our record. What appeared to be a grand slide toward self-destruction for many people with the terminal disease of drug addiction has been halted. We stepped in and diverted it by using this method, among others."

In response to the accusation that there is a "sadistic gratification" for the purveyor of "loving brute force," Dederich commented: "I guess you just have to believe me when I say my motivations are pure. When I attack, I can't prove I'm immune to sadistic satisfaction. In the early days, I was probably less immune than I am now. I can tell you this: I don't particularly enjoy having to give anyone a haircut. It's hard work." This viewpoint corresponds with that of other older members of Synanon.

Part of the rationale for attack therapy is that the recipient does not "hear properly" in areas in which he is emotionally blocked. In fact, in sessions that I have been in, the group often gets a good laugh because a problem that has been pointed out several times to someone is often literally not heard. "Attack," in a sense, is a misnomer, even though it appears to be attack to the untrained eye. It is more accurate to view the attack as an effort to communicate some information useful to the person, information that he appears to have an emotional block to hearing. Consequently, ridicule, caricature, exaggeration, analogy, repetition, and other devices are used. The volume of the attempt to communicate is turned up high (almost to the point of screaming) at times and down low (when the person is apparently rationally listening to the group's opinions) at other times.

In some cases, what has become known in Synanon as the "carom shot" is used in a synanon. This involves telling person A what you also want person B or C to hear and learn. In the middle of delivery, a comment may be made to emphasize the point ("Do you hear what is being said to Joe, Jack?") In fact, many people appear to have obtained therapy in synanons from listening closely to what another person is receiving. And at times, a person who is "screaming" at another is also talking to himself.

The use of ridicule and exaggeration in synanon sessions appears to be an important tool in the system. The rationale for using ridicule, which also appears brutal at first glance, is that "ridiculous behavior deserves to be ridiculed." Behavior (not the self!) is examined, and if it is ridiculous, the person is ridiculed. He is often laughed at by the group for certain acts. When he begins to laugh with the group at himself, he is considered to be on the road to recovery. In Chuck Dederich's view, exaggeration is a way of holding "magnifying glasses up to the person's behavior so that he can look at himself more clearly."

Some different viewpoints on the drug-addiction symptom serve to highlight Synanon's approach to ridicule. On the one hand, the professional and public view of addiction is that it is a serious and disturbing symptom formation. And, of course, this is true. Most intelligent people have a sympathy for the victim and a compassion for his painful plight.

Synanon people deeply share this sympathetic viewpoint. However, they are convinced that this kind of commiseration or sympathy does the addict no good. In fact, it often backfires, reinforcing self-pity and continued drug use. At Synanon, they reverse the field and take this posture (which at first glance may seem cold and unfeeling):

"You stupid slob—you've run yourself into the ground by your behavior. Your tough-guy-dope-fiend style keeps getting you dropped off in a cage. You're not really bad; you're just stupid and ridiculous. Look at how ridiculous you are: like a rat, you ran up and down alleys stealing; you buy some white powder, and then you jam a needle with some fluid in your arm, conk out, and go back for more. Of course, you are killing yourself. You will either die by being locked up for life or die from an overdose in a back alley. Your behavior is ridiculous!" (Thirteen addicts died from an overdose of heroin in Los Angeles in the summer of 1964!) [Many more have died since then as a result of the increased abuse of drugs.]

This is cold, hard talk—on the surface, lacking in sympathy, yet in a definite way, it is realistic. More than that, it does not support the old pattern, which considerable unrealistic affection apparently does. The proof is that the standard, generally sympathetic counseling approach has not done the job that Synanon has accomplished with its attack therapy. Love, affection, and involvement are also certainly practiced in the organization, but these approaches have to be assessed in Synanon as they are used in conjunction with the (seemingly) tough approach. The combination of tough and soft, in proper proportion at the right time, seems to do the job.

One Professional View of Attack Therapy

Despite the apparent success of Synanon's attack therapy, it is negatively evaluated by many professionals as a "destructive approach to human behavior." An interesting vignette related by Reid Kimball reveals the paradox of professional resistance to attack therapy:

> In one synanon session, we had with us a visiting clinical psychologist, Dr. Gold, a Governor's man (evaluating Synanon), and several parole officials. This visiting group had expressed a great interest in being in a regular synanon session. They agreed, in front, that they would participate like anyone else. We happened to have some of our toughest guys in that particular synanon. In the group, among others, were myself, with eighteen years of addiction behind me before Synanon; George the Turk, with fourteen years behind him; Phil Hunt, with twelve years; and Jack Hurst, with nine years of past addiction.
>
> We had a rugged attack-type synanon, but a usual one. All of the Synanon people went at each other, but we also went after the visitors. We attacked the Governor's man for not doing his work in evaluating Synanon. We could never get to talk to him about Synanon because he was too busy chasing one of our broads around the building. We went at the psychologist, and one of the parole officers was even attacked.
>
> But here's the point. At the end of the session, the psychologist made the flat statement that this was the most 'destructive approach to human behavior' he had ever witnessed in his twenty years of practice. I said, "But we're all clean, and nothing else has worked." He stuck to his guns. This man, whom I liked, who is probably intelligent in all other areas of life, could not see any *non sequitur* in his thinking!
>
> Now, dig this. The event I described occurred back in 1960. When Chuck and I attended this gathering of drug-addict experts at the University of California at Los Angeles conference in 1963, I ran into the same psychologist, Dr. Gold. I put him on. I said, "You remember George the Turk, Jack Hurst, Jesse Pratt, Phil Hunt, and, of course, myself? You know, we are all still clean. Do you still think this is the most destructive therapy you've ever witnessed?" You know, his answer was still yes!"

Professional Therapy and Synanon

Many professionals become interested in Synanon and visit for the purpose of adapting some of Synanon's methodology to other therapeutic settings. Synanon has developed some treatment approaches, especially the small-"s" synanon, which seem to be transferable. However, Chuck believes that the utilization of Synanon's methods in another setting tends to fragment the approach and renders it less effective. More than that, it is his view that Synanon has very little to do with the standard professional schools.

"We have no argument whatsoever with the professional fraternity doing whatever they do," he said. "It's none of our business, really. However, we do not want them interfering with our business. When they attack what we do, of course, we become defensive and in some cases have to institute a counteroffensive. We do not want or need interference from professionals.

"We ourselves made the mistake of thinking of Synanon as therapy rather than an education. We are more of an educational enterprise than a therapeutic one, more of a learning process than a therapeutic process. We don't presuppose sickness as much as we presume stupidity. We say, 'If you weren't so dumb, you wouldn't be in jail all the time. The hell with your being sick.' Our starting point is not a hospital but rather a school. We currently have several hundred Synanon graduates, and we plan to graduate several hundred more.

"Synanon has run head on into several professional systems. Some have helped, others have opposed. One thorn of opposition has been the California Department of Corrections. They pulled seven parolees, Synanon residents who were staying clean and doing well in the program, out of the building. With one exception, Ted, who returned to Synanon after his parole hold was over, they are either in jail or using, and Ted's girl friend died of an overdose of drugs."

Dederich believes that the negative feelings about Synanon projected by some professional bodies are manifestations of their fear of losing their vested interest in the status quo: "I think it's mainly subliminal. We don't really constitute a threat to the California Department of Corrections, even though their efforts to smash us reveal that they seem to think so.

"We keep plugging away at our work, which seems to be hailed by many as a breakthrough. Yet, there is a cultural lag of recognition in certain quarters, particularly from the professionals. We've had all sorts of National Institute of Mental Health people and pros come through here, but nothing comes of it. We keep getting turned down on our requests for funds, even though we submit well-developed plans, in the form they seem to want them. Senator Dodd recommended that we receive federal help over a year ago, but nothing has happened.

"Even some professionals who are friends of Synanon and think they know better often tend to distort the picture. They perceive Synanon from their own limited viewpoint. The psychiatrists see a psychiatric process; the correctional people see a "halfway house"; the psychologists, depending on their school, a therapeutic process. The friendly professionals tend first to heap praise on the organization and then to conclude that Synanon has inadvertently stumbled upon their magic professional secret. One very friendly, enthusiastic psychiatrist, after a two-week visit, concluded that Synanon had inadvertently developed an extension of Freudian psychoanalysis: "Many of your people are now ready for the (true, bona fide, legal) therapeutic experience of psychoanalysis," he gleefully announced and then went on to publish his "discovery."

In another case, a prominent sociologist, wedded to a learning theory of crime causation, coauthored an article that ignored most of the Synanon process. The article essentially attempted to prove that Synanon had "unwittingly" implemented the theory he supported.

(A younger sociologist published an article in an important criminology journal in which he attempted to prove that Synanon made people dependent and was not applicable to treating criminals other than addicts. He had never visited a Synanon House or the Nevada State Prison project!)

As indicated, there are two dominant professional responses. One is the attack on a methodology that appears to be, by its sheer existence, a threat to the status quo and vested interest. The other is the friendly professional's ploy, which is to be extremely laudatory, even indicate that it is some kind of breakthrough—but one that is, of course, within the framework of his professional school.

Neither professional response honestly gives Synanon its proper due: the recognition that Synanon, as created by Chuck Dederich and his able assistants, is a new methodology and social structure, administered by a new breed of professional people. An attempt to jam Synanon into other molds clouds the issue and produces false appraisals.

The Professional Bias

Synanon seems to go against the grain of many prejudiced members of the community, who have an aversion to ex-criminal-addicts and interracial living. On another more complex level, the prejudgments of many professionals (both friend and foe) reflect another problem with which Synanon must cope. First, Synanon finds itself in the necessary position of proving to the professional community that a therapy "of, by, and for" the people works. This must be done despite the fact that there is already ample evidence (five hundred people) that Synanon does work.

Another attitude that Synanon has to battle repeatedly (especially with Synanon's professional friends) is the illusion that professionals have about Synanon's "fit" into their pet theory or institutional image. They refuse to accept the organization on its own terms, as a unique therapeutic system. The clamor of many professionals for more "scientific proof" when there is an obvious *prima facie* case of hundreds of ex-criminal-addicts who are now leading productive lives, is a smoke screen for a more subtle form of bias. I believe that the most important element of professional resistance to Synanon is the widely held belief that the professional superstructure is the only feasible one for the "bona fide," or "legitimate," treatment of emotional problems. The professional, the average layman, and even the "patients" have been convinced on a deep emotional level that only the properly schooled professional is qualified to understand and help people.

The lack of proper recognition of Synanon is tied in with the controversy over the professional therapist's acceptability and respectability. Synanon has the audacity to proclaim, by its sheer existence, that the "patients" can do the job themselves! This may be a new therapeutic revolution. It is to be expected that professionals, especially the conservative wing, will increasingly attempt to put this "uprising" down. Among other reasons, their fear may be related to a financial threat. This fear (already registered by some professionals) is, of course, absurd, since the increasing complexity of our world and social problems demands increased help from all quarters—professional therapists included. The only fall professionals may take by the ascendancy of the people's therapy role is one in status. The professional therapist (with the psychiatrist at the apex) may find the Synanon revolt of several hundred former "patients" most distressing, because it is possible that eventually many patients may be regarded as his therapeutic equal.

Professional criticism of Synanon often takes the form of what Chuck has called the "orthodoxy effect." Dr. Gold, described earlier by Reid Kimball, evidenced a typical professional response. He reacted negatively to what he considered to be an unorthodox method. He was more concerned with proper method than with results! Despite the clear, live evidence, in the person of Kimball and others, that the synanon session was constructive, Gold believed that it was destructive because it was unorthodox. Perhaps professional therapy has reached the bureaucratic stage in which orthodoxy of method is more important than the achievement of concrete therapeutic results.

Merit and logic inhere in the Synanon methodology, and this is confirmed by considerable evidence. It rests on (among other principles) *the logical foundation that if a particular social configuration of people and beliefs can produce a person's problem, another constellation of people operating within the framework of a constructive social system can ameliorate the same problem.* Such a social system for positive living has been developed by Chuck Dederich and his associates. (It may be that they have succeeded in an area in which the professional has failed because they were unencumbered by the vast body of complicated and often conflicting theory and research found in the professional therapeutic field. Moreover, Synanon was certainly not plagued by the orthodoxy effect.) In any event, Synanon works, and the existence of hundreds of clean ex-addicts and criminals should be clear evidence of success to any logical, unbiased person.

Based upon the foundation of its successful work with the hard-core criminal-addict, in response to a community demand, Synanon has recently embarked on a more ambitious program for working with a wider range of human difficulties. This new direction includes individuals who were never criminals or addicts. Most of these people are reasonably successful members of the community. For these "members" of Synanon, synanon sessions and over-all involvement with the "movement" appear to be resolving a variety of frustrations, feelings of loneliness, alienation, and relationship conflicts. This part of the program, for people with "average" human problems, has been incorporated into the over-all Synanon operation and seems to be functioning with a considerable measure of success.

The belief of some professionals in their exclusive right to treat human problems is no longer logical or practical in the light of Synanon's success. Greater cooperation between the professionals and the Synanon community of "professionals" seems clearly needed. A first step in this potentially productive cooperation would be for the orthodox professional and the public to understand Synanon, not as an extension of older institutional models, but as a new therapeutic system with a viable structure and integrity of its own. From this more logical starting point, the public and the professional community, in cooperation with Synanon, can forward the natural thrust of this vital new social movement.

Chapter 27

Alcoholics Anonymous

LESTER R. BELLWOOD

Lester R. Bellwood: b. 1920, Merrill, Iowa.
B.A., State University of Iowa, 1949. Th.M., 1952, Th.D., 1953, The Iliff
School of Theology, Denver, Colorado. Ph.D., clinical psychology,
Boston University, 1962.
Chief, Alcoholism Division, Fort Logan Mental Center, Denver, 1961–date.
Visiting Professor, Pastoral Psychology, The Iliff School of Theology,
1961–1971. Professor of New Testament and Pastoral Psychology,
Interdenominational Theological Center, Atlanta, Georgia, 1954–1961.
Books: (Co-author) *Reader's Guide to the Study of the Bible* (1957).

Alcoholics Anonymous began in 1935 in Akron, Ohio.[1] Two individuals, Bill W. and Dr. Bob S., co-founders of Alcoholics Anonymous, met and initiated a program that materialized into a fellowship called Alcoholics Anonymous. Its roots were founded primarily in religion and medicine (2, p. 160).

The early pioneers in the field found that sobriety was easiest when they tried to help other problem drinkers stay sober. They also found that spiritual values were imperative in daily living. Within three years of trial and error with the new philosophy, three promising groups emerged in Akron, New York, and Cleveland, respectively (1, pp. 16–17). By 1939 there were approximately 100 members whose experiences were published in a book entitled *Alcoholics Anonymous*. It later became the Alcoholics Anonymous textbook. By 1965 the membership had expanded to 350,000. Since then it has grown by leaps and bounds. In addition, family groups have emerged, "AlAnon" and "AlAteen," in the effort to satisfy family needs.

One short paragraph from the literature strongly suggests the therapeutic values inherent in Alcoholics Anonymous: "Alcoholics Anonymous is a fellowship of men and women who share their ex-

---

[1] Portions of this paper are to appear in a forthcoming book by the author entitled *The Mountain*.

periences, strength and hope with each other that they may solve their common problem and help others to recover from alcoholism" (7, p. 5). To a great extent, it is the interpersonal relationship in the group that helps restore the alcoholic to community, or if you wish, to sanity.

Three "Legacies" stand as foundation stones for the fellowship of Alcoholics Anonymous. They are Recovery, Unity, and Service. (7, p. 5). The first of these is incorporated in the "Twelve Steps" which serve as the heart of the Alcoholics Anonymous program and are the primary concern of this paper. The steps are essentially concerned with gaining a continuing sobriety. The second "Legacy" is formulated in the "Twelve Traditions" which embody the survival of the local group's unity. The third "Legacy" involves "General Services," including the General Services Conference, which functions primarily as a liaison group (9).

Early in the development of Alcoholics Anonymous, Dr. Silkworth conceived of alcoholism as both mental and physical in the statement "The obsession of the mind that compels us to drink and the allergy of the body that condemns us to go mad or die" (2, p. 13). This concept became basic to Alcoholics Anonymous philosophy. In a word, the physical allergy does not initiate the drinking, but the physical allergy is set in motion by the mental process that initiated the drinking. Once drinking begins, regardless of the reason for drinking, the alcoholic has no ability to control it. "We alcoholics are men and women who have lost ability to control our drinking. We know that no real alcoholic ever recovers control" (2, p. 30). "We are equally positive that once he takes any alcohol whatever into his system something happens, both in the body and mental sense, which makes it virtually impossible for him to stop" (2, pp. 22–23).

Alcoholism is likewise viewed as an illness by Alcoholics Anonymous, a progressive illness that can never be "cured" but which, like some other illnesses, can be arrested. (3, p. 9). This viewpoint reflects the attitude that there is nothing shameful about having such an illness if one faces the problem and tries to correct it. "We are perfectly willing to admit that we are allergic to alcohol and that it is simply common sense to stay away from the source of our allergy." (3). The term "progressive" emphasizes the understanding that if one is an alcoholic, his drinking problem will become progressively worse with the passing of time. One may be able to stop drinking for a limited period of time, but inevitably, if he is an alcoholic, he will drink again, with less and less control each time (4, p. 9).

Alcoholism is also recognized as fundamentally a health problem. This is to say that it is not a moral problem, not a question of character or will power (4, pp. 5–6). There is a tendency to view alcoholism with other illnesses.

> If you have tuberculosis or diabetes or heart disease, you have to recognize that you have the problem before you can do anything about it. And once you recognize the problem, you are not going to get very far by depending solely on will power or strength of character. You can't "swear off" diabetes, for example, but if you are a diabetic, you can continue to live a full, happy life by observing certain elementary precautions. (4, p. 6)

Alcoholics Anonymous also has a ready answer concerning the sin concept of alcoholism. To the question, "Does Alcoholics Anonymous regard alcoholism as a sin?" comes the answer, "As a Fellowship, A. A. [Alcoholics Anonymous] is committed to no theological concept of alcoholism" (5, p. 10).

Nevertheless, Alcoholics Anonymous has strong religious overtones in its philosophy, although Alcoholics Anonymous would never consider itself to be a religion. Perhaps it would be more logical to say that Alcoholics Anonymous is more concerned with handling feelings of guilt (repressed hostility in the Freudian sense) than it is concerned with the theological concept of sin. In fact, this idea is exactly the implication inherent in the "Twelve Steps" which serve as the heart of the Alcoholics Anonymous program. The same psychodynamics prevail as one pursues the "Twelve Steps" in Alcoholics Anonymous as predominate in the religious solution to feelings of guilt and hostility on the road to becoming "whole" or "holy."

Certainly psychotherapy is concerned in part with helping the individual deal with feelings of guilt. Religion and Alcoholics Anonymous do the same thing in a very special way. The latter two approaches are much more related to St. Paul's concept of metanoia (religious experience or conversion) than is psychotherapy. Some alcoholics may never be able to obtain help through the psychotherapy approach—some simply do not respond to it! They may, however, gain sobriety through practicing religion or entering Alcoholics Anonymous. On the other hand, other individuals may never respond to religion or Alcoholics Anonymous and must take the psychotherapeutic route. Still others find that a combination of two or all three basic approaches is necessary if they are to gain sobriety and at the same time feel good and free from internal anxiety.

Since religion and Alcoholics Anonymous apparently follow a similar (if not the same) psychodynamics on their road to wholeness it may be of value at this point to pause, and through a simple analogy point to the religious experience as a path in the direction of justification or wholeness, and then through the same analogy show how the twelve steps in Alcoholics Anonymous operate within the same spectrum.

RELIGIOUS EXPERIENCE

When we read in the Bible about God, we find that He is conceptualized variously. The Bible says that God is good; God is Love; God is power; God is eternal; and the like. All these words describing God have positive connotations: goodness, power, love, eternity, etc.

Let us consider God in terms of an analogy (see Figure 1), as a large magnet with the positive pole pointing manward (8, pp. 171 ff.). This magnet has a negative pole on the other end pointing away from man into infinity.

Theologians speak of God in this position, namely, God pointed manward with unconditional love. In such a position he can do nothing else but love.

In a human way, this analogy is comparable to my five-year-old son. Three years ago we gave him a tool chest for Christmas. He ran around the house with the hammer, pounding everything he could find, thinking he was doing a perfect job identifying with his

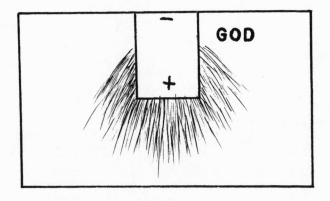

Figure 1.

father. The psychological implications were ignored when my son was told not to go near the hi-fi with the hammer. This instruction only gave him the idea, and, as soon as he had a chance, he turned and gave the hi-fi a whack and put a big "cat-eye" in it! I did not like what Tommy did, and he got a licking for it, but I still love Tommy! My love for Tom does not depend upon how well he behaves.

Theologically speaking, man is not capable of exhibiting this kind of love indefinitely, as God is able to do. Yet, similarly, God may not like what we do, but He loves us just the same, for His love is completely unconditional. When we feel rejected by God, it is we who reject Him, not He who rejects us, and frequently we do this by trying to be gods (self-sufficient) ourselves, which we shall see later.

Now that we have established the analogy in part for God's "personality" in terms of His relationship to man, let us consider a similar analogy for man's relationship to God. First, consider the behavior of magnets. When a positive pole of one magnet and a negative pole of another magnet are pointed in the direction of each other, they will attract. If one were to place a paper over the two magnets and sprinkle iron filings over the two, he would find that he could see the fields of force as they line up the magnets and interact (see Figure 2).

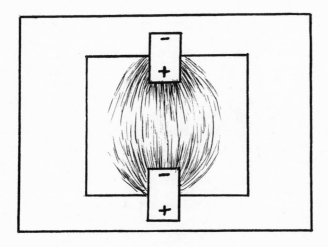

Figure 2.

When the two magnets are brought too closely to each other, they stick together. This is the counterpart of "love" on the inorganic level. The attraction is so great that it is difficult to separate them.

If one were to reverse one of the magnets, the effect would be much different. For example, place two positive poles in the direction of each other (see Figure 3). Now, cover them with iron filings. What happens? They repel each other, and the filings are seen to pull back away from the opposing poles. They refuse to attract. This is the counterpart of "disharmony" on the inorganic level. They simply will not stick together.

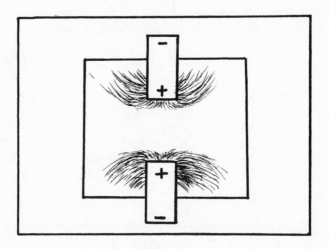

Figure 3.

Now, let us utilize the analogy to illustrate man's relationship to God. In the book of Luke we read a story about two men, a Pharisee and a publican (tax collector) who went up to the temple to pray. The Pharisee looked upon himself as a very righteous man, and he wanted everyone to know how good he was. Consequently, he stood up so everyone could hear him and prayed:

> God, I thank thee, that I am not as other men are, extortioners, unjust, adulterers, or even as this publican. I fast twice in the week, I give tithes of all that I possess. (Luke 18:11–12)

As he left the temple the Pharisee felt no different than when he went into the temple. He did not feel justified. Why? He attempted to represent himself as a god—perfect! This attitude is exemplified in the analogy: the Pharisee being magnet *a* (cf. Figure 4) with the positive pole pointed toward God, as if the Pharisee were a god himself. In other words, he revealed all of his good qualities and kept his imperfections to himself. Consequently, he made no contact with God, for like poles repel.

The publican was quite different. When he prayed, he stood afar off and did not even look up. He simply pounded his breast and pleaded, "Oh, God, be merciful to me a sinner!" and he closed his prayer and walked away. It was the tax collector who went away

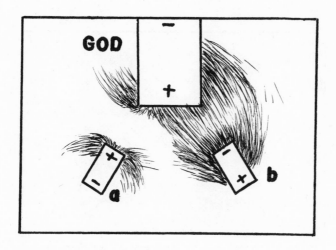

Figure 4.

justified and filled. The analogy in Figure 4 makes this very clear (cf. magnet *b*). Rather than trying to present himself before God as perfect, like the Pharisee did, the publican admitted he was an imperfect human being and refrained from boasting about his good qualities. In opening his heart to God and revealing his negative (hostile and guilty) self, he made contact immediately, for opposite poles attract.

Why did he go away justified or filled? Consider the analogy again. See what happens to the negatives (or guilt in the form of repressed hostility) as he turns them over to God. The negative forces of magnet *b*, Figure 5, are moving upward toward God. Watch them as they ascend. In a sense, the publican was saying, "God, I am not perfect, I am a sinner, and I know it—please forgive me and have mercy upon me!" and on up to God goes his confession. If one follows these negative forces, they move on out into infinity in the direction of the negative end of the magnet representing God.

Is not this why theologians can say that God can take an infinite amount of negative feelings and still love? Certainly, the positive pole of God pointing manward remains unchanged. God's ability to receive negative attitudes is infinite. What is coming from God in exchange for the publican's confession? Positive forces are moving to-

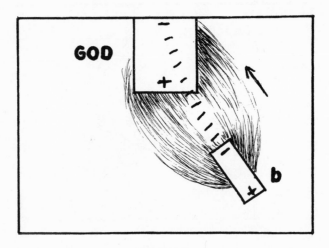

Figure 5.

ward man. Watch them move (cf. Figure 6) on down into the publican, filling him with the unconditional love "stuff" that can only come from God. God in a sense is saying, "I know you are not perfect, you were not created that way. Most important is that you are able to humble yourself in confessing it and admitting it, and I love you just the same!"

What a wonderful feeling to know that one is loved for himself! The publican no longer needs to go about wearing a mask, trying to be that which he is not—perfect. He can be himself, knowing that even though he is not perfect, he is loved by God just the same!

That is why he went away justified. He was justified because he was able to admit that he was an imperfect human being, and he was filled with the unconditional love of God in spite of it.

One cannot keep this kind of love to oneself. Once love is received, it must be given. For example, the alcoholic (as in Figure 6, magnet *a*) who chooses to handle his problem by traveling this road may return home, only to meet his wife at the door (Figure 6, magnet *b*) loaded with negative feelings of hostility directed toward him. She begins the minute he gets into the door.

"You good for nothing bum, get the hell out of here! You can't tell me you have been drunk for thirty years and in a couple weeks

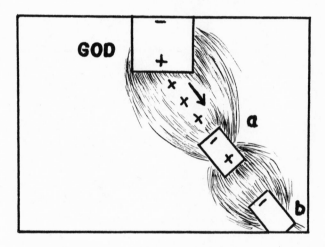

Figure 6.

of treatment you are cured! I've had enough of your lies and false promises!" And on and on she goes in the negative encounter with him.

The alcoholic cannot retort as he has in the past, with negative reactions, and withdraw only to get drunk, for his negative feelings are already directed Godward. Facing her positively, he remembers how he is loved by God even though he too is imperfect, and he responds to her likewise. He says something like this, "You may be right, honey. I know I have been very wrong, and I have mistreated you, and you have a right to hate me, but I love you anyway," and he not only verbalizes these feelings, but he begins to demonstrate his love even though she responds negatively to him. In a word, he accepts her as he is accepted by God, and immediately she is attracted to him, for opposite poles attract (see Figure 6, magnets *a* and *b*).

Now, as she is accepted long enough to see her own faults, she begins to say to herself, "What happened to that joker?" She thinks in retrospect, "There was a time when I felt that I was far better than he, but there is a love stuff coming from him that I never saw before. Somehow I am beginning to feel inferior to him!" and she steps aside from directing her hostility toward him and turns it over to God (Figure 7, magnet *b, b'*) as she vents her internal hostile feelings to God in making the confession:

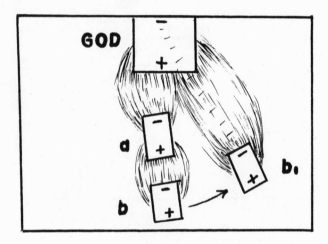

Figure 7.

"Oh, God, there was a time when I felt I was almost perfect compared to my husband, but now I feel so inferior to him!"

Then she sees herself, perhaps for the first time, when she says, "God, maybe some of the things I have been doing to him are the very things that have been keeping him drunk!" She begs, "Oh, God, forgive me a sinner." Immediately she makes contact, for opposite poles attract, and like the publican and her alcoholic husband, she too is justified or filled with the unconditional love of God even though she is unlovable, too. In humbling herself she is filled with the Glory of God! Now she and her husband together are oriented in the same direction, both imperfect, but at the same time radiating the love of God to others. I say, as Jesus said in the illustration, "Those two, the alcoholic and his wife, went down to their home justified!" With all of the alcoholic's negatives given to God under His control, the alcoholic no longer needs to get drunk to release them. Religion has saved him from the destructive power of alcohol, and it will continue to do so as long as he can be honest with God and confess his imperfections. Feelings of guilt (repressed hostility) given vent to or released in this way no longer provide the necessity for one to get drunk in order to release feelings. Drinking frequently is an escape valve for the release of repressed hostility.

It may be noted that the alcoholic had to be cleansed of his internal negatives before he could "turn his cheek" to his wife and accept her long enough for her to see her own imperfections. First, he had to have a free flow of his own negatives to God, and feel internally adjusted or justified, before he could passively sit by and permit her to level allegations at him. Her negatives had a free flow to God through him. That is why one cannot turn his cheek like a passive–aggressive personality until he first is justified or adjusted. Without the free flow of his negatives up to God, he will bottle them up, and when he can hold no more, the volcano erupts and he must get drunk to release them. Thus, Jesus was right in suggesting the passive–aggressive technique (though it is not the only approach he offered), but it is important to have one's own negative feelings under control before one attempts it.

This act of giving up one's negatives to God in the spirit of penance is an ancient one. Noah did it when he came out of the ark on dry land. He gave vent to his "shadow," so to speak, when he killed one of every animal and beast and burned it on the altar as a sacrifice to God. God "smelled the pleasant odors" and gave favor to him in return. The killing of the animals gave expression to the internal negative drives so that positive forces could be directed toward man. In yielding his negatives to God Noah received the positive from Him to give to others. This practice of venting one's hostility through killing the sacrificial animal and burning it on the altar so that God would smell the "sweet" odors and be pleased was so important in antiquity that sacrificial instructions for doing so were meticulously recorded by the priestly group in the book of Leviticus (Leviticus 26).

When people turned from the Lord and disobeyed Him or stopped following after Him, trying to be self-sufficient (gods) themselves, God refused to "smell the pleasant odors of their sacrifices." He warned them in Leviticus 26:31 and later in Amos 5:21–22 and Jeremiah 44:2 that He would treat them thus, and He did just that! Because they failed to offer their sacrifices in the spirit of penance, He refused to smell their pleasant odors and left them to destroy themselves. The Mass in the Roman Catholic church in the same way continues to be celebrated in the spirit of penance. Before the recipient approaches the elements he first must give vent to his guilt in the confessional. In humility he admits his own guilt, and he is willing to amend his life. He then is in the state of Grace and worthy of receiving the Host. Without complete release of his internal negative guilt feelings there is no such thing as being in the state of Grace.

Likewise, when the Pharisee went up to the temple to offer his prayer, he offered it in the spirit of self-fulfillment and self-righteousness. He appeared openly to be so perfect that he was almost like a god and not in need of God to cleanse him of his internal guilt. Consequently, God let him go down from the temple feeling no different than when he went up to it.

But the publican was quite different. When he offered up his prayer, he openly sacrificed or gave up his internal wickedness, and as with the early animal sacrifices, God "smelled the pleasant odor" of his giving, and sent him away feeling justified and filled with His Glory.

ALCOHOLICS ANONYMOUS

It is my opinion that Alcoholics Anonymous provides the same dynamic for helping the alcoholic as religion did for the publican or for the alcoholic and his wife in the previous section. The dynamics are identical, but the basic approach is different. Though we shall utilize the same analogy in elucidating the Alcoholics Anonymous program, let us digress momentarily to get an overview of the Alcoholics Anonymous approach. In general, their primary goals are centered around the twelve-step program, and several techniques are employed to accomplish these twelve steps, which are exemplified in a variety of different kinds of group meetings. There is the open meeting, the closed meeting, and the study group. In addition, they have a program for the family of the alcoholic called AlAnon and for the youth of the family called AlAteen.

Another important aspect of the program involves the sponsor.

Every new alcoholic who joins Alcoholics Anonymous (often called a pigeon) is assigned to a sponsor, usually an alcoholic who has completed the first eleven steps and is pursuing the twelfth step of the program. He is commonly called the "twelfth-step worker" and serves as a buddy to the new member. His responsibility is to nurture the neophyte through the first eleven steps as he himself has done, after which time he releases the new member as a mature member to reach out and do his own twelfth-step work with his own pigeon. This buddy system offers something of a symbiotic relationship for the benefit of both parties. The new convert to Alcoholics Anonymous is nourished back to sobriety and health, and this nourishing process provides the food that gives the vital energy which maintains the sobriety of the sponsor—both give and both receive abundantly.

THE OPEN MEETING

Open Alcoholics Anonymous speaker meetings may be conducted for a few persons or for several hundred people. The chairman, essentially a member of Alcoholics Anonymous with one month or more sobriety usually, however, has at least a year of sobriety. This length of sobriety for chairmanship is dependent upon the tradition developed within the group.

In addition to the chairman, there are usually three or four speakers with varying lengths of sobriety. During the course of the meeting, each speaker is called upon by the chairman to give the following information concerning himself: (1) tell what he was like before coming to Alcoholics Anonymous; (2) tell what happened to him; and (3) tell what he is like now. The meeting usually lasts one hour. Coffee is often served after the meeting, and the members socialize. The open meeting is available to anyone regardless of whether or not he is an alcoholic, and it is held for several reasons:

1. It gives new people, and those who might be searching for a solution to the drinking problem, an opportunity to hear about the drinking histories of other persons. These accounts help the alcoholic, for example, to identify his own alcoholism.

2. It lends comfort to the new person, because as others talk about themselves, the similarities are obvious, and it is reassuring to realize one is not alone and isolated.

3. Often at large open Alcoholics Anonymous meetings new people begin to realize that they are not as wicked or as bad as perhaps they had imagined previously, and they can feel accepted and for-

given as others have been who might even have had a worse background.

4. There is real hope in hearing an attractive, sober, well-groomed person describe a drinking history worse than one's own. If he can get sober and return to a normal life, there is hope for "me" to do likewise.

5. When a new member, or even an old member, listens to a speaker discuss his approach to the philosophy of Alcoholics Anonymous, the new member often gets insights into a way to put the principles of Alcoholics Anonymous to work in his own life in greater depth than before.

6. The speaker also gains as he speaks for himself. He strengthens his resolution not to drink when he makes a public declaration of his decision. Stating that one is an alcoholic in public also reaffirms this position in one's own mind. Relating one's position in regard to the Alcoholics Anonymous philosophy crystalizes and firms up his conception and makes practice of the principles easier. Often speaking at a meeting and hearing the response from other members gives one much gratification and peer acceptance. Sometimes a different self-image emerges. It is not too hard to think of one's self as being helpful to others. In many ways this thought may assuage guilt.

The nonalcoholic may take comfort in the fact that help is available if needed and that God is good to have permitted these blessings to be showered on such needy ones.

The first three steps in Alcoholics Anonymous are quite frequently accomplished in the open meeting. One of the greatest defenses of the alcoholic is denial, and he needs to work through his denial system. That process is embodied in the first step.

Step 1. We admit we are powerless over alcohol—that our lives had become unmanageable.

The purpose of this first step is to be honest. If one is not powerless over alcohol, he does not belong in Alcoholics Anonymous as a member. Contrary to being like the Pharisee in the previous section, he follows the road of the publican and admits his imperfect self— that he is powerless over alcohol (cf. Figure 2). In recognizing he is not sufficient in himself, he admits that he is not a god and cannot control himself. The admission is only the first step, but it is the foundation for building in the direction of "wholeness." "Only through utter defeat are we able to take our first step toward liberation and strength. Our admission of personal powerlessness finally turned out to be firm bedrock upon which happy and purposeful lives may be built" (1, p. 21).

Thus, admission of alcoholism is a step toward honesty, which is a necessary element in the program, honesty with oneself and about oneself. "So we try not to deceive ourselves, our friends and our fellow alcoholics about our drinking problems. For many of us this emphasis on personal honesty was a new experience" (6, p. 11).

If the alcoholic can admit he is powerless over alcohol, then there is a power to help, and that power is God—a power greater than man who will restore him to sanity.

Step 2. Came to believe that a Power greater than ourselves can restore us to sanity.

An alcoholic may say, "I am not insane," but he is urged to look in retrospect at his life and behavior while drinking and see for himself that there is no doubt that he has been insane while drinking. There is no flowering of the words, "restore us to sanity" among Alcoholics Anonymous members. They do not permit the new member to get off the "hook" in that respect. They face him squarely and say, "You are insane and 'nutty as a fruitcake' when drinking, and you had just as well admit it!" He then recognizes God who has the positive "stuff" to help his mortal being (cf. large magnet representing God, Figure 2). In a word, like the publican, he recognizes a power greater than himself who is ready to help him. This acknowledgment of God as he understands him is a most essential part of the Alcoholics Anonymous program.

Step three is the keystone to the whole program.

Step 3. Made a decision to turn our will and our lives over to the care of God as we understand Him.

In this step the alcoholic decides to turn his life over to God, and he realizes what God is. He decides whether to let God run the show or be content to run it himself. Theoretically, if he decides to run it himself, he will get drunk. If not, it is a twenty-four-hour process because it is an about-face in his thinking processes. The key words are "lives" and "will." Alcoholics Anonymous says that an alcoholic is a "self-will run riot," and in past experiences most alcoholics pray in a "Give me" fashion, and "I won't do it again, but do it my way!" His objective is to begin to understand what God's will is in his own life, and this manifestation of God's will begins in very simple things. For example, God's will for me is to be responsible for myself as a person and to assume responsibility for my station in life. For a housewife, it means to get out of bed, cook breakfast for her family, and sit down to the table sober and happy rather than drunk and snarling. It means washing the dishes after breakfast and not going back to bed in a drunken stupor. It means not leaving the washing and ironing for three or four weeks until someone else does it.

This manifestation of responsibility applies to men also as head of the household. The man goes out, and gets a job, and turns his earnings over to his family, no matter how small, whether he likes it or not, because he admits, "I have been a self-willed human being run riot!"

In step three, then, he admits that he is not self-sufficient and lays himself at God's mercy, as did the publican (cf. Figure 5). In a sense he opens his heart to God and reveals his imperfections. He recognizes he cannot handle the negative forces upon him and gives them up to God who alone can handle all evil. It is most difficult for the alcoholic to relinquish himself to God and let Him take over, admitting that he is not sufficient in himself, but when he does things begin to happen.

Thus, in the open meeting the alcoholic accomplishes the following: (1) he becomes honest about himself and his relationship to God and to people; (2) he learns what it means to have an open mind and be sane; and (3) he has to get the hang of what it means to go without drinking for 24 hours a day.

THE CLOSED MEETING

The closed meeting gives the alcoholic the opportunity of entering into the next phase of Alcoholics Anonymous. It is for the alcoholic only, and it enables him to pursue steps 4 to 12. He is given the privilege in an anonymous setting to talk through things that are painful and embarrassing and too difficult to discuss in open groups. The closed meeting may be a speaker-type meeting, large or small, in which all of the benefits of the open meeting are forthcoming. Members are apt to be much more frank about their personal histories. Additional benefits often result:

1. Everyone is encouraged to enter the discussion by sharing experiences and feelings. Often new and old members are able to experience a catharsis, and in this sharing they gain insights regarding their own lives.

2. Usually very close, warm relationships are formed among peo-

ple who attend such groups regularly. Often it is the first time in their lifetime that they have had such an experience. It gives them a sense of comfort and serenity and a feeling of belonging.

3. Sometimes the sharing of events of the past which are painful or disgusting is so calmly received by the group that the alcoholic discussing his past may get a feeling of forgiveness. Those who listen really forgive him in the same way that they were formerly listened to and accepted and forgiven by others.

There is a personality analysis and catharsis that follows in steps four and five.

Step 4. Made a searching and fearless moral inventory of ourselves.

This step is taken in a closed meeting, for often the guilt is so great that it would be impossible for him to expose some of his deeds to the public, especially to his spouse. A good Alcoholics Anonymous sponsor will soon get the idea that one does not take the moral inventory by expressing his deeds out of his head as they emerge. He will suggest that the member in question purchase a small notebook and begin to write in detail the things he has done that bother him. Yet, he does not leave out the good things. Some choose to balance the ledger as follows:

DAILY MORAL INVENTORY

Liabilities to watch for:	*Assets to strive for:*
Fear	Faith
Self-pity	Self-forgetfulness
Self-justification	Humility
Self-condemnation	Self-valuation
Dishonesty	Honesty
Impatience	Patience
Hate	Love
Resentment	Forgiveness
False pride	Simplicity
Jealousy	Trust
Envy	Generosity
Laziness	Activity
Procrastination	Promptness
Insecurity	Straightforwardness
Negative thinking	Positive thinking
Criticizing	Look for good
Eliminate the negative	Accentuate the positive

Source: Group No. 1, 1311 York, Denver, Colorado.

The personality analysis in this step consists of taking a new look at oneself in addition to the admission of alcoholism. Herein one makes a general confession of his personality defects. Such questions as the following (among others) are suggested for this inventory: (1) did my selfish pursuit of sex relations damage others or myself? (2) did I spoil my marriage and injure my children? (3) did I jeopardize my position in the community? (1, p. 24). Like the publican, the alcoholic looks at his own imperfections and prepares to give them up in confession before God, for although personality analysis and inventory are emphasized, they are not adequate in themselves; the catharsis must follow, and this catharsis is accomplished in the fifth step.

Step 5. Admit to God, to ourselves, and to another human being the exact nature of our wrongs.

Again, compared to the publican, he brings forth his confession, his pinned-up hostility (guilt feelings) flows freely up to God and out into infinite space (cf. Figure 5). An experienced Alcoholics Anonymous member will recommend that one choose wisely when he shares his moral inventory with another human being. He may even urge him to look at other resources like a doctor, nurse, minister, or counselor who has the professional oath or ethic of confidentiality. It amounts to a general examination of one's conscience in which he explores his entire life. It is like a general confession. This experience is very humiliating to both the alcoholic and the listener, and they enter into a spiritual contract between themselves and God; this experience does a very wonderful thing for both of them, for between the two there is a closeness and bond so strong that the alcoholic leaves feeling loved and forgiven. There is a great sense of contrition and absolution experienced.

Relief from the catharsis comes in step six.

Step 6. We're entirely ready to have God remove all these defects of character.

Now that he knows his defects of character and has confessed them, the alcoholic becomes ready to have them removed. This step separates the men from the boys in Alcoholic Anonymous, for some of them (the boys) have defects they cherish and do not want to give up. They may make a choice and live with their cherished shortcomings, participating in the program and accepting second best. If they do, the degree of serenity is less and they are prone to have more dry drunks with emotionally upset days, for they are not living up to their own true values. They hang on to their special desires, for example, gambling, homosexual behavior, masturbation, cheating in business, only to mention a few.

On the other hand, he may join with the men and be willing to have his cherished defects removed. As he gives freely in the confessional, his humility is received by God with a compassionate quality of love, and in return he receives unconditional forgiveness—the strength embodied in the love "stuff" that can only come from God (cf. Figure 6)—and, like the publican, he is filled. If he is willing to have God remove all his defects of character, the relief is felt. This relief is well expressed in Alcoholics Anonymous literature: "Provided you hold back nothing, your sense of relief will mount from minute to minute. The damned-up emotions of years break out of their confinement and miraculously vanish as soon as they are exposed. As the pain subsides, a healing tranquility takes place" (12, p. 52).

On the other hand, like the "boys," someone may tend to resist God's help and attempt to become a god himself, thinking he is self-sufficient and capable of handling his pinned-up feelings as he thought he could handle alcohol. God is always ready, but He can do nothing until one is willing himself to yield and let God remove his defects of character. It is most difficult to let things happen! But sooner or later, like the publican, the alcoholic must humble himself and ask God to remove his infirmities if he is to go all the way. He must not only be willing to have God remove his defects, but he must also ask for all his shortcomings to be removed. Thus, step seven.

Step 7. Humbly ask Him to remove our shortcomings.

"Oh, God, have mercy on me a sinner!" said the publican. This same kind of unpretentious searching and asking is necessary, and it must continue into action if the sincerity of meekness is real; therefore, steps eight and nine must follow.

Step 8. Made a list of all persons we have harmed, and become willing to make amends to them all.

Step 9. Made direct amends to such people wherever possible, except when to do so would injure them or others.

Once the alcoholic has made a list of those he has harmed, he will find that he no longer knows where some of them live, or some may even be dead. Others may be individuals who would be greatly harmed if amends were made. For example, if that individual were happily married, it may be very harmful to both him and his spouse to humbly ask for forgiveness from either of them for having committed adultery. If the individual is dead, some Alcoholics Anonymous sponsors suggest that their change in conduct is sufficient to merit feelings of forgiveness by the deceased one. Others may suggest that he write a letter to the dead one and mail the letter to his sponsor and in the presence of the sponsor read the letter and ask for pardon. This procedure offers a concrete act of humility and a feeling of forgiveness and absolution through the sponsor on behalf of the deceased one.

For those whom he cannot locate, he must become ready at any time in the future to be responsible for making amends if he ever meets them again. If it is in payment of a debt, the money he owes may be given to the church or charity.

In making these amends, the alcoholic removes his stifling mask and allows himself to be known for what he really is—an imperfect and incomplete human being who finds completion in the free flowing of energies between himself and God. He closes the great chasm that separates him from God, so to speak, and is filled (cf. Figures 5 and 6).

But these steps are not enough. If the gap between him and God is to remain closed, freeing him of the dreadful feeling of being "cut off" from God's redeeming grace, the alcoholic must take the next step.

Step 10. Continue to take a personal inventory and when we were wrong promptly admit it.

The process is continual of removing one's masks in the presence of God and giving up one's sinful acts, giving them to God, the only source under God's control where they are contained in limitless space, the only source where they can be exchanged for positive forces of energy—love "stuff" that comes only from God in pure form. The process is comparable to a beautiful plant (God) taking in carbon dioxide and giving off life-giving energy called oxygen. This contact with God must be a continual struggle. As St. Paul said, "Not that I have arrived, but I push on for perfection." The next step must be pursued.

Step 11. Sought through prayer and meditation to improve our conscious contact with God as we understand Him, praying only for knowledge of His will for us and the power to carry that out.

Having had a spiritual awakening as a result of these steps, like the publican, the alcoholic is justified, bubbling over with the unconditional love of God, and like the alcoholic previously discussed, he cannot keep it; he must give it to others; he is ready to take the final step.

Step 12. Having had a spiritual awakening as the result of these steps, we tried to carry this message to alcoholics, and to practice these principles in all of our affairs.

Knowing that God loved and accepted him though he was imperfect and unlovable, the alcoholic can in the same way accept another when that person is down and feeling completely rejected (cf. Figure 6, magnet *b*). As the one he seeks to help is accepted by him, he too gets a glimmer of that love stuff shining through his sponsor from God, enabling him to take the second step, namely, that of believing that there is a power greater than himself who can restore him to sanity. With the continued acceptance of his sponsor, he makes his confession to God, and like this sponsor (or the publican), he too becomes justified—filled! When he reaches the top step, he is ready to become a twelfth-step worker, and he accepts others long enough for them to know the feeling of being at one with God! This is "turning your cheek." It is a continual process of one alcoholic receiving by the strength of God and, in turn, helping another be filled and gain his sanity, his unity with God (cf. Figure 6).

STUDY GROUPS

In the same way that the Bible is a record of man's search for God, so are the twelve steps and the big book a record of the alcoholics' search for both God and sobriety, and the study groups follow the same approach as does the exegete in biblical studies. The study group is also closed, and in a sense it is a round table discussion composed of alcoholics who have gained all or part of the experiences discussed in this paper, but who also wish to make a real effort to understand and apply the twelve steps of the Alcoholics Anonymous program. Members may meditate on each word of the program. For instance, in the first step "We" is the first word. In meditation of this word in relation to oneself and the group, much insight may come. An interpretation and meditation on such words and concepts as humility, God, honesty, power greater than oneself, charity, and the like, produces all kinds of insights that change lives. These words take on new meaning that they may never have had before. What goes on in the study group may be compared to what goes on in a Bible study class in which the Bible commentary is studied to help understand the meaning of specific passages in the Bible. In the absence of a commentary, the group takes the role of the interpreters or the exegetes.

ALANON

The AlAnon family groups are open to relatives and friends of the alcoholic or to the interested public. Their meetings are conducted very much like those of Alcoholics Anonymous, except they use the Alcoholics Anonymous program in their own lives. They eliminate the word "alcohol" from the program and add the word "alcoholic," i.e., "We admit that we are powerless over our alcoholic," etc. They also accept members from families whose alcoholic may never sober up. These people learn how to live at peace in spite of that fact. Social activities are also available, and it is expecially good for re-uniting couples who need to learn to play, as well as for wives whose husbands are drunk. They pursue much of the same soul-searching as does the alcoholic in Alcoholics Anonymous.

ALATEEN

The AlAteen program is the same as the AlAnon, except it is for the benefit of the youngsters of an alcoholic. The children learn about alcoholism and how to live with an alcoholic parent. It helps them to explore their own problems and grow up. It also offers social activities conducted much like AlAnon groups.

In summary, this paper illustrated that religion and Alcoholics Anonymous have the same psychodynamics for the recovery of the alcoholic. Alcoholics Anonymous appears to be religion with its bare essentials, without the possible stifling effects of dogma and creed. It is religion in its down-to-earth simplest form, where every-one can grasp it and use it for salvation, for sanity, for wholeness, for recovery!

REFERENCES

1. Anonymous. *Twelve steps and twelve traditions.* New York: A.A. Publishing, Inc. 1952.
2. Anonymous. *Alcoholics Anonymous comes of age.* New York: A.A. Publishing, Inc. 1957.
3. Anonymous. *This is Alcoholics Anonymous.* New York: A.A. World Service, Inc. 1961.
4. Anonymous. *Alcoholics Anonymous for the woman.* New York: A.A. World Service, Inc. 1962.
5. Anonymous. *A clergyman asks about alcoholism.* New York: A.A. World Service, 1962.
6. Anonymous. *Memo to an inmate who may be an alcoholic.* New York: A.A. Publishing, Inc. 1963.
7. Anonymous. *Partners in Alcoholics Anonymous.* New York: A.A. World Service, Inc. 1964.
8. Bellwood, L. R. Transference phenomena in pastoral work. Unpublished doctoral dissertation, Department of Pastoral Psychology, Boston University, 1962.
9. Snarr, D. N. Current alcoholism treatment: a study in social ethics. Unpublished doctoral dissertation, The Iliff School of Theology, Denver, Colo., 1966.

Chapter 28

Recovery, Incorporated: Mental Health Through Will Training

ABRAHAM A. LOW

Abraham A. Low: b. 1891, Baranow, Poland. d. 1954, Rochester, Minnesota. M.D. University of Vienna, 1919.
Private practice, Neurology, 1925–1931, and Psychiatry 1931–1954 in Chicago, Illinois. Instructor in Neurology, University of Illinois Medical School, 1925–1931. Assistant Professor and Assistant Director of the Psychiatric Institute of the University of Illinois Medical School, 1931–1940. Associate Professor and Acting Director, Psychiatric Institute, University of Illinois Medical School, 1940–1941. Assistant State Alienist of Illinois, 1931–1941. Founder and Medical Director of Recovery, Inc., The Association of Nervous and Former Mental Patients, 1937–1954.
Fellow: American Medical Association; American Psychiatric Association.
Books: *Studies of Infant Speech and Thought* (1936). *Techniques of Self-Help in Psychiatric After Care* (1943). *Mental Health Through Will-Training* (1950).
Articles: numerous papers on Clinical Neurology, Histopathology of the Central Nervous System, and Clinical Psychiatry.

Psychotherapy, individual or group, is invariably based (1) on a philosophy and (2) on techniques. In years past, the field was dominated by three main philosophies and techniques: Freud's psychoanalysis, Adler's individual psychology, and Jung's approach. More recently, the psychoanalytic doctrine has taken the lead and all but crowded out its erstwhile rivals. It established its hegemony in universities and philanthropic foundations and gained unquestioned prominence in the province of psychotherapy. The doctrine appears to be in firm control in the official psychiatric organizations, in the mental hygiene activities of the national government, in the veterans administration, presumably also in the hospitals of the armed forces. Official

818

psychotherapy, in the United States today, is essentially psychoanalysis.

I reject the psychoanalytic doctrine both as philosophy and therapeutic technique.[1] In point of philosophy, I cannot share the view that human conduct is the result of unconscious drives, sexual or otherwise. To my way of thinking, adult life is not driven by instincts but guided by Will. In emphasizing the priority of Will over Drives I am merely echoing the principles and teachings of the late Professor Emil Kraepelin, founder of modern psychiatry, and those of the late Professor Wilhelm Wundt, father of modern psychology. Quite proudly I also claim to echo the voice of common experience and common sense. Whatever may be meant by drives, be they instinctual cravings (the favorite psychoanalytic term), or emotional trends, desires, wishes, yearnings, and learnings, they all eventuate in impulses, acting or ready for action. To me it is inconceivable that adult human life can be ordered without a Will holding down impulses. What precisely is meant by the term Will is amply demonstrated in the text.

In point of psychotherapeutic techniques, psychoanalysis must be accounted a failure on the evidence of its own testimony. The most startling defect is the insignificant number of patients which can be reached by the method. The Chicago Institute of Psychoanalysis, for instance, has been able to report no more than 319 patients treated six months or longer during a ten-year period (1). The Menninger Clinic of Topeka, Kansas, tops this record of poor productivity with a report (2) of 100 patients similarly treated for six months or longer in the course of ten years, 1932 to 1941. In order to fully appreciate the story told by these astonishing figures one must remember that the two institutions are generously staffed and richly financed. Knight (2), tabulating the results of treatment as published by the psychoanalytic institutes of Berlin, London, Topeka (ten-year surveys), and Chicago (five years) was unable to quote more than 660 cases treated for upward of six months in the four clinics during a ten-year period (five years in Chicago). Of this total, 363 patients were treated in Berlin, 114 in Chicago, 100 in Topeka, and 74 in London. Stating it otherwise, the productivity of the psychoanalytic techniques, as reported for four leading clinics, ranged, in point of the number of patients carried per year, from 7.4 (London) to 36.3 (Berlin). Figures of this kind admit of one conclusion only: psychoanalytic techniques are available

---

[1] This paper represents selections from A. A. Low, *Mental Health Through Will Training.* (12th ed.) Boston: Christopher, 1965. Reprinted through permission of the publishers, with some changes to conform to the style of this book.

for a small fraction only of the multitude of postpsychotic and psychoneurotic patients. The reason for its restricted availability is the egregious amount of time needed for the administration of the treatment, an over-all average of hundreds of hours being required for each individual patient. For patients cared for in private practice there is the added handicap that the time-consuming process involves a necessarily exorbitant expense. Whether the emphasis be on the time factor or the cost element, in either case the method is all but unavailable for the masses of patients.

Aside from its limited availability for numerically significant groups of patients, psychoanalysis is also, again on the evidence of its own testimony, therapeutically ineffective. Knight (2), assaying the therapeutic results obtained in 660 analyses conducted for six months or longer in the institutes of Berlin, London, Chicago, and Topeka tells us that 183 patients (27.7%) were considered "apparently cured;" 186 (28.2%) were "much improved;" 291 (44.1%) were either somewhat improved, or worse, or showed no change. Needless to say, a 27.7% yield of "apparently cured" patients, even adding the 28.2% of the "much improved" contingent, constitutes a serious indictment for any psychotherapeutic method. Oberndorf (4) is authority for the statement that 40% of the "psychotic cases treated by psychoanalysis plus institutional regime at the Menninger Clinic" were discharged as cured. He comments that this is also the percentage of those "discharged as cured from mental hospitals in the United States." It is well known, however, that the 40% figure for cures of state hospital patients represents the spontaneous recovery rate. Is it permissible, then, to draw the inference that, for psychotic patients at any rate, the results of psychoanalytic treatment are identical with their spontaneous chances for "outgrowing" their psychosis? Taking either the hint offered by Oberndorf or the disappointing figures supplied by the above mentioned statistics, the conclusion seems inescapable that psychoanalysis has failed as a therapeutic technique.

It is not intended here to criticize psychoanalysis with a view to extolling the work of Recovery, Inc. But inasmuch as the psychoanalytic method has well nigh monopolized the field of psychotherapy, it is incumbent on a diverging approach to measure its record of accomplishment against that of the recognized procedure. A few simple figures culled from my files will demonstrate that the combination of office treatment with the group methods practiced in Recovery, Inc. achieves a range of availability which dwarfs that of psychoanalysis.

Between January 1, 1946 and December 31, 1947, in a representative two-year period, I was able to examine in my office a total of 425 new patients. Deducting from this figure those patients who did not return after the initial examination (140) and those who suffered from somatic or neurological conditions (24), 261 subjects remained who were available for psychotherapy. Of this final group, 156 were given treatment for six months or longer. In other words, employing the method described in this paper, one man was able to give active psychiatric care to a considerable multiple of the patients served in a comparable period by large staffs of psychoanalytic institutions. Clearly, the Recovery method is vastly superior to psychoanalysis in the matter of availability to the masses of patients seeking psychiatric care.

As concerns the therapeutic effectiveness of the Recovery techniques, as distinguished from mere availability, it is sufficient to point to the basic character of the organization: the members know one another; they meet frequently and regularly in classes and at parties; they get together in family gatherings and consort socially; they form sewing clubs, bowling parties, and dancing teams; many of them spend evenings or Sundays together, dining or visiting theaters and amusement places. One can readily surmise what would happen if no more than a negligible 28% of the lot would finally reach the status of "apparently cured." The organization would explode in no time. Instead, the association, staffed by one physician, financed without outside assistance, shunning though not completely escaping publicity, has prospered close to fifteen years. This record speaks for itself. It needs no statistics to support its claims.

MY THERAPEUTIC APPROACHES

Imagination, Temper, and Symptoms

The central theme of today's panel[2] was fear, more particularly, the fear of making a decision. Tillie feared deciding between two pairs of socks; Maurice feared taking a book from the library; and Carol, Frank, and Don quoted similar fears of deciding, choosing, taking a stand, and reaching a conclusion. Frank surmised that all the issues and problems, conflicts and dilemmas listed by the panel members were sheer trivialities. But the fact is that Tillie, while grappling with her difficulty, developed panics and confusions and all manner of frightening symptoms. To her the danger of making a wrong decision did not

---

[2] This section is extracted from Dr. Low's talks and papers.

appear at all trivial. It loomed in her mind as a matter of momentous importance. She thought of serious consequences and grave responsibilities; she anticipated failure and disaster. In other words, her imagination was on fire.

If there were no imagination, there would be few panics and anxieties. And without panics and anxieties nervous symptoms would die away. No nervous patient would ever fear collapse unless his imagination told him that palpitations, air hunger, and chest pressure spell the danger of imminent death. Nobody would ever shiver at the thought of "another sleepless night" except that imagination paints a lurid picture of the fatal results that a mythical sleeplessness has on health. I may mention the fanciful notions that patients entertain about the dreadful effects of "nervous fatigue," and you will realize that the idea of danger created by your imagination can easily disrupt any of your functions. If this is true, it is clear that the nervous patient is served by an imagination that is out of bounds, rampant, unbalanced. If the balance is to be restored, the patient will have to acquire a working knowledge of how his imagination functions. Clearly, all I can offer is a brief address in a sketchy account of its mode of operation.

It is the tragedy of the nervous patient that after years of suffering he develops an unbalanced imagination, the first guesses of which tend distressingly and consistently to interpret inner and outer experiences in terms of insecurity. The greater tragedy is that the first guesses are accepted sight unseen without an attempt at verification. Unable to resist its suggestions, that patient becomes the victim of his imagination. An incessant stream of insecurity suggestions is poured forth with rapid-fire velocity, leading to a continuous succession of wrong opinions, conclusions, and decisions. The final result is that the patient, realizing that his first guesses tend to be either wrong or harmful, comes to fear forming an opinion, reaching a conclusion, or making a decision. In a sense his fears are based on good logic. In most instances, imagination has misled and deceived him. On a hundred or thousand occasions it told him that his sensations will lead to collapse. The suggestion never materialized. How can that imagination be trusted? Whenever a symptom made its appearance, whether palpitations or numbness or dizziness, imagination suggested invariably that this was the last gasp, that an emergency was on. The patient went into a panic, clamored for instant help, insisted that the doctor be summoned without delay. When the relatives, aware of the "nervous" nature of the spell, hesitated to call the physician, perhaps in the dead of the night, the patient passed into a violent burst of temper, and the wish had to be granted. But the moment the physician arrived, his mere presence or calm manner frequently dispelled both symptom and temper in a trice. The deceitfulness of his imagination was here clearly demonstrated to the patient. It lied to him, led him to wrong conclusions, to hasty decisions. It produced temper, caused unnecessary expense, created domestic friction. Worst of all, it undermined his self-respect and made him look ridiculous. Trusting an imagination of this kind, it would seem, is impossible.

Had Tillie permitted her imagination to be occupied with dreams and hopes, her chest would have currently swelled with pride and her heart would have habitually expanded with joy. Instead, her chest became the seat of agonizing pressure, and her heart was rocked by wild palpitations because her imagination was allowed to busy itself with fears and anxieties mainly or solely. What prevented her from keeping her imagination fruitfully occupied was her preoccupation with terrors and panics, with symptoms and distress, in short, with the idea of insecurity. And, if an imagination is more or less constantly preoccupied with ideas of insecurity, it will be deprived of the opportunity to occupy itself with those dreams, hopes, and visions from which ideas of security originate. If this happens, the imaginative balance will be disturbed, the thoughts of insecurity will drown out the ideas of security, and anxious preoccupation will cancel out the pleasurable occupations. The result will be a paralyzing fear of deciding, planning, initiating, and acting. But without decisions, plans, action, and initiative there is no possibility of developing pride, self-reliance, and self-sufficiency. It was the sustained preoccupation with ideas of insecurity that prevented Tillie from acquiring even that modicum of self-trust that prompts the trivial decisions of daily existence.

You will understand now that if the nervous patient is to regain his lost imaginative balance his preoccupations with ideas of insecurity will have to give way to occupations with thoughts of security, that is, with hopes, dreams, and pleasurable anticipations. You will also understand that hopes, dreams, and joyful anticipations are the very warp and woof of decisions, plans, and conclusions. And if you ask how you can manage to rout your preoccupations my answer will be of the simplest kind: stop listening to the threat of the symptomatic idiom and the imbecilities of the temperamental lingo and your imagination will again be able to indulge in its stimulating occupations and you will be in a position to make decisions, draw conclusions, formulate plans without fearing the dreadful consequences suggested to you by temper and symptom. Learn to use the Recovery language of self-confidence and fearlessness and your imagination will be freed of the deadweight of panics and anxieties. Thus delivered it will once again occupy itself with thoughts of security and ideas of self-sufficiency.

Temper, Sovereignty, and Fellowship

When Frank met his mother, he offered to mail the letter. Behind this offer was a desire or determination to be helpful or courteous or considerate. The act expressed the motive of service, that is, the spirit of Fellowship. Frank has frequently stated in panel discussions that he and his mother do not get along well together. They live in a more or less continuous temperamental deadlock, in an atmosphere of strife, spite, and bitterness. You may conclude, therefore, that Frank's offer was a polite gesture rather than a genuine eagerness to be of help. But in group life an insincere gesture of generosity and fellowship is far more valuable than an outspoken expression of enmity and a brutal assertion of one's sovereignty. No doubt, the rebuff offered by Frank's mother was sincere. It was based on sincere bitterness and sincere hostility. Sincerity of this kind is anything but an asset. A group is interested in peace and order. And peace and order are destroyed or disrupted by the temperamental expressions of anger, vindictiveness, and bitterness. A temperamental outburst is sincere, of course. So are murder and burglary. They are based on genuine and sincere desires to kill and rob. That the mother was sincere in her rude reaction to Frank's offer of fellowship was no credit to her. That reaction was dictated by the mother's will to have her own way, by her insistence on domination and her determination to assert her sovereign rights. As such it served the ends of unrestricted individualism, not those of rule-bound group life. It was based on the principle of sovereignty, not of fellowship.

This is not an attempt to exonerate our friend Frank. He practiced his share of rudeness and sovereignty when in a temperamental act of brusqueness he "grabbed Harriette and said let's go." Both mother and son are currently disposed to display excesses of domestic temper, exercising their disposition to assert their sovereign rights and ignoring the needs for fellowship, mutuality, and toleration. What interests us here is the close relationship that exists between the workings of an aggressive temper, on the one hand, and the spirit of sovereignty and fellowship, on the other. The members of the panel spoke of symbols and symbolic victories. One of the most pernicious symbols is that of sovereignty. Frank's mother imagined, perhaps unknown to herself, that she represented or symbolized sovereignty in her dealings with the members of her family. Her will to assert her sovereignty provoked the resistance of her son with the result that family life was turned into a battlefield of temperamental dispositions in which both mother and son craved the glory of symbolic victories and both effectively frustrated one another's ludicrous ambitions. In the end, a cruel, implacable deadlock developed in which feelings and sensibilities were ruthlessly slaughtered and fellowship was made a shambles. The realistic objects of the incessant fights were invariably such trivialities as a letter to be mailed or a sugar bowl to be filled. The symbolic goal was the craving to assert sovereign rights. The inevitable results were tears, crushed feelings, and refusals to eat or otherwise to share and to practice fellowship.

The deadlock between Frank and his mother is undoubtedly extreme. It is characterized by an extreme insistence on the exercise of unrestricted sovereignty and an equally extreme refusal to practice fellowship. Deadlocks of more moderate intensity were mentioned by the other members of the panel. Annette was in deadlock with her sour-dispositioned aunt, Sophie with her boisterous youngsters, Carol with her soft-spoken and well-intentioned husband. All of them were in one way or another embroiled in the tug-of-war of domestic temper, all of them had in previous years indulged in the cruel game of craving symbolic victories in the battle for their sovereign rights, and all of them had an unenvious record of tears shed, feelings crushed, and meals taken in the dead silence of sullen moods. But all of them would tell you in unmistakable language that for them the concept of sovereignty had been finally exposed as an empty, silly, and childish symbol and fellowship has become a living, mature, and concrete reality. Even Frank, the helpless party to a relentless and apparently incurable deadlock, was able to state that before he had his Recovery training "the deadlock led to endless quarrels because neither of us would give in. Now I keep quiet and while the deadlock persists there is no argument." In his home, fellowship is not reestablished, but the peace-destroying symbolism of sovereignty has been routed and with it Frank's symptoms of fatigue and sleeplessness. And if it is true that Recovery training is capable of laying the ghost of sovereignty, then, we may be pardoned for claiming that our system of self-help is the sovereign means for promoting fellowship.

Muscles and Mental Health

When Harriette told recent members of Recovery that she recovered her health after fifteen years of futile search for a remedy, she met with skepticism. Had she told the doubters that her main means of recapturing health was the use of her muscles, their skepticism would have turned into outright cynicism. That the mind governs muscles is a truism accepted even by the most sophisticated mentality. But that muscles can be made to mold and influence mental activity sounds incredible to the skeptic and laughable to the cynic. Fortunately, our patients do not belong to the group of "advanced thinkers," and to their plain common sense and unpolished way of viewing things the humble muscle commands as much dignity as the pretentious brain cell. They know that if in a nervous ailment central management breaks down the peripheral rank and file may be ready or can be trained to "take over." And so, when in the lives of Harriette, Frank, Christine, Phil, and many hundreds of Recovery members the machinery of central management was thrown out of gear, the muscles were trained to hold the line until management could be reorganized and revitalized. After the muscles had demonstrated their ability to keep the concern going, the self-confidence of the brain was restored, and the body regained its capacity for concerted action and balanced adjustment. Such "pinch-hitting" by the muscles for the brain may sound incredible, but skepticism and cynicism are offshoots of intellectualism, and Recovery stands for realism, plain common sense, and an unspoiled way of viewing life.

At the time when Harriette joined Recovery she suffered from a condition in which her brain had almost ceased giving directions to the muscles. If any guidance was supplied, it was in the form of fearful anticipations, gloomy misgivings, and dismal threats. The brain had retreated from active management of the body. It cowered away in abject defeatism, shivered at the thought of giving orders, and trembled at the prospect of having to take the initiative and to shoulder responsibility. There were tasks to be finished, decisions to be made, and actions to be planned, but the brain, paralyzed by fear, terrified the muscles into helpless inactivity and the inner organs into chaotic functioning. Harriette was tortured by "headaches and nausea and fatigue and dizzy spells, by weak spells and palpitations." Her ears ached and her eyes blurred and her throat choked, and for solid years her brain warned her not to walk when she felt dizzy, not to work when she was fatigued, not to eat when she experienced her nausea. The sense of hopelessness in the brain created an attitude of helplessness in the muscles. Action was held in abeyance, life was suspended.

After fifteen years of unrelieved agony, Harriette learned in Recovery that if the brain defaulted on its managerial duties the muscles can be made to "take over" and to "pinch-hit" for the cringing cerebral manager. At first she had her doubts. The method seemed too simple. When her nervous fatigue made her feel exhausted and her brain threatened that the next step meant unfailing collapse how was she to force her muscles to venture into that next step that might lead to destruction? But then she heard a patient recite in a class interview how she had routed her fears by "commanding her muscles" to do what they dreaded to do. The patient had developed the habit of growing panicky at the mere sight of a knife, fearing to do harm to the baby. During the interview I urged the patient to practice touching knives and assured her that the mere act of contacting or handling the "dangerous" object was certain to convince the jittery brain that there was no reason for jitters. The resoluteness of the muscles would conquer the defeatism of the brain. The patient accepted my suggestion, practiced touching knives, and purged the brain of its fears. "I would have never believed," the patient exclaimed, "that such a simple method could cure my fears. But it did." Other patients reported similar experiences. One patient was afraid of crossing the street. Stepping out of the house meant initiating a chain of frightening symptoms: palpitations, sweats, dizziness, muscular weakness, and dimness of vision. The brain sounded the customary alarm, warning of a dire emergency. After due instruction, the patient learned to brave the empty threat of the sensations and the defeatist babble of the brain. He compelled his muscles to walk on and convinced his cowardly cerebral manager that no danger existed and that the warning signals flashed by the brain cells were false alarms not to be taken seriously. After Harriette witnessed several class demonstrations of this kind, she decided to give the method a fair trial with the result that she worked part time after three weeks of practicing muscle control and engaged in full-time activity after another four months. The brain had been convinced by the muscles that all that was required to shake off nervous fears was to make the muscles do what the brain feared to do.

As was mentioned, Harriette was at first skeptical. But when in classes and at Recovery meetings her skepticism melted, she commanded her muscles to lie quietly in bed when she was tense and restless, to walk on when she felt exhausted, to eat when the mere sight of food produced nausea, and to speak forcefully when the throat felt choked. And after the muscles swung into action, disregarding the "symptomatic idiom" of the organs, Harriette's brain was instantly convinced that exhausted muscles can do a fine piece of walking, that a weary body can lie motionless in bed until sleep supervenes, that a stomach harried by the prospect of nausea can be made to take in food, without sending it back, and that a throat, drained of its moisture and contracted to a pinpoint, could be induced to voice a well-modulated speech. With continued practice of systematic muscle training the brain finally was rid of its defeatism and invigorated by a newly gained conviction, and it could muster the courage to resume leadership and to reinstate the ancient set of rules, policies, and principles for healthy conduct. Harriette's muscles had reeducated her brain.

Had Harriette retained her skepticism she should have refrained from practicing muscle control, and defeatism would have nullified or retarded her cure. Unfortunately, too many patients persist in their skepticism, scorning the use of a method that appears "too simple" to promise results. One such patient recently tried to challenge my statements about the role of the muscles in shaping conduct with the question, "But, doctor, I don't suffer from palpitations or dizziness or fatigue. My trouble is an obsession. How can muscles cure an obsession?" The obsession from which the lady suffered was one of jealousy. The patient knew that her husband was a model of matrimonial loyalty, but she could not shake off the thought that he was unfaithful. She was told: "I grant that yours is what is called an obsession. But if you ponder the meaning of the word you will realize that what obsesses your brain is an idea. You know from experience that ideas come and go. How is it you cannot get rid of your idea? How is it that it 'obsesses' you and occupies your attention all the time? The reason is that the actions of your muscles feed this idea and reinforce it incessantly, preventing it from leaving the brain as ideas ordinarily do. Command your muscles not to act on the obsession, and it will die of inanition. What you do is keep the thought of jealousy alive by means of your muscular action. You rummage in the pockets of your husband's clothes to find evidence of his philandering. When you arrive home you search rooms, garret, and basement to discover telltale objects left by an unwelcome visitor. You spy on your husband's activities, telephone his office numbers of times to check on his whereabouts, scrutinize his mail and notebooks, and keep a close watch on every one of his movements. When he arrives in the evening, you subject him to a relentless bombardment of quizzes, questions, and suspicions. All of this is done by your muscles. Every search, every act of watching, every sequence of questioning intensifies your tenseness and keeps your attention forcefully riveted on the obsessive idea. That idea would die a natural death within a short time, as ideas commonly do, if you permitted it to expire. But the action of your muscles keeps it alive, prolonging your suffering and refusing to let your brain find its normal equilibrium. The surest way to make the obsession depart from your brain is to command your muscles not to ask questions, not to telephone your husband's office, not to launch into endless searches of rooms, pockets, drawers, and notebooks. In your case, the mucles, if properly restrained, would not only reeducate the brain, they would also give it the much-needed breathing spell and would relieve it of the well-nigh intolerable tenseness under which it is placed through the action of your muscles."

I could quote numerous other examples illustrating the many uses to which the method of muscle control lends itself in its task of either convincing the brain that defiance of symptoms is possible and harmless or relieving it of pressures caused by morbid preoccupation with disturbing ideas and impulses. But I shall close this discussion with the assurance that what Harriette did can be done by every nervous patient and that the simplicity of the method which she used ought to be no occasion for skeptical shrugs and cynical sneers. Precisely because the method is simple it is a prompt, effective, and convincing one.

Realism, Romanticism, and Intellectualism

Annette felt tired and thought the "fatigue was physical." She then formed the idea that her nerves were "exhausted and shriveled and incapable of performing their job." After she was told in classes that nervous fatigue has its source in the patient's sense of discouragement and self-disgust, she "didn't like that very well because I knew how my muscles felt." With this she formulated the familiar philosophy of nervous patients, which can be condensed in two sentences: I feel tired; hence, I am tired, and I think my muscles are exhausted; hence, they are. On the basis of this philosophy, patients are convinced that what they feel is real and what they think is right. And it is the supposed reality of what they feel and the presumed rightness of what they think that keeps patients from ironing and dressing and preparing breakfast. Protesting solemnly that their nerves are "incapable of performing their jobs," these persons do a perfect job of coddling their feelings and pampering their thoughts. Pronouncing their coddled feelings real and their pampered thoughts right, they prepare the groundwork for manufacturing a self-made incapacity.

I want you to know that this is a philosophy—confused and absurd it is true—but a philosophy, nevertheless. My patients claim they suffer from frightening sensations, overpowering impulses, torturing thoughts, and devitalized feelings. But I tell them that this is a half-truth at best; that what they actually suffer from is their philosophy. And if their philosophy is based on the assumption that in their spells and tantrums their feelings are real and their thoughts are right, well, that is precisely the philosophy of temper. In the ordinary burst of temper, whether it be presymptomatic or postsymptomatic, one feels the insult or injury was a "real" outrage and thinks he is "right" in considering it a deliberate hurt.

If I speak of a philosophy, I do not refer to a complex system of thought as described in textbooks. What I have in mind is what has been called the philosophy of life. Let me add immediately I know three philosophies of this kind only: realism, romanticism, and intellectualism. If in the pursuit of your daily activities you coddle your feelings, you will act as a romantic; if you pamper your thoughts, your conduct will be that of an intellectual. Your behavior will then be governed by feelings whose telltale story has been hastily believed or by thoughts whose immature suggestions were uncritically accepted. In either case, your action will be guided by the subjective promptings of your inner experiences instead of by the objective requirements of outer reality. If you were a realist, you would first consider the actual facts of the prevailing situation and would not hesitate to suppress your thoughts or shelve your feelings if you found they conflicted with the realities of the situation.

A philosophy tells you which goals to choose and how to aim at them. You who are readers of our Recovery literature know that goals are of two kinds: group and individualistic. The realist aims at group goals mainly. His ambition is to adjust his conduct to the requirements of group life. In the instance of the visit to the bakery shop he considered himself a member of the group of shoppers. He knew that by expressing his feelings of irritation or his thoughts of resentment he was bound to arouse the enmity of some members of that group. And antagonizing the group meant maladjustment. If his goal was to create good will in the group, he had to curb his individualistic inclinations to express his inner responses. He exercised control and remained adjusted. To the romantic and intellectual person the good will of the group means little. Group standards are odious restrictions to their craving for individualistic expression. In the episode at the bakery shop the romantic would not have hesitated to voice his indignation with a candid and perhaps studied indifference to the sensibilities of others. He prides himself on being frank and aboveboard. "What is wrong about expressing a feeling?" asks the romantic enthusiast for frank expression, and forthwith, without scruple or hesitation, he rolls off a list of his likes and dislikes regardless of whether they are offensive, tactless, and out of place. He will tell you, without mincing words, that your furniture is not properly arranged or that if he had planned a house like yours the rooms or entrances or exits would have been differently placed. If it is a female romantic, she will intimate plainly that she has no taste for your jewelry and that her way of cooking a roast is different and "if you want to get a real coat let me take you to my tailor." It is all an expression of feelings, and if in the process feelings of others are hurt, well, it is about time they got used to language that "comes straight from the shoulder." Presently, this unrestrained talker will steer the conversation into the channels of sickness, hospitalization, operations. She will revel in gruesome recollections of the "excruciating pains" she suffered without being able to convince her husband or physician that the pain was "real." What agonies she went through. She felt pain and tugging and pulling in the lower abdomen. "It was there. I felt it all the time. But they thought it was my imagination. Finally I got my physician to take me to the hospital, and on the operating table they found adhesions all over." Her feelings had told her she had a tumor or something of the sort, and it was "really there."

I could go on indefinitely describing the amusing, though by no means harmless, mouthings of these romantic souls. I could portray their lust for complaining, their zeal for being considered a martyr. But it would merely illustrate the fact that their philosophy is one of reckless expression of feelings. These feelings are coddled and treasured and magnified and thrust at every innocent listener who consents to be an audience.

I shall now give you a brief account of the intellectual mentality, the counterpart of the romantic soul. His stock in trade is the insistence, repeated and repeated ruthlessly and tirelessly, that he is right, that you better take his advice, that he could have told you how to avoid trouble if you had only cared to listen to him. Thinking that he is right, he promptly assumes that others are wrong. Hence, he delights in correcting the statements and opinions of those about him. He is critical, aggressive, meddlesome. He not only knows things but knows them better than others. His views are advanced and modern, theirs are standpattish and outmoded. His supreme delight is to change things, to reform laws and institutions, to do away with the old and to create something new; hence, he is impatient with tradition, custom, and standards. He knows how to arrange things, how to plan them, how to predict and prevent. Enjoying a self-appointed monopoly in correct thinking, he is eager to mend and "reform" the defective thought processes of others. These others are backward, benighted, reactionary. He is forward-looking, enlightened, progressive. The essence of his attitude is that he knows and is right and that the others are ignorant and wrong. And if they are wrong it is his duty to tell them. There is no reticence about this intellectual. He talks and argues and fights for his opinions. His pet idea is "free speech," not only in the political scene where it may have a legitimate place, but also in social and domestic contacts where it merely serves the purpose of shocking settled convictions and established views. Waiting in line at the bakery shop, the intellectual would or might let loose a stirring tirade of criticism against "that bunch of stuffed shirts" and their "red tape." He might inveigh against the greed of the "vested interests" and the oppression of the common people. Voicing their thoughts and opinions, particularly if these are shocking to the lethargy of the standpatters, is a consuming passion with these fight-thinking and enlightened intellectuals.

I do not wish to be misunderstood to imply that my patients are generally addicted to a romantic or intellectual philosophy of life. Presumably, some of them are, but so are some members of every group. At any rate, I am little concerned about the political, economic, or social views of my patients. What interests me is their philosophy with regard to symptoms and temper. The fact is that my patients, prior to receiving training in Recovery, have been stubbornly romantic about their symptoms and emphatically intellectual about their temper. They coddled their defeatist feelings of "really" being exhausted and of "really" not having slept a wink for months and pampered their thoughts of having the "right" to wail and complain and make extravagant demands on relatives and friends. What the panel members demonstrated convincingly is that persistent and systematic training in the realistic principles of Recovery is the superb means of ridding our patients of the pretentious pseudophilosophies of decadent romanticism and arrogant intellectualism in their dealings with their common inner experiences.

External and Internal Environment

Annette was jostled by a street car rider and as a result felt irritated and tense for hours and ultimately developed blurred vision, tightness in the abdomen, disturbance of appetite, and general discomfort. She recounted this example when dealing with the topics of constitution, environment, and temper. Undoubtedly, the jostling man was her environment. But what he jostled was Annette's muscles. It was nothing but a jostle, a jar, perhaps a jolt. How is it possible that a mild encroachment of this sort produced serious derangements of vision, appetite, abdominal function, and general well-being? Was Annette's constitution so weak that a trivial push from the outside could cause a violent upheaval of her inner organs? It does not seem at all likely that mild pressure against her muscles should occasion such a severe inner reaction.

The jostling street car rider was environment to Annette. But by the same token, Annette was environment to the jostling man. His muscles pushed her muscles. And it will be useful for you to know that men and women are environment to one another and that the one acts on the other by means of muscles. Even if they speak or merely look, the speaking and looking are done by the muscles of the mouth and the eyes. But if environmental effects proceed from muscle to muscle, how is it they reach down to the inner organs and even to the depths where the thoughts, moods, impulses, and sensations of the personality are embedded? For Annette did not merely respond with organic distress (vision, digestion, and tenseness); she was also irritated, fearful, "felt hurt and stepped on," and doubted whether she "could ever start out again in this world." Her muscles were merely jostled, but her inner organs were profoundly upset, and her personality was thrown out of equilibrium. How was it possible for a trivial environmental event to release such widespread effects?

You who have gone through the process of Recovery training know that the careless street car rider did not merely jolt Annette's muscles; he also jolted her temper. And temper is the bridge over which environmental irritations can reach across the muscles to the inner organs and to the depths of the personality. Along this road it penetrates to the domain that we call internal environment.

Roughly speaking, everything that exists or lives outside your muscles is external environment, everything that is inside your muscles is internal environment. Your home and its furniture, your father and mother, your friends and neighbors, your employers and employees together with a host of innumerable things, conditions, and persons make up your outer environment. But inside you there is the inner environment, far more potent and vital, more readily disturbed and shaken than anything outside you. This inner environment is made up of your internal organs, on the one hand, and your personality functions, on the other. The latter are your feelings and moods, thoughts and decisions, sensations and impulses. Let your outer environment be disturbed by war, bereavement, fire, or financial loss, and the chances are that you will bear the shock and emerge from it unscathed. But let your impulses be deranged, your sensations get out of control, your feelings become the seat of fear, envy, and jealousy, and your thoughts the prey of torturing obsessions, and the resulting commotion is likely to unsettle your nervous constitution.

Annette experienced another jostling episode a year later when a woman pushed her in front of a show window. She felt irritated again, but this time for a moment only. The next moment she laughed, and the irritation passed. There was no effect on the inner organs, no jolting of her personality functions. You will instantly realize the difference. In the first instance, in the street car, the environmental irritation was reacted to with temper; in the second instance, before the show window, the response was directed and mitigated by a sense of humor. The sense of humor, born of indifference to irritations even if they are severe, prevented the emergence of temper which takes annoyances seriously even if they are trivial.

We may conclude that the trivial irritations of external environment—they comprise the bulk of irritations in general—can be approached either with temper or with a sense of humor. If the approach is temperamental, the inner organs and the personality functions of the internal environment will be thrown into commotion; if the approach is humorous, the internal environment will be spared the anguish of frustration and the agony of disordered functions. The jostling or jolting will be felt by the muscles only; it will be prevented from spreading there to work havoc with emotions and sensibilities. But in order to prevent this spread you must learn how to control your temper and to develop a sense of humor. In Recovery you have learned that temper is your worst enemy, humor your best friend.

Feelings Are Not Facts

I want you to know that your feelings are not facts. They merely pretend to reveal facts. Your feelings deceive you. They tell you of danger when there is no hazard, of wakefulness when sleep was adequate, of exhaustion when the body is merely weary and the mind discouraged. In speaking of your symptoms your feelings lie to you. If you trust them you are certain to be betrayed into panics and vicious cycles.

I said that your feelings lie to you, that they deceive and betray you. How can that be? How can feelings be true or false? If you are sad what has that to do with truth, deception, or treachery? Feelings are either experienced or they are not. They are present or absent but never true or false. Thoughts alone possess the quality of truth and falseness. If the patient's feelings tell lies, they do so because an incorrect and deceptive thought is attached to them. The deception is accomplished by the thought, not by the feeling. The panel members expressed this relation between thought and feeling with convincing plainness. One after another they stated that before joining Recovery they thought of their panics as dangerous, but now they think of them as merely distressing. You see, a panic is a feeling of extreme distress which annexes either the thought of danger or that of harmlessness. The panics experienced by patients are not pure feelings, they are overlaid and modified and taken captive by a thought. If the annexed thought is that of danger, a vicious cycle will develop and the panic will be prolonged. If the thought is that of security, the panic will be stopped abruptly. It all depends on whether the patient will accept the physician's thought of security or his own thought of danger. If this be so, then, it is no longer a question whether the physician's thought ought to prevail or the patient's feelings. It is no longer the problem of thought versus feeling but of one thought versus the other. The patient is not asked to change his feelings or to discard them or to disavow them. He is merely asked to substitute the physician's thought for his own. You will now understand the meaning of my statement that the Recovery slogan "Sensations are distressing but not dangerous" symbolizes the close union between patient and physician. If it is assumed that the physician approaches the patient with an objective thought and the patient reciprocates with a subjective feeling the two could never meet. Feelings cannot be exchanged or shared. If the patient were nothing but distressed or sad or despondent, the physician's thought could hardly reach him. Communication and mutual understanding would be blocked effectively. But if the feeling experienced by the patient is reduced to a "quarter feeling" of despair, associated with a "three-quarter thought" of danger, then the physician's thought of security can easily meet the patient's thought of danger. It can modify or eliminate it. In Recovery this has been done with singular success. As the panel members quoted themselves: In former years they entertained their own thoughts that the panic was dangerous. Now they accept the physician's thought that it is merely distressing.

The Will Says Yes or No

Claire, on the Saturday panel, recounted how several weeks ago her husband told her he had to leave town for a number of days. She knew it was a business trip that could not be postponed. Nevertheless, she was thrown into a panic at the prospect of being left alone. She felt a heat wave sweeping over her body, her throat choked, her heart raced, and her entire body felt limp. She was tense and dizzy and weak. She said nothing and could hardly have said anything because she was terror stricken. Her husband noticed the disturbed feelings and upbraided her for being selfish and inconsiderate. In the course of the panel discussion she stated that her husband "obviously didn't care how I felt." Later she added that she was able to stop her feelings by applying her Recovery training. She spotted the panic as an instance of temper and self-pity, hence, as sabotage. The spotting produced instant relaxation. "I was surprised," she said, "that I was able to stop and control my feelings as quickly as I did. I think I am learning how to handle my feelings."

Claire became terrified at the thought of her husband leaving town. The terror meant to her that her feelings were disturbed. The disturbed feelings were noticed by the husband who upbraided her presumably for failing to control her feelings. That suggested to Claire that her feelings were not properly appreciated. Recovering her composure, she was surprised to find that control of feelings was easy. In the end she concluded that her Recovery training had served her well in the matter of handling her feelings. After listening to this report of an incident in which feelings fairly leaped over one another, I must confess that the dexterity with which Claire manipulated feelings is surprising indeed. And I shall ask: did Claire deal with feelings? or did she play on something which she merely called by that name?

What happened to Claire was that she suffered a scare. Previous to the scare she was reasonably calm. Being calm, her condition was that of relaxation. Her thoughts were relaxed. They were focused on the little household cares of cooking and shopping, or they reviewed the trivial happenings of the preceding day or she dwelt on the funny dream she had the night before. There was no stewing over issues, no worry about problems, no conflict of ideas, no confusion of plans. The feelings were in the same state of relaxation, and she experienced neither fear nor anger, nor excessive joy nor immoderate grief. The relaxed thoughts produced a serene spirit; the relaxed feelings gave rise to a mood of comfort. Whenever a person is serene and comfortable, his inner organs tend placidly and peacefully to their functions of circulation, respiration, digestion, and elimination. Hence, no violent sensations, no choking, no air hunger, and no nausea. We may say that when Claire was serene and comfortable her sensations were just as relaxed as were her thoughts and feelings. With no disturbance rocking the body there was no occasion for the impulses to become turbulent and impetuous, so that the total of her experience (thoughts, feelings, sensations, and impulses) was that of calm, rest, and composure. We conclude that prior to being struck with terror Claire's total experience was that of security, producing a state of relaxation.

I want you to understand what is meant by the words "total experience." Our body has only two ways of experiencing a situation. No matter what is the nature of the situation, it is approached either with a sense of security or one of insecurity. If your attitude happens to be that of security, your entire body will partake of that experience. Your thoughts, feelings, sensations and impulses, your inner organs, outer muscles, and skin, even your tiniest fibers and most minute particles of tissues will share in the total experience of security which now governs your body. Experiencing security, they will all be largely devoid of strain, tenseness, commotion, and excitement. Barring certain organic diseases, no human experience is possible, even thinkable, in which thoughts express security and impulses are restless and erratic. Nor is it feasible that at one and the same time feelings should be relaxed and sensations disturbed and muscles taut. The just prevailing sense of security may be mild or exalted; the experience of insecurity may be moderate or severe. But whatever may be its degree or intensity the entire body is affected. It is a total experience.

A total has parts, and the total experience has its part experiences. I have mentioned them already. They are thoughts, feelings, sensations, and impulses. These are the dominant parts of the total experience. If any of them become disturbed, the disturbance will spread to the other members of the team. If any of them is pacified, the entire team will regain calm and peace and the disturbance will be stopped. This calming and stopping of disturbances is what is generally referred to as "control" (of disturbances). You will now understand that if you wish to control the total experience of insecurity you must use a method which will control, that is, stop and calm any one of the dominant parts of that experience. Control one dominant part, for instance, the confused thoughts, and the rest of the team (feelings, sensations, and impulses) will follow suit. The dominant part which Claire chose for control was her feeling of terror and despair. She claims that after this feeling was calmed and stopped the sensations, thoughts, and impulses quieted down and she relaxed. But I shall ask: how can feelings be stopped, calmed, or controlled? Which method did Claire use for controlling them? Feelings are spontaneous; they rise and fall and run their course, and no deliberate effort will ever put a halt to their spontaneous progression. Obviously, Claire did not control her feelings but some other dominant part of her total experience of insecurity.

That feelings and sensations cannot be stopped, calmed, or controlled by deliberate effort ought to be familiar to you because I have emphasized the fact on numerous other occasions. I told you repeatedly that thoughts and impulses alone are subject to control. Evidently, when Claire "applied her Recovery training" she applied it to her thoughts and impulses, not to her feelings or sensations. I shall repeat: two inner experiences only are subject to control: thoughts and impulses. I shall add that one factor only is capable of controlling them: the Will. The inference is that when Claire put a check on her total experience of insecurity the feat was accomplished through the intervention of her Will. It was her Will that exercised control over her thoughts, perhaps also over her impulses, perhaps over both. Emphatically, it did not and could not control feelings and sensations.

You remember I mentioned frequently that the Will has one function only: it rejects or accepts ideas and stops or releases impulses. In either case, it says either yes or no to the idea or the impulse. Suppose an idea suggesting danger lodges itself in the brain. It is then for the Will to judge and decide whether or not danger exists. If the Will accepts (says yes to) the idea of danger, then the thought of danger will mobilize feelings of insecurity and will release in their wake rebellious sensations and vehement impulses. The total experience will then be that of insecurity. Conversely, if the Will decrees that no danger threatens, the thought of insecurity will be discounted and feelings, sensations, and impulses will retain their customary equilibrium. You will understand now that ideas rising in the mind offer suggestions to which the Will replies with yes or no. This has been called the denying and affirming function of the Will. The same function may be exercised by the Will in response to impulses releasing them with a yes and restraining them with a no. How is it that this process of denying and affirming can be used for thoughts and impulses only and not for feelings and sensations? You will grasp that concept readily if you will consider what precisely the words yes and no mean when employed in connection with an inner experience. When the Will disposes of the thought of danger by rendering the verdict no; the denial can be expressed, as by saying, "No, there is no truth to this suggestion of danger. Perhaps there is not even a probability or possibility of it." Similarly, when an impulse presses for action and the Will interposes its veto, it says in essence, "No, this impulse is undesirable, and its action will prove unwise and harm-harmfulness, wisdom or folly are possible in the instance of feelings and sensations. If a person is seized with grief or stimulated by joy ful." No such ratings in terms of truth and falseness, desirability and it would be senseless for the Will to claim that the joy is false or the grief impossible. Feelings are either experienced or not experienced. Their existence, wisdom, and probability cannot be denied or affirmed. The same holds for sensations. If the head aches it would be absurd for the Will to object that "No, this is no headache. It is unwise, untrue, or improbable." Clearly, if the Will is to intervene in order to control the total experience of insecurity, its no cannot be directed to feelings and sensations. Instead, it must address itself to thoughts and impulses.

We can now sum up our analysis of Claire's reaction. When her husband announced his planned trip, the idea of danger leaped into Claire's brain. The thought of danger mobilized feelings of insecurity, threw sensation into violent uproar, and released a host of turbulent impulses (to cry out in despair or shout in anger, to argue, protest, run). When this happened, Claire's Will was inactive, and the thought of insecurity was accepted. The result was that the body was thrown into the total experience of insecurity. Suddenly she remembered her Recovery training and presumably recalled the Recovery motto that sensations are distressing but not dangerous. Now the thought of "no danger" dominated her brain, and she decided to ignore or deny the existence of danger. Her Will had been alerted and said no. The no calmed her thought processes, and the calm communicated itself to sensations, feelings, and impulses. The total experience was one of security. When Claire noticed that her body had relaxed so miraculously, she felt the need for explaining the miracle, and in doing so she employed the clumsy and incorrect language of the man in the street. According to this language, feelings are subject to control. Had she used the Recovery language, she would have surmised that her total experience of insecurity had been remedied by the intervention of the Will, which said no to the idea of danger with the result that one dominant part of the experience was brought under control and spread the effects to the other parts. Claire had done the right thing but, trying to explain it, called it by the wrong name.

Sabotage Method No. 1

The concept of sabotage is basic to the philosophy of Recovery. The nervous patient sabotages his own health, his social adjustment, his efficiency and equilibrium, and—the most pernicious form of sabotage—the physician's authority. The trouble is that the patient, engaged in a systematic effort of obstruction, plies his trade in such a subtle and almost underhanded manner that he is not aware of his own plottings and machinations. Formerly, I believed that the patient weaves his obstructionist plots from the depths of subconscious motivations. This level of motivation absolved him of all suspicion of deliberate conspiracy. Gradually, however, a good deal of conscious contrivance became increasingly obvious. The patient asks the innocent-sounding question, "Don't you think my condition could be the result of a glandular trouble?" That this question is a diagnostic statement and therefore an attempt at sabotage is clear to the physician. But is it equally clear to the patient? Is he conscious that his question challenged the physician's diagnosis. It is safe to say that at the precise moment when the inquiry is made the thought of antagonism or obstruction may be absent from the questioner's mind. But, if we survey the patient's mental activities beyond the immediate scene and trace his meditations no farther back than to the bus trip which he made to the doctor's office, the picture changes radically. While on the bus he was preoccupied with the diagnosis given him on the occasion of his previous visit. He was told then that his condition was of a nervous nature, that it implied no danger, that the combination of office treatment and group management would eliminate his complaints. Now, on the bus, he views the physician's pronouncements with a critical eye. It seems preposterous to him that his "unbearable" fatigue should be labelled "just nervous," i.e., innocent and harmless.

Why then was he asked by other physicians to take a rest, to stop working? True enough, his present physician is competent, highly recommended, and undoubtedly successful. But Drs. J. and F. were no numbskulls, either, and the one diagnosed a mild anemic condition, and the other blamed the fatigue on a low blood pressure. And the doctor who writes the health column in the morning paper suggested yesterday that fatigue states are frequently caused by a lowered metabolism which, in many instances, can be traced to a glandular deficiency. Why should all these possibilities be ignored? The ruminations continue in this vein until the train of thought is interrupted by some incident that diverts the patient's attention. The sabotaging activity is no longer pursued. Leaving the bus, the patient enters a restaurant to eat lunch. He reads the paper, gives some fleeting thought to all kinds of topics and observations, and the subjects of complaints and diagnosis sink to a lower level of consciousness. When he faces the physician, his diagnostic doubts may still be removed from the upper strata of his conscious awareness. But are they buried in the subconscious? They were mulled over and rehearsed just half an hour ago and are quite active and fresh in memory although not in the forefront of conscious meditation. They wait merely for the proper occasion to get revived. When the physician opens up with the introductory question, "How are you today?" the patient's slumbering antagonism is quickly aroused, and the thoughts recently rehearsed during the bus ride are promptly sprung on the physician. That antagonism may not at the present moment be glaringly conscious. But it was in the limelight of awareness a short time ago. It did not have the time to sink down to the subconscious level. We may safely call it half-conscious or quasi-conscious.

Clearly, if sabotage is to be controlled and eliminated, it must be stopped at its source and origin. It originates at times and in places outside the physician's office, in the bus, at home, on the street, in the workshop. In the presence of the physician the sabotaging thoughts burst forth spontaneously with little reflection and hardly any deliberation. But in the absence of the physician the sabotaging is done reflectively and deliberately. If a person is spontaneous, his utterances are blurted out and poured forth impulsively. Usually there is neither time nor incentive to revise the spontaneous performance. On the other hand, when the patient sabotages in clear reflection, he has the time and occasion for correction provided he has also the incentive to correct. Recovery, with its untiring insistence on a total effort, supplies the patient with the needed incentive. But the patient's endeavor is bound to be vague, groping, and ineffectual unless he is supplied with adequate insight into the devious ways in which his own sabotaging tricks operate. Armed with both incentive and insight, he will be properly equipped for the long, drawnout and grueling battle against his sabotaging propensities, the *enemy number one* of mental health. Of the many disguises behind which sabotage hides the most important ones will be mentioned. As may be expected, the most common form is one which is frequently encountered in ordinary conversation: Literalness. Essentially, this device makes use of the technique of rejecting a statement made by the speaker without opposing it openly.

Example 1. The patient reported that at a card game his mother corrected him every few minutes. He was provoked, threw the cards on the table, and precipitated a violent argument. He slept poorly that night and awoke in the morning all exhausted. He was told to avoid drawing the temperamental conclusion that he is right and mother wrong. His reply was, "I think that mother is wrong but not that I am right." It was not easy to make the patient see the obvious truth that the question raised in an argument is who is right and who is wrong; that if the one party to the controversy is declared to be in the wrong it follows inevitably that the other party must be right; that if he thought the mother was wrong it was obvious that he felt he was right. "Can't I think the one thought and not the other" the disputant continued. "Not any more," he was told, "than you can think of light without darkness, good without bad, love without hate. Once the pair of the team of opposites is thought of, the other pair is called up automatically." The patient was then shown that he could have used his own common sense to realize that he was literal and listened to the letter instead of to the meaning of the physician's statements. If he had done that he would have demonstrated a will to conquer his temper. Instead, he distorted common sense and debauched logic and sabotaged the will to get well.

Example 2. A lady exclaimed in utter frustration, "I can't plan. I get flustered when I begin and then I do not know what to do next." The physician remarked, "Of course, if you say you cannot plan . . ." but was unable to continue because the lady interrupted him sharply, "I don't mean to say that I cannot plan. It is merely difficult for me to make a decision because I have no determination." She was told bluntly that her manner of reasoning was devoid of logic; that the sharp distinction which she chose to make between planning, making decisions, and having determination was superficial sophistry, a literal differentiation meant to confuse the issue instead of clarifying it. Being a college graduate and possessed of such keen logic as to be an artist at word juggling, she ought to employ her logical capacities to analyze her own statements in terms of sabotage. Her aim ought to be to get well, not to stage a senseless and futile debate with her physician. The result was that she produced a new literalistic perversion of logic. She shouted, "I do not mean to debate with you, I merely wish to make you understand my point of view." Whereupon she was told politely but firmly, "Whether I understand or misunderstand you is of no significance. The thing that counts is that you make every effort to understand me."

Brief examples: A woman patient reported in astonishing frankness about her wild temper outbursts. She related a series of uncalled-for acts of spite and vengefulness, interlarding the recital with such comments as, "Of course, I know it's my fault . . . I am just a nag . . . What I need is a good licking, I guess." When the examiner warned her not to indulge in an orgy of self-blame, she burst forth, "I don't blame myself; I am just telling my story."

A patient was told not to get sore at herself because that was her main form of temper. She replied, "Doctor, I don't get sore at myself. I am just disgusted with myself." Another patient was warned not to be irritable, whereupon she rejoined, "I am not irritable. I am just upset by what my daughter says."

In all the situations quoted in these examples, the patients display a tendency to block the physician's effort, to combat his views, to reject his suggestions by means of a literal misinterpretation of the words he uses. Once the patient's attention has been called to his favorite methods of sabotaging he is in a position to correct his habits. In Recovery, corrections of this kind are made frequently and effectively.

REFERENCES

1. Institute of Psychoanalysis, *Ten Year Report.* Chicago; 1932–1942.
2. Knight, R. P. Evaluation of the results of psychoanalytic treatment. *Amer. J. Psychoanal.,* 1941. **98,** 434.
3. Low, A. A. *Mental health through will training.* (12th ed.) Boston: Christopher, 1965.
4. Oberndorf, C. P. Consideration of results with psychoanalytic therapy. *Amer. J. Psychiat.,* 1942, **99,** 374.

Editor's Note: Other methods of sabotage dealt with by Dr. Low in his book are: ignoring or discrediting the initial improvement; disparaging the competence, method, or diagnosis of the physician; failure to practice spot diagnosis; failure to spot emotionalism and sentimentalism; and failure to practice muscle control.

The following article by Dorothy Kerchner[1] and Douglas Goldman[2] is a discussion of Dr. Low's will training in practice.

RECOVERY, INC.

Recovery, Inc. is an organization of local groups developed first by Dr. Abraham Low in Chicago between 1937 and 1950. It originated in Dr. Low's group psychotherapy sessions. These sessions were directed to preparation of patients for independent and productive lives outside of psychiatric hospitals and helped some patients to overcome hermitlike withdrawal.

In 1950, Dr. Low conceived the idea that the groups could be more self-sufficient, that the patients themselves could take over much of the function of resocialization and rehabilitation without taking over the medical psychiatric function of therapy. Since 1952, the groups have developed further inside and outside the Chicago area. Since 1954, when Dr. Low died, others have taken up the interest in the work, and it has continued to expand.

The techniques applied in the Recovery movement are thoroughly described and documented in a book by Dr. Low, *Mental Health Through Will Training*. The meetings follow a more or less set pattern. They begin with the reading of a chapter from Dr. Low's book or the playing of a tape by Dr. Low which presents one or more examples of symptoms susceptible to the Recovery technique with comments by Dr. Low. The meeting is then given to a period of "'examples" presented by members themselves and followed by comments from members of the group and the leader. Discussion of examples lasts for approximately an hour and is followed by an informal social period, directed to further discussion that might stimulate the more timid participants to discuss problems with the group leader and other members.

---

[1] Dorothy Kerchner: b. 1919, Philadelphia, Pennsylvania. R.N., Good Samaritan Hospital School of Nursing, 1942. B.S., College of Mount St. Joseph on the Ohio, 1952. M.A., in psychiatric nursing, New York University, 1962. Assistant Professor of Nursing, College of Mount St. Joseph on the Ohio, 1964–date. Director of Nursing Service, Longview State Hospital, 1962–1964. Past Chairman of N.S.A. section, Eighth District of Ohio State Nurses Association. Area Leader, Recovery, Inc., greater Cincinnati group.

[2] Douglas Goldman: b. 1906, New York, New York. B.S., 1926, M.B., 1928, M.D., 1929, M.S., in pathology, 1929, University of Cincinnati. Assistant Clinical Professor of Psychiatry, University of Cincinnati, 1950–date. Clinical Director, Longview State Hospital, 1937–1962. Chairman, Department of Psychiatry, Good Samaritan Hospital, 1954–date.

Group leaders are members whose improvement from psychiatric illness has advanced to an adequate degree that they may have extra training and indoctrination. This additional training comes from others experienced for a longer time in the application of the principles set by Dr. Low. Group leaders from various parts of the country periodically meet to discuss further development of the technique. A number of psychiatrists act in an unobtrusive, advisory capacity. The group hopes to maintain a nonauthoritarian point of view so that the idea of self-help among patients continues to be emphasized in the work of re-socialization and rehabilitation.

Dr. Low developed a special vocabulary for use in the work of the meetings of the Recovery groups. The important words are:

Example: An emotional and psychologic reaction involving disability and discomfort to the patient and preventing his normal participation in work or social activity.

Temper: A relatively acute form of emotional reaction which takes a number of forms: (1) Angry or aggressive temper, a reaction of resentment, open hostility, impatience, and disgust outwardly directed. (2) Fearful or retreating temper dominated by feelings of fear, a sense of failure, inferiority, and guilt which are inwardly directed.

To *spot:* The verb "to spot" is synonymous with the verb "to recognize" in the usual colloquial sense. The members of Recovery groups learn with each other's help to *spot* disturbed feelings and sensations as the various forms of angry or fearful *temper.*

Sabotage: This word represents the breaking down by the patient under conscious or unconscious motivation of any rehabilitative activity or accomplishment.

Endorsement: This term means the giving of credit for good performance against the resistance of adverse emotional and psychologic background. It can come from others or from the patient himself.

Briefly described *examples* as presented at Recovery meetings indicate the nature of this form of activity.

1. A housewife had finished her domestic chores and had decided to go to the park near her home for a walk and to enjoy the beautiful weather. She had always previously been afraid to go out alone, but since she had improved her mental state, she was now able to go out alone with fewer symptoms arising. She was even able to carry on a conversation with a friend whom she met. After walking, she noticed that she had forgotten to change from her housedress before going out and worried about what her friend would think of her. The Recovery activity had trained her to react to such discomfort by *spotting* her

fearful temper and feelings of inadequacy. It was simple to recognize that a housedress was not inappropriate during working hours and that symptoms were a minor residual of her illness. The patient brought this to the next Recovery meeting as an example to be discussed in considerable detail.

2. Another instance had to do with a patient who was not following the psychiatrist's direction either in performance or the taking of medication. The group pointed out that the patient was *sabotaging* his own improvement. The various reasons for this in the patient's life situation could be discussed superficially in the group in relation to *angry and fearful temper* with encouragement to better performance.

Recovery, Inc. is maintained rigidly as nonsectarian, nonreligious, nonpolitical, but with many affiliations that encourage patients in hopeful, useful, social activity. People of many faiths can meet together in rooms rented or donated for use in churches, synagogues, schools, lodge halls, and other community-oriented institutions. No economic segregation or other forms of inappropriate differentiation of human beings are practiced. About 10,000 men and women are at present affiliated with the Recovery movement. These are members of over 500 groups in the United States and Canada. Individual groups must be kept relatively small, preferably with less than 30 members; when the activity expands beyond this number, groups usually divide to accommodate the geographic convenience of the members. A continuous program of leader training makes this division possible. The groups usually have the sponsorship of psychiatric social workers, psychiatric nurses, and psychiatrists whose functions are to maintain a kind of security in the purpose of the movement and to help avoid the pitfalls of going beyond the purposes of rehabilitation and resocialization. The movement is strictly oriented to assist and follow-up on the work of the psychiatrist but under no circumstances to replace him.

Conclusion

An Eclectic Evaluation
of Psychotherapeutic Methods

FREDERICK C. THORNE

Ideally, all new methods and claims thereof should be evaluated against the background of existing scientific knowledge for the purpose of discriminating the exact operational steps involved. After an operational analysis of exactly what is taking place, it becomes possible to differentiate the component processes and to distinguish between what is old and what is genuinely new. Old methods keep turning up under new titles, and there is an almost infinite number of permutations and combinations in which old methods can be combined with the claim that something new and different has been added.

Any clinical case may be studied from many different operational viewpoints, each selecting a different focus of operations (such as perception, learning, affects or motivational modifications) and attempting to modify behavior by a variety of manipulations of the learning process. Underlying all clinical manipulations, however, it must be assumed that the primary clinical objective is to modify the learning process, either by unlearning, learning, or relearning desired patterns. The basic issue resolves itself down to (a) what is to be learned (unlearned or relearned) and (b) how is this to be accomplished?

All therapy and counseling implies that behavior is to be changed, either by basic personality modifications or by specific instrumental learnings. The clinical problem is how to arrange conditions so that learning can occur. The purpose of this critique is to extract the operational features of the methods described in these volumes and to evaluate the underlying assumptions and claims.[1]

---

[1] The editor had asked Professor F. C. Thorne to provide a systematization and overview of the contributions in *Direct Psychotherapy: 28 American Originals* alongside the exposition of the views he had expressed in many of his previous publications. Although sharing many of Professor Thorne's ideas, the editor sees a number of issues and evaluations differently. The differences arise particularly in viewing the contributions of humanistic, existential, and

OPERATIONAL CLASSIFICATION OF CLINICAL CONCEPTS

Most of clinical psychology and psychiatry is still in the prescientific era of individual exploitation where each new generation of theorists and practitioners proceed to rediscover older facts and methods and give them new names, all without proper reference to historical accumulations of established knowledge. This situation is intolerable because science cannot grow in an orderly manner without proper classification and codification of concepts and techniques. Only confusion can result from a situation where newer theories and findings are not related operationally to existing knowledge.

The field of psychotherapy reminds us of a headless horseman galloping off in all directions at once. The fields of abnormal psychology, psychiatry, and psychoanalysis are now more than 65 years old, with increasingly large numbers of people working therein. A large number of theories and methods have evolved and been combined in many permutations and combinations. Instead of coining new vocabularies and rushing in boldly to establish proprietary claims to new schools, the innovator would be more scientifically sound to relate his theories and methods to existing knowledge. We need fewer wildeyed enthusiasts loudly proclaiming new developments and more mature clinicians who know the field thoroughly.

Much depends upon the way journal editors handle manuscripts proclaiming the discovery of new methods. For some years, the *Journal of Clinical Psychology* has encouraged operational report writing. Manuscripts involving new and esoteric vocabularies redefining older concepts have been returned to the author with the editorial demand that they be related to existing knowledge and stated operationally. In contrast, some other journals appear to open their pages to esoteric terminologies and rehashes of older methods under the illusion that something novel and exciting is being presented.

THE PROLIFERATION OF PSYCHOTHERAPIES

In the few short years since the field of psychotherapy became widely open to clinical psychologists, a period of intense activity has

religious approaches to psychotherapeutic conceptualizations and effectiveness. Such disparity of views is unavoidable in the scientifically primitive stage of the current psychotherapeutic scene, where the opinions are preponderant over validated knowledge. Maybe the differences between "tough-minded" and "tender-minded" thinkers are related to basically irreconcilable temperamental and emotional determinants of the *Weltanschauung*. Ed.

resulted in the appearance of many new systems and schools of psychotherapy with new names, vocabularies, and more or less impressive theoretical rationalizations. Indeed, it appears almost as if each new aspirant to the field has coined his own system to the point where some cynic has pointed out that the situation resembles "The Rover Boys Let Loose in the Psychotherapy Laboratory."

Due to the professional prestige which accrued in the past to Freud, Adler, Jung, and other innovators in the field, there is high motivation among young clinicians to achieve recognition by discovering a new method. Probably this motivation explains why so many workers are attracted to inventing new variations without bothering to consolidate and become proficient in what is already known.

The difficulty with endless permutations and combinations of existing methods which are given new names and unproven claims for efficiency is that confusion ensues when new developments are not related to each other and to existing knowledge. At this stage in the evolution of methods of psychotherapy, the broad outlines of the field are now pretty well established and much is known about a great many techniques. In order to consolidate this knowledge, it is essential to make an operational analysis of all methods in order to objectify their nature. All new developments should be related operationally to the established armamentarium and thereby take their place.

Instead of individualistic proliferation of infinite variations of existing methods under new names, the scientific therapist should relate his practices to existing knowledge, acknowledging theoretical antecedents, eschewing unnecessary terminological complexities, and other overpretentious claims.

CULTISM AND PROPRIETARY METHODS

Elsewhere (8), I have enumerated the signs of cultism, and such criteria must be applied to each new development in clinical practice to discriminate contributions which are eminently scientific from those which are only pseudoscientific. The criteria of cultism include general failure to relate new developments historically and acknowledge theoretical antecedents, coining esoteric new vocabularies operationally unrelated to basic science factors, establishing proprietary schools and groups dedicated to the advancement of the method, failure to conduct proper standardization and outcome studies, preoccupation with cultistic methods to the exclusion of established clinical knowledge, uncritical enthusiasm and claims for own methods, improper advertising, and unsuitable ego involvement on the part of advocates.

While there can be no criticism of scientists who choose to limit their studies to specific methods or topics, so that they become bona fide specialists in their area, serious criticism should be directed toward cults who develop their proprietary methods and claims outside the established practices and safeguards of science. The bona fide specialist is to be distinguished from the cultist on the basis of his conservative and scientific modes of operation. The recent notoriety and undesirable publicity attendant upon the activities of Dr. Timothy Leary in relation to psychedelic drugs illustrate what can happen when an otherwise responsible scientist goes overboard. It is a matter of professional concern to study the personality factors causing a respected scientist to change into a mystical charlatan. The profession of clinical psychology should waste no time in publicly dissociating itself from the activities of Dr. Leary and others still within our fold who are tending in such directions.

SZASZ, CULTURAL RELATIVITY, AND THE MYTH OF MENTAL ILLNESS

The theory of cultural relativity has had a long history, particularly in reference to the question of who is normal. The so-called mentally disordered often consider themselves normal and the rest of the world pathological, but in the long run the weight of mass opinion usually carries the day. Persons who deviate widely from established tradition, or who do not run their affairs with reasonable prudence, typically are declared mentally abnormal when their activities prove dangerous to themselves or to society. Although a few people originally considered abnormal have later turned out to be genuine prophets, most persons judged pathological probably are genuinely abnormal in the sense of not being able to get along with the majority of society.

However, in the long evolution of the law, standards of what are considered bad or antisocial or abnormal have progressively loosened until behaviors that were once considered absolutely bad and pathological are now viewed more tolerantly as manifestations of human variability. There has been a marked reduction in the area of things considered morally bad, with a corresponding enlargement of the area of mental illness or simply of the range of what is considered normal.

These trends have been reflected in the fields of psychiatry and clinical psychology in attempts to apply cultural relativity theory to mental disorder. Carl R. Rogers (4) (and later proponents of relationship therapies) stressed the importance of trying to enter the worlds of the mentally disordered, experiencing with the schizophrenic, and of abandoning the dichotomies of good–bad, normal–abnormal, sane–insane through the adoption of accepting, nonjudgmental attitudes which ignored issues of diagnosis. Other psychologists, reacting to classical methods of psychiatric and institutional methods of handling psychotics, raised questions of who was right, an inhuman society or the sensitive patient who was simply reacting to an intolerable Fate.

Szasz (5) stirred up a veritable hornet's nest when he questioned the applicability in psychiatric fields of models of illness derived from physical medicine. He denied the existence of mental illness, substituting the concepts of cultural relativity and disturbances of human relations. Szasz severely criticized current medical methods and responsibilities in procedures for the commitment and institutionalization of mental cases, attacking the validity of the whole psychiatric approach and stimulating very critical attitudes in the general public who sympathized with his viewpoint though being incompetent to judge its validity.

The practical result of such trends has been a period of great instability and confusion as the old gods have been attacked without substituting anything very well proven in their place. Idealistic zealots of all faiths have been attracted to the banners of Rogers, Szasz & Co., along with a lesser following of solid scientists. The basic issues and facts too often have become lost in a welter of semantic confusion in which idealistic hopes have been confounded prematurely with the morbid realities of what psychological disability actually is no matter what names it is called.

No one wishes to treat the mentally disabled with anything less than the most up-to-date humanism. However, all things have to be kept in proper relation to each other. Historically, the fact is that no one has ever treated the mentally disordered more effectively than modern psychiatry. When and if superior methods are evolved, psychiatry will be first to welcome them. It remains to be proven, however, that theology, philosophy, or any other discipline can come up with anything better than has psychological science.

Clinical psychologists should not allow themselves to be drawn into dialectic arguments over unprovable issues. Mental disorder is what it is, and the realities of societal evolution are what they are, idealists to the contrary. It would be folly to abandon what hard-won knowledge we have in favor of dialectic debates over intangibles. To be certain, errors and abuses are present in our thinking, but let us not destroy the discipline to get rid of its fallacies.

Humanism has been oversold as the panacea for all clinical problems. Man's inhumanity to man is certainly a major cause of conflict and breakdown. However, it is not the only cause nor even the major cause. Many of the greatest human efforts have been stimulated by adversity, and frustration seems to be an essential precondition for certain types of creativity. There is no evidence that perfect conditions in the environment inevitably produce the highest accomplishment. To the contrary, human achievement often has been highest under conditions of deprivation and lowest under conditions of surfeit and luxury. Idealists often visualize the perfect Utopian conditions that would result from some projected socialistic reform, only to discover such things as that "love is not enough."

The profession must not be distracted from its objectives by reformers who would have us abandon the old in favor of unproven idealistic alternatives. Elsewhere (12), I have undertaken an ideological analysis of the contentions of Szasz, demonstrating that many of his arguments are invalid, overdrawn, or specious. Although social relativity concepts have modified scientific thinking importantly, they are not about to overturn the established body of scientific facts. Quibbling about semantic alternatives does not remove the personal and social disabilities resulting from mental disorder and must not be allowed to confuse treatment issues. The eclectic viewpoint protects the clinician from going off the deep end by providing knowledge concerning the indications and contraindications of all known methods and thereby avoiding uncritical adherence to every new fad that comes along. We all know "clinical faddists" who "fall" uncritically for every new cult.

All psychological theories and their therapeutic applications involve certain underlying assumptions concerning the nature of man and the optimum conditions and directions of his development. Consequently, it must be emphasized that every clinical action has its outcomes and their related costs. By costs we mean the actuarial accounting of what it costs, in terms of actual life outcomes, to act or develop in one way or another. No action is without its consequences and costs.

Unfortunately, the costs of certain therapeutic goals have not been objectively demonstrated and assessed. For example, Christian philosophy advocates altruism whereas Ayn Rand stresses rational selfishness. Freud explained all behavior in terms of the metapsychology of the unconscious repression of instinctual drives, a determinism of the unconscious, whereas behavior therapy is based on environmental determinism. Ellis' rational therapy stresses cognitive factors whereas Rogerian nondirective therapy emphasizes affective factors blocking growth. Adler and Dreikurs stress teleoanalysis of the goals and life styles of the person whereas Frankl studies freedom of will, will to meaning, and the meanings of life. Each one of these and all other systems, if logically carried out to its underlying goals, would result in entirely different behavioral outcomes, and their survival values, both personally and socially, remain to be determined.

Consider, for example, the outcomes of advocating such diverse therapeutic goals as "the pursuit of happiness" vs. "social responsibility" or altruism. Permissiveness is considered necessary for the pursuit of happiness, which may end up with pampering, nonexistence of ordinary external limits or controls, egotism, narcissism, impulsiveness, and short term goals, i.e., the spoiled brat or recent "hippie" types. In contrast, social responsibility requires self-control, selflessness, regard for others, self-sacrifice in the service of others, and movement toward the greatest social good. What has become of the modest, self-effacing, quiet, generous, helping child, who was seen but not always heard, and whose ultimate success consisted in making himself useful rather than always seeking what he could get out of life. Is that so bad?

Serious questions arise as to what life goals are indicated for specific persons. Goals that are commendable and realistic for one person may be destructive and unrealistic for another, depending upon his resources. Consider, for example, the universal advocacy of self-expression as a life goal. The current goal of some therapists appears to be that all people must achieve complete self-expression in order to become actualized. Consider also the costs of such complete self-expression. A moron who keeps his mouth shut may appear more intelligent than he is, and non-self-disclosure may thereby become a defense mechanism preserving at least the semblance of normality. On the contrary, the moron who expresses every thought and whim quickly reveals his enormous inadequacies. Similarly, consider the social consequences of complete self-expression by a moron. Society can often assimilate the moron who is quiet, helpful, and self-effacing, but the moron who is loud, noisy, boisterous, uncouth, and crude may quickly outlive his welcome everywhere. So which is preferable, for the moron to be obnoxiously self-expressive or passively inconspicuous? These questions are goal decisions that may have to be made before the start of training and rehabilitation.

These same considerations apply to the advocacy of complete sexual expression and freedom. Sexual expression always has its costs, it may not be universally the ultimate experience of life, and its free expression may involve conflicts as destructive as its repression.

The purpose of these qualifications is to warn the therapist against the uncritical acceptance of any one set of values or goals with neglect of the indications for other values and goals. The clinical decision will usually depend on realistic actuarial accounting.

DIAGNOSIS AND THERAPY

The clinical method in science depends upon a number of basic principles that must be stated and restated because they are too often ignored.

1. Etiology, the study of causation, is basic to all diagnosis. Diagnosis is the recognition of a specific type of etiology which determines the cause–effect relationship in any particular case.

2. Historically, knowledge about therapy developed earlier and more rapidly than knowledge about diagnosis. Many therapies were developed empirically with no rationale or specific indications. Because therapies could be developed empirically, and applied intuitively, prescientific clinicians have argued that therapy could be practiced independently of diagnosis.

3. Diagnostic grasp depends on discovering why and how the person got that way, and what can be done about it. If etiologic formulations are correct, specific therapeutic plans may be made.

4. All behavior modification in psychotherapy occurs through learning, unlearning, or relearning. The principal diagnostic question is what and how behavior is to be modified. Ideally, the client himself should develop insight into what behavior needs to be changed and be motivated to seek help for symptoms or patterns which he is unable to change for himself. More commonly, society working through various authorities or even the therapist recognizes that changes need to be made and tries to influence the client to accept reconditioning as in his own best interests.

5. No one universal panacea or method of case handling is indicated in all cases. Although certain methods, such as nondirectivism, may be safer and indicated in more cases than others, such methods are not specific for all kinds of disorders.

6. The clinical objective should be to discover the specific etiologic factors operating in a particular case and then to utilize specific methods of therapy indicated for that kind of a condition, i.e., to use specific methods as indicated in specific conditions.

7. The "shotgun" approach is not the same as the eclectic method. In the shotgun method, the clinician uses anything he can think of,

blindly, in the hope that some method will succeed. In contrast, the eclectic approach attempts to select specific methods to fit specific conditions based on known indications and contraindications.

8. The principal objective of therapy is to control or ameliorate the primary factors causing a condition. In general, symptoms will disappear if the prime factors are removed.

Valid therapy depends upon valid and reliable diagnosis to uncover the factors underlying disorder and to know what to do at all stages of case handling.

CASE HANDLING: A LEAST COMMON DENOMINATOR

Psychological practitioners have been slow to recognize the tremendous difficulties inherent in differentiating discrete methods of case handling and in objectively assessing their results. In every clinical field, the prescientific era is characterized by a proliferation of proprietary methods, with each practitioner developing his own techniques, and with a confusing mass of often contradictory claims concerning the purported benefits from special methods.

The most blatant error consists in claiming therapeutic effects where, in fact, none may exist. This error is initiated when a practitioner labels himself as a therapist when his efforts have not yet been demonstrated to have any therapeutic effect.

The error is elaborated when a method is claimed as therapeutic when no genuine therapeutic effects have been demonstrated. Clinical experience indicates that it takes 50 years or more before therapeutic claims of any particular school can be scientifically proven or disproven. For example, psychoanalysis has attained great prestige for more than 60 years with many of its basic tenets largely unvalidated. Thus, it may take 50 to 100 years for a plausible erroneous claim to be disproven.

Operationally, the most parsimonious approach would be to designate all practitioners as case handlers until their methods were actually proven to have objectifiable therapeutic effects. Similarly, it would be most parsimonious to designate all techniques as case handling until such time as therapeutic effects could be demonstrated. Let us be intellectually honest with ourselves and think of ourselves as simply case handlers until we can demonstrate objectifiable therapeutic results. There are too many eagers and Horatio Algers currently loose in the psychotherapy laboratory.

BEHAVIOR THERAPIES

The current respectability of learning theory in basic science psychology has led to many attempts to devise systems of psychotherapy based on practical learning and retraining methods. These methods all depend upon mechanistic-behavioristic theories emphasizing the stimulus-response paradigm and assuming that all learned behaviors can be unlearned and relearned. All behavior therapies tend to be ahistoric, i.e., denying the relevance of past history and concentrating on the removal of present symptoms. Most behavior therapies ignore or deny the relevance of classical personality dynamics and depth psychology by concentrating on the retraining of specific behaviors regardless of their causation.

Haugen (Vol. One, p. 244) describes a variant of reciprocal inhibition therapy in which attention is directed to the state of the organism at the time treatment is instituted. Haugen believes that the client reacts most optimally when in a state of calmness induced by training in progressive relaxation. After the patient has learned the techniques of relaxation, these techniques are gradually applied to increasingly complex situations, such as work situations, social problems, etc.

Phillips "assertion-structured" therapy (Vol. One, p. 35) seems difficult to comprehend because of his utilization of new terminology and semantic abstraction complications. Basically, he states that we must deal with psychological states and their meanings (assertions). Phillips introduces the semantic abstraction of "interference" to describe the use of learning techniques to break up maladaptive patterns. He attempts to "structure" the situation more clearly so the client understands what is expected of him, including sets of rules for "right" behavior and the setting of limits. Phillips is particularly concerned with the dynamics of "circular" reactions and of interrupting the cycle at suitable points. Schedules of reinforcement are utilized to produce operant conditioning, as are cybernetic feedbacks to "control the effects."

Some behavior therapists tend to treat the patient like a mindless animal organism who is subjected to an authoritarian reconditioning instigated by a directive therapist who assumes the responsibility of knowing what is wrong with the patient and what should be done for him without securing the permission of the patient or even his cooperation. Indeed, the control by behavior therapists of methods capable of reconditioning clients against their will or even without their knowledge is akin to the mind-washing techniques of Fascism and Communism and should be limited to the most competent ethical personnel.

The use of operant conditioning and behavior therapy to secure ideological and attitudinal reorientation involves ethical issues that should be scrutinized by the professions of psychology and education. There can be little objection to programmed teaching or behavior modifications in subjects where the facts are known (such as mathematics, the physical sciences, or foreign languages). Larger questions of validity arise in the social sciences where fact has not been established in many areas into which ideological bias may creep. Many clients of the more extreme therapies, such as psychoanalysis or Rational Therapy, act as if they had been brainwashed in the sense of having become thoroughly indoctrinated with an ideology the validity and applicability of which to any specific case is open to question. Who is Skinner, for instance, to assume the responsibility of programming the masses in directions which he happens to think correct?

As an early advocate of directive therapies, I have recommended attempting ideological/attitudinal reorientation in selected cases but with the utmost caution to let the client comprehend the various alternatives and ultimately make his own choices. Every clinician has encountered essentially uncured patients who have been indoctrinated with psychoanalytic concepts and who go on mouthing them for the rest of their lives without showing any basic improvement. And in many cases, such patients actually become worse where the indoctrination has been so erroneous as to lead to grosser maladjustment.

Implosive therapy (see Stampfl and Levis, Vol. One, p. 83) is a form of behavior therapy theoretically related to Harry L. Hollingsworth's redintegration theory which stated that conditioned reactions tend to be "redintegrated" by any stimulus associated with the original noxious stimulus. A "danger signal" paired with another neutral stimulus tends to produce a higher order conditioning, resulting in a radiation of such symptoms as anxiety. This concept can be used to explain the "free floating" quality of anxiety reactions. In implosive therapy, conditioned neurotic reactions are treated by deliberately reintroducing the noxious unconditioned stimulus and related stimuli and extinguishing the conditioned reaction through nonreinforcement. The effect is intensified by training the subject to imagine danger signals himself and to stimulate himself with noxious stimuli whose effect will not be reinforced as in the original traumatic situation. It is claimed that many conditioned reaction symptoms will quickly extinguish when not reinforced.

Historically, it is interesting that Hollingworth was treating clients by the same methods under a different name in the early 1920's. In the early 1930's, I observed the late Prescott Lecky treating a severe anxiety state. The patient was hypersensitive to noise and had to stay in a quiet room all the time. Dr. Lecky had the client administer loud noises to himself whenever he felt able to tolerate the resulting anxiety until the reaction was extinguished.

The propositions of Stampfl and Levis need to be evaluated scientifically, particularly with reference to conditions of imminent severe decompensation in cases where the patient is potentially dangerous to himself and others. Stampfl and Levis admit that such cases often get worse before they get better, and the long term results need to be evaluated.

CONDITIONED REFLEX THERAPY

Underlying Salter's conditioned reflex therapy (Vol. One, p. 106) is the (unproven) assumption that all psychopathology results from a conditioned inhibitory state of the organism. Excitation is considered to be the natural state of all living things; conversely, inhibition results in a state of non-self-expressiveness or even non-Being. Excitation particularly involves affective impulsive expressiveness. Salter differentiates excitatory and inhibitory "personality" types characterized by the presence or absence of free affective-impulsive expressiveness. Salter draws heavily from Pavlovian theory in postulating the mechanisms of conditioning whereby the "inhibitory type" is produced by repressive forces in family and society.

Salter's depictions of excitatory and inhibitory types have considerable face validity even though his general theory remains scientifically unvalidated. The inhibitory person is pictured as grossly restricted in action potentialities: anxious, defensive, submissive, low in self-sufficiency, conflictual, and generally paralyzed in action.

Although Salter labels his approach as "conditioned reflex," it is actually an affective-expressive approach which commands the client to drop his inhibitions and practice expressing the Self and particularly feelings and emotions. This is an active-directive reconditioning approach, theoretically rationalized as utilizing disinhibition to return the organism to a state of excitation.

Salter advocates six techniques for practicing self-expression including (1) deliberately uttering feelings and emotions (*feeling talk*), (2) expressing feelings motorically (*face talk*), (3) expressing emotions by contradicting and attacking, (4) expressing the self more actively through greater use of the pronoun I, (5) expressing self-regard more actively, such as by agreeing with praise, and (6) improvising more often to become more spontaneous and flexible. Salter largely disregards past historical antecedents and concentrates on getting the client to be more excitatory and self-expressive.

Salter cites only anecdotal evidence supporting his claim that excessive inhibition is the cause of all psychopathology. Here again, many uncontrolled factors are operating, including catharsis (to some degree), suggestion, acceptance, clarification, nonjudgmental approach, persuasion, and retraining. To the degree that any particular case manifests the "inhibitory personality," such methods may be indicated. What about the cases that are already excessively excitatory and expressive in asocial directions? What about other etiologic factors known to operate? Salter's model has definite applications but, like all other panoramic claimants, it cannot be accepted as a universal panacea for all therapeutic indications.

SPECIALIZED BEHAVIOR MODIFICATION METHODS

Typical behavior therapy methods tend to be directed toward modifying specific symptoms or target behaviors without regard to their etiology or causation. The therapist in a more or less authoritarian manner decides what behaviors are unhealthy or undesirable and then proceeds to modify them without the client's permission or even the client's knowledge as to what is being attempted. Although such methods may be directed toward one symptom or target behavior, any number of behaviors may be modified through more complex programs of behavior modification.

Attempts to extend the behavior modification concept to the whole therapeutic milieu are not new, having been explicated by Abraham Meyerson as early as 1939 in his "total push" method of maximizing the resources of the environment to stimulate chronic schizophrenics back to reality. More-sophisticated behavior modification methods continue to appear, but the underlying assumptions that all behaviors are learned and can be modified by differential reinforcements are the same.

Taulbee and Folsom (Vol. One, p. 165) present such a more

sophisticated approach in their "attitude therapy," which utilizes a structured environment in which carefully selected prescriptions of attitudes are used to reinforce adaptive behaviors and extinguish maladaptive behaviors. The five distinctive attitude modalities are active friendliness (AF), which provides tender, unsolicited loving care and attentions; passive friendliness (PF), in which such loving care is available but not forced on the patient; kind firmness (KF), which assigns the patient time-filling tasks firmly but kindly; matter-of-fact (MOF), which recognizes the patient's disabilities matter-of-factly while offering rehabilitative opportunities; and the no demand (ND) attitude, which makes no demands except expecting compliance with four basic limiting conditions involving remaining in treatment, not harming the self or others, and complying with medications.

Taulbee and Folsom show great sensitivity to providing the optimum conditions in which the patient can learn best what attitudes are offered and expected of him. I consider that the basic contribution of attitude therapy is in describing more-sophisticated ways of mobilizing the entire environment in the program of behavior modification rather than in inventing a basically new approach.

In my paper (Vol. One, p. 190) I have described a method of group behavior therapy developed in a hospital for insane criminals which utilizes the ward therapeutic communities to systematically modify criminalistic ethics and behaviors. The method depends on identifying target sociopathic behaviors and then developing strategies and tactics whereby the group therapist attacks and modifies the ideologies and life styles underlying the criminal ethic. A syllabus of planned strategies for modifying target behaviors is outlined for the purpose of dealing with the most commonly encountered causes of maladaptive behaviors, which are systematically extinguished while more adaptable behaviors are reinforced.

CONFRONTATION PROBLEM-SOLVING THERAPY

Garner has developed a sophisticated version of eclectic directive therapy in his confrontation problem-solving techniques (Vol. One, p. 328). The basic method consists in confronting the client with directive statements reflecting some aspect of his problems and following each statement by a question asking the client what he thinks about what the therapist has just said. This technique of inducing the client to become engaged in the process of therapy by soliciting his reaction to each directive statement made by the therapist has many potential values, not the least of which is the safety-valve effect of discovering whether the client is understanding the therapist correctly and what his reaction is. Misapprehensions can be corrected on the spot. However, a potential danger is that the client's short-term interpretation may not be the same as his longer-term reactions after he has had time to assimilate the deeper significances of what was said. This defect is characteristic of all methods which place too much emphasis on immediate client responses to what goes on in case handling.

Garner makes a scholarly presentation of all the different methods of influencing the client which may be adapted to the confrontation technique, including literally all the classical methods from persuasion (DuBois) to interpretation of the unconscious (Freud) to operant conditioning (Skinner). Garner's discussion makes a large number of claims concerning the alleged benefits from utilizing the confrontation modification of this eclectic array of techniques appropriated from the literature which would lead the reader to conclude that this is an omnibus method capable of taking over the best features of all other classic methods of face-to-face interviewing with the added advantage of the confrontation question.

The crux of the confrontation technique undoubtedly hinges upon the therapeutic relevancy and the skill whereby the therapist selects the crucial things to react to in his confrontation comments. This aspect places a tremendous responsibility on the therapist to be competent in utilizing all possible approaches and methods which may be relevant in uncovering and dealing with the client's problems. This responsibility is the central problem of all eclectic directive methods which utilize a large number of relevant techniques according to their indications and contraindications.

The confrontation method can be considered essentially as a refinement of the eclectic-directive methods described by me in 1950 (6) with the added modification of the question eliciting the client's reaction after every confrontation. This method depends upon continuous clinical diagnosis relating the meanings of what the client says and does to therapeutic interventions and confrontations introduced by the therapist as the result of his best judgments concerning the indications and contraindications of doing any particular thing at any particular point. This technique is tremendously more complicated than the single utilization of any of the classic methods because it requires the therapist to be master of all the classical methods that he is attempting to utilize eclectically. It remains to be demonstrated how well any one therapist can master all the different potential modes of intervention and whether the addition of the confrontation question produces any added advantage. Incidentally, I had also utilized the confrontation question at selected points to make certain that the client was understanding critical issues, but not as an integral part of every confrontation statement.

I believe that emphasis on problem-solving is an important contribution to healthier and more efficient life management. The life management theme has been advanced by me since 1950 and later in my emphasis on studying the global unit of the-person-running-the-business-of-his-life-in-the-world. This approach gives careful attention to all pertinent life problems on the basis of the general principle that mental health consists in solving life problems well whereas ill health inevitably involves a breakdown of problem-solving and coping abilities. My theory of existential anxiety postulates that the success/failure ratio in the life of any person constitutes a kind of a lifetime batting average and that anxiety is an existential reaction to the general failure of a person's life management activities.

"RATIONAL" REEDUCATIVE THERAPIES

Efforts to instill "right" living through selected programs of educational and philosophical indoctrination long antedate their formal application in counseling and psychotherapy. Recognition of the importance of ideological content was widely accepted among laymen for centuries prior to any attempt to include such factors in scientific counseling. In 1950, I (6) presented the first formal discussion of ideological-attitudinal reeducation in a chapter entitled "Maximizing Intellectual Resources."

In 1957–1958, Ellis (Vol. One, p. 295) published the first two articles expanding ideological-attitudinal reeducation into a formal method of psychotherapy based on the postulate that ideological misconceptions inevitably lead to maladaption and reactive emotional disorders. In succeeding publications, Ellis (1) developed a very active-directive technique of diagnosing irrational ideas and forcefully confronting the client with the implications of his misconceptions. Ellis extended this approach to the treatment of sexual problems by rejecting conventional morality as stultifying and recommending sexual liberalism, even to the extreme of advocating legally compulsory premarital sex experience. Unfortunately, with his aggressive promotion of such ideas in popular books, Ellis seems to have moved away from more conservative scientific evaluation of his methods and claims.

Between 1950 and 1957, Anderson (Vol. One, p. 257) developed a rational-reeducative approach entitled "Assumption-Centered" psychotherapy directed at rationally evaluating and correcting the assumptions and expectations upon which actions are based. Anderson was among the first to recognize that each person develops expectations or anticipations concerning what he is "entitled to" (entitlements) which can lead to frustration if they are unrealistic. She further developed a personality theory based on the postulates that each person is "inescapably grandiose, prideful, vain and egotistical," characteristics that are necessary for psychological survival. With the postulate, like that of Ellis, of the primacy of thought over emotion, assumption-centered methods seek to discover what is maladaptive in the ideas, attitudes, and values of the client and to correct them in a reeducative process. As in many other psychotherapeutic theoretical systems, Anderson's underlying theory has not been validated generally, and possibly it is limited in its assumptions and applications.

Weitz (Vol. One, p. 485) offers a "problem-centered guidance" theory that is centrally concerned with detecting areas of problem behavior and correcting them with rational-interpretative solutions of difficulties. Unfortunately, from my point of view, his utilization of a new terminology to revive older concepts hardly helps the clarification of his position. His approach appears as a restatement with some novel refinements of general rational-reeducative methods.

Storrow's Verbal Behavior Therapy (Vol. One, p. 67) seems to me to be another variant or restatement of the basic rational-reeducative approach. Basing his conception on modern learning theory, Storrow emphasizes verbal stimuli as important tools in teaching the client new modes of behavior. He lists a series of learning techniques for removing "positive" symptoms which resembles Herzberg's "task-oriented" therapy. Storrow apparently regards his contribution to be in developing verbal methods of facilitating behavior therapy.

Ayn Rand and Nathaniel Branden offer further refinements of rational-reeducative therapy in their Objectivist philosophy, which has important implications for psychology and therapy. Rand postulates rational self-interest as the prime motive and stresses that this can only be implemented successfully through maximizing cognitive resources. In a series of papers entitled "Check Your Premises,"

Rand indicates how current erroneous ideologies can lead to malad-justment unless corrected.[2]

The Reality Therapy of Glasser (Vol. Two, p. 562) may also be considered as a variant of rational-reeducative therapy based on the assumption that distorted perceptions of reality underlie all psychological disorders. Glasser states that all disorder stems from the inability of patients to fulfill essential needs based on denial of the reality of the world around them. Glasser advocates forceful confrontation of the client with reality, helping the client to fulfill his needs more adequately by coping more effectively with reality. Assuming that need patterns are the same throughout mankind, Glasser stresses the involvement of the therapist in teaching the client responsibility through discussions aimed at bringing the client closer to reality. This task of bringing the client closer to reality is accomplished by correcting misperceptions of reality rationally and otherwise maximizing intellectual resources in problem-solving.

INSIGHT THERAPY

The fact that mental patients tend to show lack of insight into (a) the fact of their abnormality and (b) the inner process factors causing abnormal behaviors has led to methods of psychotherapy designed to produce various levels of insight into both the fact of abnormality and its causes. Behind insight therapies lies the unproven assumption that insight is a curative agent that can produce better contacts with reality and make possible corrective adjustments.

Indeed, the implicit assumption underlying psychoanalysis is that analysis and interpretation of the unconscious undercuts repression mechanisms, rendering inner process dynamics conscious, and supposedly releasing the person from the tyranny of his unconscious. It has taken more than fifty years for clinical experience to disprove the allegedly curative effects of psychoanalytic-type insights as relatively recent statistical studies indicate the large incidence of failure

---

[2] See the series of articles in the *Objectivist Newsletter,* published by the Nathaniel Branden Institute, 350 Fifth Avenue, New York, N. Y. The *Objectivist Newsletter* began publication in 1961 at 120 E. 34 St., New York, N. Y. The most important citations were from the *Objectivist Newsletter,* 1962, **2,** 1, 2, 20, 25. See F. C. Thorne, & Pishkin, V. *The Ideological Survey. Journal of Clinical Psychology,* Monograph Supplement #25, July 1968, for a detailed review of the philosophical-psychological concepts of Ayn Rand and Nathaniel Branden. See also Rand, A. *Atlas Shrugged.* New York: Random House, 1957, 936–993 for the original exposition of the objectivist philosophy.

(50% or more) of psychoanalytic cases. Every clinician knows of "completed" psychoanalyzed cases where "insight" has produced no alleviation of symptomatology.

Furthermore, serious criticism has been directed by Rogers and the nondirectivists against the whole historical approach to personality study on the grounds that maladjustment is in the present and how the person got that way is relatively inconsequential therapeutically. Here again, insight into the etiology or causation of many mental conditions does not inevitably result in amelioration.

In spite of general disillusionment with insight therapy, new attempts of utilizing it are proposed, such as Blake's "Illumination" (Vol. One, p. 464). Once again a term has been devised to describe an older method. Operationally analyzed, Blake uses exhortation and logical reasoning to convince psychotic patients with no insight that they are mentally ill and that their troubles are psychological in nature. As Blake returned to an academic career after four years in a mental hospital situation, he could not provide statistical evidence for his method; it remains in the stage of a pilot project. The description of the "illumination" method provides some very clever refinements of persuasion as applied to this limited problem of catalyzing insights in psychotic patients, and we would have no criticism of his presentation if he would relate his modifications historically to classical operational methods. Particularly with reference to paranoid patients, for example, some doubts may be offered as to their efficiency until such time as real confirmatory evidence is reported that indicates genuine results with methods which older clinicians have long since abandoned.

Blake's illumination method represents an attempt to mobilize all possible methods of inducing or persuading the patient to develop insights into the nature and causes of maladaptive behaviors. This approach is essentially a cognitive one to rationalize the causes of misbehaviors on the assumption that recognizing their nature will inevitably result in corrective adjustments on the part of the patient—an assumption that is not universally true. Blake's techniques include attempts to (a) convince the patient, (b) compare the patient with others, (c) contrast present with past behaviors, (d) force quandaries, (e) challenge or confront the patient, (f) needle the patient, and (g) discuss "tricks of the mind"—all of which involve relatively superficial and authoritarian efforts to "talk" the patient into relinquishing maladaptive behaviors and learning more adaptive behaviors. Blake's main assumption appears to be that persuasion and insight methods can be made more effective through more sophisticated applications. Although we admit the value of more sophisticated applications, our sole dependence on such methods has definite limitations, and it remains to be demonstrated objectively whether Blake has achieved anything over and above the competent eclectic use of such time-honored techniques.

INTEGRITY THERAPY

"Moral" therapies have an ancient historical background stemming from the discovery by primitive man that acts have consequences in the form of failure to achieve or punishment for wrong-doing. It did not take long for the mind of primitive man to formulate the concept of some higher controlling force (God) who inevitably punished misbehavior. Man soon became as anxious over wrongdoings that were not immediately evident (because concealed) as for manifest misbehavior. Down through the ages, efforts were made ranging from witchcraft to modern theology to devise methods for propitiating angry gods and begging their forgiveness. The concept of sin, defined as deliberate wrongdoing, became a central point of the theologies that predicted hell and damnation for anyone who broke God's law. In the Middle Ages, the connection between sin and mental disorder was established in the Christian doctrine that said insanity was the inevitable result of unrepented sin and in itself prima facie evidence of influence by the devil.

The natural antidote offered by all moral therapies is the commandment to do no wrong. And, if one has done wrong, to repent and beg for forgiveness, and not to repeat the sin again. Moral theology seeks to rehabilitate the sinner and the mentally ill by leading him to the truth and to teach prophylaxis by preaching the right ways of living. Hence, Moses brought forth the Ten Commandments, and ever since moral philosophers have been trying to refine the list of right behaviors.

Inevitably the attention of psychological scientists was drawn to the influence of the dichotomy of good–bad, right–wrong, black–white, God–devil on psychic life. Freud conceptualized the forces of conscience as superego whereby the Reality Principle was internalized to direct the ego to control the forces of the id. Anxiety, according to Freud, resulted when an overtyrannical superego became unable to maintain repression over id impulses which threaten to emerge and disrupt existing defenses.

The analogy was drawn by Mowrer that the Freudian superego captivates the ego, destroying the autonomy of the ego, and thus implying that one goal of therapy was to attack the overrepressive superego and overthrow its tyrannical control.

Mowrer (Vol. Two, p. 515) offers an opposing hypothesis to the effect that the id (or psychological hedonism) captivates the ego, which then ignores its conscience (superego) and proceeds to deliberately act wrongly, resulting in anxiety when wrongdoing is discovered or guilt if the person conceals what he has done or even depression if the person comes to hate himself because of deliberately ignoring conscience and doing evil.

The reader should note here the similarities of Mowrer's theory with classical theologies which postulate a self capable of self-control through will power, of the ability to know and distinguish right from wrong, of acceptance of responsibility for doing what is right, and of inevitable guilt and punishment for wrongdoing, either by God or by the person himself who has internalized such prescriptions. Mowrer contends that secret violations of good faith, contract abrogations, concealment, cheating, infidelity, and disregard of conscience inevitably cause conflict, anxiety, guilt, self-hate, and feelings of failure. Mowrer's model, therefore, is a variant of classical moral philosophies reconceptualized in terms of modern scientific symbols.

The validity of Mowrer's theory hinges on the age-old recognition that punishment inevitably results from wrongdoing. If the client can be shown where he has been making mistakes, and persuaded not to repeat them in the future, much needless trouble and anxiety and guilt can be avoided. Mowrer's prescription is "Confess your Sins" and get them off your conscience, make restitution, and "Sin ye not in the future." The direction to make amends and restitutions may have the usefulness of Herzberg's "tasks," as discussed in Herzberg's article in *Developments on Four Continents,* in preparation.

Mowrer's approach can be expected to be necessarily a moralistic judgmental approach which could be quite threatening to guilt-ridden alcoholics and others who know only too well how wrong they have been. Mowrer suggests that this effect can be minimized by not being stern and rejecting but instead showing the understanding of one who has been through the same troubles himself and is now offering himself as a model for rehabilitation.

Clinical experience indicates that "moral" therapies, as almost all current methods, have limited applicability and therapeutic successes. Probably more "moral" therapy has been attempted in the history of mankind than any other kind, with general lack of success in preventing war, crime and personal unhappiness. The clinical indications and contraindications of moral therapies need to be studied and established more exactly.

Incidentally methods of psychological tutoring that I have developed (11) extensively apply the hypothesis that health and success derive from doing many things right in life. Conversely, existential anxiety is postulated as the inevitable reaction to the threat of self-actualization which results from error and failure. Mowrer's integrity theory and therapy may be regarded as but a special case of my wider position.

All the so-called "moral" therapies tend to become "hung up" over the related issues of sin, guilt, and scrupulosity. Theology is primarily concerned with sin and often has had to deal with excesses and even fanaticism developing over excessive guilt in relation to sin. Father O'Flaherty's scrupulosity therapy (Vol. One, p. 221) represents a cognitive attempt to assuage excessive guilts related to undue preoccupations over "sinful" acts and impulses. Apart from the issue as to whether a less absolutistic interpretation of religion would not have avoided stimulating such conflicts in the first place, it remains to be demonstrated objectively whether intellectual exercises can exorcise deep affective conflicts. Certainly much time and effort must be invested in cognitive defenses against obsessive-compulsive conflicts that might have been entirely avoided by a less demanding morality. The clinical question arises whether paralyzing conflict is best resolved by strengthening cognitive defenses against unacceptable impulses or by removing the source of the conflict entirely by desensitizing the unacceptabilty of the forbidden impulses which usually are only relative to some authoritative standard of conduct. This appears to be a case where having created a conflict, it becomes necessary to develop methods for its resolution.

THERAPY #52: THE TRUTH

An age-old adage contends that "people are problems" and "people make their own problems." Irrespective of social credos that command love for the unlovable, social applications of the law of diminishing returns tend to limit how much society (or its representatives) can invest in a person who is nonproductive or too disruptive. Somewhere a balance must be reached in protecting the rights of both the individual and of society. Indeed, in a society that is leaning over backward to protect individual rights, an opposite clamor is arising to give at least equal protection to the rights of society.

Much hinges in therapeutic approaches upon the underlying philosophical approaches concerning what is true and realistic. The classical authoritarian-regimentarian approach stemming from theological morality laid down strict codes with drastic punishments for wrongdoing. A contemporary application of this approach is Mowrer's integrity therapy, which contends that guilt arises from deliberate wrongdoing and that the client must purge himself from sin if he wishes to be healthy and happy.

Nondirectivism and other permissive client-centered therapies are based on the underlying postulates that every life is infinitely valuable in its own right, independent of how it is lived, and that good will triumph in the end if it just can be unblocked. Closely related are the recent social psychiatries of Szasz, Pratt, Bandura, and Sullivan, which deny the medical model of illness and explain deviations as disorders of social interrelationships or even of socially imposed restrictive rejections.

Mainord's "Truth" therapy involves a very practical combination of Mowrer's morality-integrity approach with a modified version of gamesmanship-social interaction theory. Mainord adopts a sort of "Truth or Consequences" approach in which the client is constantly confronted with the consequences of being dishonest or illogical, utilizing the learning theory approach of rewarding adaptive behaviors and punishing maladaptive problem solutions. It is interesting that late in the 1930's Prescott Lecky (3) had developed his Self-Consistency theory, which postulated that anxiety and guilt resulted from inconsistency and that the problem of therapy was to point out the causes of inconsistency and help the client to become self-consistent.

Mainord argues that since maladaptive behaviors are learned in a social context, corrective learning also must occur in a social context, utilizing the therapist as a model of consistent behavior and the group therapy situation as a training center for uncovering and retraining maladaptive behaviors. Each client entering therapy is required to (1) accept everything as his personal responsibility, (2) be absolutely truthful with the group, and (3) assume responsibility for the rest of the group as well.

The group therapy sessions are treated as adjustment workshops in which each participant is held strictly to reality principles, encouraged to bring out problems truthfully and completely, with behaviors judged to be negative exposed to critical scrutiny to demonstrate their maladaptiveness and with adaptive behaviors being positively reinforced.

Mainord utilizes challenging, judgmental statements to confront patients with the realities of the situation and the implications of their maladaptive behaviors. For example, the confrontation "You're not sick, you're crazy" forces the client to reevaluate his self-concepts and to try to see more clearly how he got into trouble. Behavior conflicts and self-concept inconsistencies are forcefully called to the client's attention whenever they occur, with the literal confrontation "Now, who's screwing who? . . . You are screwing yourself. . . . Don't blame others, blame yourself. . . . You are creating your own problems by your own inconsistencies."

Although the use of direct confrontations to force the client to review his contributions to conflict arousal and self-concept inconsistencies dates back to Lecky (3) and my work (14), Mainord's great contribution consists in organizing the whole therapeutic environment to carry out the program on a 24-hour basis. Whereas the typical social environment tends to punish maladaptive behaviors by rejection and institutionalization, Mainord creates a therapeutic workshop in which conflictual or inconsistent behaviors can be brought out into the open, analyzed realistically, and resolved by more adequate coping behaviors for the formerly traumatic situations.

Mainord's contention that judgmental attitudes and forceful confrontations with reality principles can be very effective therapeutically under conditions of strict fairness demands careful consideration in contradiction to nondirective injunctions against making judgments and directly influencing the client. When utilized skillfully and nonthreateningly, judgment and correction can challenge the client to self-review and self-discovery and actually enhance client activity. This discovery was made first by Lecky, who confronted clients with the inconsistency between their self-concept ideals and their actual behaviors, and later by me in utilizing psychological tutoring to show the client how he creates his own problems.

CHARACTER-BUILDING THERAPY

Ernest M. Ligon has behind him a lifelong devotion to character research which has not received the general professional recognition it deserved in an era when behavioristic researchers were more concerned with molecular psychophysiological subfunctions than with the broader dimensions of positive mental health. Ligon's concern has been with the connection of character and positive mental health and the development of methods for the study and measurement of character.

At this point, a few words should be said about the general atmosphere of psychological science in America between 1920 and 1970. Behaviorists had routed the subjectivists who insisted in talking about consciousness, mind, will, purpose, and volition. Behavior determination was postulated to come from the unconscious (Freud) or from environmental conditioning (Watson, Skinner)—both mechanistic principles. Studies of character were relegated to peripheral fringes of scientific psychology or turned over completely to education and religion. Indeed, the work of Ligon and others probably did not become too widely recognized because of theological orientations.

The time has come when the study of character, purpose, and volition must be returned to scientific psychology and psychiatry, which has only recently turned from the exclusive study of psychopathology to the much broader field of positive mental health. Indeed, more than 25 years ago, I advocated the development of a science of psycho-sanics or positive mental health which later led to publication of the book *How to Be Psychologically Healthy* (10), which incorporated the accumulated experience of the mental hygiene movement, including the work of Ligon.

Ligon's approach (Vol. One, p. 433) consists in giving clients positive things to do with little or no emphasis on symptoms and problems. The main therapeutic strategy is to build character by instilling high convictions, rehabilitating value systems, maximizing personality responses for self-expression and social adjustment, and giving the person a real purpose in life. Character development is the central core of positive therapy.

Whereas psychopathology has always focused on negative behaviors, character building stresses positive potentials. Personality resources are inevitably strengthened by any mastery of appropriate technical and social skills that may be developed. The first step consists in trying to develop a sense of purpose in the client to motivate him in positive direction. Often, the young person must approach life as a smörgasbord in which there are many potentially interesting things to do and each young person must find what is suitable individually. There is no easy road to discovering one's purpose in life, and patient counseling often is indicated to keep the client experimenting with potentially positive directions.

The second step consists in evolving a set of personal convictions which will stand as guideposts for living and value decisions. These convictions should be acquired by each person for himself rather than being imposed by authority even though human wisdom has achieved a distillate of value systems that have proven valuable. This development results in a sound and tenable philosophy of life.

The third step consists in developing breadth of effective social *vision* whereby each person learns his place in society and how he can improve social conditions.

Character building usually involves intense psychological tutoring concerning all details of personal-social adaptation involving training in many types of skills. To some extent such skills are taught by home, school, and society, but usually such training has been incomplete or sketchy, and when such is the case the therapist takes over to finish the job.

ROLE PLAYING AND LIFE STYLE RETRAINING

Kelly's fixed role therapy (Vol. One, p. 394) is a very subtle technique of reeducation involving retraining of general attitudes and values, new role dimensions, and life style patterns. Although Kelly's presentations of the technique have been couched in "personal construct" theory terms, the actual mechanisms turn out to involve a sophisticated version of psychological tutoring. Any thoroughgoing analysis of both personal construct theory and fixed role therapy must involve a systematic operational analysis and translation into basic science terminology. Like many other innovators, Kelly has coined many new terms, become involved in high-level abstractions in attempting to rationalize what he is doing, and otherwise written about his work in a rich elegant style that sometimes may becloud the basic issues.

The least common denominators of Kelly's system seem to involve (a) self-concept retraining, (b) social-perceptual retraining, and (c) the personal construct approach to the study of ideological-attitudinal constellations. As applied to fixed role therapy, Kelly starts out by having the client write up a "self-characterization sketch" that presumably reveals the basic outlines of his self-concepts, including the nuclei of his neurotic problems and interpersonal difficulties. The second step consists in having the therapist write up a "role enactment sketch" describing a hypothetical person characterized in terms of more healthy self-concepts, social perceptions, roles, values, and life styles. The third step consists in asking the client to take a vacation from himself and attempt to act out the role suggested by the hypothetical personality of the enactment sketch. The assumption is that if the client is enabled to enact the new role faithfully, this success will result in systematic retraining on many levels of adjustment.

The crux of the fixed role method relates to the validity of the new "self" suggested by the therapist in his "role enactment sketch." This method is a very directive technique in which the therapist assumes responsibility for making some diagnoses concerning what is unhealthy about the client based on the therapist's analysis of the "self-characterization sketch." The therapist furthermore accepts responsibility for suggesting a more healthy life plan, including a more tenable self-concept, new perceptions of the self and others, new roles presumably leading to greater self-actualization, and detailed coaching concerning how to enact the new characterizations of the self. Kelly offers detailed suggestions concerning how this permissively oriented psychological tutoring can be accomplished in the 5 to 10% of clinical cases in which he believes it to be indicated.

On the positive side, both personal construct theory and fixed role therapy reflect Kelly's own great sensitivity for the distinctively personal nuances of life, his respect for individuality, and his ingenuity in devising subtle ways of influencing people painlessly. Notice that fixed role therapy does not involve any painful probing of the maladjusted past and no overt regimentation or authoritarian directiveness. It is almost as though Kelly introduces psychotherapy in the form of an intriguing and painless game, i.e., he simply suggests that it might be interesting to experiment with some new roles and personal constructs that presumably have helped others with similar problems. Published excerpts of these methods indicate that Kelly is masterful in construction of more healthy enactment sketches with which the client may experiment.

On the negative side, three main criticisms may be directed against Kelly's work. The first criticism relates to the general abstruseness of Kelly's approach, his attempts to reconstitute a whole new system out of elements that are generally well known and accepted, his creation of an esoteric new terminology and somewhat pedantic descriptions of the supposed new systems, and his reliance on non sequiturs to enhance the general validity of the approach. To the extent that basic science knowledge about self-concepts, social perceptions, and role playing are valid, then Kelly's system derives validity from these operationally well-known elements. Kelly has a habit, however, of bringing in tangential concepts and getting involved in dialectic abstractions which tend to cloud the basic issues and may add little to support the validity of his contentions. For example, Kelly gets off the track in his concern with "the scientist as the paradigm of man," "that what a scientist does, man can do." This argument seems to involve (a) a somewhat grandiose identification of "a scientifically minded psychologist" as sort of a modern

Wise Man who knows best what the client should do, (b) the unproven assumption that the scientist inevitably runs his life better and hence should be regarded as a model for healthy behaviors, and (c) the assumption that any scientist (therapist) has the skills necessary to understand and literally enter the life situation of the client and thereby to help him, whereas obviously many therapists of the past have been singularly obtuse in failing to understand the problems of clients. Certainly, the fact that some psychological "scientist" has achieved the status marks of, say a Ph.D., membership in the American Psychological Association, and American Board of Examiners in Professional Psychology certification is no validation of his abilities as a therapist or diagnostician.

The second criticism of Kelly's approach concerns the validity of the diagnoses of self-concept status, social perception status, and role-playing status on which both his theory and therapy depends. Ideally, assuming correct diagnoses and valid formulation for retraining, one could accomplish much by broad character retraining. However, the validity of its application in any particular case remains to be demonstrated. In fact, this approach is a most difficult and technical method, and few contemporaries possess the necessary competence and experience to make it work.

The third criticism involves the standard difficulties of assuming the responsibility for being directive and authoritarian in a therapeutic situation wherein the therapist skillfully avoids overt regulation and acts out a deceptively passive role. The fixed role therapist actually is being very directive and authoritarian when he undertakes to analyze the client's self-characterization sketch and then to construct an enactment sketch that suggests an entirely new self, role, and character for the client to try to enact, involving everything from new perceptions of self and others, new roles, and new life styles, to new values for living. We have no quarrel with Kelly's contention that the psychological scientist may be the most logical person to undertake such training, but we would criticize the seeming ease with which he makes such suggestions without first stating very clearly and openly what is actually involved.[3]

---

[3] It is a very significant commentary that many learning theorists, such as Skinner and to lesser degree, Kelly, who presume to make practical applications in applied and clinical psychology, never seem to take time out to do some soul-searching concerning their own personal qualifications for assuming the mantle of the Grand Kleagle of the new behavior conditioners trade. Who is to say who has the qualifications to condition whom and how? Under what fiat are the behavior programmers operating which gives them such powers over the lives of others?

TRANSACTIONAL ANALYSIS

Transactional analysis (Vol. One, p. 370) is an important development in the new school of social psychiatry which postulates that maladaptive interpersonal relations constitute an important source of psychopathology that can be understood only by detailed observations and transactional analyses of clinically significant interactions.

Eric Berne's historical introduction provides interesting insights leading to his invention of transaction analysis and game theory. His story provides another example of the benefits to be derived from deductive theory-centered approaches in preference to client-centered inductive approaches.

Steiner compares the transactional analysis (TA) theory of Child, Parent, and Adult ego states with Freudian ego–superego–id theory and other ego psychologies. Transactional analysis utilizes a structural analysis of the interactions of two or more people to differentiate the contributions of the Child, Parent, and Adult ego states of the parties involved. Child ego states represent integrational fixations in which the stimulus-bound, pleasure-pain-determined integrational milieu continues to be cathected essentially unchanged into adult life. The Parent ego state represents an unaltered interjection of parental or authority values, thus providing a mental content parameter consisting of externally conditioned imperatives for action. The Adult ego state involves high-level problem-solving integrational states in which the cerebral computer is able to deal with situations flexibly and appropriately, autonomously, and without interference by irrelevant lower level considerations.

Transactional analysis deals with transactions, including games, as the basic units for study. Transactions always involve the ego states of the participants, which are differentiated by structural analysis. Transactional analysis seeks to discover the psychological meanings of social actions which cannot be understood until the underlying ego states and ulterior motives are understood. The raw data of TA are interpersonal communications and interactions. Communications proceed smoothly as long as the underlying ego states and motives are parallel or complimentary but become interrupted when cross states or motives operate at odds with each other.

Berne's second important contribution was his discovery of the dynamic social significance of the "games" that people play on each other which can have important clinical results. A "game" consists of (1) a transactional unit consisting of a unified series of interactions with a beginning and an end, (2) ulterior motives involving different psychological and social levels, and (3) a payoff for both players. The motivations for playing games come from stimulus hunger, structure hunger, and position hunger.

Stimulus hunger is satisfied by actual or symbolic "stroking," i.e., by being paid attention to and thus gaining a biologic advantage. Structure hunger involves the need for a social matrix within which one can react with others, where the gain is a social advantage. Position hunger involves a need to vindicate one's lifelong existential position, which may be a Child, Parent, or Adult Ego state.

Berne and his colleagues have described a large number of games that people play based on observations of personal and group therapy. Their contribution is in calling attention to situational-existential factors too long ignored in psychiatry.

TUTORIAL COUNSELING

Tutorial counseling is an adaptation of the eclectic viewpoint to specific techniques for making available detailed psychologically oriented tutoring to clients who have sufficient personality resources to benefit from a compilation of mental hygiene principles and teachings. The hypothesis is that clients will benefit from having available the latest psychological information on how to be psychologically healthy and manage life better.

Tyson (13) made the first compilation of mental hygiene teachings based on an extensive review of the literature up to 1950. Since then, bibliotherapy has been utilized as a mental hygiene adjunct by many clinicians such as Karpman (2).

I have summarized (11) the ideological content underlying my applications of psychological advice and tutoring covering a wide range of levels of integration and life management problems. The rationale of this method is that positive mental health depends upon managing many aspects of life well. Success in any area contributes to positive mental health, whereas failures contribute to existential failure and anxiety. Essentially, the health of any life is a reflection of the healthiness of component areas of adjustment.

Although the problem of measuring the effects of psychological tutoring involves tremendous difficulties, a method is available for assessing the results of any form of educational or therapeutic indoctrination. This method is actuarial costs, in which groups holding different ideologies, or acting out different beliefs, are assessed as to various outcome criteria, such as the level of education attained, socioeconomic status attained, incidence of various forms of such mental disorder as neurosis, psychosis, suicide, alcohol, delinquency, divorce, etc.

Cain's paper (Vol. Two, p. 611) presents an anecdotal, rather impressionistic account of his version of what is basically an eclectic approach utilizing what are essentially total push methods for modifying alcoholic behavior. Cain makes a number of technical suggestions that he considers pertinent to the specific problems of the alcoholic.

PASTORAL COUNSELING

Various claims have been made concerning the alleged values of spiritual counseling on the basis of the doctrinal teachings of different theologies. The pastoral counseling movement has grown rapidly in size and in the number of clergymen who are trying to help their parishioners in solving life problems. To the degree which the pastor is trained to use the standard methods of psychotherapy, pastoral counseling becomes a valuable lay adjunct to the mental health movement. However, when pastoral counselors claim special benefits from "spiritual" counseling, it is necessary to evaluate the methods and results scientifically to discover whether anything extra has been added beyond the well-known suggestive and supportive methods which are active in other therapies. Since it is known that all methods have some successes, probably due to simple supportive effects, it remains for pastoral counseling to demonstrate the mechanism of operation of special methods.

Burroughs' description of spiritual therapy (Vol. Two, p. 717) does not provide sufficient data either for an operational analysis of exactly what methods are being used or for an objective appraisal of the results. His assumptions concerning the "reality of the soul" and of "spiritual illness" are an example of mystical claims that are untestable and unprovable. Irrespective of what he claims to be doing, and of the validity of his hypothesis, it has been long known clinically that religion, alcohol, and drugs may be used by some insecure, anxious, dependent personalities. Such individuals tend to react well to supportive authoritarian handling. When the pastoral therapist has a strong likeable personality, he can often accomplish wonders with selected alcoholics who need friendship and acceptance. However, any disruption of such a relationship usually results in regression and return to alcohol. Burroughs does not report the follow-up data which, incidentally, are also missing in the reports of many contemporary psychotherapists.

It is very difficult to evaluate the claims that have been made by pastors developing individual variations or combinations of the classic therapies with their own versions of spiritual counseling. Characteristically, pastors of all faiths tend to claim superiority for their own approaches in the absence of any comparative objective studies. The area is surfeited with semantic difficulties in operationally defining such concepts as God, spirit, sin, evil, salvation, etc., which have no objective criteria. No two writers seem to use the terms in exactly the same meanings if, indeed, they are objectively definable. [Of course, some psychologists, philosophers, and theologians firmly believe that most important realities are beyond rational grasp.]

Tweedie's presentation of Christian psychotherapy (Vol. Two, p. 641) consists of a rational-logical synthesis of contributions from the psychotherapy literature, which he has been able to use in his own practice. His commentary consists largely of generalizations and anecdotal observations that are characteristic of psychoanalysis, lay, and pastoral counseling literature. It remains for proponents of such systems to provide objective evidence that they can make valid contributions over and above standard psychotherapeutic methods, considered scientific by the consensus of current practitioners.

Vayhinger under the designation of behavioral pastoral counseling (Vol. Two, p. 678) appears to be advocating a common-sense, down-to-earth method of dealing with real people, with real problems, by realistic methods. We are unable to distinguish any distinctive methods apart from the common sense that a wise professional, who at the same time is a warm "good guy," can bring to the solution of problems in people who are of lesser ability and experience. Obviously, the quality of such therapeutic interactions must be a function of the maturity and psychological sophistication of the pastoral counselor, and of the meaning his sacerdotal role has for the believing counselees. We prefer to designate any methods as "case handling" rather than therapy until such time as beneficial effects can be demonstrated objectively.

SPECIALIZED GROUP PSYCHOTHERAPIES

Therapy groups have formed around just about every known method of psychotherapy, involving both selected groups of patients and selected groups of methods. The success of the Washingtonian movement in the 1850's and of Alcoholics Anonymous in the 20th century led to general recognition that (a) interactions of recovered laymen can be therapeutic when organized around a plausible rationale and (b) special kinds of cases should be treated in groups.

Dr. Abraham Low's (Vol. Two, p. 818) anecdotal descriptions of ways of case handling utilized by Recovery, Inc. illustrate some very practical considerations in helping former mental patients of all socioeconomic levels. Dr. Low starts by pointing out that some intensive methods, such as psychoanalysis, are prohibitively expensive and extremely limited in their applicability, even assuming that some valid results can be demonstrated. It remained to develop group psychotherapy methods capable of dealing with large numbers of former mental patients who required further supportive case handling. The professional reader should be cautioned against regarding Dr. Low's contribution as an academic treatise, which it is not. It does communicate, however, the kinds of matters that Dr. Low found profitable to discuss in the Recovery sessions. It is particularly revealing to consider the use by Dr. Low of special terms to convey psychological mechanisms to lower class patients. For example, Dr. Low speaks of the various ways in which patients can "sabotage" treatment, not only in terms of classical Freudian resistances, but in terms of the "games" that patients learn to play with their therapists.

On a more informal but still well-planned and skillful basis, the Synanon movement as described by Yablonsky (Vol. Two, p. 747) provides a milieu therapy involving many of the principles of rational and behavior therapies. As with Alcoholics Anonymous and other lay organizations conducted by people who were once themselves disordered but have since been "cured" by participation in the movement, Synanon provides an accepting, understanding environment staffed by people who know what they are talking about through having lived through problems themselves. Synanon and similar movements tend to minimize and break down defensiveness by developing an unusual kind of rapport and communication in which the "in-group" recognizes its own kind and its own problems and develops its own vocabulary and modes of communication.

Synanon demonstrates new applications of authority, directiveness, and "attack" therapies which appear to be well-tolerated and effective modes of changing behavior when they are expertly utilized. In direct and even brutal ways, the clients are forced to face reality, their defenses and maladaptive patterns are rigorously attacked and torn away, their self-concepts are openly examined, and they are pushed into new modes of behavior. All this is in direct opposition to professional methods, such as psychoanalysis, and, indeed, Synanon has been severely criticized by professionals for opposing established principles. Nevertheless, in our opinion, such movements as Synanon deserve the most extensive opportunity to demonstrate their methods, which should be studied closely by professionals. The notorious inability of many professional psychologists and psychiatrists to deal with "offbeat" groups such as adolescents, beatniks, psychopaths, drug addicts, and other character disorders indicates the need for fresh approaches of which Synanon appears very promising.

The dynamics of group therapy now have been well studied, and objective methods are available for studying their nature and results. The great problem remains, however, of determining whether the therapeutic mechanisms at work are identical with the rationale claimed by any therapist. Group therapies of all types involve many common denominators, such as suggestion effects, catharsis, desensitization, abreaction, ideological reorientation, and supportive effects, which need to be parcelled out before claims can be made for special effects of added ingredients.

ECLECTIC THERAPIES

The first systematically eclectic textbook in the fields of personality counseling and psychotherapy was *Principles of Personality Counseling* (6). This book represented a development and expansion of a series of papers entitled "Directive Psychotherapy" which had been published between 1945 and 1950. The choice of the title "Directive Psychotherapy" was dictated by our opinion that the nondirective approach was being too uncritically presented and accepted by the client-centered movement and to emphasize that important directive methods existed. By 1950, we recognized that the term "directive" was too limited and nondescriptive of our methods, which were more properly designated as "eclectic." Consequently, the book *Principles of Personality Counseling* made an eclectic operational analysis of all recognized methods existent at that time (1950), together with underlying assumptions and a statement of their indications and contraindications. Between 1950 and 1960, the eclectic approach was expanded into a formal system of practice with the books *Principles of Psychological Examining* (7), *Clinical Judgment* (8), *Personality* (9), and *Tutorial Counseling* (11). By 1966, I also had laid down the basic structure of a comprehensive integrative psychology emphasizing hierarchical levels of integration and the psychological state as the primary datum for study and behavior modification.

SOME INVALID CLICHES CONCERNING ECLECTICISM

Historically, eclecticism has been increasing in professional significance since the late 1940's, at which time few if any clinicians labeled themselves as "eclectics." By 1967, many sources (cf. 14) indicated that a majority of American clinical psychologists were designating themselves as eclectic.

Eclecticism has gained ground even though it is not a flashy, intriguing new system, overtly seeking conquests in the form of converts. Novices in the field tend to be overenthusiastic and uncritical concerning whatever school they happened to be exposed to first. And every new spectacular development, such as Behaviorism, Gestalt psychology, or Freudianism in their heydays, tends to attract new adherents in much the same manner as the Pied Piper. Genuine clinical maturity is required to maintain a detached perspective in evaluating the claims, the indications, and the contraindications of new developments.

Eclecticism has been subjected to critical attacks by some who do not even comprehend its essential tenets, but who keep parroting a number of standard cliches that have been advanced by critics:

1. Eclectics have been described as "confused," apparently on the grounds that they have not been able to make a definite choice between competing systems. This invalid criticism fails to comprehend the very point behind eclecticism, namely, that no system is a universal panacea and hence the necessity for critically evaluating and utilizing what is valid and indicated in all systems.

2. Eclecticism has been depicted as involving a "grabbag" or "shotgun" approach, utilizing methods haphazardly or indiscriminately. Although this criticism may be true of some incompetent applications, it does not truthfully reflect the eclectic method at its best; expertly discriminating the advantages and the disadvantages, the indications and contraindications of each method specifically in particular applications.

3. Eclecticism has been criticized as involving professional nihilism whereby the clinician has become disillusioned and wanders about experimenting with new methods indiscriminately. It is true that many clinicians have become disillusioned with existing systems, such as psychoanalysis. This disillusionment should not, however, involve

total rejection but only more exact understanding of indications and contraindications.

4. Eclecticism has been attacked as involving "blind," "cookbook" applications of clinical methods willy-nilly. This criticism fails to comprehend the basic requirement that the eclectic understand and apply knowledge of indications and contraindications competently. Eclecticism is far from being "blind"; to the contrary, it involves the exact opposite.

5. Eclecticism has been criticized as being attractive to novices and beginners who have not really mastered any major method, such as psychoanalysis. At its best, eclecticism requires the highest clinical competence, involving mastery of all major approaches.

6. Eclecticism often has been relegated to secondary status by cultists, such as, for example, psychoanalysts, who often behave as though they regarded themselves as an elite guard. Thus, the eclectic is often looked down upon whereas, actually, his position is the most valid and tenable.

7. The eclectic is viewed as lacking any systematic, comprehensive background for clinical practice. This criticism has been answered, recently, by me; I propose a comprehensive integrative psychological state. This approach does not require being "grounded" on some particular school of psychology because it derives its inspiration and subject matter from the actual clinical raw data of the case and situation at hand. The etiologic (causative) principles are "given" in the raw data and do not have to be derived deductively from some school of psychology.

8. Eclecticism has been criticized as too complex and impossible of comprehension by the average clinician who cannot master all the schools of psychology. This criticism is invalid because modern operational approaches simplify the study of the various schools of psychology and differentiate their respective contributions. The beginner can and must master all pertinent information in the field.

REFERENCES

1. Ellis, A. *Reason and emotion in psychotherapy.* New York: Lyle Stuart, 1962.
2. Karpman, B. Objective psychotherapy. *Clin. Psychol. Monogr.,* 6, 1950.
3. Lecky, P. *Self-consistency.* New York: Island Press, 1951.
4. Rogers, C. R. *On becoming a person.* Boston: Houghton-Mifflin, 1960.
5. Szasz, T. S. The myth of mental illness. *Amer. Psychol.,* 1960, 15,

113–118. Also, *The myth of mental illness*. New York: Hoeber, Harper, 1961.

6. Thorne, F. C. *Principles of personality counseling*. Brandon, Vt.: Journal of Clinical Psychology, 1950.

7. Thorne, F. C. *Principles of psychological examining*. Brandon, Vt.: Journal of Clinical Psychology, 1955.

8. Thorne, F. C. *Clinical judgment*. Brandon, Vt.: Journal of Clinical Psychology, 1961.

9. Thorne, F. C. *Personality*. Brandon, Vt.: Journal of Clinical Psychology, 1961.

10. Thorne, F. C. *How to be psychologically healthy*. Brandon, Vt.: Clinical Psychology Publishing Co., 1965.

11. Thorne, F. C. *Tutorial counseling*. Brandon, Vt.: Journal of Clinical Psychology, 1965.

12. Thorne, F. C. An analysis of Szasz' "Myth of Mental Illness." *Amer. J. Psychiat.*, 1966, **123**, 652–657.

13. Tyson, R. *Current mental hygiene practice*. *Clin. Psychol. Monogr.*, **8**, 1951.

14. Wildman, R. W., & Wildman, R. W., Jr. The practice of clinical psychology in the United States. *J. Clin. Psychol.*, 1967, **23**, 292–295.

Name Index

Abramovitz, C. M., 34
Ach, N., 336, 361
Adler, A., 22, 259, 300, 373, 818, 849, 853
Adolph, P., 655
Albee, G., 522
Alexander, F., 9, 11
Alger, H., 855
Allers, R., 3, 643
Allport, G. W., 663, 680, 681, 682, 684, 693, 698
Anant, S. S., 523
Anderson, C. M., 2, 14, 18, 863
Aquinas, 623
Arbuckle, D. S., 490
Ard, B. N., 301
Aristotle, 623, 625, 698, 717
Arnold, M. B., 698
Augustine, 623
Ayllon, T., 352
Azorin, W. A., 543

Bach, G., 777
Bacon, F., 4, 114, 625
Baer, D. M., 301
Bailey, P., 3
Bakan, D., 659
Baker, J. N., 300
Ballou, S., 300
Bandura, A., 130, 139, 869
Beck, A. T., 300, 301
Becker, J. N., 300
Becker, W. C., 524
Bellwood, L. R., 18, 745
Bender, J. F., 125
Benedek, T. F., 344, 345
Berne, E., 300, 374, 380, 875, 876
Bernreuter, R. G., 446
Bertrand, J. F. T., 441
Bindra, D., 4
Binswanger, L., 698
Blake, J. A., 721, 865
Blanton, S., 722

Bleuler, E., 275
Bockoven, J. S., 167, 522
Boisen, A., 651
Bonhoeffer, D., 536
Bonime, W. R., 259
Boring, E. G., 2
Boudewyns, P. A., 102
Bowers, M. K., 685
Brady, J. P., 87, 89
Branden, N. 863, 864
Breen, G., 301
Breuer, J., 399
Breznitz, S., 300
Brown, D., 339
Buber, M., 424
Buddha, 751, 753
Burkhead, D. E., 300
Burkhardt, J., 35
Burroughs, G. W., 19, 638, 877

Cain, A. H., 12, 19, 514, 613, 877
Calder, R., 626
Callahan, R., 301
Cameron, D. E., 19, 357
Campbell, C. H., 2, 3, 5
Cark, R. K., 509
Carkhuff, R. R., 25
Carlson, W. A., 300
Carnegie, D., 444
Carnell, J. E., 664
Carrera, R. N., 102
Casriel, D., 518, 540
Charcot, J. M., 399
Chase, S., 618, 625, 626
Cherbonnier, E. B., 622
Christ, 616, 654, 655, 710, 711, 712, 739, 753, 778, 805
Clark, G., 664
Clinebell, H. J., 682, 692, 721
Cohen, L., 354
Colby, K. M., 17
Conrad, J., 613
Cooke, G., 301

885

Coons, W. H., 300
Cressey, D., 749
Crowder, T., 182
Curran, C., 686

Dabrowski, K., 528
Dante, 623
Darley, J. G., 503
Darwin, P. L., 301
Davidson, P. O., 354
Davies, R. L., 300
Davison, G. C., 300, 301
Dederich, C., 534, 535, 544, 751, 754,
   762, 763, 765, 771, 772, 773, 774,
   776, 777, 779, 781, 783, 784, 785,
   786, 788, 789, 791, 792, 793
Descartes, 717
Diamond, L., 301, 773, 774
Dignam, R., 352
di Loreto, A. A., 300
Diven, K., 109
Dodd, T. J., 791
Dollard, J., 19, 98, 357
Dorsey, J. M., 300
Drakeford, J. W., 518
Dreikurs, R. 23, 853
Dreyfus, F. A., 17
Driesch, H., 697
Dubois, P., 19, 861
Dunlap, K., 3, 124, 126
Durant, W., 625

Earle, P., 166
Egyedi, H., 3
Ehrenwald, J., 347
Einstein, A., 624, 626
Ekstein, R., 373
Eliot, T. S., 685
Ellenberger, H. F., 528, 533
Elliot, O., 523
Ellis, A., 2, 9, 14, 18, 301, 322, 651,
   666, 862
Ellis, H., 624
Ellson, D. G., 108
Ellsworth, R. B., 526
Emerson, R. W., 622, 751, 778
Endore, G., 518
Epictetus, 296
Erb, W. H., 6
Erickson, M. H., 108
Eysenck, H. J., 4, 23, 301, 681

Fagan, J., 430, 431
Fairbairn, W. R., 373
Federn, P., 372

Ferenczi, S., 19
Fisher, C., 354
Fisher, V. E., 468
Fitzgerald, F. S., 614
Fliess, W., 5
Folsom, J. C., 34, 168, 859, 860
Ford, D. H., 19, 374
Frank, J. D., 140, 301, 336, 345
Frankl, V. E., 23, 34, 124, 300, 643,
   644, 645, 698, 699, 721, 853
Franklin, B., 451
Freud, S., 5, 14, 17, 20, 184, 259, 260,
   263, 297, 338, 340, 345, 347, 354,
   372, 373, 374, 399, 428, 635, 638,
   645, 648, 649, 652, 659, 663, 681,
   751, 778, 818, 849, 861, 866, 871
Friedman, L. N., 300
Fromm, E., 259

Gardner, G. E., 332
Garfield, Z. H., 301
Garner, H. H., 860, 861
Gatchel, R. J., 300
Geer, J. H., 300
Geis, H. J., 301
Gershon, S., 300
Ginott, H. G., 300
Ginsburg, S., 666
Glass, D. D., 300
Glasser, W., 2, 12, 21, 130, 134, 300,
   514, 524, 528, 540, 562, 864
Glicken, M. D., 301
Gliedman, L. H., 301
Goethe, 723
Goldiamond, I., 352
Goldman, D., 745, 843
Goldstein, K., 423
Golias, G., 52
Goodman, P., 424, 425
Gordon, R. E., 334
Gottesman, L. W., 25
Goulooze, W., 657
Greenberg, I., 301
Greenson, R., 348
Grinker, R. R., 20, 22, 373
Grossack, M., 301
Gullo, J. M., 301
Guthrie, G. M., 100

Haley, J., 300
Hamer, C., 749
Hanson, P. G., 301
Harlow, H. F., 507, 543
Harper, R. A., 69, 301

Harrington, G. L., 562, 595, 596, 597, 598, 601, 602, 606, 608, 609
Harrington, M., 2, 3
Hartman, B. J., 301
Hartmann, H., 374, 377
Hastings, J. E., 300
Hauck, P., 301
Haugen, G. B., 34, 856
Havens, J., 681
Hayakawa, S. I., 618
Heath, D. H., 523
Heerema, E., 644
Hefferline, R. F., 424, 425
Heidegger, M., 373, 646, 698
Heine, R. W., 24
Herr, V. V., 638
Herzberg, A., 21, 863, 867
Hilgard, E. R., 68
Hiltner, S., 693
Hinton, J., 624
Hippocrates, 17, 279
Hogan, R. A., 101
Hollingsworth, H. L., 857, 858
Holmes, O. W., 752
Hommer, L. E., 302
Horner, R. F., 183, 189, 352
Horney, K., 259, 373
Hudgins, C. V., 107
Hudson, J. W., 301
Hulme, T. E., 653
Hunt, P., 790
Hurst, J., 749, 765, 790
Husserl, E., 698

Imber, S. D., 301
Imboden, J. B., 359

Jackson, D., 360
Jacobson, E., 34, 246, 249
James, W., 665
Janet, P., 19
Jansma, T., 656
Jaspers, K., 638, 639
Jellinek, E. M., 721
Johnson, H. K., 3
Jones, M., 523
Jones, R. G., 300
Jordan, B. T., 300
Jourard, S., 528, 540
Jung, C. G., 19, 373, 663, 679, 818, 849
Jurjevich, R. M., 107

Kamiya, J., 301
Karno, M., 352

Karpman, B., 876
Karst, T. O., 301
Kellerman, J. L., 725
Kelly, G. A., 27, 80, 300, 873, 874
Kempler, B., 300
Kerchner, D., 843
Kierkegaard, S., 635, 646, 698
Kimball, R., 773, 775, 776, 778, 793
King, A., 613, 623
Kinsey, A. C., 126
Kirchner, J. H., 745
Knight, R. P., 819, 820
Knox, J., 647
Kogan, J., 430
Korzybski, A., 259
Kraepelin, E., 819
Krasner, L., 352, 519
Krippner, S., 301
Kris, E., 374
Krishnamurti, 259, 373
Kubie, L., 357

Lafferty, J. C., 301
Lago, F., 781
Lang, P. J., 300
Langworthy, O., 339
Lao-tse, 751, 753, 778
La Pierre, R. T., 3
Lazarus, A. A., 11, 23, 34, 300, 301, 525
Lazarus, R. S., 301
Leary, T., 850
Lecky, P., 300, 858, 869, 870
Leslie, R. C., 681
Lesse, S., 345
Levis, D. J., 101, 103, 545, 546, 857, 858
Lichtenstein, H., 358
Liddell, H., 246, 247
Ligon, E. M., 18, 715, 870
Lincoln, A., 594
Lind, D. L., 87, 89
Litvak, S. B., 300, 301
Loewald, H., 348
Loewenstein, O., 374
London, P., 130, 657
Longfellow, H. W., 752
Low, A. A., 4, 18, 745, 819, 844, 879
Lowenfeld, J., 100
Ludwig, E., 3
Luther, M., 108, 222

McBrearty, J. F., 301
McEachern, D. L., 300

McFarland, R. L. A., 509
McKenzie, J., 658
Maeder, A., 684
Mahler, C. A., 524
Mainord, W. A., 34, 528, 534, 540, 869, 870
Marquart, P., 647, 655
Marx, K., 647
Maslow, A. H., 319
Masserman, J. H., 340
Matarazzo, J. D., 352
Maultsby, M. C., 301
May, R., 646, 698, 699
Mead, G. H., 539
Meares, A., 17
Meehl, P. E., 20, 99
Meerloo, J. A., 745
Meichenbaum, D., 301
Menninger, K. A., 13, 167, 168, 718
Meyerson, A., 859
Middleton, J., 781
Milby, J. B., 187
Miller, J. G., 505
Miller, N. E., 98, 100, 357
Milton, 623
Montherlant, H., 614
Moreno, J., 518
Morita, S., 23
Mowrer, O. H., 1, 5, 13, 18, 21, 23, 98, 101, 123, 129, 130, 135, 139, 140, 163, 329, 352, 503, 513, 514, 526, 643, 649, 653, 659, 660, 745, 867, 868, 869
Mulder, J., 645
Murray, J. A. C., 657, 673
Muthmann, A. M., 301

Narramore, C., 655
Nash, E. H., 301
Natenberg, M., 3, 5
Nettler, G., 523
Neufield, I., 301
Niebuhr, R., 622
Nisbett, R. E., 300
Noah, 805
Norborg, S., 665

Oberleder, M. F., 170
Oberndorf, C. P., 820
O'Connell, W. E., 301
O'Flaherty, V. M., 34, 221, 868

Parker, J. B., 300
Parlour, R. R., 162

Patterson, W. E., 183
Pavlov, I. P., 107, 109, 124, 259, 297
Payne, R. W., 354
Perls, F. S., 423, 425, 426, 427, 429, 430, 431
Perls, L., 430
Peterson, N. L., 655
Pfister, O., 652
Phillips, E. L., 2, 14, 34, 300, 856
Piaget, J., 341, 376
Pike, J. A., 622
Pinckney, E. R., 3
Pinel, P., 19, 546
Pishkin, V., 864
Pivnicki, D., 24
Plato, 623, 625, 697, 751
Polster, E., 430
Post, J., 15, 16
Post, T., 301
Powers, W. T., 509
Pratt, J., 790
Pratt, S., 162, 517, 869
Premack, D., 302
Prescott, L., 300, 869, 870
Pribram, K. H., 438
Prinzhorn, 638
Progoff, I., 645
Pursglove, P. D., 430

Rachman, S., 3
Rand, A., 852, 863, 864
Rank, O., 259, 373, 424
Rapaport, D., 374
Rashkis, H. A., 336
Ravenette, E. T. A., 301
Ray, A. A., 300
Reich, W., 424
Reissman, F., 526
Rice, O. R., 622
Rimm, D. C., 300
Rioch, M. J., 25
Ritter, B., 301
Rivers, W. H. R., 115
Robbins, B. S., 19, 259
Rogers, C. R., 319, 493, 540, 659, 667, 865
Rose, J., 468
Rotter, J. B., 300
Rubenfeld, S., 100
Ruesch, J., 300
Runestam, A., 645, 656, 665

Sachs, H., 5
St. Gregory, 233

St. Ignatius, 221, 222, 225, 226, 228, 239
St. Paul, 228, 797
St. Thomas, 751
Salter, A., 2, 3, 22, 34, 107, 108, 109, 110, 123, 124, 858
Saslow, H. L., 352
Satir, V., 300
Saul, 647
Schacter, S., 300
Scher, J., 359
Schmideberg, M., 16
Schofield, W., 68
Schultz, J. H., 248
Schwab, E. A., 300
Schweitzer, A., 594
Scott, J. P., 523
Scott, N. A., 614
Seguin, C. A., 17
Selesnick, S. T., 10
Seliger, R. V., 721
Semmelweis, I. P., 4
Shapiro, M. B., 301
Sharma, K. L., 301
Shepherd, I. L., 430, 431
Sherman, S., 301
Shoben, E. J., 98, 651
Silkworth, B., 796
Simkin, J. S., 430
Singer, B. A., 301
Singer, J. R., 300
Skinner, B. F., 6, 130, 246, 302, 338, 352, 857, 861, 871, 874
Slack, 352
Sletten, I., 300
Sloane, R. B., 354
Smith, V. H., 14
Solomon, H. C., 521, 522
Solomon, R. L., 100
Spiegel, H., 23
Spielberger, C. D., 300
Spinoza, 717
Sroufe, L. A., 300
Stampfl, T. G., 34, 131, 525, 857, 858
Steffy, R. A., 301
Steiner, R., 373, 875
Stekel, W., 19, 300, 652
Stenmark, D. E., 187
Stevenson, I., 19
Stieper, D., 300
Stone, A. R., 301
Storrow, H. A., 2, 13, 34, 863
Strong, E. K., 446

Sullivan, H. D., 329
Sullivan, H. S., 259, 539, 543, 869
Sulzer, E. S., 74
Sundland, D. M., 300
Szasz, T. S., 130, 851, 852, 869

Taft, G. L., 300
Taulbee, E. S., 34, 166, 167, 170, 859, 860
Thompson, M., 784
Thoreau, H. D., 751, 752
Thorne, F. C., 26, 193, 300, 847, 864
Thornton, E. E., 684
Tillich, P., 635, 727
Tompkins, S., 328
Tooley, J., 517
Tournier, P., 656, 661, 669
Travers, R. M., 300
Trexler, L. D., 301
Truax, C. B., 25
Tweedie, D. F., 23, 638, 878

Ullmann, L. P., 519
Urban, H. B., 19, 374

Valins, S., 300
Vander Linde, L., 652
Van Dusen, W., 424
van Kamm, A., 490
Van Til, C., 664
Vaughn, R., 684, 687
Vayhinger, J. M., 24, 878
Velten, E., 300
Vittoz, R., 19
Voltaire, 666

Wagner, E., 301
Walder, E., 468
Wall, H. W., 100
Wallace, C., 657
Walters, O., 643, 646, 647, 652, 662
Waskow, I. E., 161
Waterink, J., 643
Watson, G., 622, 871
Weil, K., 774
Weinberg, G., 537
Weitz, H., 485, 863
Wells, H. K., 3
Wells, H. S., 624
Weston, D., 301
White, E., 644, 650, 662
White, R., 647
White, V., 651

Whitehorn, J. C., 341
Wiener, D., 300
Williamson, E. G., 503
Wilson, A. E., 102
Wohlgemuth, A., 3
Wolpe, J., 131, 246, 247, 248, 302, 305, 329
Wortis, J., 5
Wright, H. W., 166, 183

Wundt, W., 819
Wynne, L. C., 100

Yablonski, L., 18, 528, 745, 781, 879
Yontef, G. M., 425, 430
Young, M. F., 312

Zajonc, R. B., 301
Zingle, H. W., 300
Zubin, J., 354

Subject Index

A.A. *See* Alcoholics Anonymous

adult education, fosters mental health, 784

aggression: forms of verbal, 201; as childish interaction, 201–2

AlAnon, 816

AlAteen, 816

alcoholics: as victims of momism, 613–14, 617; as immature, 613; semantics important to, 618; strong tendency to anxiety in, 620; abound in guilt, 723, 736, 737; filled with self-hatred, 724; strong dependency needs of, 724; do's and don'ts in therapy of, 725–26; fail to recognize their need for therapy, 727; as inveterate liars, 727; most frequent psychopathological traits of, 727; as skilled con men, 727; drinking after recovery, 729, 741–43; facing same temptations as drug addicts, 773; prone to denial of reality, 808; considered as "self-will run riot," 809. *See also* Alcoholics Anonymous, alcoholism, spiritual therapy with alcoholics

Alcoholics Anonymous, 18, 636; demonstrates increase of willpower in a group, 243; developed self-help when professionals failed with treatment, 526; slogan of, 526, 633; recovery program of, 537; fulfills needs of members, 581; not needed by recovered alcoholic, 611; a rejector of, 623; a rejection of religious aspects of, 633; its head in psychology and heart in religion, 694; as a spiritual therapy, 721; helped the founder of Synanon, 751, 752; roots in religion and medicine, 795; considers spiritual values imperative in life, 795; three legacies of, 796; religious overtones in, 797; shares with religion and psychotherapy concern about guilt feelings, 797; parallels between methods of religion and, 798–810; twelve steps as primary goal of, 806; twelve steps explicated, 808–15; honesty with oneself and about oneself as essential in, 809; responsible behavior demanded by, 810; example of moral inventory of, 811; AlAnon and AlAteen programs of, 816

alcoholics recovery program: definition of recovered alcoholic, 611; as concerned with present and future, 602; as goal oriented, 612; as reeducational, retraining relationship, 612; as essential in searching for a goal in life, 612, 615; intensive effort required in, 612; adjustment to current society identified as mental illness in, 612; rejection of the insipid character of contemporary culture in U.S. in, 613; basic question of what is the most you can do and contribute to life in, 613; not an easy, comfortable program in, 613; childish aspects of alcoholics rejected in, 613; American men considered psychological freaks in, 613; duration of treatment in, 614; criteria of recovery in, 615; reality becomes better than intoxication through, 615; individual alone cannot free himself in, 616; three or four group members optimal in, 616; characteristics of participating alcoholics in, 617; about seventy alcoholics treated in, 617; educative counseling and reading, heart of, 618, 623; semantics as fundamental role in, 618; withholding opinions harmful to patient in, 619; seven categories of self-analysis in, 619–20; physical symptoms changing during interview in, 620; writing thoughts down therapeutically effective in, 620–21; escape reading helpful in, 621; intellectual revival important in, 621–22; "eter-

891

nal verities" in, 623; three case histories in, 623–36; religious conversion associated with overcoming alcoholism in, 624–27; features of "total push" methods in, 877

alcoholism: sobriety reinforced by therapy, 211; confusion of authorities about, 611; treatment for, 611–36, 717–43, 796–817; individual alone cannot free himself from, 616; criteria of recovery from, 615; recovery through religion from, 616, 624–27, 631, 633–36, 639, 717–39; intellectual blocks may cause, 621; escape reading helpful against, 621; wife's role in, 628–31; as a spiritual illness, 719–20; vaguely defined and definable, 719; medical approach ineffective in, 720; pseudotranscendency in, 722; personality deterioration in, 722; a definition of, 739. See also alcoholics, Alcoholics Anonymous, alcoholics recovery program

alienation: as basic psychiatric problem of our era, 523; as a concern of integrity therapy, 523

American direct psychotherapists: as pioneers, 1; resisted by Freudians, 3; soft culture rejected by, 613

American men, considered as psychological freaks, 613

American Psychoanalytic Association, suppresses unfavorable research, 7

anaesthesia: to sound and pain, produced by hypnosis, 108

anhedonia, 99˙

anxiety: desensitization in felons, 199–200; guilt as source of, 269; arising from failure to maintain self-image, 272, 276; defined as excitement minus oxygen, 427; as a source of mental illness, 646; arising out of threat to essential religious values, 646; as necessary human experience, 646; as mental liability and asset, 647; out of sin against God, 648; as dread of wrong decision about the future, 648; as pain of a sick soul, 649; in alcoholics, 727, 798; in recovered psychotics, 821–23; imagination as a source of, 822; redintegration theory explanation of "free floating," 857; postulated as resulting from self-inconsistency, 869; arising out of unsolved life problems, 876

assertion-structured therapy, 2; originating in a child guidance center, 35; steers clear of Freudian preconceptions, 35, 39; influenced by operant behavior and cybernetics, 36, 41, 44, 45, 64; as ahistorical, 36; as short term, 36; deals with observable behavior and social interaction, 36, 48; environmental consequences as a crucial datum in, 36, 44; conflict (disconfirmation) of assertions, 37, 61; redundancy of behavior, 37; four early concepts of, 37; approach and avoidance variables of conflict, 37; overcoming conflict as primary goal of, 37; discards life histories, 38; changing assertions, relationships, or environmental factors to lead to solutions, 38, 56; therapist as part of patient's environment, 38; interference as therapeutic mode, 38–41, 45; interference as unauthoritarian, 39; clarification (restructuring) basic to improvement in, 39, 58; example of structuring, 39–40; simplifying the distracting abundance of data, 41; conceptualization of makes it behavior therapy, 41; emphasis on solutions rather than pathology in, 41, 42; reinforcement as a cardinal concept, 42; shaping or fading the behavior as central concern, 42; rejects medical model of pathology, 43; drives and inner forces disregarded, 44, 64; as a planning of behaviors rather than a studying of conflict, 44; feedback utilized in, 45; loops of behavior elements, 45–48, 57, 62; therapist is active in, 48; two illustrative cases, 48–61, 61–64; reinforcing desired behavior in, 51; assertions exemplified, 50, 51, 53, 60; summary, 64–65; offers parsimonious solutions, 65; seems difficult to understand, 856

assertive responses, training in, 22

association, as more productive when directed than "free," 19

assumption: equal belief, 264; of right or wrong as value system, 265; includes actor-reactor implications, 267

assumption-centered psychotherapy: concept of human being as prideful and egotistical as basic to, 257; rooted in personal disenchantment with Freudism, 258; frustrated entitlement, a fundamental concept in, 258; interpersonal implications postulated in all behavior in, 259, 262; dynamics considered to be below awareness in, 259; gradual growth of insights for, 259; common features with many systems, 259; Judeo-Christian insights predated the findings of, 260; organically determined behavior considered equally important as psychodynamics in, 260; theory of, 261, 275; psyche assumed as basic to consistent behavior in, 262; value system seen as basic to behavior in, 264–66, 268; thought assigned primacy over feelings in, 267–68; case illustrations for, 268–69, 270, 286–87, 289–91; grandiosity found as basic psychological dynamism in, 259–73; repetitive behavior results from guilt prevention, according to, 273; practice of, 275–87; psychotics, organics, associative disorders inaccessible to, 275–76; qualifications for accepting patients for, 275–78; patient's behavior problems primary focus in, 281; patient expected to work on his own in, 281; elements of initial evaluation in, 281–82; interview emphases in, 281–86; factual data rather than patient's feelings are sought for in, 282; failure to adapt to authority, rather than rejection in childhood seen as etiologically important in, 282; asking clarifying questions in, 283; disturbing symptoms and also signs of grandiosity inquired into in, 284; confrontation of patient with tentative statements in, 288; realistic changes expected in, 288; recapitulation of psychotherapist's beliefs in, 291–92; therapy considered an adventure in honesty in, 292; as a rational-reeducative approach, 863. *See also* grandiosity, psyche, self-image

atavistic regression in psychotherapy, 17

atheist: no such a thing as an, 626; Freud as an, 638

attack therapy: in Synanon, 747, 766, 772–77, 785–90; as an act of love, 787

attitude therapy: systematizes attitudes of therapeutic personnel, 166, 169; assumes that maladaptive behavior was learned, 166, 169; utilizes principles of reward and punishment, 166; rooted in milieu therapy, moral treatment, conditioning, and psychoanalysis, 166; no patient considered hopeless by, 167; members of family involved in treatment by, 168, 174; works through a team-centered approach, 169, 170; discards medical model, 169, 170, 173; uses principles of learning, 170; based on an evolving treatment philosophy, 170, 171; treats hospital as an environment, 171; sees treatment as a relearning process, 172; demands a reality-oriented value system from therapists and patients, 172; holds patient responsible, 172; description of treatment team in, 173; makes for uniform interaction with patient, 173; leading patient to reality as treatment goal of, 174; five treatment modalities in, 174; insight unnecessary for improvement in, 175; understanding and acceptance basic to all five treatments, 175; treatment by active friendliness in, 175–76; treatment by passive friendliness in, 176–77; patient left alone to reorganize himself in, 177; treatment by kind firmness, 177, 180; treatment by matter-of-fact modality, 177–79; treatment by no demand attitude, 179–80; antidepressive program in, 180–84; evaluation of different treatments of depression, 183; medications ineffective in, 183; as applied to geriatric patients, 184–87; improvement statistics for, 188; as a better mobilization of existing resources, 860

aversive therapy, as explained to felons, 211

authority: adaptation to crucially important in childhood, 282

behavior: unaffected by psychoanalysis, 21; includes thoughts and feelings, 68; two ways of modifying, 68; rather than thinking emphasized in operant group therapy, 159; reinforcement only of positive, 160; basically determined by values, 264–66; primary focus of assumption-centered therapy, 281; operates in two realities: objective and symbolic, 486; as continuous and unsegmented, 486–87; behavior product as unit of, 487–89; as main focus of reality therapy and in Synanon, 577, 771, 788

behavioral pastoral counseling: prejudices against, 679; relies on multitudes of religious leaders, 679; as common sense and reality oriented, 68; values and goals considered as important as emotional, intellectual, and social factors in, 684; uses power of healing inherent in faith, 684; based on conscious and real factors, 685; uses religious forms with discrimination, 685; enables client to choose freely his style of life, 685; illustrations of, 686, 688–91; relationship to secular therapy, 685–87; religions as resources for, 692–94; parishioners have easy access to, 693; relates sufferers to a higher power, 695

behaviorism as dogmatically irreligious, 642

behavior modification: equivalent to psychosocial functionalism, 517; practiced by Synanon and Daytop Village, 518; used by "total push" method 30 years ago, 859; as unwarranted usurpation of individual rights, 874. See also behavior therapy

behavior psychotherapy. See behavior therapy

behavior therapy, 35–66, 67–82, 83–105, 107–28, 129–64, 166–89, 190–220; concentrates on environmental stimuli, 70; based on learning theory, 70; growing vigorously, 70; as parochial and dogmatic, 519; evangelical fervor in, 519; as one of many therapies, 520; classical (Wolpean), 527; as the fourth psychiatric revolution, 546–47; suffers from a truncated view of man, 641; based on assumption of environmental determinism, 853; as ahistoric, 856; focuses on removal of symptoms, 856; patient treated sometimes as mindless mechanism in, 856; therapist assumes that he knows better than patient what is wrong in, 856; involves sensitive ethical issues, 857; in Synanon, 879

Bernreuter Scale, 446

Bible, as basic authority for spiritual therapy for alcoholics, 722

bibliotherapy, 876

body language, as closer to truth than words, 427

bracing: as continued state of tension, 245; as continual emergency reaction, 247; facilitates psychopathological developments, 248

brainwashing: Freudwashing, a variety of, 28; of a psychiatrist, 258; of patients, 857; used in Synanon, 778; suspected in psychoanalysis and rational emotive therapy, 857

case handling, a more appropriate name for prescientific psychotherapy, 855

character: three dimensions of (purpose, courage, social convictions), 434; as measured by achievement of maximum potential, 434; development basic to positive psychotherapy, 871

Christianity: not a ticket to security but to anxiety, 647

Christian psychotherapy: relates Biblical faith to psychotherapy, 643; as a challenge to research rather than final answer, 643; as allied with Christ as the Great Physician, 654; has to be ultimately directive, 655; different concepts of, 654–57, 664–65; gives meaning and unity to life, 657; avoids pushing Christians into hands of secularists, 658; three prominent practitioners of, 660–64; treats sick person and not the sickness, 661; provides for exposition rather than imposition of values, 668; many methodological approaches can be used in, 669; prayer and use of Bible specific to, 669; therapist prepares himself by prayer in, 670; four phases of counseling process in, 670–74; transformation of the person sought in, 672; based on Christian anthropology, 674; claims superior efficacy, 674

Christian religion: neglected by behavioral scientists, 260; insights predated many psychiatric concepts, 260; involvement in mental health movement, 642; conversion experiences in compared to psychotherapy, 662;

church offered resources for a sound mind for 2000 years, 678

church, as a bridge to religion, 635

claustrophobia, treated by disinhibition, 110–18

client-centered therapy: as basically Freudian, 659; as an impossible ideal, 667; emphasizes affective factors, 852

clinical impressions, cautioned against, 101

community mental health. *See* community psychiatry, community psychology

community psychiatry: as alternative to mental hospitals, 522; five meanings of, 522; and small-group movement, 523; as third psychotherapeutic revolution, 546

community psychology, five meanings of, 522

compliance: an innate behavioral tendency, 339; compared to plant tropism, 339; appearing between infant and mother, 339; primary and secondary, 339–42; noncompliance can be critical and uncritical, 343–44; as basic to suggestion and autosuggestion, 346

compulsive behavior, as prevention of and not caused by guilt, 273

compulsive cleansing: not same as religious scrupulosity, 232; as inept gesture, 233

conditioned reflex therapy, 2, 22; is diametrically opposed to psychoanalysis, 107; associative reflex as better term for, 107; refocuses on reactions overlooked by Pavlov, 107; considers hypnosis and conditioning identical, 107; excitation, inhibition, and disinhibition as basic concepts in, 109; excitatory personality as the goal of, 109; inhibition as cause of maladjustment in, 109; makes an individual out of a type, 109; six reconditioning techniques in, 110, 859; self-praise recommended in, 110; disinhibition treatment of claustrophobia, 110–18; disregard of childhood history in, 113, 859; treatment successful in a few sessions in, 110, 114, 117, 124, 127; self-training and self-therapy used in, 116–17; inhibition, the only diagnosis in, 123; treatment of shyness, anxiety, stut-

tering, homosexuality in, 124–27; traumas disregarded in, 118; therapist asserts his authority in, 119, 120; therapist shows "insulting disinterest" for patient in, 119; the unproven assumption of, 858; as an active-directive reconditioning approach, 858; many other uncontrolled factors operating in, 859

conditioning: equated with hypnosis, 107; words used as conditioned stimulus in, 107, 108; produces auditory hallucinations, 108; compared to set of gears, 118; for anxiety tolerance in felons, 199; neurosis in animals, 246; as hang-up of behaviorists, 297; psychotherapy and verbal, 354; as root of neurosis, 644

confidentiality: not promised in operant group therapy, 144; kept in the group in integrity therapy, 531

conflict: of assertions, 37, 61; approach and avoidance in, 37; overcoming of, 37

confrontation problem-solving therapy: used to help patient unlearn maladaptive modes, 330; technique of, 330–44; statement and question regularly presented in, 330; reiteration of statement serves as a challenge in, 330; as a psychodynamically oriented therapy, 331; change in symptoms or better social functioning as goal of, 331; authoritarian approach frees from anxiety in, 331; selecting the confrontation statement in, 332–39; the question as key to therapeutic effectiveness in, 347; the question prods problem-solving attitude in, 346; operant conditioning in, 348–53; relief as a reward in, 348; theoretical constructs of, 355–61; case applications of, 361–67; as an eclectic directive therapy, 860; misunderstanding by patient can be checked on the spot in, 861; was foreshadowed in eclectic counseling, 862. *See also* compliance

conscience: hypertrophied in scruples, 222; misuse of syllogism of, 228; as guide to mental health, 514

constructive alternativism: as tentative mapping of reality, 395; assumes relativity of truth, 395, 399

contract: therapeutic, 387; and goal of

institution, 387; psychology adopted in integrity therapy, 517, 533; in integrity therapy, 531; between psychiatrists and psychotics, 595

conversion: reached through reading, 624–27; psychotherapeutic value of, 721

criminals: treated by behavior therapy, 190–220; provide vicarious pleasure for some professionals, 782; tacitly reinforced by professionals, 782

curative factors in psychotherapy: involvement, 12; active struggle, 2, 13; confrontation of patient, 10; recuperative ability, 16; relationship, 17; "therapeutic eros," 17; humanness, 17; relaxation, 17; homeostatic powers, 17; hope, 17; strengthening moral and religious convictions, 17; excitation, 19; mastering of a challenge, 19; improvement of behavioral responses, 19; performance of therapeutic tasks, 19, 20; punishments and rewards, 19; faith in therapist, 23; interference, 38; relief, 348

cybernetics, 36, 41, 45, 61

cyclothymia, genetic factors in, 520

Daytop Village, 137, 139; compared to integrity therapy, 516, 521, 528; practices behavior modification, 518; rejects psychopharmacological medications, 521; as part of community psychology, 523; concerned with alienation, 523; places proper stress on feelings, 540

death: made more bearable by religious practices, 691–92; a cutting point between two modes of existence, 699

democratic procedures with prisoners, 209, 215

denial of reality common in alcoholics, 808

dependency: discouraged in verbal behavior therapy, 78; unenhanced by directiveness, 162; prolonged by psychoanalysis, 296; strong in alcoholics, 724

depression: and Mowrer's guilt therapy, 101; treated by kind firmness, 174, 180–84; lessened by menial tasks, 180–82; inventory of, 182; externalizing hostility necessary for lifting of, 183; medications ineffective in treatment of, 183; arising out of failure of

self-image, 272; and helplessness, 272; arising out of moral failure, 514

dereflection, 34; in therapy for scrupulosity, 221, 240–41

desensitization: gains hold less well than with implosive therapy, 103; in vivo in RET, 301; as a tedious process, 525

diagnosis: considered irrelevant, 123, 523, 586; misleads doctor and patient, 595; as antitherapeutic, 595

direct psychotherapy: takes self-healing into account, 16–17; discards Freudian ceremonials, 17; deals with pathology, 18; discards insights, 18; forerunners of, 18–19; basic difference from Freudian analysis, 20; insight demoted in, 20–21; more economical than psychodynamic methods, 21; neglects dreams, 22; stresses healthy rather than sick aspects, 22–23; discards mental illness model, 23; widely applicable, 24; human rather than technical process, 25, 27; an educational experience, 25; either directive or nondirective, 27; avoids clandestine indoctrination, 27–28

dreams: in compliance with therapist, 352; confirmatory, 353; not solicited in gestalt therapy, 428; analysis used in Christian psychotherapy, 672

drug addicts: similar to alcoholics, 773; need self-respect and respect of others, 785; might be hurt by sympathy shown, 785; endangered by self-pity, 789

drugs: sobriety reinforced through therapy, 211; presented as brain poisons, 211; appeal to self-interest against, 211; make one subhuman, 750

dynamic. See psychodynamic techniques, psychodynamic therapy

eclectic evaluation of psychotherapy methods: operational analysis proposed as basic step in, 847–49; psychotherapy considered to be in prescientific stage, 848; myth of mental illness related to, 850–54; values and goals need be settled beforehand, 853; assumed that no method is universally applicable, 854; not to be identified with "shotgun" approach, 854–55, 881; major error of claiming therapeutic effects without proof, 855

eclecticism: saves from spurious theory, 260; fails to provide direction to observations, 260; some invalid cliches about, 881–82; on the rise, 881; not seeking converts, 881; arises out of clinical maturity, 881; as a trial to evaluate and utilize the best features of special therapeutic systems, 881; demands competent and discerning application, 882

eclectic therapies: developed out of directive therapies, 880

ego: boundaries, 377, 391; strength, idly talked about in psychoanalysis, increased through confession and commitment, 536

ego states, 375–78

electrical stimulation, 6

Emmanuel movement, a religious forerunner of psychotherapy in U.S., 638

emotions: conditioned to words, 108; "constipation" of, 109

entitlement as fundamental concept of assumption-centered psychotherapy, 258

essence: defined as fundamental substratum of being, 697; example of, 699

essential therapies: grounded in basic concepts of human nature, 696; combine existentialism and Catholic philosophy, 699; an illustrative case of, 700–708; conceived as God working in both client and counselor, 708; the technique becomes unimportant in, 708

esthesiogénie, 6

excitation, a basic concept in conditioned reflex therapy, 109

existence, defined as changeable, emerging aspect of being, 698; example of, 699

existential impotence fostered by psychoanalysis, 514

existentialism: tends to overlook man's limitations in social settings, 490–91; in religious therapy, 638; assumptions of, 698–99; considers objective and subjective aspects as a unit, 699

extinction, in Freudian and in systematic desensitization, 527

facial talk, 110

feeling talk, 110

feeling: changed by doing, 112; well-being arises out of behaving well, 142, 148; given secondary importance in assumption-centered therapy, 282; overstressed in psychoanalysis and client-centered counseling, 540; of secondary importance in Recovery, Inc., 829–30, 834–36

felons, as usually psychologically unsophisticated, 218

fixed role therapy: used in verbal behavior therapy, 80; involves client in calculated venture, 394; client as principal investigator in, 394; embedded in personal construct theory, 394; understanding of "role" essential in, 398; does not strive for insight, 399; an ontological venture rather than an epistemological exercise, 399; employed with particular patients only, 400; no diagnostic category needs to be excluded from, 400; technique of, 400–21; seen as sophisticated psychological tutoring, 872; as a very directive technique, 873; as a way of influencing people painlessly, 873; therapist plays a deceptively passive role, 874. *See also* constructive alternativism, personal construct theory

flight from reality, 175

Freud: going beyond, 2; warnings against, 3; nonscience of, 3; uninterested in psychotherapy, 5; considered his patients as his victims and tormentors, 5; mistaken about reasons for maladaptation, 297; combined Charcot and Breuer in his method, 399; his aim of psychoanalysis, 424; atheism of, 638; fantasized about false guilt, 649; considered guilt as repressed hostility, 797; assumed a determinism of the unconscious, 852; mechanistic principles of, 871

Freudian: psychoantics, 3; blinders on therapists, 4, 14; self-praise abundant, 4; precepts, 7, 16; lore, 14; neglect of patient's interests, 13–15; "depth-centered prejudices," 14; maze of presuppositions, 17; moral ambiguity, 18; vagaries unvalidatable, 26; preconceptions rejected by Phillips, 35–39; metaphysical quicksands,

107; dead horses of birth trauma, 124; dominance decreasing in U.S., 129, 638; concepts superfluous in operant group therapy, 163; misperception of traumas as determinants of behavior, 296, 514; failure to distinguish neurotic and healthy superego, 513; nondescript morality, 514; denigration of morality, 517; coldness contrasted with closeness in integrity therapy, 544; domination of clinical psychology, 545; supervisor imposes ideology on trainee, 565; mistaken belief about transference, 589; "free" association less productive than directed one, 619–20; client-centered therapy as basically, 659; resistance as Low's sabotage, 879. See psychoanalytic

Freudism: as mysticism, 3; psychopathy of, 3; hoax of, 3; pseudoreligion of, 3; resistance to criticism, 3; paraphernalia of, 7; subtle influence of, 13; accepted in childlike way by psychiatrists, 258; as naturalistic, positivistic philosophy, 638; dominates American psychiatry, 818. See also psychoanalysis

Freudwashing as a subclass of brainwashing, 28

frustration-hostility-aggression hypothesis, 200

frustration tolerance, increased by stresses and patience, 213

Gamanon, helps find meaning in life, 617

games in transactional analysis, 380–84

generalization of stimuli not easily achieved, 507–8

general practitioner: urged to deal with mental illness, 244; a psychotherapy suitable for, 244–53

geriatric patients: emotionally troubled, 184; reality treatment of, 184–87

Gestalt therapy: originated by Perls, 423; succinct definition of, 424; combines existential philosophy and phenomenology, 424; an achieved gestalt frees for another, 425; awareness as primary tool of, 425; self-regulation as a basic postulate of, 425; intellect is deemphasized in favor of senses in, 406; body language considered a

better truth signal than words, 426; intellectual shell around patients to be resolved in, 427, 428; seeks insights not of why but of how and what, 428; does not search for dreams, 428; does not dredge the past, 428; primary task of getting patient to accept himself, 429; thinking distinguished from experiencing in, 429; resources of, 430–31; experiencing as best method of learning of, 431; focus on nonverbal communication in, 431

God: mistaken offense against, 223, 230; rejecting childish ideas about, 625, 636; "try on the idea of for size," 625; semantic difficulties in accepting idea of, 636; dwelling in the psyche, community, and universe, 639; mental illness as alienation from, 639; anxiety as sin against, 647; can heal any ailment, 654, 673; at work in client and counselor, 708; as experienced in religion and A.A., 798–815; construed into punishment agent, 866

grandiosity: as basic to psychological dynamics, 259, 263; basis of, 263–64; or the prideful self-system, 263; right beliefs basic component of, 263–64; masks of, 269; not manifested by overassertiveness, 269; as need to be special, 270; as excessive fear of failure, 270; as supercolossal vanity, 270; in saving face, 271; as cause of anxiety, 272; expressed in self-devaluation, 272; expressed in perfectionism, 273; as cause of some suicides, 274; rather than "poor self-image" needs correction in therapy, 275; deliberately inquired about in therapy, 284; expecting changes in others as, 285; causes difficulties in life, 287, 292; as human predicament, 291; as the great psychological secret, not infantile sexuality, 292

group, increases willpower, 243

group behavior therapy with offenders: goal of, 190; setting for, 191; minimal staff participation in discussions in, 191; rationale of, 192; reinforcing positive, ignoring negative responses in, 192; therapist sets guidelines in, 192; directive counseling employed in, 193; evaluation criteria of, 193; criminal self-concept corrected in, 193–95; striving for self-consistency in, 194–95; building up self-controls in, 196–97; improving work attitudes through, 198–99; the imprisonment anxiety desensitized in, 199–200; training for coping with hostility, 200–202; sexual drive control and sublimation taught in, 202–4; training for nondirective human relations in, 204–5; undercutting paranoid thinking by, 205–6; the usage of medications clarified in, 207–15; primacy of security considerations clarified in, 208; democratic procedures reestablished in, 209, 215; psychological rehabilitation asserted as primary condition for release, 210; sobriety regarding alcohol and drugs reinforced in, 211; dealing with felons' complaints against administration in, 213–15, 217–18; "prison ethic" undermined through, 212–15; dealing with an obscene patient in, 216–17; need for professional leadership of, 218, 219; relating to community problems is essential to success of, 219

group therapy: 129–64, 166–89, 190–220, 370–93, 515–61, 611–36, 747–94, 795–817; with felons, 190–220; has advantages over individual therapy, 524; joys and disadvantages of, 525; for alcoholics, 611–36, 795–817; varieties of, 806; many therapeutic effects included in, 880

guidance: as problem solving, 485–511; two concepts of, 485–86; serenity as purpose of, 485; counseling as one facet of, 486; components of, 486; in schools shifting to group counseling, 524

guilt: as source of anxiety, 269; arises from violated values, 270; compulsive behavior as prevention of, 273; prevention causes repetitive behavior, 273; as one of three primary stress feelings, 284; is inevitable during personality changes, 288; underlies some mental illness, 440, 646, 649; as universal human experience, 648; is manifested in inferiority complex, 648, 650; as a wound to personality, 648; is contrasted to sorrow as clean wound, 648; as punishment by psyche for flaunting its laws and demands, 648; as dread of wrong decision in the past, 648; Christians vacillating between concepts of, 649; as sin or as neurotic self-condemnation, 649; Freud's fantasy about false, 649; arising out of unadmitted sin, 650; as manifestation of inferiority feelings, 648, 650; as pain of a sick soul, 718; abundant in alcoholics, 723, 727, 736, 737; considered as repressed hostility by Freud, 797, 805; psychotherapy, A.A., and religion share concern about, 797; assuaged by helpfulness to others, 880

hate: as psychological virus, 200
homosexuality: confusion among physicians about, 120; preposterous psychoanalytic preconceptions of, 126; not found by Freudians in themselves, 126; nonsense of hereditary origin of, 126; no incest taboos needed to explain, 127; as threat to prisoners, 199; determined by grandiosity, 269; the demon of "latent," 620

homosexuals: basic features of, 127
honesty: demanded of patients, 140; patient rewarded for, 157; psychotherapy as adventure in, 292; demand for in integrity therapy, 516; demand for in Synanon, 751, 766; essential for recovery from alcoholism, 809

hope: as anticipation of future reinforcement, 503

hospitalization: based on social nuisance rather than "mental illness," 131

hostility: training for coping with, 200–202; reduced by nondirective relationships, 204; expression of not encouraged in reality therapy, 580; vented in Synanon, 750

humor as patient's best friend, 834

hypnosis: camouflaged in psychoanalysis, 2; precursor of direct therapy, 18; equated with conditioning, 107

illumination method: applied to psychoses, 464; inducing insight into sick condition as goal of, 465; improvements noted after, 465; speeds up remissions, 466, 467; elements of brainwashing in, 467; too drastic for use with neurotics, 468; less shocking than other attack therapies, 468; therapist preferably an extrovert, 469; establishing rapport in, 469–70; checking degree of insight, 470; systematic check on reported symptoms in, 471; employing doubt as a wedge in, 471; illustrations of seven techniques of, 472–83; solidifying the progress by follow-up procedures, 483–84; as superior to nondirective methods with psychotics, 484

imagination, curbed in patients, 822

implosive therapy, 83; treatment of the radio compulsion case by, 84; application of learning theory in, 84–86, 89–90, 91–95, 98–101; illustration of basic theory of, 84–87; treatment of hysterical blindness by, 87–90; treatment of wastebasket case by, 90; gradual extinction of anxiety-eliciting cues in, 91; strong aversive stimuli presented later in, 91, 93; determination of conditioned stimuli in, 92; psychoanalytic hypotheses useful in, 92, 94; patient forced to face anxiety cues in, 93; implosive scenes in, 92–95; use of harsh words harmless in, 95; procedure in, 95–98; introducing the patient to, 95; training of imagination for, 96; establishing therapist as director of imagery, 96; personal meaning of imagined scenes not required of patient in, 96; words are supplied to the patient in, 97; theory of, 98–101; leading the patient to approximate traumatic stimuli, 100; ten areas of psychopathological cues in, 101; experimental studies in, 101–3; as superior to conventional, milieu, and desensitization therapy, 102–3; as strenuous procedure for therapist, 525; as related to theory of redintegration, 857

improvising as cure for indecision, 110

impulsivity, as associated with minimal brain damage, 273

indecision arising out of former wrong decisions, 822

Industrial Revolution, suppresses human ingenuity, 397–98

inferiority complex as manifestation of guilt, 648, 650

inhibition: as basic concept in conditioned reflex therapy, 109; as only diagnosis for Salter, 123

insecurity, decreased by learning, 453

insight: therapeutic ineffectiveness of, 11, 109, 116, 241, 265, 501, 502, 568–87, 590, 597, 605, 865; demoted in direct psychotherapy, 20; about past as evasion of responsibility, 152, 590; unessential to improvement, 175; three important RET insights, 306; intellectual and emotional, 307; fixed role therapy does not strive for, 399, 420; in Gestalt therapy about how and what, 428; derived from problem identification, 501; justification by faith compared to Freudian justification by, 660; fake, 770; as bread and butter of psychotherapeutic trade, 771

insight gathering in psychoanalysis, 2, 10

integrity groups. See integrity therapy

integrity therapy, 14; right where psychoanalytic wrong, 14; encourages examination of moral failures, 514; behavior modification principles in, 516, 545; as a therapeutic community, 516; Synanon and Daytop Village akin to, 516, 521, 528; honesty, responsibility, and emotional involvement, three common terms in, 516; contract psychology adopted in, 517, 533; imputed smuggling religion into professional circles, 517; as nontheistic but essentially religious, 517–18, 544; part of small-group movement, 519; concerned with alienation, 523; basic presuppositions and precepts of, 527–29; four factors of mental illness and health, 521, 527; considers neuroses to arise not out of unreasonable fears but out of dishonest behavior, 527; goals are positive rather than extinctive in, 527; positive operant conditioning in, 528; intake interview in, 529–34; no notes, anamnesis, or diagnostic work in, 529; therapy starts at once in, 529; sharing own experiences with newcomer in, 530, 551; pressure on evasive applicants in, 530; truth-telling is rewarded in, 530; group rules in,

531–32; confidentiality in, 531; no subgrouping allowed in, 531; probationary six meetings in, 532, 547; no visitors at weekly meetings of, 532; honesty considered socially functional in, 533; dubbed nudity therapy, 534; application of responsibility in, 534–39; Commitment Book used in, 536; ego strength increased through confession and commitment in, 536; emphasis on restitution in, 536; might have been called action therapy, 536; slogan "act right, feel right" in, 536; insisting on keeping the word in, 538; mature person considered an actor, not only reactor, 538; new social identification through, 539; emotional involvement through, 540–43, 550–51; ritualistic embracing or kissing in, 542–43; taboo against physical aggression, 543; Freudian coldness contrasted with closeness in, 544; wayward adults offered socialization in, 544; no graduation from, 545; a case history in, 546–52; "psychosurgery" (disclosure of secrets) in, 551; self-change in, 552; as mutual-help process, 552; as peer-group model of therapy, 552; as subculture and a way of life, 552; involvement as sharing pains, joys in, 552; ground rules of, 552–54; suggestion and guidelines for, 554–56; common features with psychological tutoring of Thorne, 868

intellectual: blocks, causative in alcoholism, 621; revival important in recovery from alcoholism, 621–22; prejudices against religion, 679

interpersonal: checklist, used in evaluation of therapy outcomes, 183; postulated in all human behavior, 259

involvement: with patient as prerequisite of psychotherapy, 514; as sharing of pains and joys, 552; means emotional relationship with patient, 576

irresponsibility, synonymous with mental illness, 584

Jacobson's relaxation technique, applied to anxieties, 249

Jewish traditions as a comfort in mourning, 691–92

lay therapists, 24

learning theory: in verbal behavior therapy, 70; in implosive therapy, 84–86, 89–90, 91–95, 98–101; in attitude therapy, 170–72; in relaxation therapy, 245; and assumptions-centered therapy, 259; combined with religious concepts, 638

life history, disregarded in reality therapy, 579

life purpose: essential for an alcoholic to find, 612–15; not easily discovered, 871

logotherapy, 34

man: as incurably grandiose, 259–74; as self-talking and self-indoctrinating creature, 298; as gullible, 298; as self-propagandizing, 298; exaggerates importance of other's attitude to him, 298; tends to disparage himself instead of only his traits or behavior, 298, 313; prone to crooked thinking, 299; escalates a desideratum into necessity, 304; practices self-denigration, 305; as unique, 434, 438; as universally prone to guilt, 648; nature never totally known, 696–97; as forever emerging, 698–99; as carrier of the image of God (soul), 718; achieves more in adversity, 852

masochism: reinterpreted as psychological survival, 274; as maintenance of values, 274

matriarchy: post-Christian in U.S., 613; dedicated to permissiveness, 613; produces predominantly childish men, 613, 614; cripples American men emotionally, socially, spiritually, 613; closely associated with alcoholism, 613–14, 617, 629; projected in contemporary religion, 694

meaning of life: deepest psychotherapy is to help find the, 434; integrates personality, 436

meaninglessness of life, as pain of a sick soul, 719

medical model of psychopathology, discarded by therapists, 23, 43, 142, 148, 169, 173

medications, clarified use of, 207, 215

mental energy, positive and negative uses of, 435

mental health: values are basic to, 23–

24; religion essential to, 23; as acquisition of self-controls, 197; work ability as, 198; not dependent on sexual release, 202; does not always mean attractive personality, 405; shown by strong character, 434; gained by achieving one's maximum potential, 435; as enhanced by social involvement, 443; not highly correlated with religious convictions, 440; as good life and strong conscience, 513, 514; four factors of, 521, 527; as responsibility (fulfilling basic psychological needs), 575; faith as basis of, 651; pictured as rational behavior in Synanon, 784; as fostered by adult education activities, 784; consists in solving life's problems well, 862, 876

mental hospitals: obsolete and bankrupt, 521; as human warehouses, 522; supplanted by community psychiatry, 522; training patients for a better world, 597, 600

mental illness: as refusal of responsibility, 10; myth of, 23, 850; resulting from denied values, 23; equated with social bothersomeness, 131–33; defined as social threat, 132; unproductivity as basic feature of, 132; guilt as source of, 135; presaged by inability to work, 198; four factors of, 521, 527; as irresponsibility (failure to fulfill basic psychological needs), 575; as a concept rejected by reality therapy, 582; involves breakdown of problem-solving ability, 862

milieu therapy: as utilized in attitude therapy, 166; definition of, 167

minimal cerebral deficit: clinicians are blind to, 260; as component of impulsive suicide, 274; leads to stress proneness, 276; brought disrepute to psychotherapy because of disregard of, 277

MMPI, used in evaluating psychotherapy, 101–3, 183

modeling used as remedial device, 139

momism. See matriarchy

moral: treatment as incorporated in attitude therapy and described, 166, 167; integrity inseparable from integrity of mental life, 513; immaturity damages personality, 513; fail-

ures examined in integrity therapy, 514; responsibility as way to mental health, 514; effort required of patients, 514; designation disparaged and respected, 517; order called for in psychotherapy, 642; inventory, 811

morality: denigrated by Freudians, 514, 517; essential psychologically, sociologically, and humanly, 517; as major concept in reality therapy, 583, 592; a working definition of, 592–93

Morita therapy, 18; avoids considering the past, 21; stresses healthy functions, 22; leads to resignation, 23

mourning: relieved by Jewish traditions, 691–92

muscular tension, higher in neurotics, 246

naturalistic superstitions strangle religion, 639

neurosis: of animals pertinent to human anxiety, 246; arises from dishonest behavior, 527; metaphysical problem found under every, 643; noogenic, 644; faulty early conditioning as a root of, 644; as result of conflict and predisposition, 644; stress need not cause, 644; brought about by spiritual factors, 645; caused by concept of sin, 651; called disease of the bad conscience, 652; remedied by restoring ethical ideals, 652; as medical euphemism for a state of sin, 658, 666

neurotic: as predominantly egocentric, 615; fear, as pain of a sick soul, 719

nondirective: human relations, reduction of hostility through, 204–5; precipitates counselor's fanciful view of client's past experiences, 496

nudity therapy, a dub for integrity therapy, 534

null hypothesis, does not apply to human affairs, 405

objectivist philosophy as a rational-reeducational psychotherapy, 863–64

operant behavior, 36, 41

operant conditioning: and cybernetic thinking, 48; applied in assertion-structured therapy, 36, 41, 44; applied in relaxation therapy for anxiety tensions, 246, 249; applied in implosive therapy, 87; applied in RET, 302; applied in confrontation problem-solving therapy, 348–55; applied in integrity therapy, 528

operant group psychotherapy: functions best with institutional supports, 137; behavioral changes seen as arising from consequences in, 137; based on a teaching community, 137; best practiced in groups, 137; therapist as primarily a teacher in, 138, 139; therapist as mainly manipulator of reinforcements, 138; modeling used as remedial device in, 139; desirability of self-disclosure qualified in, 140; verbal reinforcement as the main tool in, 140; honesty, responsibility, and mutual interest as chief demands of patients in, 140; description of an intake interview in, 140; selection of patients for, 414; therapy clearly focused on patient's defects, 142; everything retranslated into patient's responsibility, 142; "sickness" and victimization denied in, 142; feeling well postulated on behaving well in, 142, 148; medical model discarded in, 142, 148; patient denied freedom to be silent in, 143; responsibility for other patients demanded in, 143; no promise of confidentiality given in, 144; patient must earn everything he gets in, 145–49; staff avoids doing what patients can in, 145; good functioning demanded outside group meeting, 149; the function of group meetings in, 149; detecting discrepancies between professed code and actual behavior as the basic therapeutic strategy in, 149, 152; starting the group in, 149–53; examples of interchanges in, 150–51; therapist must stick to his guns in, 152; focus is on current behavior and current interpersonal problems in, 152; pursuit of historical why's blocked in, 152; patient's autonomy predicated on responsibility for behavior in, 153; medication considered counterindicative for discharge from, 153; therapist is the ultimate arbiter in, 153; leader's work taken over by group members in, 153; motivations disallowed as excuses in, 153–54; as-

signment for honest behavior given in, 157; emotionally strong words recommended in, 157; therapist deals with personal problems only in the group in, 158; evidence is required for all statements in, 159; psychotic behavior disappears when attention is not paid to it in, 159; emphasis is on behavior not on thinking in, 159; only positive behavior is reinforced in, 160; clinical result of, 160–61; judgmental attitude did not bother patients in, 161; others can be trained in, 162; directiveness does not enhance dependency in, 162; no need for Freudian concepts in, 163; dubbed "brutality therapy," 534; seen as combination of integrity therapy and gamesmanship-social interaction theory, 869; similarity with adjustment workshops, 869

paradoxical intention, 34
paranoid thinking: common among criminals, 205; undercut through therapy, 205–6
paraprofessionals, 525
past history of patient: avoided in Morita therapy, 21; blocked in operant group psychotherapy, 152; not considered, 580; considered psychologically irrelevant in Synanon, 770–71
patient: evasiveness, 12; behaving like an upset child, 50; example of overemotional, 52, 58; gives up, 52; lacks self-direction, 58; angry at pressure, 60; lacks rigorous thinking about himself, 64; advised to stop blaming and start living, 79; forced to assume personal responsibility in life, 79; supplied with words, 97; considered as basically a social reject, 133–34; must give up socially objectionable behavior, 136; denied freedom to be silent, 143; must earn anything he gets in operant group therapy, 145; expected to snitch, 158; not bothered by judgmental attitudes, 161; the geriatric, 186–87; dealing with an obscene, 216–17; as his own Skinner box, 249; behavior contrary to conscious self-image, 280; expected to work on his own, 281; may lose symptoms but still be sick, 286;

confronted by tentative statements, 288; dealt with tenderly, 288; expected to move, 288; compliance, compared to plant tropism, 339; as principal investigator, 394; potential focused on in reality therapy, 580; asked not the why but the what of his behavior, 581; must see that troubles are in himself not with others, 586; symbiosis between psychotherapist and, 595; trained for a better world, 597, 600; easy hospital life does not provide incentive for change in, 597; accepted, but his symptoms rejected in reality therapy, 599; asked to give up crazy symptoms, 599; Freudian withholding of opinion may be harmful to, 619; accuses therapist of being "too damn Freudian," 624; not an object to be manipulated, 668; each one as a special case, 671; must accept responsibility for condition, 672; can be damaged by therapist's religious crudeness, 685, 687–88; suffers from his philosophy, 830; sometimes treated as a mindless organism by behavior therapists, 856; temper as worst enemy, humor as best friend of, 834

pecking order in prison, 201

penance: for scruple, seen as a mistake to correct a mistake, 231; as shadow boxing in the scrupulous, 231; distorted into masochism, 231

penitential: shadowboxing, 231, and masochism in the scruple, 231

person, not an unscientific concept, 397

personal construct theory: underlies fixed role therapy, 394; postulates anticipations as determinant of psychological reaction, 395; behavior of scientists as paradigm for patients in, 396, 406; contrasted with behavioristic approach, 397, 399; speaks of persons rather than organisms, 397; sees a person through his constructs, 397; role defined in, 397, 406; envisions a society of the inquiring man, 398; not a cognitive theory, but of human process, 398, 415; man finds himself in his actions, according to, 398; other psychotherapies in, 398–99. *See also* fixed role therapy

personality: created as one lives, 418; compared to onion with layers and thick-walled ball, 425; enhanced by social effectiveness, 441, 444; primarily a social phenomenon, 539; improvement based on doing right, 581; guilt as a wound to, 648

phobias, 234

physical aggression: taboo in integrity therapy, 543; taboo in Synanon, 750

physiologic therapy for the "neuroses." *See* relaxation therapy for anxiety tensions

placebo effect, enhanced by prestige of the healer, 140

positive psychotherapy: major conviction that emphasis on positive actions is more helpful therapeutically than emphasis on sick aspects, 433; symptoms disregarded in, 433; developed character indicates mental health in, 434; considers that deepest psychotherapy is to help find meaning in life, 434; postulates positive and negative uses of mental energy, 435; character development is the core of, 435; postulates that purpose integrates personality, 436; man is unique, 436; examples of, 437–39; considers that social skills enhance effectiveness of personality, 441, 444, 446–50; scientific decision-making should be taught in, 442; believes that social involvement enhances mental health in, 443; provides skills for growth in character strength, 445; use of one's uniqueness is skill for character growth, 445, 447; found that lay scientist skills eliminate many maladjustments, 449–53; systematic observation removes biases, 450–51; pro-con technique provides objective overview, 451; method of characteristic differences reduces emotionalized conflicts, 451; sociogram reveals relationships objectively, 452; found that learning decreases insecurity, 453; teaches that relativistic viewing of one's knowledge avoids upsets, 454; learning how to influence increases social adaptation, 459–62; conclusion, 462; "the best defense is a good offense" is the golden text of, 462; character building basic to, 871. *See also* character

pride, 539

printed word as arid medium, 431

"prison ethic": undercut in therapy, 212; shown as personal immaturity, 212; to be supplanted by democratic processes, 212, 214

problem-centered guidance: serenity, the purpose of, 485; theory of, 486–89; objectives of, 489–91; unconditional regard and acceptance not essential to, 490; stresses and frustrations bring about the need for, 492–93; the process of, 494–509; application of tests in, 496–97; warning against mistaking symbolic representation for adequate description of reality, 497–500; effective problem identification leads to insight in, 501; insight not considered sufficient for remediation in, 501–2; counselor intervenes if corrective behavior lacking in client, 502; maps to reach productivity, self-actualization, and serenity provided in, 503–4; counselor suggests means to solutions in, 504; counselor manipulates events symbolically or directly in, 504; translation into action may be called therapy in, 505; new modes of attack on problems achieved in, 506; generalization of learning completes, 506–7; evaluation by behavior standard as final step in, 508–9; is not a formal problem-solving procedure, 510

professional leadership, essential for therapeutic work with felons, 218

progressive relaxation, used in anxiety, 244–53

psyche: assumed to be basic to consistent behavior, 260; determined by nervous system and long dependency period, 261; uniqueness of each, 261; developed after birth, 262; patterned for child by adult culture, 262; interpersonal experiences basic to, 262; assumptions are the substance of the, 262; basic to consistency and dependability of behavior, 262; major goal of living seen in survival of, 263; as computerized reservoir of assumptions, 266; or essential "I", 266;

punishes sternly breaches of its laws, 648

psychiatric: problems always complex, 73; revolutions (four), 546; labels dispensed with in reality therapy, 574; diagnosis misleads the doctor and the patient, 586, meaningless for treatment and antitherapeutic, 595; organizations are dominated by Freudians, 818

psychiatry: provides no viable solution for guilt feelings, 650; Christian contrasted with pagan-rooted, 657; wild theorizing of, 700; neglects the spiritual dimensions, 721, 723; can be made superfluous by the Bible, 722

psychoanalysis: useless, 1, 605–6; harmful, 1, 2, 3, 7; an exercise in futility, 2, 7; ineffective, 2, 107, 295, 819–21; psychoanalytically-oriented therapy more effective than, 2; as hypnotizing, 2; dwelling on the past in, 2, 9, 20, 21; past traumas used as resistance in, 2; slavish regard for, 2; blunders of, 3, 423; as wish hunting in the unconscious, 3; as successful error, 3; considered as induced delusions, 3; failure of, 3, 4, 864–65; fraud in, 3; fallacy of, 3; not better than spontaneous remission, 4, 17; the scandal of, 4; accepted uncritically by professionals, 4; waste of time and finances for, 5, 819–20; left Freud neurotic, 5; lack of validation of, 5, 7; suggestion in, 6; spontaneous remission effects in, 6; and Skinner's pigeons, 6; corrective therapy for, 15–16; implants its own psychopathology, 16; induces "hypochondria of the mind," 16; failed with psychiatrists and psychologists, 2–5; exaggerated veneration of method in, 16; as transfer of therapeutic delusions, 16; deprives patients of benefits of spontaneous remissions, 17; considered as metaphysics, 19; stultifies therapists in training, 20; fails to affect behavior, 20; sickens the patient deliberately, 22; is needlessly complex, 24; scholastic pedantry of, 25; inferior to learning theory, 27; smuggles *Weltanschauung* into patient, 28; rejected by Phillips, 35; has outlived its usefulness, 107; an explanation for failure of, 109; influenced attitude therapy, 166; a psychiatrist disenchanted with, 258; is shallow and superficial, 295; does not provide patient with real cause of troubles, 295; focuses on irrelevant information, 296; encourages prolonged dependency, 296; teaches patient questionable assumptions, 296; leaves patient bogged down in irrational assumptions, 296; falsely assumes that traumas determine behavior, 296; misses important current thinking by focusing on the past, 298; only a limited range of patients accessible to, 299; RET insights deeper than in, 306; a case failure of, 312; the therapist supposedly used by patient as a screen in, 329; origin of, 371; likened to years of study of coughs or treatment of common cold, 371; appears irrelevant to medical practice, 372; inapplicable to severe mental disturbance, 372; prevents assimilation of other views, 423; aim of, 424; alleged moral neutrality of, 513; fosters existential impotence, 514; group therapy has advantages over, 524; extinction of fears in, 527; idle talk of ego strength in, 536; overstresses significance of emotions, 540; as second psychiatric revolution, 546; six main differences between reality therapy and, 582–95; mistaken about transference, 582, 589; as morally unrealistic, 592; as a different way of working with people than reality therapy, 594; as a bridge mistaken for a way of life, 635; shows perverted thinking about religion, 638; egocentric attitude to life in, 639; specific brazenness to display psychic entrails in, 639; prevents surrender to being, 639; is long on analysis and short on synthesis of personality forces, 641; is dogmatically irreligious, 642; psychologizes most mental disorders, 643; can be detrimental to religiomoral conflicts, 656; leads to dismal consequences, 659; as a pernicious doctrine, 660; has no better rate of cure than state mental hospitals, 820; monopolized the field of psychotherapy, 820; basic

tenets largely unvalidated after 60 years, 855; its patients as if brainwashed, 857; many clinicians disillusioned by, 881. See also Freud, Freudian, Freudism, psychoanalytic, psychoanalyst

psychoanalyst: treats rather than cures, 13; emphasis on unconscious useful to, 21; subject to rigorous indoctrination, 24; insight as bread and butter of, 771; as cultist, 882. See also Freud, Freudian, Freudism, psychoanalysis, psychoanalytic

psychoanalytic: disdain for other therapies, 1, 5; Establishment, 1; ritual, 6, 17; lack of involvement, 12; training as transfer of therapeutic delusions, 16; therapist described, 69; theory used in implosive therapy, 92, 94; methods imprecise, 107; preposterous preconceptions about homosexuality, 126; rigidity brings about revolt, 130; concepts disregarded in operant group therapy, 163; narrow view of the ego, 374; dynamics less clear than of TA, 386; misconceptions abandoned, 514; therapy questioned, 562; therapy as failure, 565, 623; therapy as getting psychiatric kicks, 579; dominance unfortunate for American psychiatry, 587; therapy urges patients to live down their potentials, 612; therapists as defeatists, covering up personality deterioration in their culture, 612; withholding of opinion may be harmful to patient, 619; dominance decreasing in U.S., 638. See also Freud, Freudian, Freudism, psychoanalyst

psychodynamic techniques, produce undynamic effects, 514. See also psychoanalytic

psychodynamic therapy: assumptions of, 69; insight as the principal agent of change in, 69; emphasizes understanding, 69; leads to mediocrity, 612

psychological: rehabilitation as precondition of release, 210; tests in guidance, 496–97; self, identified with pride system, 260; determinism is stultifying, 635

psychopathological: cues, ten areas of, 101; disorder defined as maladaptive learning, and as social maladjustment, 131–34; developments facilitated by tenseness (bracing), 248; underplayed, healthy behaviors focused on, 596

psychopathology: of psychoanalysis transferred to patient, 16, 22; rejected medical model of, 43, 142, 148, 169, 170, 173; ten cues of, 101; and heredity, 520; and biochemical factors, 520; and ecological variables, 520; as contract between psychiatrists and patients, 595; of alcoholics, 727; understressed by positive psychotherapy, 871

psycho-sanics or science of positive mental health, 871

psychotherapeutic: theory, 14, moderately relevant to practice, 17; complexity does not guarantee effectiveness, 25; contract negotiated with patient, 74; revolution against Freudian dominance, Synanon as a start of a new, 129, 793; innovations are sometimes redundant, 129, may be illusory, 130; contract clear in TA, 387; unwritten contract broken in reality therapy, 595; failure ascribed to the doctor in reality therapy, 601; priesthood championed by unwise churchmen, 657; value of religious conversion, 721; prejudices against Synanon, 793–94; process defined as learning, unlearning, or relearning, 847

psychotherapist: as not very important, 16; narcissistic delusions in, 17, 279; as active architect of behavior change, 48; describes problem, 52; ties behavioral elements, 52; suggests, 56, 58, 63; recapitulates, 58; should not interpret prematurely, 60; directs patient to be practical, 61; tentative definition of, 68; as source of reinforcement, 74; communicates personal experiences to patient, 75; hypothesizes about patient's symptoms, 91; as director of imagery, 96; asserts his authority, 119, 120, 331; disillusioned by what is learned in training, 129; as a teacher, 138; as manipulator of reinforcements, 138; as ultimate arbiter, 153; cannot have any other relationship with patient,

279; not to be a kind figure primarily, 281; can be misled by patient's misperceptions, 282; mistaking baby-sitting for psychotherapy, 286–87; expects movement from patient, 288; as social reinforcement machine, 353, 354; authority diagram essential for, 388; confronts actively in TA, 390; blunders of clinically insensitive, 401; suggests means to solution, 504; qualities of effective, 576–77; symbiosis between patient and, 595; as affected by parochialism, 637; a puffed-up, 637; self-infatuated, 637; perversion of thinking in a, 638; doctrinaire mentality in a, 639; coming to view religion positively, 642; as the new clergyman, 657–60; the delusion of ethical neutrality of, 663; influences patient's choice of life philosophy, 663; as an active moral agent, 665; can damage patient by his religious crudeness, 685, 687–88; may only prolong maladjustment, 693; as a model for the patient in spiritual therapy, 723; tacitly provides symptom reinforcement in criminals, 782; the most pernicious sabotage is that of authority of, 840; until efficacy is proven case handler is a better name for, 855. *See also* psychotherapeutic, psychotherapy

psychotherapy: replete with superstitions, 4, 6; abounds in unvalidated assumptions, 4; needs demythologizing, 4; should be de-Freudianized, 4; ignorance about, 7; as problem solving, 8, 13, 286; "delightful brainpicking" in, 9; "objective reviewing" in, 9; confrontation of patient in, 10; of adolescent delinquents, 10; commiserating with patient in, 11, 12; futility of passive approach in, 11; as assistance to nature, 17; as determined by patient's faith in therapist, 24; subscientific level of current, 26; or behavior change, 65; attempt at definition, 68; as psychological treatment technique, 68; impinges upon intact organism, 68; varieties of, 69; shaped by its theory of personality, 130; as closely tied to moral issues, 134; Dejerinian, abandoned, 244; not a catharsis, 281; as a learning experience, 281; focuses on patient's behavior, 281; failure to clarify as major hazard of, 282; as adventure in honesty, 292; viewed as ideology, 328; the left wing-right wing polarity in, 329; three patient behaviors in, 329; and verbal conditioning, 354; as translation into action, 505; professional, failed with alcoholics, 526; four revolutions of, 546; as special kind of teaching, 575; getting psychiatric kicks as, 579; admitting irresponsibility as precondition of improvement in, 581; not needed by recovered alcoholic, 611; educative for alcoholics, 612; a bridge on which one cannot live forever, 634; role in reality quite modest for, 637; inseparable from religious context, 638; enhanced by religion, 638, 640; as collaboration in mutual philosophic faith, 638; if too reflective prevents surrender to being, 639; transcendent reality marks difference between religious confession and, 639; as an outgrowth of psychoanalysis and behaviorism, 641; long on analysis and short on synthesis of personality forces, 641; the third force in, 642; moral order called for in, 642; turning to religion in, 642; a Christian's involvement in, 642; can be a means of grace, 655; futility of secular, 655; sometimes akin to Christian conversion, 662; cannot satisfy deeper spiritual hungers, 662, 663; implies values, 664–67; can suffer from overemphasis on techniques, 668; as an art, 669; unexhausted in its techniques, 669; little proof of helpfulness of, 681; and religion, both relieve conflicts, 687; neglects spiritual dimension of personality, 721; could be made superfluous by the Bible, 722; therapist's personal faith essential in spiritual, 723; need for unrecognized by alcoholics, 727; insight as bread and butter of, 771; as professional prerogative, denied by Synanon, 778–79; a new profession (Synanists) in, 778; Synanon as a unique system of, 793–94; shares with A.A. and religion the concern about guilt, 797; invariably based on

a philosophy and techniques, 818; as dominated and monopolized by psychoanalysis, 818, 820; differences of opinion on, 847–48; in scientifically primitive stage of development, 848; new names used for slight innovations in, 847–49, 855; proliferation of approaches to, 848–49; criteria of cultism in, 849; cultural relativity confuses issues in, 850–53; humanism oversold as panacea in, 852; assumptions on the nature of man underlie every system of, 852; stress on happiness or responsibility would lead to different outcomes in, 853; diagnosis considered prerequisite for systematic, 854–55; case handling, a more appropriate name for, 855; claiming therapeutic effects without proof as a major error in, 855; proposal for actuarial evaluation of methods of, 876. See also psychotherapist, psychotherapeutic

psychotics: treated by operant group therapy, 129–64; treated by attitude therapy, 166–89, illumination method, 464–84, reality therapy, 562–610, Recovery Inc., 818–46; changed by disregard of their sick behavior, 159; have unwritten contract with psychiatrist, 595; reality therapy shows higher discharge rate of, 596

rational-emotive therapy: basic postulate of—humans troubled not by events, but by their views of them, 296; sees man as born to act and think foolishly, 297; enumerates forty innate predispositions hampering realistic adaptation, 297; considers Freudism and behaviorism misleading, 297; vulnerability to negative feelings and introjection of criticism seen as basic reasons for maladaptation in, 297; parents not considered main traumatizing agents in, 298; crooked thinking discerned as cause of emotional trouble, 299; found to be more effective than psychoanalysis or other therapies, 299; A-B-C theory of personality, the essence of, 299; criticism of, 299; helps deal with basic emotions, 300; similar principles announced by other ther-

apists, 300; many psychologists experimentally confirmed that thoughts determine emotions, 300; research vindication of homework assignments in, 301, 307; voluminous clinical support of, 301; considered as the main cognitive therapy, 301; induces patient to attack his maladjustment-creating philosophies, 301; considered as emotional reeducation, 302; includes features of reciprocal inhibition and operant conditioning, 302; technique of, 302–12; starts with symptoms and responses (consequences), 302; some of the irrational ideas combatted in, 303; uses a form of scientific thinking, 304; teaches patients to give up on superhuman expectations, 305; is holistic and humanistic, 305; its thoroughness prevents recurrence and substitution of symptoms, 306; its insights deeper than in psychoanalysis, 306; homework report in, 310–11; not exactly short-term treatment, 312; an illustrative case of, 312–18; overgeneralizing discouraged in, 313; limitations of, 318–20; The Institute for Advanced Study in, 319; paraprofessionals can use, 319; can be used as bibliotherapy, 320; stresses cognitive factors, 853; as ideological-attitudinal reeducation, 862
rationalization, as defense of grandiose self-image, 268
rational therapy. *See* rational-emotive therapy
reading: as escape found helpful to alcoholics, 621, 623; leads to a conversion, 624–27; gives confidence, 624
reality, as treatment goal in attitude therapy, 174
reality therapy, 2; beginning with doubts about conventional psychiatry, 526, 563, 568; the first case of, 563–68; confrontation with present reality in, 565, 569; developed against psychiatric training and reading, 566; basic concepts of, 568–73; basic pathology—inability to fulfill own needs, 568, 596–97; meaningful involvement with others leads to fulfillment of basic needs, 569; the essential human must care for pa-

tient, 570; basic needs—to love and be loved, and be and feel worthwhile, 571–72; worthwhileness comes from satisfactory behavior, 572; responsibility defined as fulfilling own needs, 573; dispenses with psychiatric labels, 574; responsible means mentally healthy, 574; self-respect gained through self-discipline, 575; as a special kind of teaching, 576, 594; involvement means emotional relationship in, 576; concerned with behavior rather than attitudes, 577; the patient decides if his behavior is responsible in, 558; not concerned primarily with making the patient happy, 579, 597; unhappiness considered the consequence not the cause of behavior, 579; not interested in patient's history or unconscious mind, 579, 582–83, 587, 590–92; patient's wide potential kept in view in, 580; others not blamed for patient's failures in, 580, 586; expression of hostility never encouraged in, 580; doing right considered basic to personality improvement, 581; precondition of improvement—patient admits irresponsibility in, 581; six basic differences from conventional (Freudian) therapy, 582–95; concept of mental illness rejected in, 582, 584; concept of tranference discarded in, 582, 589; morality is major consideration in, 583, 592–94; no causative psychological agent (trauma) presupposed in, 584; concepts of irresponsibility and mental weakness supplanting "mental illness" in, 584, 587; treatment—for better functioning in life and not for mental sickness, 585; diagnosis produces no difference in treatment, 586; focusing on inadequacies hinders involvement, 588; involvement rather than transference in, 589; important unconscious area is what patient is doing now, 591; as a different way of working with people than conventional psychiatry, 594; three requirements of, 594; on a psychotic ward, 595–602; breaks unwritten contract between psychotics and their doctors, 595; increases discharges of psychotics, 596; every staff member is important for treatment by, 596; focus on potentially healthy behaviors in, 596; involvement of staff with patients on ward essential in, 599; patient accepted but symptoms rejected in, 599; failure of patient ascribed to the doctor in, 601; treatment of a psychotic in, 602–10; as a variant of rational-reeducative therapy, 864

reciprocal inhibition: involved in relaxation therapy, 247; deconditioning in, 247; or counterconditioning, 527

Recovery, Inc.: rejects psychoanalysis outright, 819; has higher rate of recovery than Freudian analysis, 820; imagination curbed in, 822; indecision conceptualized as result of past precipitous decisions, 822; patient advised to switch to pleasurable anticipations, 823; even an insincere gesture of helpfulness is desirable, 824; individual sovereignty disparaged, the spirit of fellowship encouraged in, 824–25; patients considered fortunate in not being "advanced thinkers," 826; stands for common sense, as opposed to intellectual skepticism and cynicism, 826; action of muscles may relax the mind, 826–29; no coddling of feelings and assuming that one's thoughts are always right in, 829–30; patients considered to be suffering mainly from their philosophy (assumptions), 830; recommends suppressing feelings and thoughts if dictated by reality, 830, 834–36; group considerations are more important than individual inclinations in, 830; temper considered patient's enemy, humor his friend, 834; feelings are not facts, patients told in, 834; temper and self-pity "spotted" as sabotage of recovery, 836; control of thoughts and impulses thought possible and not of feelings and sensations, 838–39; will conceived as accepting or rejecting thoughts and stopping or releasing impulses, 838; sabotage, a basic concept of, 840; sabotage considered more conscious than unconscious, 840; sabotage of physician's authority considered the most pernicious in, 840; methods of sabotage, 840–43

redintegration, 100

reinforcement: cardinal concept in assertion-structured therapy, 42, 51; hope and fear as anticipation of, 503; of positive responses, 192

relapse into psychopathology due to incomplete extinction, 100

relaxation: therapeutic effects of, 18; as untensing emotions through body, 34, 826–29

relaxation therapy for anxiety tensions, 244–53; compulsive, phobic, and depressive patients also treated with, 245; frequency and time involved in, 245; based on learning theory, 245; as postulated on interaction between brain and organism, 245; as based on facilitating, learning effect of mental state, 245, 247; animal neuroses are pertinent to, 246; Skinner box behavior modifications also relevant to, 246, 249; reciprocal inhibition has implications for, 246; inducing a nontense state in organism is the chief feature of, 247, 248; voluntary relaxation has to be learned thoroughly, 248; as different from J. H. Schultz' relaxation, 248; relaxing makes tension aversive through, 249; organ functions improved with, 249; interpersonal improvement through, 249; Jacobson's relaxation techniques are basic to, 249; basic rule—graduated application of, 249–50; family cooperation enlisted for, 250; a case illustration of, 251–52

religion: contains energizing symbols, 25; is important in recovery from alcoholism, 624–27, 694, 795; perverted Freudian thinking about, 638; enhances psychotherapy, 638, 640; strangulated by naturalistic superstitions, 639; intellectual prejudices against, 679; definitions of, 680; extrinsic and intrinsic, 681; healthy and sick, 682–83; goes beyond naturalistic professional skills, 686; and psychotherapy, both relieve conflicts, 687; maternal and paternal values in, 694; as one of the foundations of A.A., 694, 795, 797, 798–810; as a secret source of support for the believer, 710

religious: obligation is false in the scruple, 224; a new way of being, 517–18, 747, 756–57; aspects of A.A. rejected, 623, 633; context of every psychotherapy, 638

resistance: past traumas used as, 2; as Freudian superstition, 7; attacked in RET, not only "analyzed," 309; sabotage as a synonym for, 836

responsible: means mentally healthy, 574; behavior demanded by A.A., 810

responsibility: demanded of patients in operant group psychotherapy, 140, 142; determines the freedom enjoyed by patient, 153; mental health by way of moral, 514, 574; stressed in integrity therapy, 534–39; stressed in reality therapy, 573–74; defined as fulfillment of own needs, 573; for his condition has to be accepted by the patient, 672

restitution: emphasized in integrity therapy, 536

RET. See rational-emotive therapy

revolutions, four psychiatric, 546

sabotage: as a basic concept of Recovery, Inc. therapy, 840; as more conscious than unconscious, 840; methods of, 840–43

sacramentals, as remedies for failures of human nature, 232

sacraments: seven, of the church, 711–14; psychotherapeutic effects of, 712

Salvation Army: helps finding meaning in life, 617

schizophrenia: genetic factors in, 520

scientification: of human functions deplored, 27; schematization unavoidable in, 33; personalistic psychotherapy as antidote to, 34

scruple: conceptualized as mental evil, 211; defined, 222, 229; in St. Ignatius and Luther, 222; as caused by errant emotion, 221, 222; the ultimate cause of, 222–23; beginning in deciding if one did not sin, 223, 230–32; as false religious obligation and emotional compulsion, 224; rejecting confessor's reassurance because of, 224, 226; two kinds of, 225–27; as

doubt about doubt, 225; as emotionalized thinking, 226, 234; presents conditions for endless argument, 226; false logic in a, 227, 228–29; as logical entrapment, 229; baiting as temptation to argue with a, 229–30; as self-baiting, 230; as raising a doubtful situation to a certitude, 230; examples of, 222, 224–27, 235, 239; makes for penitential shadowboxing, 231; as finding sin where there is no sin, 231; as compulsive cleansing, 232; may lead to behavioral oddities, 233; may lead to inhibitory disabilities, 233; as individually colored, 236; may be used by God to arouse a tepid soul, 236; troubles culturally and religiously refined persons, 236; inept counselor may aggravate a, 236; more women seek help for, 237; men show counterphobic defenses against, 237; Protestantism has built-in defenses against, 237; Protestant forms of, 237; therapy for, 238–42; as distorted decision of conscience, 238; counselee advised to give names to, 238–39; hard to give up, 241; has to be rejected right from beginning, 241. See also therapy for scrupulosity

self-actualization: through productivity, 198; not achieved in psychoanalysis, 295; map to reach, 503–4; as a mark of a fully functioning person, 717

self-analysis, seven categories of, 619–20

self-baiting in the scruple, 230

self-change in integrity therapy, 552

self-concept: corrected in criminals, 193–95; presented as backbone of personality, 194; striving for consistency of, 195–96; undermined by drugs, 211; inflated in each person, 263

self-consistency, striving for, 194–95

self-control: defined, 197; building up of, 196–97

self-denigration, as practiced by humans, 305

self-discipline builds self-respect, 575

self-disclosure, qualifications regarding, 140

self-esteem: largely a function of social

approval, 136; based on holding right beliefs, 264

self-expression, doubted as universal need, 853

self-hatred fills alcoholics, 724

self-identity, based on roles and expectations, 266–67

self-image: grandiosity, as basic to psychological self-preservation, 259, 260; built on personal value systems, 264; defended by rationalizations, 268; Synanon considers it very important for addict to get a correct, 772

self-pity: as main obstacle to psychotherapy, 75; arising from blocked resentment, 271; may ruin a drug addict, 789; as sabotage of therapy, 836

self-praise: abundant among Freudians, 4; recommended as reconditioning, 110

self-respect: gained through self-discipline, 575; gained through responsibility, 600

self-training, utilized in conditioned reflex therapy, 116–17

self-worth, result of worthy behavior, 572

semantics: major role in recovery of alcoholics, 618; may lead to religious conversion, 618

senses, disregarded by many people, 427

serenity: as purpose of guidance, 485; map to reach, 503–4

sexuality: training for controls of, 202–3; clarification of misperceptions of, 203

sign learning, 352

sin: unreasonable apprehension from, 221–31; reestablished as psychological concept, 651; no humanistic resolution of, 653

Skinner box, patient as his own, 249

small-group movement: encompasses integrity therapy, Synanon, Daytop Village, 519; compensates for losses in family and community closeness, 523–24, 544; functions as family, churches, schools, and community, 544

sobriety: stressed with prisoners, 211; an empty, negative concept, 634

socialism: suppresses human ingenuity, 397–98

socialization: of wayward adults in integrity therapy, 544

social psychiatry. See community psychiatry

sociogram: used in positive therapy, 452

spiritual: dimension of personality as cause of neurosis, 645; side denied by psychologists, and conceived specifically by humanists, 645; considered inaccessible to pathology, 645; problems lie under emotional problems, 654; defined as the sphere of morality and religion, 662; hunger cannot be satisfied by psychotherapy, 662, 663; minimized in favor of sexual conflict by Freudians, 663; illness, or sickness of soul, 717, or disbalance, 718; homeostasis or balance, 718; illness is self-inflicted, as a choice to serve self, 719; need to make God central, own person peripheral, 719; dimension disregarded by psychiatry, 721, 723; concepts implanted in Synanon addicts, 753. See also spiritual therapy with alcoholics

spiritual therapy with alcoholics: thousands of alcoholics helped by, 717; acknowledges divine participation in lives of men, 717, 726; based on reality of the soul, 717; free will is a fundamental concept in, 719; alcoholism considered a spiritual illness in, 719; A.A. as a, 721; Bible as the basic authority for, 722; spiritual conversion, not abstinence, as the goal of, 722; seeks beyond individual's comfort, 722; tries to actualize latent capacity rather than penetrate the secrets, 723; therapist's personal faith as essential in, 723; therapist as the model for the patient in, 723; therapist need not be a recovered alcoholic in, 724; as Christ-centered, not client-centered, 725; osmosis of love in, 726; general procedure in, 727–29; specific procedure in, 729–30; finds the problem not in the bottle but in the person, 727; avoids office setting for, 728; note-taking advised against in, 728; summary of, 731; only partial verbalization possible of processes in, 731; case histories of,

732–39. *See also* A.A., alcoholics, alcoholism, spiritual

spontaneous remission: a benefactor of psychoanalysts and psychotherapists, 4, 6, 16, 17; tied to relative failure of avoidance behavior, 100

stress: from threat to value system, 270; proneness as consequence of neurologic limitations, 276; expressed in three primary feelings, 284

Strong interest inventory, 446

substitution of symptoms: canard of, 23; influenced by therapist, 23

suggestibility, high in humans, 298

suicide: as senseless, impulsive act, 273; as failure in adaptational demands, 274; psychotherapy counterindicated for, 274; for preservation of value system, 274; and underlying grandiosity, 274; arising out of lack of emotional involvement, 572

superego: Freudians fail to distinguish neurotic from healthy aspects of, 513

superstitions: abundant in psychotherapy, 4, 6; Freudian, 7; professional about Synanon, 783–94

symbol: emotional potency of, 24; cleansing power of, 232; may be mistaken for reality, 497–500

symptoms: a classification of, 72–73; physical, changing during interview, 620; disregarded in positive psychotherapy, 433

Synanon, 18, 137, 139; considered more drastic than illumination method, 468; compared to integrity therapy, 516, 521, 528; as a behavior modification practice, 518; rejects psychopharmacological medications, 521; as part of community psychiatry, 523; concerned with alienation, 523; has many nonaddict members, 526; provides a redemptive way of life, 526; criticized as brainwashing, 534; stresses feelings appropriately, 540; compared to a tribe, 544; helps find meaning in life, 617; helped 600 addicts until 1965, 745; its story of courage, 747; as a new kind of group therapy, 747, 749, 753, 766–72; as a new way of being religious, 747, 756–57; as a new method of attack therapy, 747, 766, 772–77, 785–90; animosity toward, 748; not drugs, but

clean living discussed in, 750; truth and honesty as part of therapy in, 751, 766; synanons serve to vent hostilities, 750, 770, 785–86; cursing not condoned outside synanons in, 751, 777; manifesto of, 752; has an autocratic family structure, 752, 755; spiritual concepts implanted in addicts by, 753; no mind-changing drugs allowed, 753, 779–80; some views shared by "square" society, 754, 783; varied reactions to, 754; as a corporation producing "clean-man days," 755; past traumas disregarded in, 757; a welcome to, 757–62; classes and seminars taken seriously in, 759, 784, 791; stupidity, unwillingness to learn seen as basic features of drug addicts and criminals, 760, 773, 777, 791; indoctrination in, 762–66; drug addict considered an infant emotionally, 765, 785; synanons (group therapy) as driving force in, 766; as emotional battlefield, 766; fake insight rejected in, 770; as pseudoanalysis, 771; past history considered irrelevant in, 770–71; in contrast to professional therapy, overt behavior as the focus in, 771; getting a correct self-picture as very important in, 772–89; artful ridicule used in the "haircut" in, 773–77, 788–89; discards professional therapy, 778; brainwashing used in, 778; a new profession, leaders of, 778; works opposite of psychoanalysis, 778; some professionals impede progress of, 779, 784, 792–93; phony hipsters not tolerated in, 780–81; techniques more effective than professional ones, 781; professional superstitions and, 783–94; justification of attack therapy in, 785–90; British system (providing drugs) condemned by, 782–83; laughing at one's wrong behavior seen as sign of progress in, 789; no argument wanted with professional fraternity, 791; even NIMH lagging in support of, 791; as threat to professional vested interests, 792–93; as therapy "of, by, and for the people," 792; as a unique therapeutic system, 793–94; might be a start of a new therapeutic revolution,

793; professionals, blinded by training in orthodox methods, overlook the results of, 793–94; as a new social movement, 794; as combination of mileu therapy with rational and behavior therapies, 879

TA. *See* transactional analysis
tachycardia, decreased with relaxation therapy, 249
teaching, as the best way of mastering a subject, 243
temper: as worst enemy of the patient, 834; as sabotage of therapy, 836
Tennessee Self-Concept Scale, used in evaluating psychological treatments, 183
tensions: are learned unadaptive reactions, 250; can be unlearned, 250
Thanatos, as self-destructive drive, denied, 273
therapeutic community: in prison ward, 190–220; as challenge to "prison ethic," 212, 214; of integrity therapy, 516; in Synanon, 879
therapeutic contract: a literal, 162; as alliance to resist therapy, 768
"therapeutic eros," 17
therapy for scrupulosity, 221–43; chief snare seen in deciding if one did not sin, 223; counselee advised to study logical fallacies, 228–29; doing the opposite of scrupulous urge in, 233–34; four phases in, 238–42; precision of behavioral reactions is essential in, 238–40; ignoring the scruple as, 240–41; advantages of group application of, 242. *See also* scruple
Therapy #52—The Truth. *See* operant group psychotherapy
thought has primacy over feeling, 267
Time Reference Inventory: used in evaluating therapy outcomes, 183
transactional analysis: development of, 370–74; started with listening to patients instead of teachers, 371; basic three ego states discerned in, 372, 373, 374, 375–78, 390; structural analysis as diagnosis of ego states, 372; group therapy as natural matrix for, 372, 388; conversations become transactions in, 372; many psychologists had said it differently, 373;

theory of, 374–86; derived from psychoanalysis, 374; a wider ego psychology than psychoanalytic, 374; deals with observable not hypothetical ego variables, 374, 378; Child deemed one to eight years old, 375; characteristics of Child ego state, 375; characteristics of Adult, 376; characteristics of Parent, 376; Child considered stimulus-bound and manifested in schizophrenics, 375; Adult state analogous to computer, 376; high and low permeability of ego state boundaries in, 377; contamination of ego state boundaries in, 378, 391; transaction as the unit of, 378, 388; complementary, crossed, and ulterior transactions, 379–80; games observed in, 380–84; three hungers (stimulus, time-structure, position) underlie payoffs in games, 380–81; stroking need appeased in recognition, 380; games as exchange of strokes, 381, 382–84; "racket" as patient's existential position, 381; script or patient life plan, 382; Child as motor of personality, as manifested in the script, 384; clinical applications of, 386–92; therapeutic contract clearly defined, 387; treatment proceeds rapidly in, 387; authority diagram essential for therapist in, 388; ailing group means an undiagnosed game being played, 389; therapist confronts actively in, 390; sometimes resembles children playing, 392; as a good example of deductive theory-centered therapy, 875; corrected neglect of situational-existential factors in psychiatry, 876
transference: as one of Freudian superstitions, 7; termed a "metaphysical concept," 245; fostered by undirected fantasies and free associations in psychoanalysis, 308; volatile involvements of, 401; is disregarded in reality therapy, 580; mistaken Freudian belief about, 589
trauma: only approximated in implosive therapy, 100; left undiscovered in successful treatment, 118; of birth, idea ridiculed, 124; mistaken as determinant of behavior by Freudians,

296, 514; not presupposed in reality therapy, 584; as considered irrelevant in Synanon treatment, 757

traumatic symbol, acting outside awareness, 108

tutorial counseling, as application of mental hygiene principles, 876

two-factor learning theory in implosive therapy, 98

unconditional regard unessential in guidance, 485

unconscious: psychoanalysis as wish hunting in the, 3; increase of resistance by emphasis on the, 21; as therapeutic pitfall, 21; eschewed by Phillips, 35, 38; as a scientifically barren concept, 35; dynamics of behavior hidden in the, 259, 266; dealt with efficiently in RET, 309; an analogy of, 425; disregarded in reality therapy, 573, 583; repression of now more important than of the past, 591; sabotage in therapy is more conscious than, 840

unhappiness, as the consequence not the cause of behavior, 579

value system: as basic determinant of behavior, 264–66; causes guilt when violated, 270; maintained at the price of masochism, 274; implied in psychotherapy, 664–67; neutrality is a myth, 665, 666; exposition rather than imposition through Christian psychotherapy, 668; demanded from treatment personnel, a realistic, 172

verbal behavior therapy, 3, 67; manipulates environmental stimuli, 68; as clinical application of behavior therapy, 70; applies learning theory principles, 70; combines both behavior and dynamic techniques, 70; uses words as conditioned stimuli and reinforcers, 70; focuses on observable and reportable behavior, 71; behavior between interviews crucial in, 71; the opening phase in, 71–75; adapting patient to, 71; special meaning of diagnosis in, 72; classifies symptoms into positive, negative, and central,

72–73; specifying goals in, 73; negotiating the contract with patient in, 74; therapist as a source of reinforcement in, 74; patient is taught how to learn in, 74; creating the therapeutic climate in, 75; self-pity considered a major obstacle in, 75; therapist uses personal examples too in, 75; middle phase of treatment in, 75–77; focus is on central symptoms in, 75; treatment techniques for positive symptoms in, 76; treatment techniques for negative symptoms in, 77; the closing phase of treatment in, 77–78; termination planned from beginning of, 78; discouraging dependence on therapist in, 78; confronting patient with termination in, 78; a case study in, 79–81; patient has to stop blaming and start living, 79; stress on personal action against problems in, 80; medication as adjunct therapy in, 80; focusing on effective life in, 80; "fixed role" therapy in, 80; as a variant of rational-reeducative approach, 863

Washingtonian movement, 878

Watts riots, produced by specific culture, 265

Weltanschauung: smuggled into patients by Freudians, 28

will: power increased through group participation, 243; human life not driven by impulses but by, 819

words: as conditioned stimuli and reinforcers, 70; supplied to patient, 97; as "bells of associative reflexes," 108; have meanings other than those in dictionary, 397; more self-deceiving than body "truth buttons," 427

work: attitudes corrected in felons, 198; as self-actualization, 198

writing thoughts down is therapeutically effective, 620–21

YMCA, helps find meaning in life, 617

yoga, sitting exercises, 18

Zen, sitting exercises, 18